North Carolina beaches

Glenn Morris

A visit to

national seashores,

state parks, ferries,

public beaches,

wildlife refuges,

historic sites,

lighthouses,

boat ramps

and docks,

museums,

and more

THIRD EDITION

North Carolina beaches

THE UNIVERSITY OF NORTH CAROLINA PRESS / CHAPEL HILL AND LONDON

First edition 1993
Third edition 2005
Manufactured in the
United States of America

Set in Century Old Style
and Franklin Gothic
by BW&A Books, Inc.

The paper in this book meets
the guidelines for permanence
and durability of the Committee
on Production Guidelines for
Book Longevity of the Council
on Library Resources.

This book was published with the
assistance of the Blythe Family Fund
of the University of North Carolina
Press.

Library of Congress
Cataloging-in-Publication Data
Morris, Glenn, 1950–
North Carolina beaches / Glenn
Morris.—3rd ed.
p. cm.
"A visit to national seashores, state
parks, ferries, public beaches, wildlife
refuges, historic sites, lighthouses,
boat ramps and docks, museums,
and more."
Includes index.
ISBN 0-8078-5618-5 (pbk. : alk. paper)
1. North Carolina—Guidebooks.
2. Atlantic Coast (N.C.)—Guidebooks.
3. Coasts—North Carolina—
Guidebooks. 4. Beaches—North
Carolina—Guidebooks. 5. Recreation
areas—North Carolina—Guidebooks.
I. Title.
F252.3.M658   2005
917.5604'4—dc22   2005003447

09 08 07 06 05
5 4 3 2 1

FOR KIP MORRIS

Contents

Cape Hatteras National Seashore, 100

FEATURE ARTICLES

Preface

I am often asked, "What's your favorite beach?" and I have no favorite—but I do lean toward some. Personal preference is everything in choosing a destination, and fortunately, there's so much on the North Carolina coast to enjoy and appreciate, any traveler can find a place in the sun that suits him or her.

This book is a series of north to south impressions of North Carolina's coast. It compiles what I find interesting as I wander the extremity of the state—vignettes, I hope, that might entice you to visit. It's a marvelously complex coastline that is neither easy to live on nor simple to travel along, where life still has a special flavor, slightly briny with a little bit of grit.

I was fortunate to have the help of many professionals in researching and writing this book. I give particular thanks to Greg "Rudi" Rudolph of the Carteret County Shore Protection Office for timely updates on coastal issues; to John Taggart of North Carolina Parks, a patient tutor on the Coastal Reserve system; and to Christine Mackey, director of tourism programs for the state of North Carolina, and the tourism staff for great direction and prompt answers. Fred Annand, associate director of the North Carolina chapter of the Nature Conservancy, and Chris Canfield and Walker Gorder of Audubon North Carolina were extremely helpful as well.

Local tourism officials were indispensable to my research. Willo Winterling of the Currituck County Chamber of Commerce, Quinn Capps of the Outer Banks Visitors Bureau, Karen Sphar of the Southport–Oak Island Chamber of Commerce, and Mitzi York of the Brunswick County Chamber of Commerce were repeatedly helpful.

Anyone who visits our national seashores, national wildlife refuges, state parks, historic sites, and aquariums will find the staff eager to help and educate. My effort was greatly eased by their professionalism.

Thanks, too, to David Perry, Paula Wald, and Mark Simpson-Vos of the University of North Carolina Press for their help and support. I reserve special appreciation for the sharp eye of Bethany Johnson, the copyeditor, for an excellent and thorough read.

I am especially grateful that my wonderful companion and wife, Ginny Boyle, wholeheartedly supports playing in the sand. Every wanderer needs an anchor, and she is that for me.

Glenn Morris
October 2004

North Carolina beaches

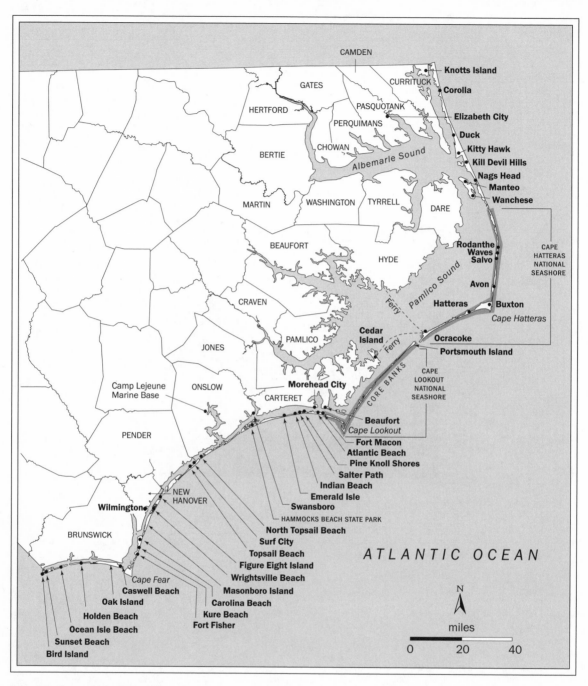

Map I-1. Coastal North Carolina

Introduction

This book is a companion for a journey along North Carolina's 320-mile-long coast. Whether you are in an armchair in Ohio or Pennsylvania wondering about the Outer Banks, or lazing on the beach at Corolla and curious about the self-proclaimed "golf coast" of Brunswick County, *North Carolina Beaches* offers an answer to the question, "I wonder what it's like there?"

One of the principles guiding this book is that the most difficult thing about planning a trip is deciding where to go. Accordingly, I have tried to paint portraits of the coast that capture the qualities that make each place distinctive. Many things go into creating a place's personality—the natural setting, the architectural character, the rhythm and pulse of traffic, the sort of folks you meet there, and so on. One place may be a great "fit" for some people and not for others. The difference between a great vacation and a week at the beach (which still beats a week at home) starts with finding a place that suits you.

The revised edition has changed a good bit in response to changes along North Carolina's outer coast. While many of these are the result of a growth in tourism, natural forces, such as storms and chronic erosion, have had their impact as well.

The first edition emphasized detailed information on public access because it was not widely available then and the public access program was relatively new. Today, most North Carolina coastal communities know that easy-to-find and -use public access makes them a more tourist-friendly destination. They readily provide this information. It is here as well, although the necessity is diminished.

North Carolina Beaches still serves as a mile-by-mile guide to the outer coast. It still includes locations for parking (accessways), ferries, federal and state parks and preserves, private preserves open to the public, and other difficult-to-categorize locations that are worth a visit. Where it is available, I have included information, such as addresses, hours of operation, phone numbers, and web addresses, which did not exist at the first publication.

North Carolina has a complicated coastline. There's an inner coast, where the sound waters touch the mainland, and the outer coast, where waves break on sandy shores. There are nearly 4,000 miles of estuarine shoreline—the inner coast—in the state, but only 320 miles of what is commonly known as beach. To go to the beach in North Carolina, your destination, in almost every case, is the string of low sandy islands, known as barrier islands (barriers to the open ocean), separate from the mainland. This book is about those beaches.

North Carolina's barrier islands shelter the shallow waters of its great bays or sounds. North to south these sounds are Currituck, Albemarle, Roanoke, Croatan, Pamlico, Core, and Bogue. They comprise the second largest estuary in the nation, after the Chesapeake Bay. They also give the state the sixth largest coastline in the nation and, by one measure, twenty-two "coastal counties," that is, counties that border on tidal waters. The islands and the sounds vary substantially in size. In the northern half of the state, the difficulty in bridging the large sounds still limits travel and commerce. Along the southern coast, the sounds are not as wide and are more easily crossed.

Land and water meet in an astonishing array of complex edge patterns: pine savannas, hardwood forests, sweeps of salt marsh, low and high swamps, even abrupt bluffs touch the wide brackish water of the sounds, bays, and estuaries. The text notes some of the best opportunities to enjoy firsthand the ecological diversity of the coast.

It is easy to see by studying a map of the jigsawed coast that traveling the region is neither simple nor quick. In fact, as one wag declared, it is only direct for fish and birds.

The awkwardness of travel resulted in relative isolation well into the middle of last century (one reason the Wright Brothers chose Kill Devil Hills is that it was way off any beaten track), which left the coast relatively wild and natural far longer than any comparable coastline.

The absolute isolation of the barrier islands began eroding in the 1930s with the first bridges and regular ferries. This opened the beaches to easy visitation, spurring tourism and initiating a modest second-home real estate boom. The building increased in tempo as paved roads, instead of sand roads, became the norm on the barrier islands. Development was paired with a preservation effort to establish national seashores, and today 130 miles of the 320-mile coastline is managed by the National Park Service. I find it remarkable that the North Carolina coast not only has few locations with "urban" densities but in many places you can still feel crowded if another person is *visible* on the beach. We're spoiled, and I like it.

The most striking attribute of the North Carolina coast is its great variety. There are wild, untamed beaches and forests, actively preserved historic towns, and no-frills fishing villages. There are sleepy beaches snoozing in their own world, family beaches with museums and arcades, and young and restless beaches with a plugged-in seaside syncopation.

If you know what you like, you can find what you are looking for, and then, make your pick.

Geomorphology of the Coast

Nearly every visitor to the Outer Banks thinks the islands are something special—a fact every coastal geologist knows. It is their distance from the mainland—they are *way* out there—that sets them apart. If they were closer to the mainland, as are most barrier islands on the East Coast, their existence and configuration would be more commonplace and better understood geologically.

Barrier islands exist worldwide where any gently sloping coastal plain borders the ocean. In the United States, every southeastern state has barrier islands, and it is the lack of them, as in the case of South Carolina's Grand Strand, that is exceptional.

Coastal geologists theorize that the ancient Outer Banks formed when the gradually rising sea level forced a landward migration of ancient dune ridges that had become islands. Island building probably began after the last period of glaciations, approximately 12,000 years ago. At that time, sea level may have been as much as 200 feet lower than it is today, and the Atlantic coast was at least 90 miles east, in the neighborhood of the continental shelf.

The melting ice caps raised sea level steadily, gradually slowing within a few meters of the present level 4,000 to 5,000 years ago. As sea level climbed, the shoreline inched landward across the continental shelf, moving vast quantities of sand before it in the form of beach deposits. River sediments from coastal plain deltas were pulled into the wave zone and also moved along the shore.

When sea level remained steady for a time during the period known as the Holocene, an age of comparative stability, wind and waves worked these large masses of sand and sediment into the precursors of our present barrier islands. The islands were considerably wider than they are today. Behind the prehistoric beach was a gently sloping, forested coastal plain, carved by the Cape Fear, Neuse, Tar, Roanoke, and Chowan Rivers and their principal tributaries.

Sea level began rising again, albeit at a much slower rate, 2,000 years ago. The ocean eventually breached the formative barrier islands, flooding the forested coastal plain behind them. It also inundated the floodplains of the ancient coastal riverbeds, creating the sounds.

This hypothesis, known as "barrier ridge drowning," seems to explain the geological idiosyncrasies of the Outer Banks. Fossil evidence discovered on the ocean side of the barrier islands of an extinct species of oyster normally inhabiting brackish waters strengthens the argument for this scenario by proving the migration of the island over once-inland oyster beds. Also, the mainland coast has the intricate patterning characteristic of flooded river valleys.

The islands "migrated" landward before the rising sea level in a sequence of steps still repeated today. When the ocean breaches the islands, it fills in the shallow sound waters with sand and sediment. If left alone, this new fill will support pioneering vegetation and, given time, become forested. Wind and wave action leverages the dune line landward. The wind blows the dune sand; it covers the established forest (as it does on the west side of Jockey's Ridge State Park), filling in the soundside marsh. Like a Slinky crawling over itself down a flight of stairs, the entire barrier island rolls over, retreating before the rising sea.

We see island migration in the shearing of sand from a dune line, storm surge overwash on a road, or a sand-filled ground-level room of an oceanfront home. When the beach moves, an oceanfront home must move as well. Over decades (though sometimes overnight), the actual shape of the entire island changes. The ocean blusters, the wind blows, and the islands do not argue; they respond passively.

Barrier islands also have locations that are comparatively stable and protected. Historically, these have been the places of the most permanent settlement. But for how long? The Cape Hatteras Lighthouse ruled $1/3$ mile of beach 100 years ago, and by the 1990s it had to be moved. Diamond City on Shackleford Banks was wiped out in a single storm. On the other hand, although most of the coastline retreats in a similar manner, many historic settlements weather on.

Here is an irony: if a beach were barren, wild, and natural, with no artificial structures on it to act as a frame of reference, how would anyone know, from one year to the next, if the island had moved? Without a fixed reference, the islands would appear stationary and unchanged, but our "permanent" houses, docks, and roads are really our yardsticks of the coastal process. The islands push against our permanence and show us to be renters, not owners. We can cling to our castles built on these magnificent sands, but all we can really do is rail at the winds in protest.

Historical Perspective

By the time the first English-speaking peoples attempted settlement in the New World on Roanoke Island in 1585, Native Americans had fished, hunted, and farmed on nearly every island along the coast. Because they had no written language, they left no written record, and our knowledge of them comes from either firsthand accounts of explorers or the investigations of archaeologists and anthropologists.

John White, an artist on the 1585 expedition whose drawings document the explorers' first glimpse of the New World, reported more than twenty Native American villages near Roanoke Island. These were most likely allied with or related to the Hatteras tribe, the first group to meet the European explorers and settlers. According to White, the Native Americans cleared villages out of the maritime hardwood forests on the soundside of the islands. They centered the village on a sweat lodge, which served as a common gathering place. Evidence favors the theory that while these local peoples were self-sufficient and traded minimally, the sounds and rivers in no way restricted their mobility. At least one of the islands in Currituck Sound, Monkey Island, served as both a summer fishing village and a burial ground, as did Permuda Island in Stump Sound in Onslow County.

The English settlement attempts were not the first forays by Europeans on these shores. Spain gained, then lost, the early advantage in the exploration and settlement of North Carolina. In 1520 Pedro de Quexoia sailed from the West Indies to the Cape Fear region. A passenger, Lucas Vázquez de Ayllón, returned in 1526 with 500 men, women, and slaves and livestock to settle the "Rio Jordan," thought to be the Cape Fear River. Ravished by disease, the settlement soon withdrew to the South Carolina coast. Fever followed the relocation, killing Ayllón in October 1526, and the 150 survivors called it quits, boarded ships, and sailed to Santo Domingo.

In 1524 Florentine navigator Giovanni da Verrazano, sailing in the service of France, recorded the first exploration of the North Carolina coast. He landed in the Cape Fear region and made detailed observations as far north as Hatteras, producing a glowing report to Francis I. In 1582 Englishman Richard Hakluyt published the account under the title *Divers Voyages touching the Discoverie of America and Islands Adjacent.*

Hakluyt's report engendered English ambition for the profitable possibilities of the "New World."

On March 25, 1584, Queen Elizabeth I granted Sir Walter Raleigh a patent for the exclusive rights to and rewards of a New World colony. Raleigh secured investors and supplied a two-ship expedition commanded by Philip Amadas and Arthur Barlowe and piloted by the Portuguese navigator Simón Fernandez. The expedition entered Pamlico Sound through "Wococon" Inlet (present-day Ocracoke Inlet) on July 4, 1584.

Shortly thereafter, Barlowe and a few men sailed north to an island Native Americans called "Roanoke." The first encounter with Native Americans went well. When the expedition returned to England, it took along Manteo and Wanchese, the first Native Americans to visit England.

Barlowe's subsequent report increased Raleigh's desire to attempt to colonize the New World, which had been named "Virginia" in honor of the unwed Elizabeth. He again rounded up investors, and on April 9, 1585, Sir Richard Grenville, Raleigh's cousin, with Ralph Lane along as "lieutenant gourvernour" set sail from Plymouth in seven ships and with 108 men to make the first colonization effort in "Virginia." The fleet reached Hatteras on July 22, 1585, and by August 17 had disembarked on Roanoke Island. Only ten months later in 1586, pressed for food and supplies and by deteriorating relations with the native inhabitants, Sir Francis Drake evacuated the colony, leaving eighteen men at guard in the fort they had built.

The report of Lane's group intrigued Raleigh, and undeterred by efforts to dissuade him, he organized yet another expedition. This time, they would do it right by settling to farm and build a community in the deep-water region of the Chesapeake Bay. Raleigh enlisted John White, the artist who had illustrated the explorations of the 1585 expedition, as "Governor" of the "Citie of Ralegh in Virginia." Women and children, livestock, and supplies were part of this package.

Raleigh's "second colonie" left England in the spring of 1587 led by the *Admirall*, piloted by Fernandez. During the crossing, White clashed with Fernandez over the continuation to the Chesapeake region. When they reached Hatteras on July 22, 1587, they quickly proceeded to Roanoke Island to pick up Grenville's men, but the men were missing and the fort destroyed. Fernandez refused to sail north as planned, so White ordered the colonists to disembark on Roanoke Island.

It was a struggle from the start but not without its benchmarks. On August 18, White's daughter Eleanor and her husband, Ananias Dare, gave birth to Virginia, the first child of English-speaking parents born in the New World. This joy aside, the colony ran low on food and supplies, and White reluctantly agreed to sail to England for provisions. The colonists promised to leave a sign if they abandoned Roanoke Island for the mainland.

The threat of European wars stranded White in England until 1590. When he returned to Roanoke Island, he found the settlement in shambles and the letters "CRO," believed to indicate the Indian village of Croatan, carved in a tree. The colonists were never found; the colony was lost. White returned to England, and colonization attempts on North Carolina soil ended. In 1607 colonization efforts successfully shifted north to Jamestown in the Chesapeake region.

Compared to the Chesapeake Bay, coastal North Carolina's population grew slowly, disadvantaged by treacherous ocean waters to the east, shoaling inlets, shallow sounds, and the lack of deep-water ports. Except for the deep-water Cape Fear River region, early settlement in North Carolina spilled over from Virginia, where deep-water supply was safely established.

Communities did grow along the sounds in the eighteenth century. The town of Bath incorporated in 1706, followed by New Bern in 1710 and Beaufort in 1723, each a port town but none with favorable deep-water access to the open ocean.

During these early years, the coast was plagued by piracy. Both Stede Bonnett and Edward Teach, better known as Blackbeard, had their pirating terminated on the North Carolina coast.

Growth quickened in the Cape Fear River region at Brunswick, established in 1725, and Wilmington, established around 1735. As early as 1732, the population of Brunswick was 1,200. The shallow sound waters limited the prospects of the early sound cities, but Wilmington thrived on its deep-water port. Newcomers pushed inland, and trade routes linked ports with new inland cities.

Agriculture, timber products, and fishing sustained the economy of eastern North Carolina until the Civil War. The large older cities served as market centers. The coastal region continued to grow and prosper, tied firmly to dependence on agriculture, large landholding patterns, and slave labor.

By the time of the Civil War, North Carolina had two major ports, Wilmington and Morehead City, each linked to the Piedmont by railway. Fort Macon guarded the channel serving Morehead City and was quickly seized by the Confederacy. Confederate forces moved swiftly to construct Fort Fisher in order to secure the more reliable deep-water port of the Cape Fear River.

Union ships blockaded the North Carolina coast beginning around 1862, but the erratic shoreline provided refuge for shallow-draft blockade-runners that smuggled arms and supplies across the sound waters. There were skirmishes along the Outer Banks at Hatteras Island, and Roanoke Island was captured in 1862. The famous Union ironclad ship *Monitor* swamped while being towed from Hampton Roads, Virginia, and sank offshore from Cape Hatteras; it has recently been located, and salvage operations have begun.

While the war ended the antebellum social order, it did not change the coastal economy. Life in the coastal region remained limited by its waters and enriched by its lands until the middle of the twentieth century.

In the 1870s the sparsely populated barrier islands caught the eye of two different groups of people: wealthy northern industrialists and mariners who sailed the outlying waters. Both effected profound change. The industrialists discovered the seasonal waterfowl populations in Currituck and Pamlico Sounds and purchased thousands of acres for private sport.

Meanwhile, the loss of life due to shipwrecks spurred the federal government to improve the lighthouses and to establish the U.S. Life-Saving Service. Beginning with the first stations in 1874, the life-saving service eventually established a network along the entire length of North Carolina's barrier islands. The stations and their crews (and the post offices that followed) put the barrier island hamlets on the official U.S. postal map. Their rescues became the stuff of legend on the Outer Banks.

In 1900 two brothers named Wright arrived from Ohio and began their quest for heavier-than-air flight at Kitty Hawk.

Significant change came to the Outer Banks with the bridges and ferries of the 1930s and the beginning of World War II. Through 1942, German U-boats ravaged merchant shipping off Cape Hatteras, giving the area the nickname, "Torpedo Junction." After the war, the automobile and bridges, increased leisure time, inexpensive land, and a solidly growing economy started the second wave of settlement on the barrier islands. Yet it is amazing that after more than 400 years of visitation and habitation, the best-selling commodity in the region is still its wild and distant character.

Historical Touring

Part of any "things to do at the coast" list should include mixing some history with pleasure. The coast abounds with the opportunity. The Fort Raleigh National Historic Site in Manteo and the Wright Brothers National Memorial at Kill Devil Hills, two of the nation's most important sites, are within 10 miles of each other.

US 17 travels through the eighteenth-century centers of commerce and government. This historic link between Williamsburg, Virginia, and Charleston, South Carolina, weaves inland from the coast, and nearly every community along its passage, including Edenton, Washington, New Bern, and Wilmington, made a mark on the early history of the state. Many are attractive small towns, rich in early architectural detail (see "US 17, the King's Highway").

In New Bern, the Tryon Palace restoration and the equally exquisite but more demure residential areas are an architectural treasure trove. The residential areas showcase more than two centuries of culture and artistry. Here you can sample the flavor of one of the most extensive "period" neighborhoods between Norfolk and Wilmington.

Beaufort is an example of how most of North Carolina's coastal communities acknowledge their history by living in it instead of trapping it under glass. The homes and churches are still intact because of continual use. There is a similar charm and vibrancy to Swansboro and Southport, towns tied to the rivers and sea; they are still alive and well, restored and recycled for another century of use.

Wilmington is full of interest for the cultural tourist. Historic markers dot the downtown district, a charming area where quaint restaurants and riverside walks complement the antebellum buildings.

The legendary saga of the U.S. Life-Saving Service has been memorably preserved, mostly in the recycling of its buildings as residences, restaurants, or businesses. However, at Chicamacomico Life-Saving Station in Rodanthe, a resonant history is told and highlighted by scheduled reenactments of actual life-saving drills. More of the Outer Banks's explosive history is told at the Graveyard of the Atlantic Museum in Hatteras and at the North Carolina Maritime Museum in Beaufort, which details many facets of traditional coastal life, from decoy carving to boatbuilding.

There are, of course, four towering, historic, brick lighthouses, two of which are open for climbing

(Currituck Beach and Cape Hatteras) and a third, Bodie Island, that will be. Not to be slighted is the enduring tower at Ocracoke, wonderful Old Baldy at Bald Head Island, and the modern powerhouse at Oak Island.

Any trip to the coast can be enriched by a historical side trip along the way. If you don't want to stop, then watch for the enduring buildings that have marked the passage of centuries; they are landmarks of time as well as place.

The Access Issue

In June 2004 a one-year survey conducted by the North Carolina Shore and Beach Preservation Association, in conjunction with the North Carolina Division of Coastal Management and Sea Grant, came up with really good news: Public access is widely available along the ocean shoreline in the state.

The survey identified more than 550 public access locations, 6,356 parking spaces, and 43 public restrooms near the beaches—evidence of the success of the state's public beach access program.

Beach access will never go away as an issue, but it is less problematic than it was in the early 1980s, when, for the most part, there was little public access. Since then, the Division of Coastal Management, supported by the General Assembly, has worked with local communities to overcome the problem and has done so handsomely.

Beach access is now accepted as a necessity in coastal planning and as an essential element in creating a tourism-friendly environment. Improved access benefits a community not only by facilitating tourism and its accompanying revenue but also by reducing conflicts between private landowners and the visiting public who simply want to get to the beach. Today, every coastal community proclaims its access locations by public signs or in published material. If the access is there, and much more of it is, it is increasingly easy to find.

During the formative years of the program, it quickly developed three types of access sites: regional, neighborhood, and local, which are described below in the section on "How to Use This Book." The guidelines are fluid since site conditions and funding determine the exact mix of improvements. Development of accessways occurs as land and money become available. Funding is a perennial problem; there is never enough to go around, particularly along the coast where land values are soaring.

The crux of public access is parking. Most oceanfront communities provide adequate public access for pedestrians if they live or rent on the front two rows back from the beach. After that, not everyone has a reasonable, safe walk. The practical matter is that in some locations, much more needs to be done to provide people with safe, convenient parking near a public passage to the beach. Typically, the largest cost of a project is land for parking.

A surprising ally in the quest for access is the U.S. Army Corps of Engineers, the agency responsible for maintaining navigable waters. The corps enters the equation when a community solicits funding for a beach nourishment project. By law, part of the price is public access every ½ mile of beach that is nourished with public money. The rule is hard and fast—access every ½ mile, no more, no less—and it does not matter if the community is essentially private. This is the reason there are now public access locations in Pine Knoll Shores on Bogue Banks.

There is less urgency with soundside access, but it is no less important. Sound access permits people to reach a traditional place of livelihood and recreation. The same process at oceanfront communities, including Corolla and Nags Head, has funded several terrific sound access locations.

The North Carolina Division of Coastal Management provides an online access locator at <www.nccoastalmanagement.net/Access/sites.htm>.

Handicapped Access

The handicapped visitor to the coast will find improving access in most locations and municipalities that are very cooperative in assisting. Most regional access facilities and many of the larger neighborhood access areas constructed since 1990 are accessible to the handicapped.

Here is something more important: Most coastal municipalities, in cooperation with Easter Seals North Carolina, can loan beach-adapted wheelchairs to those who need them during a visit. The participating locations may be found in *Access North Carolina*, published by the Division of Vocational Rehabilitation of the North Carolina Department of Human Resources. (This publication contains a complete survey of the accessibility of public parks, recreation areas, and historic sites across the state.) The list of municipalities may be viewed online at <http://dvr.dhhs.state.nc.us/DVR/pubs/accessnc/accessnc.htm>. Adobe Acrobat viewer is necessary to see the list. If you want to call ahead, check with the local police or fire department of the town you intend to visit. These professionals handle the program for most of the coastal communities.

Many access sites have dune crossovers with ramps that make them accessible to people in wheelchairs. However, not all of the dune crossovers have ramps that extend to the beach. Depending on the nature of the beach, the ramp may terminate at a gazebo overlook or a deck.

Most state parks and recreation areas are accessible to the handicapped; however, not all of these areas provide access to the beachfront. All National Park Service properties are accessible, but while some trails in national wildlife refuges may be negotiable by wheelchair, many are not.

Enforcement of handicapped parking regulations varies among individual local governments. You must have a valid handicapped license plate to park in a designated space. In some locations, the fine for violating this regulation can be as much as $100.

Access North Carolina is available free of charge by contacting the Division of Travel and Tourism, North Carolina Department of Economic and Community Development, 4324 Mail Service Center, Raleigh, NC 27699-4324, 919-733-4171 or 1-800-VISITNC. It is also available free of charge by contacting ACCESS North Carolina, North Carolina Division of Vocational Rehabilitation, 2801 Mail Service Center, Raleigh, NC 27699-2801, 919-733-5407.

For more on handicapped access, see "How to Use This Book" below.

Beach Rights Issues

Although a landowner may legally deny access across his or her property to the beach, once you get to the beach, you have the right to be there. North Carolina case law has repeatedly upheld the right of citizens to use the "foreshore," that is, the wet sand beach, which is covered by the reach of high tide and exposed by the retreat of low tide. This portion of the oceanfront is reserved by the doctrine of public trust for the use of all. A 1983 ruling of the North Carolina Supreme Court reaffirmed this principle: "The long-standing right of the public to pass over and along the strip of land lying between the high-water mark and low-water mark adjacent to respondents' property is established beyond the need of citation. In North Carolina private property fronting coastal water ends at the high-water mark and the property lying between the high-water mark and the low-water mark known as the 'foreshore' is the property of the state."

The legal principle supporting this right is the common-law doctrine of public trust, a derivative of the English common law of sovereign rights, whereby the sovereign retains certain rights to be enjoyed by all citizens of the state. In the case of North Carolina, the state retains the rights to certain uses of land or waters that cannot be abrogated in any way by the state or any individual.

The battle will never be over, it seems. In July 2003 the state received a technical victory in a closely watched case from the Whalehead subdivision in Currituck County. In that case, the plaintiffs, homeowners in the subdivision, maintained that they had the right to exclude the public from the dry sand beach, that part of the strand between the mean high-water line and the vegetation or the dune line. Traditionally, this patch of sand has been public domain in North Carolina. The Superior Court judge in the case ruled that the plaintiffs did not have the right to sue the state, a technical victory and one that the plaintiffs vowed to appeal. The same plaintiffs have sued Currituck County over the use by the public of parking lots and dune crossovers in Whalehead subdivision.

This latest case is evidence that the battle over beach access is never-ending. The legal issues affecting the coast are complex and will likely always generate lawsuits. However, the right of the public to use the wet sand beach is assured.

Parks, Preserves, Reserves, and Refuges

Many government agencies and several private organizations have large public landholdings— seashores, parks, reserves, refuges, and historic sites—on the coast. Nearly all of them welcome visitors; some have interpretive facilities and regular programming, while others have few roads and only restricted or difficult access. These properties provide a different perspective because of their natural, historical, and cultural importance, and they have separate listings in the text.

Cape Hatteras and Cape Lookout National Seashores are the most prominent public lands on the coast. Between them, they protect nearly one-half of the state's oceanfront mileage. Complementing the seashores, but serving a different purpose, are the seven wildlife refuges of the U.S. Fish and Wildlife Service.

The U.S. Department of Defense has huge acreage in its military bases, target ranges, and landing fields. The best known are Camp Lejeune and New River Air Station at Jacksonville and Cherry Point Marine Air Station at Havelock. The target range at Stumpy Point and the Naval Auxiliary Landing Field at Bogue (there is another that is closed near the town of Atlantic) can provide high-energy punctuation to a low-key region. Visitation policies at the military sites vary, but the bases are open and the guards stationed at the entrance gates will direct you to the appropriate location for registration.

The U.S. Coast Guard maintains active bases to serve the major inlets of the state and deeper waters with heavy boating traffic. The Coast Guard stations are open to the public. The Oregon Inlet Station is worth visiting just for the historically respectful architecture of the main building. The Coast Guard also maintains the lights in the lighthouses.

The state of North Carolina manages five parks, four natural areas, three aquariums, three historic sites, and two underwater archaeological preserves. It also manages ten reserves under the supervision of the North Carolina Coastal Reserve system, a little-known but very successful state program established to protect the wild and natural coast. In the words of one administrator, the reserve sites "are meant to be green space on the map." The lands and waters acquired so far encompass a diversity of habitats.

The reserve system originated in 1982, when the National Oceanic and Atmospheric Administration (NOAA) funded five years of acquisition for the National Estuarine Sanctuary Program. In North Carolina, NOAA accepted four sites: Currituck Banks, Rachel Carson, Masonboro Island, and Zeke's Island. In 1988 this program became the National Estuarine Research Reserve, which managed the use of the lands for research, education, and compatible recreational activities.

In 1988 the General Assembly established the Coastal Reserve system to allow the state to acquire and manage additional coastal natural areas that were not necessarily estuaries.

Your Child and the Coast

There are few fonder memories than being young and at the beach, but children's curiosity can place them in circumstances they may not be able to handle. Keep these precautions in mind when visiting the coast with your child.

- Keep your child in sight at all times. It takes more than "one eye open" to mind a child in the surf.
- Protect your child's skin from sunburn and eyes from glare and blowing sand.
- Protect your child's feet when crossing sand dunes, wading in shallow sound waters, or walking on piers or docks.
- Always be with your child when he or she is in the water, even in a tidal pool.
- If your child cannot swim, he or she should wear a life jacket.
- Be wary of rip currents that run parallel to the shore then suddenly out to sea. If your child is caught in one, help him or her to swim parallel to shore to break free.
- Do not let children swim near inlets.
- Never let a child wade in sound waters without a life jacket and sneakers.
- Jetties or rock groins (the few that exist) can be slippery and dangerous. Do not let your child play on them.
- Keep your child away from jellyfish on the beach or in the water.
- Hold your child's hand when walking on a pier or dock and make sure they are wearing shoes.
- Teach your child never to walk up behind casting fishermen. Be particularly watchful on a pier.
- Place your fishing tackle out of reach of small children, or keep your tackle box securely fastened.
- Tar and oil should be removed from a child's skin with mineral oil rather than paint solvents.

Highways to the Coast

I-95 is the major north-south interstate in eastern North Carolina. If you're traveling from the mid-Atlantic states along I-95, you can easily connect with US 158, US 64, US 264, US 70, and I-40, the east-west routes serving the coast.

From Raleigh, I-40 runs nearly due south to Wilmington. North Carolina highways 24, 41, 50, 55, 111, and 210 intersect I-40 and can be linked to take you to the coast. Routes that predate I-40—US 421 south from Dunn, NC 87 from Fayetteville, or NC 211 from Lumberton—are lazier and less monotonous, but still get you to the coast.

US 17 is the primary route if your trip originates in coastal Virginia or South Carolina. From Virginia, US 17 goes south to Elizabeth City before following the northern edge of Albemarle Sound to New Bern. From South Carolina, it moves inland to Wilmington and then parallels the coast as far north as Jacksonville. This route threads through the historical heart of coastal North Carolina (it links most of the features of the Historic Albemarle Tour). The appeal of history makes the route worthy of its own tour.

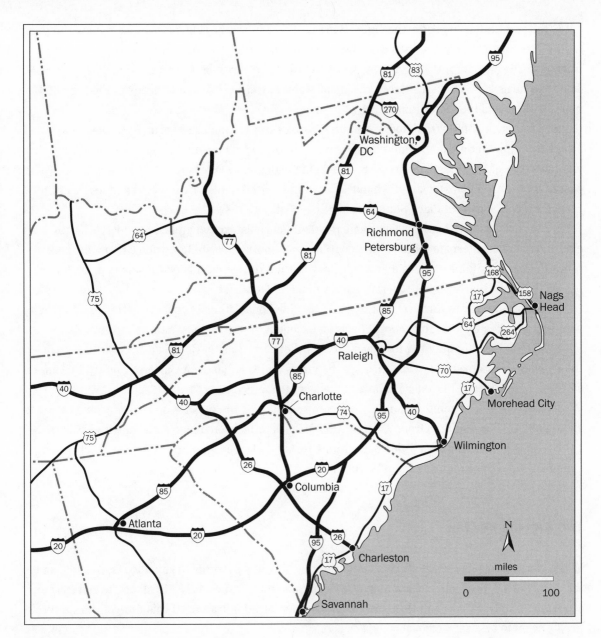

Map I-2. Routes to the North Carolina Coast

US 158 and US 64/264 serve the Outer Banks. US 158 intersects I-95 at Roanoke Rapids and goes to the Currituck mainland. This is a scenic, usually lightly traveled road until Elizabeth City. East of Elizabeth City, at Barco, US 158 merges with NC 168 from Virginia, and traffic thickens noticeably. The road turns south, crosses the Intracoastal Waterway at Coinjock, and heads to the Wright Memorial Bridge and the Outer Banks.

US 64 intersects I-95 west of Rocky Mount, 136 miles from Manteo. The road is the major east-west artery from the Piedmont and, mercifully, is much improved. There are still some frustratingly slow passages east of Williamston where US 64 is being widened to four lanes. Along the way, the route passes through Williamston and Plymouth, two communities of historic interest, and near Pettigrew State Park and Somerset Place State Historic Site, south of Creswell.

US 264 parallels US 64 as it sweeps along the mainland adjacent to Pamlico Sound. It is lightly traveled and offers an alternate route to Manteo from cities south of Washington and Greenville. It passes through several wildlife refuges and winds near Bath, a refreshing historical side trip. US 264 also passes by Swan Quarter, where there is a ferry depot to Ocracoke.

The major highway to Carteret County and Cape Lookout National Seashore is US 70, which links with I-95 20 miles west of Goldsboro. This is an excellent, well-traveled route, and from Kinston, it is a four-lane divided highway to Morehead City and Beaufort. East of Beaufort, US 70 is a route of extraordinary panoramas. It sweeps through the farms and woodlands of Carteret County, linking up with NC 12 for the trip to Cedar Island and the ferry to Ocracoke.

Travelers on US 70 going to southern Carteret County or the Onslow or Pender County resorts should use US 258 or US 58 from Kinston. US 258 goes to Jacksonville to connect with US 17 or NC 24; US 58 is a "blue highway" alternate from Kinston to Bogue Banks. US 58 can be crowded on changeover days at Emerald Isle on Bogue Banks.

The Bicycle Option

While North Carolina's coast is great country for cycling, my personal observation is that it is not for the fainthearted, especially in summer. A few desirable routes, such as NC 12 along the Outer Banks, are frighteningly narrow and throbbing with summer vacation traffic. At this time of year, it would hardly seem to be a safe, enjoyable experience.

Spring and fall months offer the best mix of good weather and low traffic for Outer Banks roads. Drivers are also more inclined to be patient during these seasons.

The Bicycle Program of the North Carolina Department of Transportation provides maps of coastal bicycling routes upon request. The maps are detailed tour guides, useful for all-purpose travel but especially geared for bicyclists. Out of eleven designated bicycling trails across the state, five include major coastal highways, namely "Mountains to Sea," "Ports of Call," "Cape Fear Run," "Ocra-

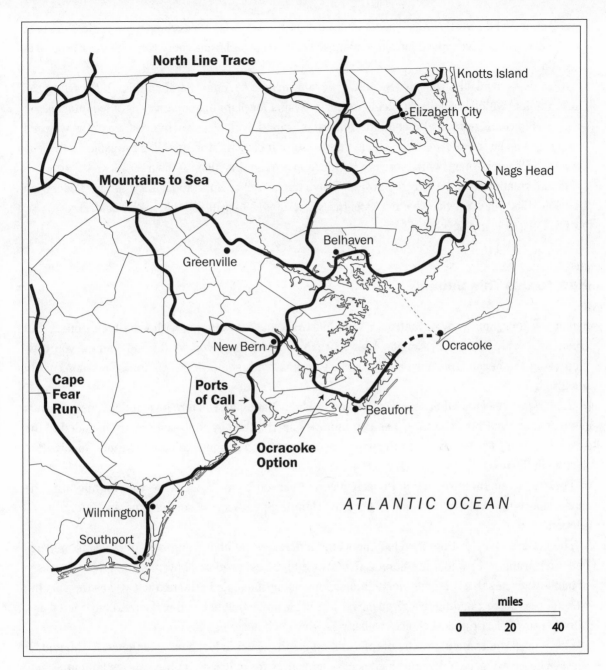

North Line Trace

Knotts Island

Elizabeth City

Nags Head

Mountains to Sea

Belhaven

Greenville

Ocracoke

New Bern

Cape
Fear
Run

Ports
of Call

Beaufort

Ocracoke
Option

ATLANTIC OCEAN

Wilmington

Southport

miles

0   20   40

Map I.3. Coastal Bicycling Routes

coke Option," and "North Line Trace." The most extensive coastal bicycling route is the "Ports of Call" route, which covers portions of the historic colonial coastal trade routes from South Carolina to Virginia.

Other maps available from the Bicycle Program include "Around Pamlico Sound: Bicycling the Outer Banks," which provides an excellent starting point for planning and gives detailed information on loops and connectors. It also contains general information on places of interest along the way and campgrounds, but no addresses or phone numbers are included. More detail is available on the "Bicycling in Beaufort" map, which traces a 6-mile loop around this historic town.

For information, contact North Carolina Department of Transportation, Bicycle and Pedestrian Division, 1552 Mail Service Center, Raleigh, NC, 27699-1552, 919-733-2804. Web address: <www. NCDOT.org/transit/bicycle>.

How to Use This Book

This book is organized by oceanfront county north to south, beginning with Currituck County and concluding with Brunswick County. I have organized entries as you would find them if you traveled along the beach from Virginia to South Carolina, with some side trips to account for county geography.

Cape Hatteras National Seashore and Cape Lookout National Seashore have independent listings distinct from their host counties. The communities surrounded by the seashore are included in the seashore listing. Carteret County, the parent county of Cape Lookout National Seashore, follows that section in the text.

There is a general introduction to each section followed by an "Access" section highlighting the most important access information, a general "Handicapped Access" section, and an "Information" section.

The "Information" listing provides important addresses and phone numbers of relevant agencies and organizations. New to this edition is the "Web addresses" section. I have included web addresses of public agencies that offer additional information about the topic in the text, as well as the specific web address corresponding to a given entry. The list is not meant to be all-inclusive; I have acted as a filter to provide a "first, best choice" website serving each location.

I have used the same hierarchy of information for the specific locations mentioned in the text. If there is no known access, handicapped access, or source for information, the entry is left out.

My hope is that the text provides a word picture of what is waiting at each location. It is meant to be a casual description of the specifics and feeling that make a destination memorable. It is sprinkled with anecdotal and historical information that should tease you to go there and find out more!

"Access" sections give general information about the comparative availability of practical public access while providing some specific information. Access is now a good business practice, and for the most part, this information is available locally and in great detail.

The "Handicapped Access" section qualifies the level of accessibility of a site for handicapped visitors, which for the purposes of this book means people who must use wheelchairs. Many dune crossovers along the coast are boardwalks that meet federal handicapped accessibility standards. These are continually updated. Those locations listed as fully accessible to the handicapped have facilities such as restrooms, gazebos, or overlooks that are built to accommodate wheelchair travelers. Locations described as "negotiable" are possibly accessible to the handicapped; they are not barrier-free but are not totally inaccessible either. The accuracy of this assessment for any individual will, of course, vary, but it is an attempt to provide some information about each location's accessibility.

The following terms are frequently used throughout the book in descriptions of facilities at access sites.

Regional access sites are the largest access sites and offer the most facilities. They are the most reliable locations to plan to visit since they generally are designed for nearly all types of users, including those with special needs. Nearly all regional access sites are fully accessible to handicapped travelers. A typical regional access site has from 40 to 200 parking spaces, restrooms, outside showers, water fountains, a gazebo or seating area overlooking the beach, and a dune crossover.

Neighborhood access sites usually have between 10 and 50 parking spaces, a bike rack, a dune crossover, and trash receptacles. They may or may not have off-road-vehicle access and lifeguards.

Local access sites generally have limited parking, which may or may not be paved, and a dune crossover.

A *dune crossover* is a controlled route through the dunes to the beach. Once you find an access site, the dune crossover is usually evident. Dune crossovers may be sand paths or wooden boardwalks, and they may have either steps or ramps for visitors in wheelchairs.

In the Cape Hatteras National Seashore section, the term *ramp* generally denotes an access location to the beach. Since much of the access serves off-road vehicles, most ramps are reinforced for this purpose.

Unimproved access areas are usually unpaved, with room for one or two cars at best, and they have a signed dune crossover.

Maps and charts accompany the text. The charts provide a graphic representation of the basic features at each main location. They are meant to serve as an "at a glance" reference; specific information is found in the text.

The maps correlate with the text, noting the major routes serving a location, regional access sites, and major landmarks. They should guide you directly to the main locations mentioned in the text. Fishing piers are shown on the maps to help orient you on the beach.

Three appendixes follow the text. Appendix A is a categorical listing of types of destinations or agencies with their mailing addresses, phone numbers, and web addresses. Appendix B lists civic or cultural happenings along the coast, arranged by month, and includes phone numbers and websites for more information on each event. Appendix C compiles a monthly listing of fishing tournaments you may want to enter, including the location of each tournament and a phone number or website for further information.

Although every effort has been made to provide the most accurate, up-to-date information, things change frequently along the coast. Unfortunately dates, hours of operation, admission fees, and even addresses and phone numbers change. However, given the general easy-come, easy-go atmosphere of the beach, I hope you'll take any such inconvenience in the appropriate manner—with a grain of salt, or should I say sand. . . .

Access Guide

Currituck County

I first went to Currituck County in 1962 on a fishing trip with my father and grandfather. We drove all day from Greensboro to Aydlett to stay in the home of our fishing guide hosts. For two days, the fishing on shallow Currituck Sound was all day and nonstop. Our knowledgeable guides navigated through a bewildering maze of low islands and only seemed to stop over grassy beds teeming with eager fish.

I hold another vivid memory from that day: the sight and sound of military jets swooping low over the narrow barrier beach that separated Currituck Sound and the Atlantic Ocean. Our guides took it in stride; the commonplace navy strafing runs earned no more than a passing glance between fishing stops. I'm glad I held on to that memory because it, more than the vanished sand roads and relocated horses that used to run free, is a flashback that gauges the magnitude of change that has come to Currituck.

The Currituck County coastline extends almost 27 miles south from the Virginia border, a windswept, narrow, low-profile barrier peninsula between Currituck Sound and the Atlantic Ocean. Parts of it remain as wild as they have ever been: there are still a few of the immense, actively moving, sand dunes; there are thickets of stable forest and thousands of acres of marshy wetlands. North of Corolla, some of the most "natural" miles of barrier island in the state are permanently held as parts of the North Carolina National Estuarine Research Reserve system and the Currituck National Wildlife Refuge. On these remote parts of the barrier, one can still see some of the "wild horses" of Currituck that once roamed freely in the shadow of the Currituck Beach Lighthouse. Much of the area is ideal for waterfowl—always has been—and each year, approximately one-sixth of the Atlantic flyway migratory waterfowl population comes to Currituck.

South of Corolla is one of the newest and "hottest" vacation beaches in the state. The hospitality industry, in the form of vacation rental construction, has been working at a feverish pitch for two decades. This is in stark contrast to the slower, more seasonally measured way of life that is traditional in this distant corner of North Carolina.

Recalling military attack training at treetop level over some of the priciest coastal real estate in North Carolina meets with head-shaking skepticism today. Those who do remember such local color are greatly outnumbered by those who have "discovered" Currituck Banks recently. In fact, the last two decades of the twentieth century wrought more alteration to Currituck County than perhaps did the previous two centuries. The solitude of Currituck's oceanfront peninsula and the unrushed rural character of the roads leading travelers there are now gone.

For most of recorded history, Currituck life has been a blend of agriculture on the mainland and fishing and hunting in the waters of Currituck Sound. This shallow embayment, approximately 30 miles long by 4 miles wide at its greatest width, is the central physical feature of the county. It separates the county land into three distinct parts: the mainland west of the sound, Knotts Island, and the peninsula barrier beach east of the sound. The last is known variously as Currituck Banks or the North Banks. These three land segments are so fundamentally different in nature and character that it can be said that they have the sound and the county courthouse in common and not much else.

Mainland Currituck County is split into two well-drained and farmable upland ridges by the North River's Great Swamp, which drains into Albemarle Sound. Knotts Island, in north-central Currituck, is two-thirds marsh (most of this is national wildlife refuge) and one-third coastal plain forest and farmland. Knotts Island is actually a peninsula extending southeast from Virginia; roads tie it to that state, while its link to the rest of North Carolina is principally by boat or ferry. Currituck's peninsula barrier beach extends southeast from Virginia for nearly 23 miles. It is a sandy, narrow spit that has intermittent stands of maritime forest on its western half if divided lengthwise, most of which is fronted with marsh.

Currituck Sound is not only the most prominent feature on the county map; it is also central to the popular (and somewhat romanticized) county history. The water is clear and not so deep; much of the sound is less than 4 feet deep and rarely deeper than 6 feet. At these depths, sufficient sunlight reaches the bottom to support an abundant covering of aquatic herbs and grasses. This is both superb habitat for fish and excellent forage for waterfowl, especially swans, geese, and ducks. Currituck Sound, rimmed with marsh and filled with food, is everything a migratory bird could wish for as a stopover.

Native Americans found the abundant fish and game important and established both permanent and seasonal settlements in and around Currituck Sound, some of which were on the small islands. In fact, the county name is a corruption of the Algonquian word *Coratank*, which means wild geese. Europeans took a cue and followed the Algonquian pattern of farming, fishing, and hunting. Currituck Sound was such a resource that, during the nineteenth century, hunting waterfowl for the commercial market and guiding sportsmen grew into a cottage industry.

Railroad expansion south from Norfolk made Currituck Sound more accessible, and word of the incredible hunting rippled north. As the twentieth century began, Currituck County was renowned by eastern seaboard sportsmen as one of the finest places for duck hunting in the country. Concurrently, a land rush of sorts began as sportsmen purchased vast tracts of marsh and sound to secure exclusive hunting rights by creating private hunt clubs. The "worthless" oceanfront of the peninsula banks was purchased as well. By the early twentieth century, private hunt clubs owned much of the 27-mile peninsula barrier beach between the Virginia state line and present-day Duck in Dare County.

The oceanfront land was used primarily for open range grazing by the few people who lived on this very isolated parcel of North Carolina. Before the hunt clubs employed residents as caretakers, cooks, and guides, the only steady employment on the peninsula banks was with the U.S. Lighthouse Service or as a surfman at one of the five life-saving stations built by U.S. Life-Saving Service.

As for the clubs, the actual buildings ranged in style and appointment from rustic to genuinely lavish, epitomized today by the restored Whalehead Club at Corolla. Sadly, the Currituck Shooting Club, founded in the mid-eighteenth century and considered one of the oldest continually operating private sports clubs in the country, was lost to fire in the spring of 2003. It was the oldest of several remaining remnants of what some refer to as the golden age of waterfowling at Currituck.

By the late 1960s and early 1970s, vacation-home development pressure began to chip away at the area's solitude. Holding development back was the lack of a road—even public rights-of-way —to Corolla from the Dare County line. Folks who lived north of Duck either drove on the beach or followed a primitive sand track to Corolla.

The proposal to extend NC 12 to Corolla in 1984 brought a flurry of debate, planning, and maneuvering over what would happen in this highly valued length of undeveloped Currituck. Among other things, the National Audubon Society and the Nature Conservancy purchased large tracts of land as set-asides for wildlife, including the much-beloved feral horses that once freely roamed the area. Some of those lands became part of a new Currituck National Wildlife Refuge, configured, ironically, from marsh and water once reserved for private hunting. Other lands and marsh became part of the North Carolina Estuarine Research Reserve.

More recently, tourism in Currituck County exploded. The building boom has now hammered to the very shadows of the Currituck Beach Lighthouse at Corolla. Thankfully, all this construction, while tough on my memory of a time when horses and scantily clad sunbathers roamed free, has not altered the fundamental simplicity of the place.

It will be obvious that the southern portions of Currituck Banks are quite tony. In some locations, ornate, oceanfront rent-a-mansions (3 stories, 7-plus bedrooms *and* pool, sleeping 16-plus) stand porch line to porch line behind the dunes. It seems that only the sunblock-slathered could slip between them to the sea. While a national chain hotel opened in 2003, the chances of another between Dare County and Corolla do not seem likely. In "greater Corolla," several self-contained properties are marketed as resorts that offer services, exclusivity, and amenities—pools and private pedestrian oceanfront access, for example—to guests who rent houses there.

"Downtown" Corolla—once little more than the lighthouse and an adjoining tree-covered settlement of clapboard homes, solitude-loving souls, a small post office, and a few stores—remains pleasantly unimproved in spite of its elevation to a multistate coastal destination. The recent growth has clustered along the thread of NC 12, which splits the very narrow peninsula. While Corolla is one of my favorite places on the Outer Banks, I offer a word of caution to those who may be used to bustling boardwalk beaches: nightlife in Corolla is the sound of crickets and surf and the flash of the lighthouse.

The village is 24 miles north of the Wright Memorial Bridge and 55 miles from the Currituck County Courthouse across the sound, a separation that is increasingly problematic as the number of permanent residents increases. As of this writing, highway and planning officials are exploring the possibilities of a highway bridge to the mainland from Corolla. In June 2004 the North Carolina Ferry Service launched a pedestrian-only service between Currituck and Corolla, with the school-age children who live in Corolla having priority seating on certain ferries during the school year.

While the distance from the Wright Memorial Bridge is not great, the traffic on two-lane NC 12 to Corolla in high season can make it seem that way. The road is the spine of the North Banks, linking all services and residential areas there. "Quick" errands elsewhere can turn annoying quickly. This is the flip side of greater Corolla's out-of-the-way appeal. Although gaining houses and year-round residents and no longer isolated, Corolla is not convenient in the sense that goods and services are at all times, well, convenient. As of the summer of 2004, there were more than 3,200 rental houses, one grocery store, one drug store, and fewer than 20 restaurants on Currituck Banks. Plan on the fact that going out to eat will take a while, especially if you go to one of the many fine restaurants in the resort communities of Dare County.

Finally, the Currituck oceanfront is gorgeous; the accessibility of the sound through outdoor service providers is unequaled. There is history to take in and miles of wild habitat to explore, but there's not a lot of neon, never was, and it is hoped, never will be.

Back Bay National Wildlife Refuge and False Cape State Park in Virginia regulate access to the Currituck Banks from the north. Only residents of the North Bank communities of Swan Beach and Carova Beach who wish to drive to Virginia Beach along the beach may obtain a permit.

Access

Currituck County provides and maintains oceanfront access in the Whalehead Beach subdivision south of Corolla. There is also ocean and soundside parking at the Currituck Beach Lighthouse in Corolla.

There is a regional access with restrooms, boardwalk, and dune crossover near the entrance to the Currituck Club development.

There is also a regional beach access with showers and restrooms at the northern edge of the parking lot of the Hampton Inn and Suites at the southern end of the county.

Access for the extreme North Bank settlements of North Swan Beach and Carova is by four-wheel-drive vehicle only. Ramp access to the North Banks for vehicles is provided at the north end of Corolla at the Tasman Drive access site.

In 1986 the county adopted a comprehensive ordinance restricting vehicular access to the beaches of Currituck. The main points of the ordinance are as follows:

— You cannot drive on the beach from May 1 to September 30 between the Dare County line and the Tasman Drive access ramp, where a paved public road exists parallel to the beach.

— You can only drive on the foreshore or wet sand beach and no faster than 15 miles per hour when pedestrians are present.

— There are exceptions for commercial fishermen "engaged in the use of or setting seines" in the ocean.

There is a boat dock and pier into the sound at the Currituck Beach Lighthouse in Corolla. Public piers, boat tie-ups, and a boat ramp are also available at the former Whalehead Club, just south of the lighthouse. The North Carolina Wildlife Resources Commission maintains boating access sites into Currituck Sound at Poplar Branch at the end of NC 3, $7/10$ mile off of US 158 north of Grandy, and into the Intracoastal Waterway approximately one mile east of Coinjock on SR 1142.

Handicapped Access

Currituck County does not presently provide specific handicapped access facilities other than ramps. Corolla has private facilities that are handicapped accessible. The grounds of the Currituck Beach Lighthouse and the soundside boardwalk are manageable by wheelchair. Several of the dune crossovers in the Whalehead Beach subdivision meet federal handicapped standards.

The Corolla Fire Department loans a beach wheelchair with advance notice by calling 252-453-8595.

Information

Contact the Corolla/Currituck County Chamber of Commerce, 6328-E Caratoke Highway, P.O. Box 1160, Grandy, NC 27939-1160, 252-453-9497.

Web addresses: <www.currituck chamber.org>; <www.nccoastal management.net/Access/sites. htm>

Knotts Island

There are at least two truths about Knotts Island: first, it may be the least acknowledged part of North Carolina; and second, the quiet isolation suits residents just fine.

If this sends you scrambling for a map, then look at the northern tip of Currituck Sound in the northeast corner of the state. The peninsula that extends south from Virginia, between the Currituck mainland and the peninsula banks south of the Virginia line, is Knotts Island.

This insular hamlet is an island only in the loosest sense of the word. Princess Anne Road from Virginia becomes NC 615 at the state line. It crosses Corey's Ditch, a narrow tidal creek linking the North Landing River and Back Bay, the western and northern estuaries that surround the high ground of Knotts Island. Knotts Island Channel completes the boundary, rippling between Currituck Banks and the east edge of the island.

Historically, Knotts Island is the driest ground between what were once some of the finest duck ponds and fishing waters in the country. Most of the island's high, forested, or farmed acreage is along the eastern third, where there are two communities, Knotts Island and Woodleigh. Local roads lead from NC 615 east to private docks in Knotts Island Channel.

Knotts Island proper includes a post office, several small stores, an elementary school, a beautiful church, and scattered residences among farmed land. It is rural, with a greater concentration of homes near the water's edge than inland. All but a few of the homes are permanent residences, and those that are not are either private hunting club holdings or vacation homes.

The drive to the island on NC 615 is through handsome tidewater forests and farmland. There is more of the same on the island.

The roadway passes through the expansive marshlands of Mackay Island National Wildlife Refuge, surrounded by vast stretches of tawny marsh grass and, in winter, groups of dabbling ducks enjoying the safe haven.

Even though the island sits in a direct line for the sprawl of Virginia Beach, it still has the feeling of a waterman's island: quaint, literally and figuratively insular, and charming for its out-of-the-mainstream perseverance and a simpler pace of life. The number of Virginia commuters is increasing, but many of these are islanders who are pursuing better jobs on the mainland. The island has yet to be hit with the splat of subdivisions that has gobbled so much of Virginia Beach that was once rural Princess Anne County. As Princess Anne Road becomes widened to accommodate traffic, though, building may eventually leap across Corey's Ditch.

Before the widespread availability of cell phones, there were several twists to everyday life that

	Fee	Parking	Restrooms	Lifeguard	Camping	Showers	Beach Access	Hiking	Trail	Handicapped	Boating	ORV Access	Fishing	Programs	Historic	Sand Beach	Dunes	Upland	Wetland
Knotts Island	•	•									•		•		•			•	•
Mackay Island National Wildlife Refuge	•	•						•	•		•		•					•	•

made Knotts Island living adventuresome. Local phone service belonged to Virginia Beach; it was a long-distance call to the county courthouse in the village of Currituck across the sound. The post office was friendly and well informed, a useful place to pick up information, though outsiders need not try. While young children attend school on the island, older children must cross the sound to go to school in Currituck. The scheduling of the free ferry to Currituck coincides with school hours. Any annual maintenance that would take the ferry out of service happens in summer when school is out.

When the ferry is scheduled for maintenance, ferry officials post notices along Princess Anne Road (NC 615) prior to the last mainland detour to Moyock to warn tourists of the service interruption.

Currently, Knotts Island is a tight-knit community; islanders who marry "off islanders" may even refer to their spouses as outsiders. Most of the families who call it home have ancestors who made their living behind a plow and on the waters of Back Bay and Currituck Sound guiding hunters and fishermen.

It's an easy place to visit, and there are more offerings that appeal to tourism like a local winery that's flourishing in the tidewater soils. The island roads are lightly traveled and could be profitably explored by bicycle. While services are increasing, unless you are making plans for an extended hunting or fishing trip, Knotts Island is best sampled as a day getaway or scenic detour from the more congested highways through mainland North Carolina and Virginia. It is one of the more curious corners of the state, still out of the way and underappreciated.

Access

Knotts Island is a community of private owners. There are no designated public access locations within the hamlet itself.

Information

Contact the Corolla/Currituck County Chamber of Commerce, 6328-E Caratoke Highway, P.O. Box 1160, Grandy, NC 27939-1160, 252-453-9497.

Web address: <www.currituckchamber.org>

Mackay Island National Wildlife Refuge

After visiting with Kendall Smith, the acting superintendent of Mackay Island National Wildlife Refuge, at the Joseph P. Knapp visitor contact station, I hustled across Corey's Ditch to the Charles Kuralt Trail viewing station on the marsh causeway. Smith had scheduled a flyover "count" of the refuge this early November day and told me to be waiting at this location when the plane came by.

I heard the plane, and then all I could see was a honking, tornadic swirl of greater snow geese. It was a stupefying sight—thousands of stout white birds with black-tipped wings spiraling upward. Then as the plane passed, they unwound, settling back onto a pond hidden from view by marsh vegetation.

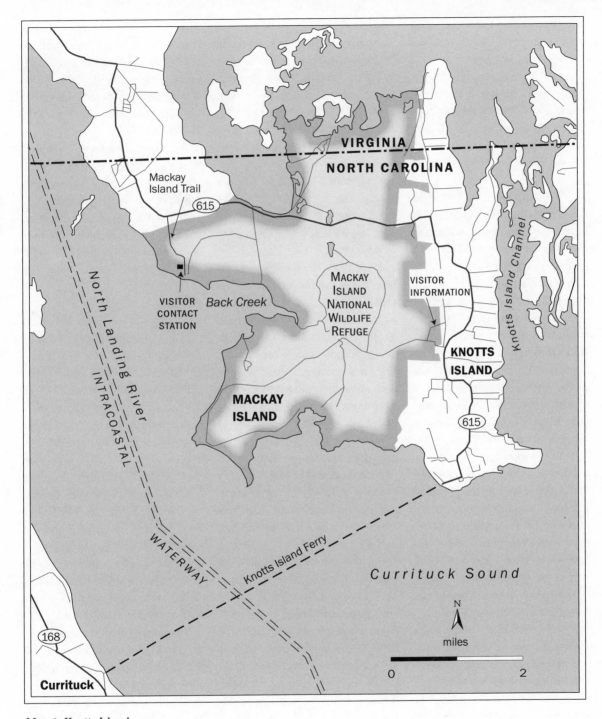

VIRGINIA

NORTH CAROLINA

Mackay
Island Trail

615

MACKAY
ISLAND
NATIONAL
WILDLIFE
REFUGE

VISITOR
CONTACT
STATION

Back Creek

VISITOR
INFORMATION

KNOTTS
ISLAND

Knotts Island Channel

MACKAY
ISLAND

615

North Landing River

INTRACOASTAL

WATERWAY

Knotts Island Ferry

Currituck Sound

N

miles

0   2

168

Currituck

Map 1. Knotts Island

It was over, and I shook my head at what seemed to be the preposterous notion of a flyover count. I never did learn the exact numbers, but it was the most impressive display of goose down that I ever hope to see. My other visits to Mackay Island have not been so animated, but no less interesting in a quiet way.

In 1961 the U.S. Fish and Wildlife Service secured an adjacent complex of wetlands, ponds, and high ground known as Mackay Island, creating a national wildlife refuge for migratory waterfowl. Today, 8,138 acres comprise the refuge: slightly more than 850 acres in Virginia and the remainder in North Carolina.

Mackay Island proper is one of the largest of several patches of high ground within the refuge boundaries. The North Landing River and its tributary, Back Creek, separate Mackay as an island. It is not the island it used to be, however. The main refuge road once crossed a bridge over Back Creek, and canoers and boaters could pass under the bridge and continue completely around the island, but since a culvert crossing replaced the bridge, boaters/canoers must portage the refuge road to make the loop.

Narrow, twisting tidal creeks thread the refuge. Most of them are subject to the characteristic wind tides that govern water levels in Back Bay, the North Landing River, and nearby Currituck Sound. Indian Creek once formed a free-flowing east boundary between the refuge and the homes and farms of Knotts Island, but it has silted and is slowly filling in as marsh.

Unless you have a boat, the practical northern limit of the refuge is the NC 615 causeway, the main road to Knotts Island. This causeway is one of the best locations for bird-watching in the refuge during migratory periods in fall and spring. The Great Marsh Trail, located along the causeway, is a $\frac{1}{3}$-mile loop for year-round hiking and bird-watching.

More than 140 species of birds have been sighted at Mackay Island, including a spectacular wintering population of greater snow geese. The refuge is also home to deer, raccoon, nutria, and mink. The management team permits limited trapping and hunting within the refuge. These activities are regulated yearly, with the numbers of hunters and days of hunting determined by the refuge mandate to provide waterfowl habitat.

Much of the land of Mackay Island came indirectly from the estate of Joseph Palmer Knapp, publisher and outdoor sportsman. Knapp constructed a mansion, since torn down, overlooking the North Landing River on Mackay Island and spent many winter hours hunting and fishing the waters of Currituck Sound. A great benefactor of the county, he was active in maintaining an environmental vigil over the ecology of the sensitive, shallow sound waters and once donated $50,000 to control pollutants on the North Landing River that were threatening the waters of Currituck Sound and Back Bay. Committed to conservation and game management, he established the "More Game Birds in America Foundation" in 1930, which later became Ducks Unlimited.

His role as benefactor extended to the people of Currituck as well. He was instrumental in providing the first free lunch program in a public school system in the state and built the Currituck School, now renamed as the Joseph P. Knapp Junior High School.

Access

The refuge office is located off of NC 615 and is open all year, 8 A.M. to 4:30 P.M. weekdays. Corey's Ditch, the Great Marsh Trail, and the canal adjacent to the north bank of the causeway are open all year. You are permitted to drive the Mackay Island Road and walk or bicycle the Mackay Island Trail (4 miles) or the Live Oak Point Trail (6.5 miles) from March 15 to October 15 during daylight hours. Mackay Island Road is open for walking and cycling to the first gate from October 16 to March 14 during daylight hours. The trails and marshes are closed at this time for resting and feeding migratory wildfowl.

Visitors will find several access points along the causeway of NC 615 for boating or fishing in the surrounding waters. You may fish in all canals and bays only between March 15 and October 15. A valid North Carolina fishing license is required.

Information

For information, contact Mackay Island National Wildlife Refuge, P.O. Box 39, Knotts Island, NC 27950, 252-429-3100.

Web addresses: <http://southeast.fws.gov>; <http://mackayisland.fws.gov>

Knotts Island Ferry

The free ferry from Knotts Island to Currituck holds approximately 18 cars and takes about 50 minutes to cross the sound. During the summer (June 15–August 30), the ferry departs Knotts Island every 2 hours beginning at 7 A.M. and ending at 7 P.M.; Currituck departures begin at 6 A.M. and continue every 2 hours until 6 P.M. During the winter schedule, there are only five daily departures from the island beginning at 7:30 A.M. and ending at 5 P.M. and from the mainland beginning at 6:30 A.M. and ending at 3:45 P.M. The winter schedule serves schoolchildren who attend mainland schools from Knotts Island. Remember two things before heading to Knotts Island from Virginia Beach or the mainland. One, any repairs to the ferry are performed during the summer; if the ferry is out for maintenance, the closing of the route is well posted. Two, the ferry fills quickly during summer weekends; if you secure a place in line, stay there. It is a first-come, first-served system.

Information

To check the schedule, call the ferry dock at 252-232-2683.

Web address: <www.ncferry.org>

Currituck Banks

North of the village of Corolla, NC 12 becomes North Beach Road, and it makes a final eastward curve as it bends around Ocean Hill subdivision, turning toward the ocean. There is an access ramp and once it is crossed, the Currituck Banks becomes the last frontier, roadless, scattered homes, wild lands, and miles of soft sand beach. It is nearly 11 miles to the Virginia line, and at the soft sand speeds, it takes about an hour's trip one way.

Informally known as the "four-wheel-drive area," the northern end of Currituck Banks is an unvarnished time capsule, gussied up in recent years by new homes built for people who simply want to live out of crowd's ways.

The drive passes oceanside through the preserves of the Currituck Banks National Estuarine Research Reserve and the upland portion of the Currituck National Wildlife Refuge, where one can see the famed wild horses, formerly of Corolla, safely relocated. It passes Lewark's Hill (also known as Penny's Hill), one of the great mendanos or moving sand dunes of the Outer Banks that has pushed its way over the abandoned community of Seagull, which thrived when

New Currituck Inlet was open more than a century ago.

There is Wash Woods, the stumps of a drowned forest emerging from the beach, but mostly there are miles of gently undulating shoreline, tracked by vehicles, as vacationers have a chance to use the four-wheel options of their sport utility vehicles. In point of fact, during the summer, traffic on the Currituck Banks can be downright dangerous.

Long before the land rush to Corolla, speculators subdivided much of the North Banks into vacation lots. Would-be developers dredged finger canals into the island, a practice no longer permitted. The primary communities north of Corolla are Swan Beach, North Swan Beach, and Carova Beach. There are points of interest; for example, at North Swan Beach, the old Wash Woods Coast Guard Station has been converted to a private residence. And you may also see some free-range cattle, although the practice was outlawed in some locations on the Outer Banks during the 1930s. The practice may still continue to a limited extent today well north on the banks. There is a sense that little has changed in these communities because access, from north and south, remains difficult. It's an understatement to say that there are many miles of curiosity-provoking beach north of Corolla and a lot of local color, too. If you go, you will be a drive-by visitor.

While Virginia Beach offers

	Fee	Parking	Restrooms	Lifeguard	Camping	Showers	Beach Access	Hiking	Trail	Handicapped	Boating	ORV Access	Fishing	Programs	Historic	Sand Beach	Dunes	Upland	Wetland
Currituck National Wildlife Refuge							•	•					•			•	•	•	•
Nature Conservancy Tract							•	•					•			•	•	•	•
Currituck Banks Research Reserve							•	•			•	•	•			•	•	•	•

the most convenient services, residents of this area must obtain permits to drive through False Cape State Park and the Back Bay National Wildlife Refuge.

It is accurate to say that nowhere else on North Carolina's coast has a road been such an agent of change as in Currituck County. Its beaches are some of the most popular on the Outer Banks, but they are being crushed by their own celebrity. Additionally, there are a lot of people who romanticize "four-wheeling" as recreation and head to Currituck Banks because it still retains a wild appeal. This natural appeal is a selling point, but at times, the crowds spill over into the northern terrain and nudge all solitude aside.

I am fortunate enough to remember when Corolla was empty and unpaved, and the only route to it was a washboard road behind the dunes. It is hard to imagine Corolla empty, but the day I buried my car to the axles in soft sand next to the Currituck Beach Lighthouse, it was. I waited an afternoon before salvation arrived in the form of a random pick-up truck. At that time,

there were fewer than 100 year-round residents living between my mired vehicle and Virginia—maybe no more than thirty. But one of them came by, and he had a chain; he hauled me out for the price of a laugh.

Some things to remember: The speed limit is 15 miles per hour and *all North Carolina motor vehicle laws are enforced on the beach*. You might want to consider the following before driving over the ramp: Let air out of your tires before going on the beach. Drive a car with plenty of road clearance. Never lose momentum as you drive. Stop only on firm sand; always carry a shovel and a chain or strap, and know the tide tables before you go.

Access
You can easily drive the family car to the Ocean Hill development north of Corolla, but you should stop there since the pavement ends. Access north of this point is by four-wheel-drive vehicle only at the designated ramp at Tasman Drive at the north end of the Ocean Hill development.

Information
Contact the Corolla/Currituck County Chamber of Commerce, 6328-E Caratoke Highway, P.O. Box 1160, Grandy, NC 27939-1160, 252-453-9497.

Web addresses: <www.currituck chamber.org>; <http://southeast. fws.gov>; <http://mackayisland. fws.gov>; <www.ncnerr.org>; <www.nccoastalmanagement.net/ Access/sites.htm>

Currituck National Wildlife Refuge

This is a sleeper refuge, little known and genuinely all over the map of the north Currituck Banks, and it includes every possible habitat type remaining there.

Several separate parcels of land comprise the 4,104-acre refuge. The northernmost components, due east of Knotts Island and fronting Knotts Island Bay, include the 1,142-acre Currituck Marsh tract and the 247-acre Station Landing tract. Continuing south, between the North Swan Beach and Swan

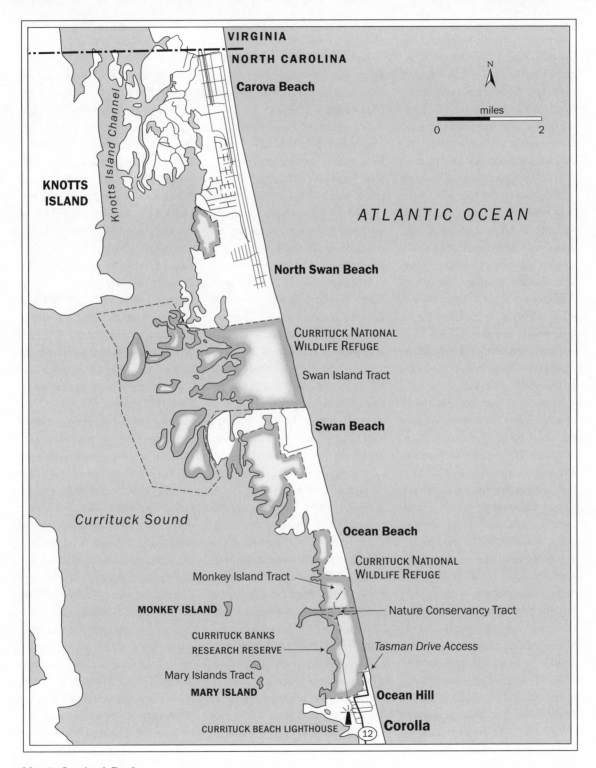

Map 2. Currituck Banks

Beach sections of Currituck Banks is the 1,390-acre Swan Island Unit, one of the original components acquired by the Nature Conservancy in the late 1970s. The South Marsh Unit, about 800 acres, is west-southwest of Swan Beach and farther south is the three-part, 380-acre Monkey Island Unit.

Monkey Island is in Currituck Sound. Once the property of a hunt club by that name, the island with its clubhouse and outbuildings went first to Currituck County and is now a part of the refuge. The northern portion of the island is one of the largest egret rookeries in the state, and part of the island was a summer fishing base and burial ground for Native Americans centuries prior to Currituck's settlement by Europeans.

Adjacent to the south boundary of the Monkey Island tract is a parcel still held by the Nature Conservancy that is used in research and wildlife management studies. It is sandwiched by the Currituck Banks component of the North Carolina Coastal Reserve system, a part of the National Estuarine Research Reserve system. The three agencies, the U.S. Fish and Wildlife Service, the Nature Conservancy, and the North Carolina Coastal Reserve, own the land from the marsh to the mean high-tide line. All three prohibit vehicular access on their property, and inland routes north from Corolla are plainly posted as off-limits. The multiple owners will probably thwart any plans for a road north from Corolla, ensur-

ing the integrity of the tracts for research and wildlife habitat.

If you are driving on the beach, the refuge boundaries are plainly marked with the national wildlife refuge logo.

The refuge, particularly the Swan Island tract, has always been ideal habitat for wintering migratory waterfowl. The land is typical of the North Banks, a transitional area between northern and southern maritime vegetation. For example, both bayberry (*Myrica pensylvanica*) and its southern relative wax myrtle (*M. cerifera*) grow here. The higher elevations and forested portions of the site support deer, fox, raccoon, feral hogs, and horses. The marsh is habitat for muskrat, river otters, mink, and a portion of the Atlantic flyway waterfowl population that winters in Currituck. Refuge managers have confirmed nestings of the piping plover, an endangered species, in the dunes within the refuge, prompting them to closely monitor vehicular traffic there during the nesting season, June through July.

The popular wild horses of Corolla have been relocated here. While this is much better for the horses, it is rough on the refuge. As an experiment to observe the effects the horses have on the refuge, management staff have enclosed a 150-acre flat area behind the frontal dunes in the Swan Island tract. The fences keep horses out in order to see what happens to native vegetation without the presence of grazing animals.

It has taken a long time and quite an effort to put this refuge together. In the late 1970s the Nature Conservancy purchased approximately 1.7 miles of oceanfront and upland property from the Swan Island Club, a private waterfowl hunting club established nearly a century earlier. The property included about 800 acres of upland and about 1,390 acres of marsh, flats, and wetlands. (The historic hunt club and its outbuildings on Swan Island, southeast of Knotts Island in Currituck Sound, were not sold.) The Conservancy transferred Swan Island and the property it had purchased from the Monkey Island Club farther south to the U.S. Fish and Wildlife Service to launch the refuge for migratory waterfowl. The refuge was officially established in 1984.

Since the flurry of those initial years, the holdings have increased to their present acreage. The refuge is being managed to maintain nesting habitat not only for migratory waterfowl, but also endangered species such as the piping plover and the loggerhead turtle.

Currituck National Wildlife Refuge is administered by the Mackay Island National Wildlife Refuge staff on Knotts Island, which is a 1 1/2-hour drive away by the most direct route, along the peninsula beachfront. The distance makes it awkward. In any event, you can't reach the Currituck National Wildlife Refuge except by driving a four-wheel-drive vehicle on the beach or by boat. There is a boat landing in

Waterlily, and if you head slightly northeast from there, you'll hit the Monkey Island portion of the refuge.

You may bird-watch, picnic, and walk in the refuge. Dogs must be on a leash. You can certainly fish and swim on the beach of the refuge, but you cannot drive your vehicle farther inland than the posted signs. Because the beach is narrow, the signs are posted about 50 feet within the refuge boundary to ensure that vehicles will have a drivable route during high tides.

The refuge is so new that management officials are taking a wait-and-see attitude before further restricting refuge use. Because access is not easy, very few people other than the residents of adjoining Swan Beach and North Swan Beach mingle with the migratory residents.

One note of historical interest: in the Swan Island tract, the owner of a parcel of private property has relocated the old Wash Woods Life-Saving Station as a private residence.

Information
For information, contact Mackay Island National Wildlife Refuge, P.O. Box 39, Knotts Island, NC 27950, 252-429-3100.

Web address: <http://mackay island.fws.gov/currituck/>

Currituck Banks National Estuarine Research Reserve

On the left-hand side of North Beach Road, just before the ramp to the beachfront, is a small parking area that provides access to the Currituck Banks component of the North Carolina National Estuarine Research Reserve. A trail leads through the upland habitat of the preserve, first penetrating the walls of a shrub thicket to move into a maritime hardwood forest and then through seasonally flooded bottomlands before emerging on a boardwalk into Currituck Sound. The $1/3$-mile long boardwalk stroll is a delight, taking about 15 minutes each way at a leisurely pace, and it provides a great look at a still wild place. Midway, it crosses a $1^1/2$-mile trail that penetrates deeper into the reserve's upland acreage. Solitude is guaranteed because no one goes there.

The upland terrain exhibits the typical mid-Atlantic vegetation pattern, a dense shrub thicket and some maritime forest thriving behind the artificial dune line created by the Civilian Conservation Corps in the 1930s. Take note of the beachfront, though, because the preserve offers a superb opportunity to see exactly what Currituck Banks looked like before the sand sprouted houses and condominiums. In fact, the juxtaposition of the preserve and Ocean Hill sub-

division next door poses a timely contrast.

The preserve originated in 1984 after the Nature Conservancy gave the state approximately 960 acres of beachfront, dunes, maritime forest, marshes, flats, and islands. It became the third component of the North Carolina National Estuarine Research Reserve system. A private hunting association, the Monkey Island Club, once owned the property.

The proximity to Ocean Hill makes the preserve beachfront easily accessible by four-wheel-drive vehicle. While the primary research done in the preserve takes place within the 625-acre sound and marsh portion, 325 acres of dunes, shrub thicket, and maritime forest remain for other uses. Although the preserve has definite boundaries, many visitors will perceive it, a tract owned by the Nature Conservancy, and the southern component of the Currituck National Wildlife Refuge as one unit of land. Indeed, the three agencies charged with managing these lands have signed agreements to allow the cooperative use of the lands for research projects.

During the warmer months, there is a lot of beach activity at the southern boundary of the preserve where it adjoins the private property of the Ocean Hill subdivision, and there are no plans to alter the traditional recreational use of the property. Plans call for establishing a small day-use area for beach recreation, funded by both county

This serene sitting area on Currituck Sound is in the 954-acre Currituck Component of the North Carolina Estuarine Research Reserve at Corolla. Courtesy of the author.

and state, with restrooms and perhaps a small parking area.

Access

Access to the northern limits of the reserve is by four-wheel-drive vehicle, which by county regulation must stay seaward of the dune line.

There is a parking area on the north side of North Beach Road that leads to the access trails within the preserve. The trail is handicapped accessible once past the trailhead. At the end of the trail is a sitting area on the edge of Currituck Sound.

Information

Contact the Northern Sites Manager, North Carolina Coastal Reserve, 983 West Kitty Hawk Road, Kitty Hawk, NC 27949, 252-261-8891.

Web address: <www.ncnerr.org>

Corolla

Talk about "Hot Beach"—well, Corolla is it, and its burgeoning popularity shows little sign of abating. With the entire implied nuance I can muster, it is fair to write that when people finally get to Corolla, they have arrived. Saying anything less does not do justice to the conversion of this sleepy village to a hot destination.

In the 1980s a washboard dirt

Rods 'n' Reels 'n' Wheels

I've spent my share of time driving after fish on the beach so it seems normal to me. If you are new to the North Carolina coast, the practice may be shocking. However, it is an old custom; you cannot effectively fish in the surf along miles of the national seashores and the rest of the coast without the shelter and mobility of a vehicle. Most drivers are laser-focused, well-intended fishermen, and their vehicles are their tackle shop/campsite on wheels.

While driving on the beach is generally legal in North Carolina, in most locations there are calendar restrictions. There are a few places with year-round driving access: the northern beaches of Currituck County, Cape Hatteras and most of Cape Lookout National Seashores (excluding Shackleford Banks), and the north end of Carolina Beach. However, each of these areas may restrict beach driving in specific areas to benefit the nesting of endangered species.

In addition, many of the resort cities permit driving on the beach between Labor Day and Memorial Day but close the beach to vehicles during the summer vacation season.

Here's where it gets serious. *All North Carolina motor vehicle laws apply to driving on the beach*—all of them, including prohibitions on alcoholic beverages being open in the cab of the car and wearing a seat belt. To legally drive on the beach, your vehicle must be registered, currently licensed, and inspected. The driver must have a valid driver's license or learning permit and must have minimum liability insurance. You are also responsible for obeying the specific laws and regulations of the local government or managing agency, such as the National Park Service. Nearly every municipality that permits driving on the beach within its city limits requires that a special permit or license be prominently displayed. Permits can usually be acquired at the local city hall or police department.

You must use only the designated access ramps to reach the beach. Usually, traffic must remain on the wet sand beach, and the speed limit is 15 miles per hour when people are present. Certain portions of the national seashores may be closed to accommodate either people or the nesting of rare species of birds, such as the least tern, or pelagic turtles. The closed portions of the beach will be clearly marked. Obey those signs, or you will endanger the creatures and your wallet.

Certain municipalities prohibit vehicle access, and you may not drive on the beach within the boundaries of Pea Island National Wildlife Refuge (approximately from the old Oregon Inlet Coast Guard Station to just north of Rodanthe). The U.S. Fish and Wildlife Service administers this refuge under a different mandate than that of the National Park Service, and driving is prohibited within the refuge.

It is strongly recommended that you check with the local municipality or management agency about taking your vehicle on the beach. Accessibility by vehicles is subject to seasonal change and other local restrictions. You are responsible for being aware of those restrictions before taking your vehicle down to the water.

Most certainly, you can't drive on the beach with anything other than a car modified to permit extra-wide tires or a four-wheel-drive vehicle. Don't even think about going without a chain or rope and a shovel, and follow established roads or tracks of other vehicles. While I've never seen reckless driving, I've seen some stupid driving that left one car mired at an inlet with the tide on the rise.

	Fee	Parking	Restrooms	Lifeguard	Camping	Showers	Beach Access	Hiking	Trail	Handicapped	Boating	ORV Access	Fishing	Programs	Historic	Sand Beach	Dunes	Upland	Wetland
Tasman Drive ORV Access							•					•	•			•	•		
Currituck Beach Lighthouse	•	•	•				•	•	•	•	•		•	•	•	•	•	•	•
Currituck Heritage Park/ Whalehead Club	•	•	•				•			•	•		•	•	•				•
Whalehead Beach		•					•			•	•					•	•		
Pine Island Audubon Sanctuary								•								•	•	•	•

track wandered north to Corolla. It was a teeth-chattering, memorable passage. The road then was intermittently graveled and paved, taking a wandering course through the sparse, windswept peninsula. It split the island and was well back of the dunes for the most part, although it surged to the oceanfront to run along Lighthouse Drive in what is now called Whalehead Beach. It delivered only the curious and a few residents to a supremely isolated village. Corolla, then, was an unassuming settlement, wholly un-cinched to the vacation-driven energy of Dare County, 15 miles to the south.

The vacation land rush began with the extension of NC 12 to Corolla in 1984, and for nearly two decades the roar of new construction has been overwhelming. The beach is still terrific, but the newfound popularity and explosion in vacation rentals can make summer visits traffic-clogged to a fault.

Obviously, Corolla is much less lonely than before, but it is still a haven for beach isolationists. It is so easy to reach that I do not believe people realize that Corolla is still out of the way, particularly for people who assume that easy access equates with the availability of an abundance of goods and services.

Necessities may be found, just not on every corner or along the main—that is to say, only—road. In high season the road is crowded, charitably speaking. Most shopping, dining, and entertainment cluster in three commercial hubs, Timbuck II Shopping Plaza, Monterey Plaza, and Corolla Light Village Shops. You can find everything you need for a week at the beach, provided you have come for a week at the beach. Don't peg your vacation pleasure on sport shopping because that's not what this corner of the coast is about.

"Old" Corolla, the original vil-lage, is ever more charming because of the new construction stuffing its enlarged civic limits. The old village snoozes beneath the handsome red-brick tower of the Currituck Beach Lighthouse—much less sleepy but, thankfully, still unplugged. The more or less original streets, Carotank, First, Second, Third, Coral Lane, and Bismark Drive, are overshadowed not by the lighthouse as before but by the larger, taller vacation homes in the new developments. There is a nice tip of the hat to the old ways in the naming of some of the streets on the soundside for the families of longtime residents.

The heart of the old village is just north of the lighthouse, an appealing mix of renovated traditional buildings and new additions. When you drive into the old village, look left under some unusually fine loblolly pine trees. You'll see the offices of Twiddy and Company, Real Estate, with a sign above the door

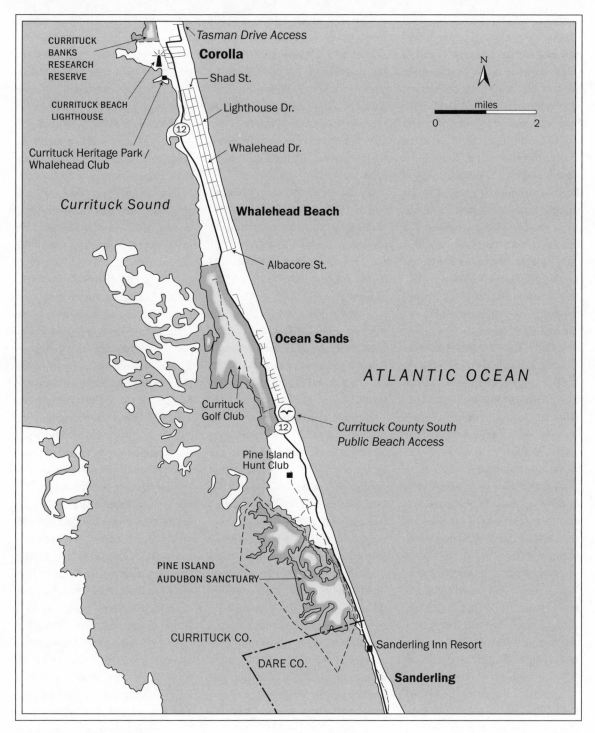

Map 3. Corolla to Sanderling

reading, "U.S. Life-Saving Station." Realtor Doug Twiddy purchased the building and moved it here in 1984, preserving a valuable structure in life-saving station history. It was the original Kill Devil Hills station, constructed in 1896, and not only did its crew witness the Wright Brothers' first flight, but a member, John T. Daniels, snapped the photograph of the century—the picture of the first motorized airplane flight. Twiddy restored the station to its original condition (the sign on the front is a duplicate of the original on display inside) and showcases first-flight historical items, as well as artifacts from life-saving days.

Twiddy also renovated the old Corolla schoolhouse immediately north of the lighthouse. Continue along Corolla Village Lane and you will note several handsome homes recycled as businesses and the Corolla Chapel, which still holds services; vacationers are welcome.

The Corolla Light resort community spreads between NC 12 and the oceanfront. To the west of the road is the Whalehead development, drawing its name and inspiration from the county-owned Whalehead Club. Paved bicycle and stroller trails thread through the soundside live oak forest leading to roads that circle the as yet undeveloped lots around the old Whalehead Club. The most startling visual contrast to the historical wildness of old Corolla is not the resort houses, however, but the bright green manicured turf of a pitch and putt course.

Corolla's great appeal is in its easy access to both the Atlantic Ocean and Currituck Sound and the recreational opportunities that come with being so close to each. Currituck Banks here is less than $1/2$ mile wide from sound to shore. The beaches are wide; the sand, fine-grained, and the early morning sun, terrific.

To the west the marsh-fringed sound beckons to the adventuresome who want to try sailing or kayaking, which, along with all-terrain vehicle rental and nature/island touring, are local cottage industries.

There are places to bike, places to blade, and a heckuva golf course, the Currituck Club. Mostly though, Corolla and environs offer a soothing place to laze, beach walk, and swim.

It is so appealing that you want to visit, and that is not always easy to do in season because the Inn at Corolla Light (website: <www.corolla-inn.com>), an idiosyncratic hostelry on Currituck Sound, offers the only nightly lodging near the old village. It is a lovely, curious space because previously it was a boutique retail complex. The individual shops are now renovated into oversized rooms. The inn has a pool, a gazebo in Currituck Sound, and such niceties as a paperback library and video collection. I found it to be delightfully available and uncrowded in the shoulder seasons, and the sunsets over the sound are an incredible bonus.

In summer, just don't be in a hurry if you want to go out to eat.

Access

Development has pressed the ability to provide easy access to the beach. Rental houses do afford access. There is also a large accessway adjacent to the hotel in the southern part of the community.

Each of the self-contained resorts and subdivisions has plentiful local access.

The primary access for visitors to Corolla is in Whalehead Beach south of the village. Two well-marked turns take you to the access parking. From the south, turn east on Albacore Street (the Food Lion grocery store at the corner of NC 12 and Albacore is your landmark). There is a dune crossover and ramp for emergency vehicles only at the end of Albacore. From the north, turn east on Shad Street (the Corolla Light water tower at the corner of Shad and NC 12 marks the turn). There is a dune crossover at the end of Shad. Whalehead Beach subdivision consists of three streets parallel to the ocean: Lighthouse Drive, directly behind the dune line; Whalehead; and Corolla Drive, the westernmost street. East-west streets with fishy names cross these three. The dune crossovers are at the east end of the fish streets; public parking is not so obvious. The county has five, very large, paved parking lots along Whalehead Drive at the intersections with Shad, Sturgeon, Perch, Bonita, and Sailfish Streets. The lots are not marked; just look for something paved and large enough for a helicopter. There is also a commitment for a new parking area at Whalehead and Dolphin Streets, near the fire department.

In the past, the sheriff's department seemed fairly easygoing about parking as long as you do not violate a posted prohibition and your vehicle is completely off the road and not blocking a drive. In fact, one deputy provides hand-drawn maps showing the parking lot locations on the backs of the warning citations he issues.

Public parking is also available at the Currituck Beach Lighthouse on Corolla Village Road—a left turn off of NC 12 just south of the lighthouse property. If you turn right at the same intersection, you will find parking at the ocean terminus of Carotank Drive.

There is also a public access area at the Hampton Inn and Suites at the southern part of Corolla.

To drive north on the beach, the access area is at Tasman Drive, but you cannot drive south on the beach from there to the Dare County line between May 1 and September 30. However, if you are in pursuit of fish for commercial activities (setting seines), you can pretty much drive your vehicle anywhere. You had better be pursuing fish in a manner convincing to local law enforcement personnel, however, or prepare to pay the $50 fine.

Handicapped Access

The Corolla Fire Department loans a beach wheelchair with advance notice by calling 252-453-8595.

The county provides ramps that meet federal handicapped accessibility standards at the eastern ends of Tuna, Barracuda, Herring, and Coral Streets in the Whalehead Beach subdivision.

The Corolla Light Village Shops have public restrooms that are handicapped accessible.

Rental cottages that have a boardwalk over the dunes may be considered handicapped accessible by real estate agents. However, check to make sure that the ramp does not extend from the second floor of a condominium.

Information

Contact the Corolla/Currituck County Chamber of Commerce, 6328-E Caratoke Highway, P.O. Box 1160, Grandy, NC 27939-1160, 252-453-9497.

Web addresses: <www.currituck chamber.org>; <www.nccoastal management.net/Access/sites. htm>

Currituck Beach Lighthouse and Lightkeeper's Quarters

I climb the Currituck Beach Lighthouse every chance I get and still can't get enough of the view. What is remarkable is how tree-covered the peninsula remains. The observation platform is about 150 feet high; if you are counting steps, it is 214. A private, nonprofit foundation, Outer Banks Conservationists, Inc. (OBC), has been responsible for the careful restoration of the lighthouse and outbuildings for twenty years under what had been a long-term lease. Last July, the De-partment of the Interior rewarded the organization's hard work with the deed to the lighthouse under the provisions of the National Historic Lighthouse Preservation Act of 2000. Restoration will continue as before, and visitors will have the breezy treat of the magnificent cat-walk view to enjoy again.

When first lighted on December 1, 1875, the Currituck Beach light completed the network of major beacons on North Carolina's Outer Banks. The Currituck light filled the gap between Cape Henry at the entrance to Chesapeake Bay and Bodie Island at Oregon Inlet, giving mariners a series of lights to guide them along the coast from Cape Lookout north.

Since North Carolina's other major beacons were painted in the black and white patterns familiar today, the decision was made not to paint the Currituck light in order to distinguish it from the others. At the base of the 162-foot tall tower (measured to the very top), the walls are 5 feet 8 inches thick—all brick. The wall thickness tapers to a mere 3 feet at the top—still all brick.

The lighthouse is open from Easter until Thanksgiving. For a $3 fee, you may climb to the focal-plane gallery and enjoy the commanding view. The fee goes toward the renovation of the lightkeeper's quarters, a large Victorian duplex on the complex grounds. Although the OBC manages the lighthouse building itself, the U.S. Coast Guard continues to maintain the lens area and the generators.

The Currituck Beach Lighthouse is open for ambitious climbers who want a towering view of the North Banks. Courtesy of North Carolina Travel and Tourism.

The lightkeeper's house was originally precut, hauled across the Currituck Sound by barge, and assembled on site in 1876. Now it is a state property included on the National Register of Historic Places. The OBC is also working with the North Carolina Department of Cultural Resources to renovate a smaller residence that was moved here to accommodate another keeper.

As you step onto the grounds of the lighthouse, look carefully at all the trees. Then, when you go inside the building, look at the his-torical photographs of the light-house: there are few, if any, trees in photographs taken during the nineteenth or early twentieth centuries. The vegetation on the light-house grounds is a comparatively new feature of the site, perhaps not more than 50 to 60 years old. Until the Great Depression, Currituck Banks was open range for grazing cattle, and as many as 6,000 cattle and wild horses cropped the vegetation on the banks. In the 1930s Works Progress Administration and Civilian Conservation Corps teams were given the task of sta-bilizing the dunes of the Outer Banks. They bulldozed an artificial (and arbitrary) dune line, planted it with beach grass and sea oats, and planted pine trees inland. Once the pines survived the grazing and sheltered the landward side of the island, other plants could success-fully germinate and grow. From the light, you are first startled by the amount of green below, the thickness of the soundside woods, and the composition of the is-land—dune to flats to shrub thicket to maritime forest to marsh.

At the west end of the parking area is a boardwalk that penetrates about 300 yards through the maritime forest, a freshwater cattail swamp, the adjoining marsh, and out into Currituck Sound. Although the walk can be buggy, it provides access not only to spectacular sunsets but also to the incredible evening song arising from the various habitats through which it passes. Note as you walk how the different habitats ease into one another—trees suddenly have sufficiently dry ground to rise out of what seems to be hopelessly soggy footing. The grasses in late summer reach 4 feet high, and the amphibian chorus announces your stroll along the length of the boardwalk, alerting the world to your intrusion. The boardwalk is a great spot to take the kids crabbing, too.

Access

The lighthouse is open 10 A.M. to 6 P.M. daily except Sunday, but it closes if there is the least hint of lightning. There are more than 30 parking spaces along the south side of the property, and across NC 12, Carotank Drive leads to an oceanfront parking lot with 30 spaces. Both lots fill up quickly during the summer.

Handicapped Access

The grounds of the lighthouse are negotiable by wheelchair, but the lighthouse is not. The boardwalk meets handicapped standards. Two handicapped parking spaces are plainly signed.

Information

For information, contact Outer Banks Conservationists, Inc., P.O. Box 361, Corolla, NC 27927, 252-453-8152.

Web address: <www.currituck beachlight.com>

Currituck Heritage Park/Whalehead Club

The Whalehead Club has remained the most lavish of the hunting clubs erected on Currituck Sound, even though for many years it was also the most forlorn. It still commands a peninsula overlooking Currituck Sound, just southwest of the parking lot on Corolla Village Road that serves the Currituck Beach Lighthouse. It is now one of the principal elements in the new Currituck Heritage Park.

In 2004 Currituck County broke ground for a new Outer Banks Center for Wildlife Education. It is between the Currituck Beach Lighthouse and the Whalehead Club. The center explores the ecology of Currituck Sound and how its natural conditions led to it becoming a haven for extraordinary wildlife populations in the nineteenth and early twentieth centuries. Particular attention is devoted to the wildlife heritage of Currituck County, once the most celebrated and romanticized location for waterfowl hunting in the United States.

It is the Whalehead Club, the zenith of what a passion for hunting can initiate, that makes the Currituck Heritage Park matchless. The Whalehead Club is truly incomparable on the East Coast.

The splendid building has been carefully restored with artifacts and personal items from its original owners. The story of the club regales visitors who take the guided tours. Pennsylvania industrialist Edward Collins Knight Jr. had two loves late in life: Marie-Louise LeBel and duck hunting. He brought them both together in opulent, eclectic, Art Nouveau style at a place he called Corolla Island. It took three years, from 1922 to 1925, and $383,000 to build this most stylish, 21,000-square-foot structure. The roof was copper, the exterior wood was cypress, the chandeliers were Tiffany, and there was a baby grand piano inside. The park-like grounds included an arched bridge over an artificial lagoon and a boathouse, both of which are restored and open for visitation. The bridge and boathouse are thought to be a reconstruction of structures noted by Knight's wife on a trip to Europe. Safe at their distant waterside retreat, the Knights sailed through the Depression with guns and party lights blazing.

When Knight and his wife died in 1936, their heirs had little use for the property, and it was eventually sold in 1940 for $25,000.

The second owner, Ray T. Adams, gave it its present name, the Whalehead Club. From that year until 1992, when Currituck County bought the property for preservation, the building steadily lost ground in a variety of uses, including as a station for the U.S. Coast

Restored to its original opulence, the once-private Whalehead Club is open as a featured component of the Currituck Heritage Park in Corolla. Courtesy of the author.

Guard, as a private academy, and then as a rocket testing station. Today, the Whalehead Club is fully restored, including a brand new copper roof—with, as specified, seven folds in each shingle—original paint scheme, and the piano. It is open to the public for tours.

Access

Following the county's purchase, you may now walk the grounds. The building is clearly visible from the lighthouse parking lot and from the public boardwalk that extends into the sound from the lot.

There are 12 parking spaces, a boat ramp, and several boat tie-ups for use at the west end of the clubhouse.

Handicapped Access

The new museum is certain to be accessible for the handicapped. At present, it is possible to use a wheelchair on the roads around the club, but the grounds cannot be easily negotiated by wheelchair.

Information

Contact the Whalehead Club, P.O. Box 307, Corolla, NC 27927, 252-453-9040.

Web addresses: <www.currituck chamber.org>; <www.whalehead club.com>

Mainland Ferry

In the summer of 2004, the North Carolina Ferry Service began an experimental ferry service between Corolla at Currituck Heritage Park and Currituck on the mainland. The pedestrian-only service is a response to the numbers of school-age children who now live in Corolla and must attend public mainland schools. The ferry substantially reduces commuting from the one-way 55-mile trip children must make to the mainland.

While school students have priority seating on certain departures during the school year, other pedestrians will be able to ride during non–school hour departures, which might also reduce the commuting chore of seasonal employees who live on the mainland but work at Corolla.

Web address: <www.ncferry. org>

Ocean Sands

The Ocean Sands subdivision, south of Whalehead Beach, covers about 3 miles of oceanfront property south of Crown Point Circle. Beach access is by rental from one of the many real estate agencies that manage the private homes in the subdivision. Ocean Sands is a very quiet subdivision; there are no through streets and very little traffic except for residents and vacationers.

Handicapped Access
Some cottages have boardwalks over the dunes that may be considered accessible by realtors.

Currituck Shooting Club

In April 2003 the Currituck Shooting Club, the oldest continually operating hunt club in the country, burned to the ground in an accident. It was one of the great historic treasures of the county.

Its roof and the top of its shingled sides were once just visible from NC 12 to the west just south of Spindrift. The club was never open to the public but was notable because it and several other clubs are responsible for preserving the wildness of Currituck Banks. The Currituck Shooting Club was founded in 1857, and the building was on the National Register of Historic Places.

The destruction was total, including guns, decoys, ammunition, and historic photographs. By chance, the historic logbooks, which recorded all the members and their guests and their take on a day's shooting, and other records of club life were off-site being restored.

The club owned more than 2,000 acres of undeveloped land in this location that formed the nucleus of the exquisite golf course, Currituck Club.

Pine Island Club

The Pine Island Hunt Club property adjoins the Currituck Shooting Club land and once extended from the sound to the oceanfront. Plans have been drawn up for a development here, and the recent construction of the Hampton Inn and Suites is a part of those original plans, which possibly include an eighteen-hole golf course and condominiums. NC 12 was realigned slightly east of its original route as a part of this proposal. The land west of the highway will remain as the Pine Island Club and, perhaps, as part of an expanded Audubon Society preserve. The lands of the Pine Island Hunt Club are not open for public visitation, except for the rather curious Pine Island Tennis and Racquet Club, which has indoor courts for handball, squash, and tennis.

Access
Except for the racquet club, there is no public beach or sound access. There is a lovely nature trail that runs from the racquet club back to the Sanderling Inn by way of the adjoining Pine Island Audubon Sanctuary.

Pine Island Audubon Sanctuary

The National Audubon Society posts nearly a mile of road frontage and 6,000 acres of forest, wetland,

US 17, the King's Highway

US 17 is the historic route through the Albemarle region, the land along Albemarle Sound where the first permanent European settlements in North Carolina flourished, having arrived in these northeastern counties as "spillover" expansion from the successful settlement of Virginia's Tidewater region. The route itself is not a direct line to the wet sand beach, as it parallels the coast far inland from the beaches. It is, however, a historic side trip, and the small communities along the route are jewels of interest—well-kept, dignified towns. You can stop, look, and learn at each of them.

Much of US 17 today follows the original track that during the colonial period made it the royal post road, the major mail route from Williamsburg to Charleston. It became known as the King's Highway (a name that persists in South Carolina).

The road touches many of the sites on the Historic Albemarle Tour (website: <www.albemarle-nc.com/hat>), and you can stitch together an informal "Colonial Tour" just by following US 17.

Elizabeth City

Elizabeth City was a late bloomer by Albemarle settlement standards, authorized by the General Assembly in 1793, more than 100 years after the founding of Pasquotank County. The waterfront community thrived after the completion of the Dismal Swamp canal in the early 1800s. Mercantile trading brought wealth to the town. Its location, however, brought the Union army in 1863, which destroyed much of the wealth by setting the town on fire.

Elizabeth City recovered from burning to regain prominence as a manufacturing and trading center by the early twentieth century. Today, the community boasts six historic districts, including an antebellum commercial district, a stunning residential district of stately homes in "Southern Colonial" revival architecture, and one embracing the traditionally black Elizabeth City State University and its adjoining residential area.

Make one sure stop, the Museum of the Albemarle, a division of the North Carolina Museum of History that details the peoples and settlement of the Albemarle, in its brand-new home on US 17.

The super secret: Squarely curious is the old Naval Airship Dock No. One at Weeksville, 12 miles south of Elizabeth City, which is 960 feet long and six stories tall with "clamshell" doors. During World War II, this hangar was built as a base for the lighter-than-air craft (dirigibles) used to protect coastal shipping. It is still home to airships today.

Hertford

I like towns that snuggle up to rivers, where cypress trees stand like moss-draped pilings between the houses and a wind-chopped sheet of broad, dark water. Hertford is such a place, and has been since 1758. You can't sail farther inland on the Perquimans River since it narrows, coils, and blocks passage past Hertford.

In 1730 Quaker Abraham Sanders built a sturdy brick house on the Perquimans River, 3 miles south of the charming community of Hertford. Known as the Newbold-White House, it is the oldest brick building in the state. It is also home to a newly constructed periauger, a two-mast sailing vessel like one originally created from a hollowed cypress log that Sanders listed in a 1750 inventory. In the summer of 2004, the periauger was launched from its boatyard at the North Carolina Maritime Museum in Beaufort, North Carolina, and eventually sailed to its new home.

Edenton

Edenton, which served as provincial capital of the colony between 1722 and 1743, is the culmination of colonial influence and power in the Albemarle. On October 25, 1774, fifty-one women met here to sign a petition supporting the "resolves" of the First Provincial Congress, an assembly celebrated as "Edenton Tea Party."

The town plan and restored historic buildings, many more than 200 years old, are Edenton's pride. The architecture of five splendid structures—the Chowan County Courthouse, St. Paul's Episcopal Church, the James Iredell House, the Cupola House, and the Barker House—fixes Edenton in your memory. The Chowan County Courthouse, built in 1767, and St. Paul's Episcopal Church, which took nearly forty years from 1736 to complete, are especially noteworthy architectural treasures. Several other restored houses, all significant to regional history, are open for tours.

Washington

Washington, North Carolina, was the first community in the United States to be named after George Washington. Its founder, Revolutionary War veteran James Bonner, renamed it from Forks of Tar River to honor his commanding officer in 1776.

The waterfront location of the town has not been kind. After Union troops torched abandoned naval stores here in 1864, the fire spread and burned many antebellum buildings. Some of the buildings listed on the self-guided walking tour survived this fire and another in 1900. The Old Beaufort County Courthouse at 158 North Market Street, now the public library, is the second-oldest courthouse in the state.

For a side trip, visit Historic Bath, the oldest incorporated town in North Carolina, which is 15 miles east. Stop at the visitors center for an orientation film before setting out on the easily walked tour of the tiny community. St. Thomas Church is the oldest existing church in North Carolina and is open for visitors. Blackbeard lived here.

New Bern

New Bern is the second-oldest town in the state, settled in 1710 by Baron Christoph de Graffenreid with Swiss and Palatine immigrants. The town incorporated in 1723, and from 1746 until 1792, it was the colonial and state capital. The city is chock-full of architectural treasures—gems such as the four-dial Baxter street clock before Baxter's Jewelry on Pollock Street and the Gothic Christ Episcopal Church. Also on Pollock Street is where pharmacist Caleb Bradham concocted "Brads drink," which after 1898 was sold as Pepsi-Cola.

The big draw is Tryon Palace, named for royal governor William Tryon, who made New Bern his capital in the 1760s. Following the Revolution, Tryon Palace served as capitol and governor's residence until 1794, when the site for both shifted to Raleigh. In 1798 the palace burned, and things went downhill from there. It was restored in the 1950s as the state's first historic site.

If I had limited shoe leather to wear away, I would walk the sidewalks of the neighborhoods between East Front Street and George Street. This is where the spirit of New Bern lives.

For additional information, contact North Carolina Division of Tourism, 301 North Wilmington Street Raleigh, NC 27601, 919-733-8372, 800-847-4862; or Historic Albemarle Tour, P.O. Box 1604, Washington, NC 27899, 252-926-2950, 800-734-1117.

Web addresses: <www.visitnc.com>; <www.albemarle-nc.com>

and marsh adjoining Currituck Sound as a bird sanctuary. Two small wooden signs mark the limits of the preserve, which starts at the Dare/Currituck County line along the "S" curve adjacent to the health club at Sanderling and extends several miles north on NC 12. Originally, the preserve was made up of nearly 2 miles of oceanfront set aside by the owner of the Pine Island Hunt Club in the early 1970s. Since that time, the preserve has increased the marsh and wetland acreage, which provides more favorable habitat to the migratory waterfowl. In return for the additional acreage, the Audubon Society released some of the original oceanfront and upland acreage.

This area is one of the most stable portions of Currituck Banks and exemplifies the full range of barrier island ecosystems. Accordingly, it supports an outstanding cross section of both flora and fauna.

Access

There is a 2¹/₂-mile self-guided trail that goes through the shrub thicket and maritime forest on the west side of NC 12. There are two observation platforms with views of Currituck Sound. The trailhead begins at the Dare County Line.

There is no parking along NC 12 as it passes through the refuge. There is no access to the beaches except by entry north and south of the refuge and walking to the preserve along the wet sand beach.

Information

Contact Audubon North Carolina, 123 Kingston Drive, Suite 206A, Chapel Hill, NC 27514-1651, 919-929-3899.

Web address: <www.ncaudubon. org/nccas_sanc4.html>

Dare County

The adjectives describing the Outer Banks of ebbing memory—remote, distant, desolate, windswept, and haunting—and those describing the Outer Banks today—jostling, crowded, engaging, lively, but threatened—apply foremost to the oceanfront of Dare County. The Dare County barrier islands comprise the state's easternmost outpost, and its beaches are synonymous with "Outer Banks." While the term almost invariably conjures an image of a favorite place between the village of Duck and the Cape Hatteras Lighthouse, it should properly include the sandy southern isles of Ocracoke, North and South Core Banks, Shackleford Banks, and Bogue Banks.

This solidly academic answer is roundly overlooked: ask 100 people where the Outer Banks are, and 90 percent will declare they fall between Virginia and Hatteras Inlet. The other 10 percent will include Ocracoke Island.

While these two de facto bookends, Duck and the Cape Hatteras Lighthouse, are a few miles and several engaging stops short of bracketing all of Dare County's oceanfront, they certainly frame the greatest length of the nostalgic and romanticized Outer Banks. There is so much to absorb here—inimitable historic threads, surprising ecological variety, a stoic, persevering population, and the graphic, unnerving starkness of a ribbon of sand precariously perched between the sky and the rolling sea.

First and foremost, Dare County is the location of more than 60 miles of some of the wildest and most accessible beach in the East, the Cape Hatteras National Seashore. Nearly all of its intriguing miles are here; the remainder is on Ocracoke Island in neighboring Hyde County. It is a resource mostly sampled as drive-by tourism from the inside of a car—miles passed are miles unexplored. One could make several lengthy visits here and only tap the shallows of its simple formula: let the beach be beach and let people be the guests. As a matter of fact, the seashore is never the same from season to season or year to year; only the tide can cover it all in a single visit.

This length of coast holds a catalog of attractions that supplement the great appeal of the vast sea and its beaches. As a historical destination, it is second to none nationally for two events that occurred here: this is where English-speaking people changed the New World by making the first attempt to establish a colony, commemorated at the Fort Raleigh National Historic Site, and this is the location where the Wright Brothers changed the world at large by making the first successful motor-powered flight.

There is a good deal more. The highest sand dune on the East Coast, by itself a state park, is open for play daily, and as a maritime historical landmark, there is the tallest brick lighthouse in the world. Except for scheduled maintenance, it is climbable, and one can read about how it was jacked up and moved away from the eroding shoreline in 1999. Overlooked and underappreciated in this mostly sunny world is the cooling shade available from several large tracts of eastern maritime hardwood forest. On the water, Dare County provides access to some of the most storied surf fishing, bird-watching, and offshore deep-sea fishing on the East Coast—the only requirement for success is showing up at the right place at the right time. Kayakers ply the sound waters around Avon, and windsurfers flock to Canadian Hole near the village of Buxton.

Every gradation between neon, unabashedly beach commercial and sun-bleached, weathered-by-the-sea summer place quilts the Dare County resort communities. The romantic magic of the place lures people here, and the debate that rages on the edge of the sea is how to best receive them and be true to what attracts them originally.

The result is a veritable sampler of options and outings. Mile for mile, the mix of patina, past, and personality makes the resort cities and public preserves on Dare's lengthy barrier islands a destination that can't be matched.

Whenever I return to these oceanfront miles, I travel with anxious anticipation about the changes I will see. This began more than 30 years ago when a campground/access area on the north end of Pea Island disappeared between my visits. Not too much later, the U.S. Coast Guard Station there became obsolete, and the arcing span of the Oregon Inlet Bridge, spanned water then sand, then more sand, until it was finally tethered in place with a great curving rock jetty.

Dare County forms the outer ramparts of North Carolina against a combination of relentless forces: wind and the ocean. They give, and they take away. It is my observation that if something is not tied down here, it will move; if it is tied down, everything around it might move anyway. The forced evacuation of the Cape Hatteras Lighthouse inland underscored this oversimplified observation. The more I return, the more I realize how temporary "permanent" is in this place.

From year to year, I never know what I will see—acute differences with my memory of the last visit or inexorable, inevitable rearrangements that portend a new alignment of land and sea. The ocean rearranges this beachfront with seeming arbitrariness, continually tinkering with the county's eastern and southern boundaries. This has always happened and select place names are the best evidence of historical changes: Bodie Island, Pea Island, and Hatteras Island have long lost their defining inlets. Way back last century, in October 1991, the sea attempted a breach of Pea Island, swallowing much of its defining artificial dune line and toying with slicing the local lifeline, NC 12. On September 18,

Once a threatened species, the brown pelican has today extended its natural range to include most of the North Carolina coast. Courtesy of Outer Banks Visitors Bureau.

2003, Hurricane Isabel did just that when it powered ashore as a Category III storm (diminished and, thankfully, downgraded from Category V) with its powerful northeast quadrant sweeping Hatteras Village. It blew out a ¹/₂-mile-wide gouge between Frisco and Hatteras Village, isolating the small community that it had devastated. Hatteras became an island once again.

Recovery of the roadway proceeded as soon as possible, but Hatteras was rocked solidly for the first time in a very long time. It is likely not to be the last time either. Isabel damaged 4,100 residences, numerous hotels, and nearly all the piers in Dare County. It also undermined NC 12 in several other locations. As a measure of public cost, the North Carolina Department of Transportation estimates that repairs to the 56 miles of NC 12 between Nags Head and Ocracoke have cost $32 million in the years between 1987 and 2003. Outer Banks residents have a dogged resignation when it comes to severe weather, but Isabel recast the thinking among long-stalwart residents.

For visitors, Isabel should be a clear signal of how tenuous life is out here. I think there is very little doubt that I will always be able to return to Dare County beaches, but the looming question is, where will those beaches be?

Part of the joy of going to Dare County from inland locations is that the drive there offers no hint that there is a beach at the end of the journey (unless you arrive by ferry from Ocracoke). The major highways, US 158 from the north and US 64 or 264 from the west, are rural drives characteristic of the eastern part of North Carolina. Along US 158, the roadside scenery is a steady panorama of farms; on US 64 and 264, the view is mostly of impenetrable coastal forests punctuated by broad swaths of farms and the crossroads clusters of small towns.

Coastal forest extends surprisingly close to the oceanfront. Both bridges serving the oceanfront from the mainland, the Wright Memorial Bridge over Currituck Sound and the new Virginia Dare Memorial Bridge over Croatan Sound, end in the forested western part of their respective destinations. In less than a mile, the trees are behind, and the view fills with the textures, colors, and shapes of the coast: dusky hues and weathered wood; the ocean waves tantalizingly screened by buildings and dunes. The tease fuels squealing childhood fervor.

The Outer Banks of Dare County are reasonably uniform in their physical characteristics and profile. They are low islands, and along much of their length the dune line built by the Civilian Conservation Corps in the 1930s offers some of the highest ground. There are exceptions. The unusual stands of hardwood maritime forest in Nags Head and Buxton on older dune ridges are important natural features that have been purchased and preserved in their unaltered condition. Another notable exception is the massive sand dunes like Jockey's Ridge of Nags Head and Big Kill Devil Hill in Kill Devil Hills.

The artificial dune line was constructed in Dare County during the Depression to stabilize the islands and to guard what would become the beachfront road crucial to the resort business. Instrumental in the success of this effort was the ban on open grazing passed by the North Carolina General Assembly. The grazing prohibition allowed sand stabilizing grasses to grow. Prior to the artificial dune line, the Dare County beaches were flat with little relief or vegetation, similar to the north end of Ocracoke today.

On the ocean side, the dune line results in a slightly steeper beach profile than would otherwise occur. Waves break with greater force in a shorter distance, carving an abrupt gradient. Many years ago, more accustomed to the tabletop flat beaches of South Carolina, I body-surfed a wave right onto the beach and used my nose as a bumper.

The ocean has claimed much of this dune ridge, although it remains the primary protection for NC 12 between Nags Head and Hatteras. It is most evident through Pea Island National Wildlife Refuge and at much of the length of the beach south of Oregon Inlet.

Not all winds and waves treat all beaches the same here. The compass alignment of the beachfront has a profound effect.

The beaches of northern Dare County to Rodanthe, south of Oregon Inlet, parallel a line that extends from north-northwest to south-southeast. The waves from winter's "nor'easters" strike almost perpendicular to the beachfront. South of Rodanthe to Cape Point at Buxton, the banks align nearly due south, and the waves from the same "nor'easters" break obliquely on the beach, paring away sound instead of pounding it free. The alignment shift also affects how prevailing winds tug at the sand and consequently affects the profile of the beachfront and dune line, which has remained fairly stable south of Rodanthe. Except for the communities, most of the oceanfront south of Rodanthe is in the Cape Hatteras National Seashore. Though access and services are limited here, it is some of the most enjoyable beach to be found.

It may seem surprising today, but people did live on Dare County's banks before there was tourism, but they did not live on the oceanfront. The commercial lifeblood of the oldest communities was the sea, but residents were wise enough to set up permanent shop where there was safe anchorage and safe housing, typically on forested tracts on the soundside of the islands.

The wooded portions of Kitty Hawk, Colington Island, Manteo, Wanchese, Rodanthe, Buxton, and Hatteras were settled by the mid-nineteenth century and are among the earliest settlements. These places are still forested (Rodanthe less so) and offer safe harbor even if the inlets, which originally sustained some of them, are problematic or closed. The first boost to sustaining settlement on the banks began in the 1870s, when the U.S. Life-Saving Service established surf stations for sea rescue approximately every seven miles along the oceanfront. Kill Devil Hills, Nags Head, Rodanthe, and Avon grew with the proximity of established life-saving stations. Many homes, stores, and even station houses associated with this era remain, outstanding and distinctive for their period architecture. Generally, though, older means wiser, and that means closer to the soundside of the island.

Although Nags Head has been known as summering place since the early nineteenth century, the location of choice then was the soundside. It took the early twentieth-century wealth of nearby inland ports such as Elizabeth City to create the leisure and resources that made summering on the oceanfront more than a flight of imagination. By the 1930s, the beginnings of the oceanfront resort business were underway. In 1932 workers paved the first 18 miles of road that would become NC 12, essentially a loop that went from an earlier causeway connecting Manteo to the oceanfront along the beach to the Wright Memorial Bridge, which had been built in 1930. At that time, private ferry service linked Roanoke Island to the mainland. The first steps to preserve the Outer Banks of Dare County as a seashore park were also made in that decade, including the construction of the artificial dune line.

At this time, large tracts of land and marsh on Bodie, Pea, and Hatteras Islands remained undeveloped and were acquired for federal use for separate purposes in the 1930s and 1950s.

The boldest land acquisition program came in the 1950s for the 30,000-acre Cape Hatteras National Seashore. The federal condemnation is still bitterly resented by some natives, but it established the basis of the booming tourism trade and protected the land from damaging development. However, it increased the value of the remaining private land, and it is on these holdings that resort building is thriving. Developers have already reached the limits and carrying capacity of the land in several of the historic communities.

As a destination, Dare County's oceanfront has two distinct personalities: the resort beach communities, which occupy approximately the northern third of the county, and those communities of the southern two-thirds of the county, which is dominated by public lands. The several communities in the southern tier, though smaller, traditional, and much less developed, have become delightful tourist destinations as a result of their history and the assets of Cape Hatteras National Seashore.

North to south, Dare's oceanfront communities begin with Sanderling, just south of Currituck County, and extend uninterrupted approximately 26 miles to Cape Hatteras National Seashore. Although the communities are distinct, it is sometimes hard to tell where one ends and another begins. In some places the ever-booming and renewing tourism visually overwhelms the older, core areas, figuratively "outshouting" them for visitor attention. Nevertheless, there is a kind of weathered serendipity that drapes over the oldest parts of each village, where the buildings have an indigenous look as though they just belong. The communities survive on more than construction and tourism, however. If you leave the oceanfront and explore the inland roads, you'll find the marinas, machine shops, and packing houses where the demanding ordinary life of the Outer Banks, much of it still associated with commercial fishing and boatbuilding, exists.

The northern communities—Sanderling and Duck—were once an easy drive along NC 12 from Kitty Hawk, but the delightful winding passage is taxed in high season by an endless stream of vacationers and construction vehicles. There is no "oceanfront" per se in these north bank communities, which were developed originally in the shelter of the soundside woods. Except for a series of engaging retail locations in Duck—boutique shopping, excellent bookstores, and restaurants—Sanderling and Duck are a series of residential developments.

South of Duck, the town of Southern Shores reaches to US 158. It is a private community with a distinctive character owed to the wonderfully anachronistic "Florida-style" flat-topped cinder-block/stucco houses originally built here in the 1950s.

The 16 miles of oceanfront between the Wright Memorial Bridge and Whalebone Junction, the intersection of NC 12, US 158, and US 64/264, host the primary bustle of Dare County's tourism. Kitty Hawk, Kill Devil Hills, and Nags Head stand shoulder to shoulder along these sands, seemingly continuous, but actually quite distinguishable. By no interpretation should it be construed that a "wall of buildings" exists along the oceanfront. If not visible because of sand dunes, the ocean always feels immediate and accessible.

While city demarcations are low-key, if nondescript, Kitty Hawk, Kill Devil Hills, and Nags Head have a different feel and offer a slightly different flavor of the sea. All are under relentless development and erosion pressure, and their responses to these community changes further differentiate them.

What they all share is a bleached, weathered look, a product of the relentless year-round wind, salt air, and sun. No building stays shiny and new in the face of these conditions. As a consequence, visitors accept these communities for what they are—jostling, energetic beach destinations.

US 158, a multilane highway west of the oceanfront, is the location for most commercial services with the exception of oceanfront hotels. The interior blocks between the commercial buildings fronting the bypass and Virginia Dare Trail (NC 12, locally known as "beach road") hold an eclectic mix of vacation cottages and smaller commercial ventures. Since the 1990s, home construction has pressed west of the bypass into the rich hardwood forests.

The landing of US 158 in Kitty Hawk happens also to be the final taxiway for travelers who are turning left on NC 12 to go north to Duck and Corolla. Northbound volume can back up traffic the 1$^1/_2$ miles from the bridge and beyond it. Both lanes can be stopped as traffic waits for the light.

Certainly, the ocean is the main attraction, but there are several must-see things here. Kitty Hawk Woods, covering the western side of that community, is a state-owned preserve of the maritime hardwood forest. The Wright Brothers National Memorial towers over Kill Devil Hills, and the Nags Head Woods Ecological Preserve protects a substantial acreage of the soundside maritime forest that is a continuation of Kitty Hawk Woods. Jockey's Ridge State Park is also in the Nags Head town limits.

Exploring nearby Roanoke Island can fill a day and part of the evening. Fort Raleigh National Historic Site is the most significant attraction. It is adjacent to the popular Waterside Theater, home to the outdoor drama *The Lost Colony*, and the commemorative Elizabethan Gardens. Roanoke Island also boasts a North Carolina Aquarium, and Roanoke Island Festival Park, harborside in Manteo, is the location for the *Elizabeth II*, a full-scale replica of a sixteenth-century sailing vessel. Summer brings a steady stream of interpretive programs, concerts, and entertainment to Festival Park.

The entire character of Dare County's oceanfront changes when you enter Cape Hatteras National Seashore. This is the quieter, wilder, and very much "outer" side of the Outer Banks. Crossing Oregon Inlet changes everything: thereafter, driving becomes miles of serenity punctuated by sleepy hamlets such as Rodanthe, Salvo, and Waves and eventually, Avon, Buxton, and at the end of the road, Hatteras.

The expanse of the unpopulated national seashore beach is home to a variety of recreational experiences, from bird-watching at Pea Island National Wildlife Refuge to swimming, fishing, kayaking, and driving on the beach. The mix makes the lure of the drive south impossible to ignore. You will queue up at some attractions, but along the national seashore, you can enjoy the luxury of having the beach (but not the catwalk of the Cape Hatteras Lighthouse) much to yourself; everyone who hungers for the possibility of miles of empty beach should visit here at least once.

Road improvements west of Manteo, including the Virginia Dare Memorial Bridge that circumvents the drive through Manns Harbor, have shortened the driving time to the beaches, but they have also shortened the transit through one of the largest pieces of Dare County. Altogether, there are 388 square miles of land and a lot more water—858 square miles—in Dare County. The land has three main segments: the barrier islands, Roanoke Island, and the mainland peninsula.

The peninsula is huge: more than 350 square miles of nearly impenetrable forests and swamps. I have forgotten where I read the memorable quotation from a local describing the entanglement that is the native vegetation here as "being so thick, a dog has to back up to bark." It probably opens up a bit on the interior, but that description is so rich that it satisfies my curiosity.

The Albemarle, Croatan, and Pamlico Sounds surround the peninsula on the north and east sides; the Alligator River forms the western boundary. This vast, unpopulated acreage, crisscrossed by timber roads and drainage canals, once belonged to timber and farming corporations. In 1984 nearly the entire mainland portion of Dare County was donated to the U.S. Fish and Wildlife Service to establish the Alligator River National Wildlife Refuge. At the time, this was the largest conservation gift ever made in the country, and it confirmed the U.S. Department of the Interior as the largest landowner in the county. This refuge permanently protects one of the most pristine tracts of coastal forest and swamp remaining in the Southeast, and it has been the location for the successful reintroduction of the officially federally endangered red wolf.

From the west, US 64 crosses the Alligator River and makes a lonely passage through the northern third of the peninsula to Manns Harbor and the Virginia Dare Memorial Bridge to Roanoke Island. US 264, an alternate route through Engelhard and Swan Quarter and eventually Washington, skirts the eastern edge of the refuge. This route is interestingly close to the Dare County Bombing Range, a multiservice target range west of the small fishing village at Stumpy Point on Stumpy Point Bay. When the military jets are flying, it can be a very entertaining passage.

Few people live on the perimeter of the peninsula, and few people even visit this portion of Dare County. Most of the visitors come for seasonal hunting and fishing—there are state game lands adjacent to the wildlife refuge where hunting is permitted. Except for two crabbing/fishing hamlets, Manns Harbor and Stumpy Point, there are few services that travelers can rely on finding.

Access

The individual municipalities and management agencies in Dare County provide beach access locations. Fortunately, this information is packed in a handy publication prepared by the Outer Banks Visitors Bureau, entitled *The Outer Banks Beach Guide*. This shirt-pocket-sized folding pamphlet details access locations and facilities, locations of lifeguarded beaches, emergency numbers, and tide tables.

The towns of Kitty Hawk, Kill Devil Hills, and Nags Head funnel great numbers of residents and visitors to the beach easily with ample and convenient parking. The access locations are clearly signed along NC 12; regional access locations are posted along US 158.

There seems to be little trouble finding an access location or park-ing space during the week, but weekends are crowded. Move out early.

Dare County provides numerous fishing and boating access locations, including boat-launching sites on the sounds. These locations are in addition to other facilities provided by the National Park Service, the U.S. Fish and Wildlife Service, and the North Carolina Wildlife Resources Commission, which are listed in the appropriate sections that follow.

In Duck, there is an unmarked basin and boat tie-up behind Wee Winks Square shopping center.

In Kitty Hawk, there is a boat ramp, docking space, and a large parking area at the end of Bob Perry Road.

On Roanoke Island, Dare County Airport Recreation Area next to the old Manns Harbor ferry dock has a boat ramp best suited for four-wheel-drive vehicles. There is a signed public boat-launching ramp just south of the Wanchese Fish Company building in Wanchese on Mill Creek. The Manteo Public Boat Landing, which includes a public boat ramp, dock, and parking area, is located at the east end of Ananias Dare Street in Manteo. The land south of the west end of the new Washington Baum Bridge is proposed as a boat launching ramp and parking area. It is informally used as such at present.

In Avon, there is a harbor located at the west end of Avon Road.

In Buxton, the county owns the harbor just south of the village and north of Billy's Seafood Restaurant.

In Hatteras, the county has two parking spaces and a boat dock easement at the privately operated Hatteras Harbor Marina, where the public may use two boat ramps adjacent to the marina for a $4 fee.

There are also public boat-launching facilities on the mainland at Manns Harbor, Stumpy Point Basin, Lake Worth, Mashoes, and East Lake.

Handicapped Access

Most of the National Park Service facilities and all of the state parks and historic sites are handicapped accessible and offer to loan beach wheelchairs upon advance request.

All the beach communities of Dare County will loan beach wheelchairs upon advance request. Contact the respective fire departments for specific information.

Handicapped accessibility to the beach varies with each municipality. All regional access locations and most neighborhood access locations are accessible to the handicapped. Some site-specific information is provided in the text. The beach communities also provide this information.

Information

For information, contact Outer Banks Visitors Bureau, One Visitors Center Circle, Manteo, NC 27954, 252-473-2138, 877-629-4386; or Outer Banks Chamber of Commerce, P.O. Box 1757, Kill Devil Hills, NC 27948, 252-441-8144.

Web addresses: <www.townof kittyhawk.org>; <www.outer banks.org>; <www.outerbanks chamber.com>

For information about Cape Hatteras National Seashore, Fort Raleigh National Historic Site, or the Wright Brothers National Memorial, contact Superintendent, Cape Hatteras Group, Route 1, Box 675, Manteo, NC 27954, 252-441-7430.

Web address: <www.nps.gov>

The North Banks

In the 1970s the northern limits of Southern Shores were the end of development on the Outer Banks. NC 12, then as now, the only route north from US 158, passed inland through Southern Shores and then began a winding passage through dense maritime forests to the nineteenth-century soundside settlement Duck, which was little more than a handful of houses, a church, a store or two, and a lovely setting on Currituck Sound. The road, the only road, continued north several more miles before running out of pavement at the Currituck County border. The route didn't stop; the road just turned to sand, making the 15 miles north to Corolla, a larger village of about the same vintage, nestled in piney woods beneath the tower of the Currituck Beach Lighthouse, an alluring temptation and an unavoidable adventure. Except for the residents (fewer than 100 received mail from the Corolla post office), fishermen, hunters, and insatiably curious, few people ventured beyond Duck—there was no reason to. Around this time, the undeveloped, unincorporated portion of the Dare

and Currituck banks came to be known as the North Banks. From the start, it was a loose description that lumped in a phrase the geography north of where most permanent residents lived. It was easily grasped and it stuck.

The term persists, but it carries a different meaning from its origins that carried a sense of disbelief at any query: there was nothing there then, and this has certainly changed now.

The once wild and undeveloped stretch of beach, some of which was used as a navy bombing range, has become lively and populated with a series of cul-de-sac streets lined with single-family vacation rental homes. A few locations, northern Dare County in particular, showcase some of the best in 1980s oceanfront development, which exhibited great care to preserve the maritime forest tree cover. There are also lengths of the North Banks where investment dollars have lined lavishly appointed houses along the oceanfront forbiddingly close to each other, effectively creating an ostentatious wall behind the frontal dunes.

Purchase and rental prices are at dizzying heights, and to a great extent, the North Banks has become exclusive by price alone. When constructed, the homes in the Palmer Island Club property, at the northern end of Dare County, were also at the northern limits of many bank accounts and for a desirable reason: the banks were so narrow at this point that only one row of houses would be constructed, guaranteeing the owners unobstructed ocean and sound views.

Nearly every building north of Southern Shores is new; most are less than 15 years old. The North Banks as a whole is experiencing a gush of celebrity as a trendy place to visit. In less than a decade, Sanderling and Duck became vacation destinations of a new order and with extraordinary demand and popularity. In slightly more than a decade, intense construction has hammered the memory of Duck as a bend in the road with Wee Winks Grocery, a fishing tackle shop, deli, gallery, and scattered second homes into oblivion.

Duck has grown up to offer an appealing mix of visual separation that insulates visitors from the feeling of being at a crowded location and has packed its roadsides with specialty indulgences. The shopping is interesting and answers the need of providing most of the familiar things that keep one from feeling too out of touch with home. Water sports, mostly kayaking and windsurfing, a natural because of the soundside location, highlight the list of off-beach activities. The irony of visiting Duck is that while it gives the impression of being distant, it becomes quite crowded, and the jostling on and off NC 12 during the summer is hardly relaxing.

Farther north, what was once a handsome back-dune shrub flat has evolved into the natty Sanderling community, driven by the same attention to environmental concerns and appearance that simultaneously made the Sanderling

Resort the yardstick for coastal resort excellence. While Sanderling is posted as a village, it is a private development distinguished by lush landscape planting that screens the houses from NC 12. The generous walkways and planting give every impression that it is a village. In the very northern part of Dare County is the grand and exclusive Palmer Island Club, a residential subdivision of one-acre lots with commanding views of both Currituck Sound and the Atlantic Ocean.

The fact that until 1984 there was a guardhouse on NC 12 at the northern border of Dare County to restrict access farther north to property owners and their guests seems incredible. Yet, the removal of that guardhouse and the paving of NC 12 to Corolla swept away the last solitude and isolated exclusivity remaining on Currituck Banks.

Accommodations for overnight visitation on the North Banks are limited to an exclusive resort or to small, upscale inn and bed-and-breakfast houses. In 2002 a Hampton Inn and Suites opened in the southern end of Corolla, becoming the first national accommodations chain to come here.

Access

Access is improving in Currituck County. There are two regional beach access locations in Corolla and several beach access points with parking in the Whalehead Beach subdivision. Corolla also has beach lifeguards at the regional beach access site near the Currituck Beach Lighthouse.

Generally, the communities of Sanderling, Duck, and Southern Shores developed as a series of private subdivisions and have no formal public beach access. Beach access is by private rental.

From Currituck County south to Kitty Hawk, the only public access is at a U.S. Army Corps of Engineers research station, located just south of the Duck Volunteer Fire Department building. There are 20 parking spaces, and in spite of the ominous signs, folks are welcome to use them.

There is one unmarked boat basin and tie-up behind Wee Winks Square shopping center in Duck.

Handicapped Access

The Sanderling Inn is accessible for the handicapped, and a boardwalk leads to a gazebo at the primary dunes.

Information

For information on Currituck County, contact Corolla/Currituck County Chamber of Commerce, 6328-E Caratoke Highway, P.O. Box 1160, Grandy, NC 27939-1160, 252-453-9497. For Corolla, contact the Currituck Visitors Center, 500 Hunt Club Drive, Corolla, NC 27927, 877-287-7488. For Sanderling and Duck, contact Outer Banks Visitors Bureau, One Visitors Center Circle, Manteo, NC 27954, 252-473-2138, 877-629-4386; or Outer Banks Chamber of Commerce, P.O. Box 1757, Kill Devil Hills, NC 27948, 252-441-8144.

Web addresses: <www.currituck chamber.org>; <www.visitcurrituck.

com>; <www.outerbanks.org>;
<www.outerbankschamber.com>;
<www.nccoastalmanagement.net/
Access/sites.htm>

Sanderling

Sanderling, a residential enclave north of Duck, is one of the most eye-appealing developments built on the North Banks during the late 1970s and early 1980s. When driving north from Duck, the telltale sign of one's arrival in Sanderling—along with highway sign—is the refined, landscaped envelope that encloses a length of NC 12. There are bike trails and a dense planting of live oaks, elaeagnus, and wax myrtle that shields the homes from the views of passersby. It is enticing and in stately contrast to the happenstance approach to the streetscape nearly everywhere else along NC 12. Fortunately, there is a figurative pot of gold at the end of this roadside rainbow, the symbolic heart of the area, the Sanderling Resort and Spa.

It's a marriage of place and attitude that began on the right foot, hit stride immediately, and has been doing a booming business since opening its doors in 1985. One of the first steps was the restoration of the 1899 Caffey's Inlet Life-Saving Station to become a restaurant, the Lifesaving Station at the Sanderling. The initial Caffey's Inlet Life-Saving Station, most likely a boathouse with quarters upstairs, was established in 1874. It was one of a series of out-

posts that were eventually located approximately every 7 miles along the coastline of Virginia and North Carolina. North from this location were Poyner's Hill, Currituck Inlet (later renamed Penny's Hill), the Currituck Beach Lighthouse, Whaleshead, and Wash Woods, which covered the coastline to Virginia. The next station south was Paul Gamiel Hill in present-day Southern Shores.

This particular station took its name from Caffey's Inlet, which opened in the late 1700s and served until a storm in 1828 shoaled it closed. The area remains one of the narrowest stretches of the North Banks. According to U.S. Coast Guard records, in 1877 surfman Malachi Corbell from this station saved two fishermen whose boat had capsized. For the rescue, Corbell received the Silver Life-Saving Medal, the first person in the U.S. Life-Saving Service to win the congressional life-saving medal.

In 1981 the building was placed on the National Register of Historic Places. In spite of its historic significance, the structure had severely deteriorated, and only a thorough renovation for the Sanderling development saved it from collapse.

It is a wonderful dining space, all the more intriguing because of the historical artifacts and nautical theme. When you sit in the rich pine interior of the three-bay boathouse, you feel the echoes of security that the sturdily constructed building projects.

The original sign from the Caffey's Inlet Life-Saving Station is

in the hands of the folks who own Owens' Restaurant in Nags Head, a building patterned in the style of a similar historic station that once stood nearby.

Access

Beach access is by private rental.

Handicapped Access

The Sanderling Inn is accessible for handicapped individuals, and a boardwalk leads to a gazebo at the primary dunes.

U.S. Army
Research Pier

The last large parcel of undeveloped land in Duck belongs to the U.S. Army. It will stay undeveloped, too, for reasons beyond the obvious importance of this location as a research station. This is the U.S. Army Corps of Engineers Coastal Engineering Research Center's Field Research Facility where scientists monitor physiographic changes along the coastline. The working end of the station is a massive 1,880-foot-long concrete pier that stabs into the Atlantic from the center of the 176-acre oceanfront site. The pier is engineered to withstand maximum ocean forces, and its purpose is to provide a study platform to collect long-term data on waves, currents, water levels, and bottom changes, particularly during storms. Many other experiments are conducted here as well, including the testing of new instruments, and it is also

	Fee	Parking	Restrooms	Lifeguard	Camping	Showers	Beach Access	Hiking	Trail	Handicapped	Boating	ORV Access	Fishing	Programs	Historic	Sand Beach	Dunes	Upland	Wetland
U.S. Army Research Pier	•						•						•	•		•	•		
Duck	•			•												•	•	•	•
Public Boating Access: Duck Landing	•										•		•						•

used as a base to study barrier island ecological trends.

The research pier is one of a limited number of sites nationwide where scientists gather data that is used to compute the long-term trends in sea-level fluctuation, in effect making it an official tidal-monitoring station. There is a continually running tidal gauge at the end of the pier that hovers above the 25-foot water depth. A small outbuilding at the end of the pier can actually be moved back into the protection of the main building on shore when severe storms threaten. The precaution is well taken, because storm waves have actually slapped holes in this concrete structure.

A number of agencies, including the National Ocean Survey and the National Weather Service, use the site. Occasionally you may see the Coastal Research Amphibious Buggy (CRAB), a remarkable self-powered, three-legged tower that rolls along the near-shore making precise measurements of the sea floor just beyond the breaking waves. It can then roll right up onto the beach and away to safe storage.

A little bit of history: the facility officially opened in 1980, but the site was acquired from the U.S. Navy in 1973. Along with it came some unusual naval artifacts—unexploded ordinance. Within my childhood memory, this was used as a tactical bombing range.

Signs posted on the property tell you everything you might want to know about the "value" of the North Banks before discovery. The warning is impressive:

> Danger. No Trespassing.
> Ammunition Dud Area. Items
> may explode when handled.
> Removal of Items Prohibited
> by Penalty of Law.

So, if you decide to visit, stay on the beach or in the parking lot.

Access

Don't let the fence intimidate you. These folks are nice and do not mind visitors. The facility is open 9 A.M. to 4:30 P.M. weekdays, and there is parking for about 20 cars. You may use the beach on either side of the pier. Do not walk through the service yard but follow the clearly worn paths that flank the buildings. Access may be restricted during ongoing experiments and certain times of the year.

Between mid-June and mid-August, at 10 A.M. on weekdays, public tours provide an introduction to oceanography, showing the types of instruments used at the station and the ongoing experiments. Should you miss the tour, stop and read the gazebo displays in the parking lot. One fascinating map dates the known migrations of Oregon Inlet—it moves around a lot more than you would suspect.

Information

For information, contact the station at 252-261-3511.

Duck

Everyone should visit Duck to see what the fuss is properly about and if it holds something for them. I find it has an inherent appeal that is part trendy and part granola, and

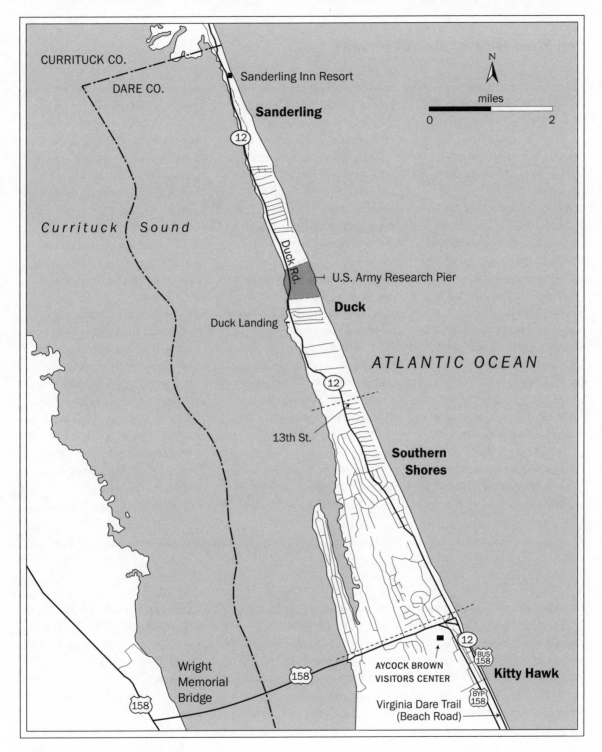

CURRITUCK CO.

DARE CO.

Sanderling Inn Resort

Sanderling

12

Currituck Sound

Duck Rd.

U.S. Army Research Pier

Duck

Duck Landing

ATLANTIC OCEAN

12

13th St.

Southern Shores

Wright Memorial Bridge

158

158

AYCOCK BROWN VISITORS CENTER

12

BUS 158

Kitty Hawk

BYP 158

Virginia Dare Trail (Beach Road)

N

miles
0   2

Map 4. Sanderling to Kitty Hawk

Just What Is Level about the Sea?

We rely on the fact that inland elevations are calibrated using the level of the sea as a reference base. The ocean is not constant—but we declare it to be zero feet and zero inches—so exactly where, then, is sea level?

This is, to borrow from *The Sound of Music*, a "problem like Maria"—that is, "How do you trap a wave upon the sand" at least long enough to measure the heights of mountains and buildings and the depths of valleys worldwide? The beach is the best place to wrestle with the notion that sea level is neither constant around the world nor static over time. It not only varies from sea to shining sea, but it also has spent much of prehistory wildly fluctuating. Take a step back, because right now evidence indicates that sea level is steadily rising.

The National Ocean Service uses a device known as a tide gauge to determine a base sea-level measure. A mechanical tide gauge is simple but seems complicated. It consists of a float inside a perforated pipe. Wire links the float to a pulley, which in turn drives a screw-operated stylus that marks a clock-operated drum. The markings on the drum provide a time graph of the level of the sea. The perforations in the pipe are below tide level to minimize float movement from passing waves. To further reduce wave interference, geologists place tide gauges at the ends of piers extending several hundred feet from the shoreline. There are about 150 such locations throughout the United States. There is one at the U.S. Army Research Pier in Duck, which is open limited hours for public visitation.

Scientists have been keeping these records for a long time, and the data reveal that tidal action varies within a month, between months, and from year to year. Because the longest cycle of tidal variation takes about 18.75 years, there needs to be a continuous recording from a tidal gauge for at least 19 years to qualify its readings as a determinant of sea level at the station of record.

Mean sea level, our base measuring reference for heights, is the average height from such a series of recordings.

That literally is a starting point, and precise surveying extends this base level across land. Eventually, it is possible to compare a carefully surveyed elevation from one location with a survey based on data obtained independently at another location. This is especially true with global satellite positioning systems. Then you hear "Uh-oh" (not really), but the results can be astonishing: sea level on the western coast

yet these terms do not fully capture its upscale and quirky personality.

Duck was "discovered" late last century by folks who were looking for a quiet outpost that offered a handful of stores and a heap of convenient solitude. At the outset, the community was barely more than a cluster of homes and a few odd stores bent around a charming "S" curve in NC 12. Today, it has grown considerably to include nearly 500 full-time residents. In 2002 the citizens approved incorporation as a separate community.

The place has been a destination for hunters since sometime in the nineteenth century, most likely early on in that century. The namesake waterfowl populations no longer aggregate here in sky-darkening abundance, however. Instead of ducks in winter, visitors flock here nearly throughout the year in pursuit of space in one of the many single-family homes available for rental. Most of the building here

of the Florida peninsula is 7 inches higher than at locations on the eastern coast. Also, the Pacific coast averages 20 inches higher than the Atlantic. (In theory, you can claim to sail up-water through the Panama Canal, climbing nearly a foot from the Atlantic to the Pacific.)

This is unleveling, to say the least, and there is no completely satisfactory reason for the variation. Water temperature and barometric pressure can chip away at constancy—water expands when heated and rises in level when the atmospheric pressure is low. Prevailing winds, water density differences because of salinity, and the shape of the near-shore ocean bottom can add up to a not so sea-level start to a cross-country measuring trip. Throw in a little spin from the rotation of the earth and its effects on currents such as the Gulf Stream (which is lower on the east side

than on the west), and you have another way to pile up enough water to alter sea level. Each of these different factors affects conditions differently in different locations; in other words, they are local but still can account for some of the intracontinental variations.

Historically, sea level changes at any given location as well. So just when you think you are on solid ground, here is the reminder that some coastlines are sinking, a fact that plays heck with a survey. . . .

Data indicates that presently sea level is rising (or the land where any given tidal gauge is fixed is subsiding). A worldwide rise in sea level is called a eustatic change.

There's no simple explanation here, either. In fact, several factors or a combination of factors might be responsible, such as a change in the amount of water held on land in the form of ice, snow, and lakes and

streams; a change in the capacity of the ocean basin through deformation, sedimentation, or volcanism; and changes in the total amount of water on the earth.

Meteorologists and coastal geologists cite a climatic warming trend that is reducing the water held as ice and snow as the most likely cause. If this is so, then it is an inexorable, unstoppable, and unmanageable change that will shake things up along the coast.

Although such a transformation is a long-term change, telltale signs will show. One of them could be the erosion of beaches as a relentless nibbling trifles the sand away.

As much as we act to the contrary, the surface of the ocean is not constant. It is on the move—upward. With this in mind, take a North Carolina geography pop quiz: How high is Mount Mitchell? It is 6,684 feet above mean sea level—for now.

is low-density and hardly noticed, as the streets with houses angle toward the ocean from NC 12. For the most part, houses were perched on the dunes, working with the existing vegetation instead of flattening the site before building. The approach has paid dividends in desirability, and while it may be a little

glitzy for some, all and all, I think Duck is a credible compromise between creating vacation dreams and balancing the realities of the natural landscape.

There is still a lovely glimpse of Currituck Sound from that memorable "S" curve that defines old Duck, but now there is even more to

look at as Duck has stretched along both sides of NC 12 with shopping, recreational, and dining opportunities that have lengthened the "village" to about two miles. This is an estimate and given only as a gauge because what matters here is the pace of travel, not the distance. In high season, traffic and time crawl as travelers strain to read tasteful, modest signage and figure out where it is they might want to go.

It can be a tough choice for first-timers because they are tempted by some of the best of the get-away-from-it-all, but not *too* far away commercial development of the 1980s and 1990s. While the new Duck has yet to weather like the old Duck, it shows every intention of becoming a minimalist concentration of commercial fronts. What binds the whole together into a sense of place is the sensitive construction that respected the existing maritime forest so one cannot see all of Duck at once. The road snakes and winds, and the shopping clusters are separate groupings along the road that blend in sufficiently to be slightly disorienting.

There has been an obvious attempt to inject an authentic flair into the architecture here. Scarborough Faire, a 1984 clustering of individual buildings linked with boardwalks, is a personal favorite. The buildings are in once-maritime forest, sited where the live oaks aren't. Boardwalks thread among the trunks linking the separate units. The complex is weathered and gray; natural leaf litter covers the ground, and it feels good to walk here. Truthfully, it makes you want to buy an official Duck, North Carolina, shirt from Grays II, which sports a turn-of-the-century ambience, with wooden porch and welcome benches.

The live oaks left behind by careful contractors make it a cool place to be. Scarborough Faire set a high

bar for retail appearance here, and I believe did much to stamp Duck as a place apart. It certainly is a nice place to dine, and Elizabeth's Café and Winery captures the spirit(s) and matches the mood and feeling of Scarborough Faire with its small seatings, fresh and innovative cuisine, and well-deserved reputation for its wine offerings (reservations recommended). Other shopping clusters, Loblolly Pines, Wee Winks Square, and the Duck Soundside Shops, fill other seasonal retail demands. Visitors must go to Corolla or Southern Shores for weekly grocery shopping.

The Waterfront Shops, a modest commercial cluster that sidles beside the water on the west side of NC 12, have a boardwalk promenade with a splendid view of Currituck Sound. There is also an unappreciated and understated glimpse into local waterfowl heritage to be gained by patronizing Duck's Cottage Coffee and Book Shop, the only freestanding building on the southeast side of the parking lot. The modest wood frame structure that has been handsomely refurbished first served as the Powder Ridge Hunt Club, a private shooting club organized during Duck's waterfowl hunting heyday in the early twentieth century. It was purchased and moved a short distance from its previous location, a waterside indentation that served as a boat slip. The fine-looking place is open seasonally as a newsstand, bookshop, and coffee house.

The northwest corner of the Waterfront Shops is the location

for one of the North Banks best-known and best-rated restaurants, the Bluepoint Bar and Grill. Completely unpretentious in decor and wonderfully casual in atmosphere, the restaurant has consistently proven to be one of the most innovative and satisfying dining locations on the North Banks. I had a delicious meal of red drum, a favorite fish of local waters and highly unusual to find on menus for the simple reason that most people who catch red drum hoard them. Reservations are a must nearly year-round. Time things right, and you can have a delicious meal served with a Currituck sunset.

A few things to keep in mind: Duck is not easy to visit in high season because of the traffic. The best way to see it is to rent a nearby house or plan to visit during the shoulder seasons when the volume of traffic subsides. While there is a thriving commercial business in water sports here, this is not the place to day-trip with expectations of swimming in the ocean. Don't let the lack of public access to the beach keep you from going to Duck, however, or you'll miss a major North Banks event.

Access

Duck is on NC 12 north of Southern Shores. While there is no public beach access, several cul-de-sac streets have lifeguards on duty during the summer vacation season.

Handicapped Access

Several of the commercial shopping areas such as Scarborough

Faire and the Waterfront Shops are accessible for the handicapped.

Duck will loan a beach wheelchair on advance reservation. Contact the fire department at 254-261-3929.

Information

For information, contact Outer Banks Visitors Bureau, One Visitors Center Circle, Manteo, NC 27954, 252-473-2138, 877-629-4386; or Outer Banks Chamber of Commerce, P.O. Box 1757, Kill Devil Hills, NC 27948, 252-441-8144.

Web addresses: <www.outer banks.org>; <www.outerbanks chamber.com>; <www.nccoastal management.net/Access/sites. htm>

Southern Shores

One cannot go or come from Duck without passing through Southern Shores, the oldest planned development on the Outer Banks. It's a gem of a community: almost completely residential, low-key, restful, and charming. In this day and time, travelers determined to reach the newer communities farther north overlook it, but it is a steady eddy in the swirl of North Banks traffic.

Southern Shores was started in 1947 by renowned illustrator Frank Stick, who began developing the approximately 2,900 acres practically alone although managed through the Kitty Hawk Land Company. The community grew slowly through the 1950s, and the first forty families created the

Southern Shores Civic Association to assume responsibility for public spaces such as town parks and beach access along the four miles of oceanfront. The parking and beach accessways are reserved for residents and their guests (vacation renters in Southern Shores are provided with access permits valid for the duration of their stay). The civic association is also responsible for community appearance issues. Southern Shores incorporated in 1979, and the community, with its golf course, marinas, and lagoons, occupies nearly all of the land between the ocean the sound south of Duck and extending to US 158. Today, it is home to 2,600 permanent residents; the summer residency increases to approximately 10,000 people.

Southern Shores has distinctive highlands consisting of old dune ridges, readily noticeable as NC 12 leaves the oceanfront and moves toward the center of the banks. The northern end of Southern Shores is an area of handsomely sited homes that are carefully placed on these back dune ridges, preserving much of the maritime forest tree cover. Thirteenth Street is the landmark that demarcates the northern limits of town. From that point, the commercial center of Duck is approximately 1.5 miles.

While the newer homes of the northern streets are attractive additions, I find the most compelling images are the distinctive, flat-roofed concrete-block "Florida homes" still visible along NC 12 slightly north of US 158. What

character! Squatting as they do behind the dunes with trim brightly painted, they evoke thoughts of the earlier Florida retirement homes that served as their inspiration. They convey a sense of a simpler time and muted wants.

An equally striking feature of these durable, block houses and Southern Shores in general is the ample lot size. The platting was generous during the early days of Southern Shores and serves the appearance of the community well today. Regretfully, it is evident that the generous lots of the original oceanfront Florida homes have attracted new owners with grander notions of seaside living, hence a new wave (pardon) of oceanfront manses. The humble block homes remaining are a wonderful foil to the new construction and, to my way of thinking, a visual reminder of the sea change in attitudes that is endemic to the coast at large.

Southern Shores's new town hall sits elegantly at the intersection of US 158 and NC 12 on a service road paralleling US 158. The building mimics the mass, detailing, and basic design of the life-saving stations that once stood along the banks and communicates this community's intent to stay in step with local traditions. Slightly west from the town hall is the Market Place, a commercial center meeting the shopping needs of residents.

Access

Southern Shores provides no public access to the beach, but it does provide parking for members of the

Southern Shores Civic Association. Only homeowners, tenants, and their guests may use the access areas. If you rent a cottage in Southern Shores, the realty agency will usually make the arrangements. To become a member, you must show proof of ownership or rental and pay a $2 fee.

Information

For information, contact Outer Banks Visitors Bureau, One Visitors Center Circle, Manteo, NC 27954, 252-473-2138, 877-629-4386; or Outer Banks Chamber of Commerce, P.O. Box 1757, Kill Devil Hills, NC 27948, 252-441-8144.

Web addresses: <www.south ernshores-nc.gov>; <www.outer banks.org>; <www.outerbanks chamber.com>

Aycock Brown Visitors Center

Traffic being what it is as one travels US 158 south into Kitty Hawk, the Aycock Brown Visitors Center at the junction of US 158 and NC 12 can come up almost too quickly to make an easy exit. However, a quick veer and visit can save time and provide the opportunity to update your tourism information. The visitors center has restrooms, picnic sites, pay phones, and easy access back onto US 158 heading south.

You can pick up various publications that highlight upcoming events and possible destinations, in addition to information on interpretive programs at the Cape Hatteras National Seashore and ferry schedules.

Locations are referenced in the publications to mileposts that are numbered 1 through 16 south from the Wright Memorial Bridge along NC 12 or Virginia Dare Trail, referred to locally as Beach Road. (NC 12 north from Whalebone Junction is signed as the Marc Basnight Highway.) There are milepost markers along US 158 as well. This is an excellent system for daytime navigation, but the mileposts are difficult to spot at night. If you seek directions, ask for a landmark in addition to the milepost reference mark.

US 158 is what I would call a high distraction highway: Many who are driving it are from out of town and are looking for a specific street, or store, etc. (Locals call them "seekers.") This fact, combined with the speed limit and multiple intersections, makes for very dicey driving. It pays to be particularly attentive because so many others are not. Left turns off and on the bypass can be hazardous, particularly at night. Plan your errand-running to avoid left turns onto the bypass from streets without traffic lights.

I personally prefer using Beach Road. While the slower speed limit drags things out a bit, there are fewer lights and much better scenery. Also, it is just plain calming, when compared to its alternate.

Access

Aycock Brown Visitors Center is open year-round 9 A.M. to 5 P.M. daily.

Handicapped Access

The visitors center is fully accessible for the handicapped.

Information

For information, call the center at 252-261-4644, or call 877-629-4386 for general Outer Banks tourism information.

Kitty Hawk

The Wright Memorial Bridge delivers travelers on US 158 into Kitty Hawk, the northernmost and smallest of the resort communities along the historic 16-mile oceanfront resort playground of Dare County. The road separates Kitty Hawk from Southern Shores to the north, and depending on the day and time of travel, stalled traffic can separate the road-weary from any remaining enthusiasm about traveling here. Northern Kitty Hawk catches a traffic back-up of people driving north to Corolla. On busy changeover days, traffic backs up from the left turn for NC 12 to the bridge, slowing access to all resort beaches north or south. My recommendation is to stay to the right as you cross the bridge, take US 158 south, and quickly turn left at the first available intersection to NC 12 south, the old Beach Road also known as Virginia Dare Trail. It is the only way to decompress. Besides, this behind-the-oceanfront-row drive provides a solid introduction to the laid-back, unpretentious personality of Kitty Hawk. It is a genuine cottage community, as casual in appearance and in attitude as any place you'll find on the North Carolina coast.

Today, Beach Road curves past the construction of a new oceanfront landmark, the Hilton Garden Inn of Kitty Hawk, on the previous parking lot of an old landmark, the Kitty Hawk Fishing Pier, which Hurricane Isabel shortened. The hotel intends to make the foreshortened pier compatible with its site plan and, ocean willing, will leave it standing.

Kitty Hawk has about 3.5 miles of oceanfront, between the old pier site and the Kill Devil Hills city limits, just beyond milepost 5. The Decharmarnel Campground on Virginia Dare Trail serves as an informal landmark of the city limits.

Beach Road paints a telling portrait of a simple, unadorned, residential oceanfront that is in a heady tug-of-war with the sea. There are a very limited number of commercial ventures along Beach Road, and the residences are small, a legacy of the town's original plotting of only 50-foot-wide lots here. There are also a few sites for trailers and campers fairly close to the beach. The town has been steadfast with height restrictions, and this keeps the scale of the Beach Road streetscape comfortable. All in all, the Kitty Hawk oceanfront doesn't

crackle with the kind of commercial energy of adjoining Kill Devil Hills and nearby Nags Head, but it settles on you comfortably like a favorite pair of cutoff jeans. Even in the peak of the July season, Beach Road is lazy with traffic, and one can dawdle through town with time to admire the weathered hominess of the cottages.

Kitty Hawk is in a tussle with the ocean. Storms have claimed multiple houses on the east side of Beach Road by collapsing them outright or washing away their septic field. Following condemnation, the vacated properties are removed, and the lots become public beach. Not so long ago, there was a continuous row of cottages along the oceanfront side of Beach Road. The vast gaps in continuity are a ready indication of how acute erosion is in Kitty Hawk. The town will be pursuing beach nourishment funding as a means to protect the remaining houses and the road itself. At any given visit, you can see a house east of Beach Road that is in tenuous circumstances.

This is an old story; the oceanfront has been creeping landward steadily here. During the late nineteenth and early twentieth centuries, the only long-term occupants of the beach were members of the U.S. Life-Saving Service, which had a station approximately at Kitty Hawk Road and Beach Road, which is just about milepost 4. Fortunately, you can get a taste of local lore and fare by stopping in at the Black Pelican Restaurant

on Beach Road just north of Kitty Hawk Road. The restaurant incorporates the renovated Kitty Hawk Beach Life-Saving Station that was constructed in 1874. This was one of the seven original stations authorized for the Outer Banks by the U.S. Congress and was included in Life-Saving District 6 along with three stations in present-day Virginia Beach. The station was relocated from its original oceanfront location in the 1970s.

The restaurant is themed on the legend of a black pelican repeatedly seen as a harbinger of rescue for those imperiled at sea, supposedly logged by W. D. Tate, the original keeper or captain of the station. Additional photographs and nautical artifacts used as decor build on the station's history, which is notable. After their historic flight in 1903, the Wright Brothers came here to the only telegraph station to declare their success to the world. A second-story deck permits a close study of the gable detailing that characterized the architectural styling of the stations.

On the west side of Beach Road, $1/4$ mile south of the Black Pelican is the 1899 Kitty Hawk Life-Saving Station. The companion to the restaurant in lore and history, it, too, was originally east of Beach Road but is now safely set back and elevated as a private residence. It is recognizable by its distinctive architecture and sign that declares its lineage as Kitty Hawk Life-Saving Station No. 2.

There is much more to Kitty

	Fee	Parking	Restrooms	Lifeguard	Camping	Showers	Beach Access	Hiking	Trail	Handicapped	Boating	ORV Access	Fishing	Programs	Historic	Sand Beach	Dunes	Upland	Wetland
Aycock Brown Visitors Center	•	•								•				•					
Kitty Hawk	•	•	•										•		•	•	•	•	•
Public Boating Access: Bob Perry Rd.		•									•		•						•
Regional Access: Kitty Hawk	•	•	•			•	•			•			•			•	•	•	

Hawk than what you'll see between Beach Road and US 158, the five-lane expressway that serves as the commercial highway for the resort villages of Kitty Hawk, Kill Devil Hills, and Nags Head. The visible beach resort, most of which has grown in the last forty years, is the newest part of the community. Historical Kitty Hawk, where generations have lived and nearly 2,000 reside year-round, extends well into the two-mile-wide maritime forest known as Kitty Hawk Woods, west of US 158. This puts most residents slightly closer to the sound than to the oceanfront. The Sea Scape golf community, along the west side of the bypass and carved out the woods and dunes there, is the peeking edge of the sequestered community. Kitty Hawk municipal center is also on the eastern edge of a sheltered forest setting; it is surprisingly lush in a place more commonly associated with sea oats and dune grasses.

Kitty Hawk Road, SR 1208, loops inland from US 158 bypass through the oldest part of Kitty Hawk and connects with Woods Road, SR 1206, deep in the extensive maritime forest. Woods Road intersects US 158. Shelter, safety, and fresh water were easily found in these woods, and so it was probably well settled by the late eighteenth century. Many sturdy frame houses, some of which are pre-twentieth century and representative of the enduring community here, are still visible on roads in the forest. The architecture reflects the need for durable year-round housing among the watermen and tradesmen who called Kitty Hawk home. Orville and Wilbur Wright stayed in such a farmhouse or "country house" when they first traveled to the desolate, windswept peninsula. Visible beside Moore Shore Road, which is off of Kitty Hawk Road, is a replica of the granite marker noting the site where the Wright Brothers built their glider (the original marker is in the town hall).

Access

Kitty Hawk Ocean Rescue has both roving and fixed lifeguard stations. Fixed stations are at the Byrd and Eckner Street accessways, as well as the Kitty Hawk Bathhouse access. Lifeguards are on duty from 10 A.M. to 7 P.M. In future years, it is likely that the lifeguard stations will increase.

Most of the major east-west streets have an access right-of-way at the beachfront. There is improved parking at Balchen and Maynard Streets, which have been widened and the shoulders reinforced for additional parking.

Byrd Street has a bathhouse, shower, and paved parking.

There is a regional access site at Kitty Hawk, south of Kitty Hawk Road on Virginia Dare Trail about milepost 4.5. It has parking spaces for 50 vehicles and a bathhouse and restrooms open 10 A.M. to 6 P.M.

There is a boat ramp, docking space, and a large parking area at the end of Bob Perry Road. There is also an unimproved access site

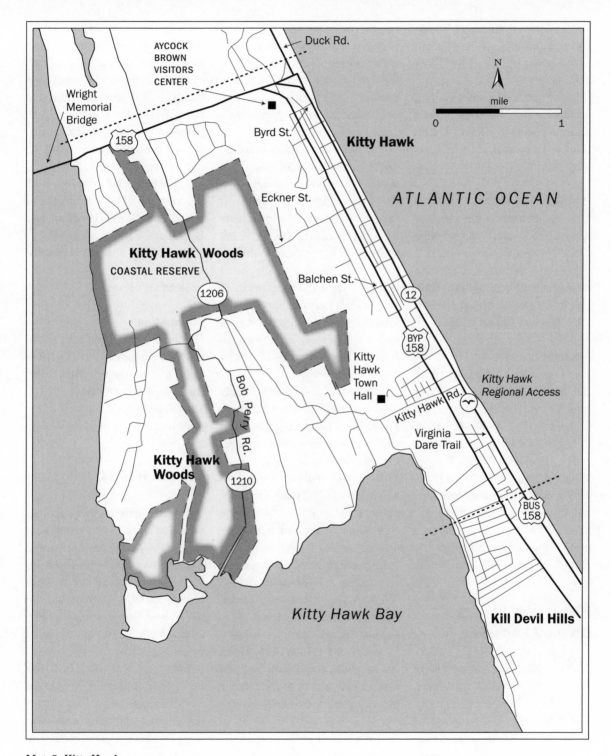

Map 5. Kitty Hawk

at the eastern terminus of US 158 (the road actually continues south at this point) near the Kitty Hawk Fishing Pier.

The town lists public parking and access at the following streets: Balchen, Bennett, Bleriot, Fonck, Hawks, Maynard, and Wilkins Streets.

Handicapped Access

The regional access site south of Kitty Hawk Road is fully handicapped accessible.

Beach wheelchairs may be arranged by contacting the Kitty Hawk Fire Department at 252-261-2666. Advance calling is best.

Information

For information, contact Outer Banks Visitors Bureau, One Visitors Center Circle, Manteo, NC 27954, 252-473-2138, 877-629-4386; or Outer Banks Chamber of Commerce, P.O. Box 1757, Kill Devil Hills, NC 27948, 252-441-8144.

Web addresses: <www.townof kittyhawk.org>; <www.outerbanks. org>; <www.outerbankschamber. com>; <www.nccoastalmanage ment.net/Access/sites.htm>

Kitty Hawk Woods Coastal Reserve

In the middle of the village of Kitty Hawk is a magnificent, little-appreciated wild preserve, the Kitty Hawk Woods component of the North Carolina Coastal Reserve. A total of 1,877 acres of maritime forest, deciduous swamp, and marsh has been set aside for safekeeping and research. The town of Kitty Hawk, with a conservation easement with the state, owns 461 acres. It is an investment in Kitty Hawk's future by saving one of the most important ecological habitats of its past.

The preserve includes upland forest on ancient dune ridges and lowland freshwater swamps between the ridges. The height of the dune ridges shields plants from the damaging effects of salt spray. Plant types found in the forest include some normally found no closer than 100 miles west, as well as plants more common in the sandy oceanside environment. The rare (for this area) hop hornbeam is also found here and in nearby Nags Head Woods.

The wildlife population is equally diverse: the upland areas have gray fox, raccoon, and white-tailed deer; the marsh environment includes nutria, muskrat, and river otter. Birding in Kitty Hawk Woods presents the possibility of seeing warblers, woodpeckers, and hawks. Wrens and other songbirds are also abundant. Deep swales provide habitat for wood ducks and the full range of familiar marsh visitors —herons, egrets, geese, ducks, swans, and rails.

Most of all, there is incredible peace and quiet in Kitty Hawk Woods with several walking trails that provide access to the interior of this important coastal reserve.

Access

The reserve is centered in Kitty Hawk and is most easily accessed from the north. From US 158, $^1/_2$ mile east of the Wright Memorial Bridge, turn south on Woods Road, SR 1206, and park at a small playground $^1/_4$ mile from US 158 next to Dominion Power. A multiuse path parallels Woods Road. Parking is located behind the playground on the north end of Woods Road.

There is also public access from the west end of Eckner Street and at the end of Amadas Road and Birch Lane. Parking is limited.

High Bridge Creek is accessible by boat from the public boat ramp on Bob Perry Road.

Information

For information, contact Northern Sites Manager, North Carolina Coastal Reserve, 983 West Kitty Hawk Road, Kitty Hawk, NC 27949, 252-261-8891.

Web address: <www.ncnerr.org>

Kill Devil Hills

Kill Devil Hills is the most populous municipality in Dare County with nearly 6,000 year-round residents. Summer visitation swells this number to as many as 50,000, as folks flock to its 4.7 miles of oceanfront to play and also to revel in its particular status as the epicenter of modern aviation.

The name Kill Devil Hills has bedeviled folks for a while. Author David Stick has written of the many possibilities, and he records what many think is the likely origin. The tale attributes the moniker to William Byrd from about 1728. Byrd, no fan of the early inhabitants, reported that the New England rum that was preferred on these sandy and isolated shores was strong enough to "kill the devil." By extension, the remark named one of the largest of the unusual sand hills characteristic of the banks here, "Kill Devil Hill." It so appeared on an 1808 map. Kill Devil Hills came to describe the adjoining community and probably became fully accepted when the U.S. Life-Saving Service so named its station in 1878.

At that time, though, Big Kill Devil Hill, where the Wright Brothers Memorial stands, was considered a noted landmark of Kitty Hawk.

It has always been dependably windy here, and the winds moved the sand around, keeping Kill Devil Hill (and its lesser neighbors) practically green-free. The large dunes migrated willy-nilly, back and forth, south to north with the annual cycle of prevailing winds. The wind, with help from free-ranging livestock, prevented any grass or plants from rooting in the sands.

None of this was known in Ohio when the Wright Brothers first wrote to the nascent weather service to find places with dependable winds to continue their experiments in flight. The weather bureau returned data on a number of possibilities, and Kitty Hawk, North Carolina, was number six on the list.

Follow-up correspondence with Joe Dosher of the Kitty Hawk Weather Bureau and former postmaster William Tate convinced the Wrights that Kitty Hawk had the right combination of abundant sand for soft landings, wide-open spaces for safety, and last but not least, isolation.

The Wrights traveled by train and ferry to Elizabeth City (where they would buy hardware, lumber, and supplies) and from there on local sailing ships to Kitty Hawk. After renting a house in the forested village (the location is noted by a marker, today), they began their experiments on the sandy, grassless flats at the foot of Big Kill Devil Hill.

In December 2003 Kill Devil Hills was squarely in the spotlight as the nation watched while the town hosted the celebration honoring the 100th anniversary of the Wright Brothers' first motorized flight on December 17, 1903. That year also marked the 50th anniversary of its incorporation as the Town of Kill Devil Hills, the very first municipality on Dare County's Outer Banks. It was a banner year for a nifty resort community that seems to be comfortable with its particular place in the sun, but is wrestling with what it wants to become. Kill Devil Hills strikes me as a town with more willingness to change than Kitty Hawk, but it is not quite sure that it likes some of the changes coming its way.

For one reason or another, Kill Devil Hills has become the de facto commercial and services community of the Dare County resorts. Travelers are more likely to find a choice of hotels, motels, and restaurants here than in Kitty Hawk or Nags Head. In fact, US 158 through Kill Devil Hills (where McDonald's only opened in 1978) has earned the local nickname of French Fry Alley.

This civic dialogue is mildly evident driving Beach Road south at the north end of Kill Devil Hills, which has a seamless transition from Kitty Hawk. The oceanfront character of the north end is "cottagy" continuing past the Avalon Pier, a landmark named for the Avalon or Avalon Beach developments, one of the earliest areas of resort subdivision. (Nearby, the east-west streets have North Carolina city names; the intersecting streets have mostly Virginia names.) The narrowness of the banks here (less than one mile) favored development that migrated from the soundside settlements. Virginia Dare Shores on the soundside was the location for an early recreation pavilion.

From the pier south to about East Fifth Street, the beach takes on a more commercial character with the appearance of national chain hotels. It is not a foreboding wall of buildings, however, and sprinkled along Beach Road, like so many painted daisies, are the quaint, weathered, shingle-sided family cottages that still have their nostalgic place at the sea. These, along with the massive rent-a-box duplexes and some condominiums, give the oceanfront an eclectic look.

The local oceanfront restaurant, Quagmires, at milepost 7.5, is a

	Fee	Parking	Restrooms	Lifeguard	Camping	Showers	Beach Access	Hiking	Trail	Handicapped	Boating	ORV Access	Fishing	Programs	Historic	Sand Beach	Dunes	Upland	Wetland
Kill Devil Hills		•	•	•	•		•						•			•	•	•	•
Regional Access: Ocean Bay Blvd.		•	•	•		•	•			•	•	•				•	•		
Public Boating Access: Kitty Hawk Bay		•									•								
Wright Brothers National Memorial	•	•	•					•		•					•	•			
Nags Head Woods		•	•					•	•	•				•			•	•	•

throwback institution. The restaurant, which has live entertainment and caters to all tastes, is a local hangout that occupies a part of the original Croatan Inn, built in the 1930s. Nearby is part of the new wave of mega–beach rental home. Old Kill Devil Hills, new Kill Devil Hills, side by side.

The most obvious holdover building along the oceanfront is the retired U.S. Coast Guard Station at milepost 8.5, East Baum Street and Beach Road. The glassed look-out station and large property make it evident.

Consider a side trip to nearby Colington Island (Colington Road is on the south side of the Wright Brothers National Memorial), a land grant to Sir John Colleton in 1663. An island of rich natural contrasts, it is home to watermen who fish and farm soft-shell crabs and pleasure-home subdivisions.

A can't-miss bet for fine dining is the Colington Café, on the left side of Colington Road as you drive to-ward the island. It is a delightful Victorian-era home with an ever-dependable, delicious menu. Desserts are a specialty, too. Reservations are advised.

Closer to the oceanfront is the Flying Fish Café at milepost 10 on US 158 bypass. Owner George Price is in his tenth year with this low-key, comfy café, open for dinner all year, that features a mix of Mediterranean and American "comfort cuisine" in an easygoing setting.

Access

Kill Devil Hills has numerous, easy-to-find public accessways and lifeguard stations. Beach access and beach safety are a community priority, and in 2004 the Ocean Rescue staffed 17 lifeguard stands and 4 mobile units. Nearly every major improved access area has a lifeguard; on-duty hours are 10 A.M. to 5:30 P.M. It is anticipated that these numbers will be maintained or increased. To a visitor, this means a lifeguard about every $1/2$ mile throughout Kill Devil Hills.

There are approximately 20 improved access locations with paved and marked parking spaces. The access areas are clearly marked on the east side of Beach Road, NC 12, at major east-west streets. Some expanded parking areas are on the west side of Beach Road. Parking is on a first-come, first-served basis, but if you arrive by 9:30, there will be plenty of room.

The following neighborhood access locations offer the most parking: Helga Street, Chowan Street, and Hayman Boulevard north of the Avalon Pier; and Fifth Street, Second Street, First Street.

Beginning with the nine streets south of Raleigh Avenue, east of the Wright Brothers National Memorial, access parking is abundant.

There is a regional access site with a bathhouse and restrooms on Ocean Bay Boulevard. To reach this site, turn east off of the US 158 bypass at the traffic light at Coling-

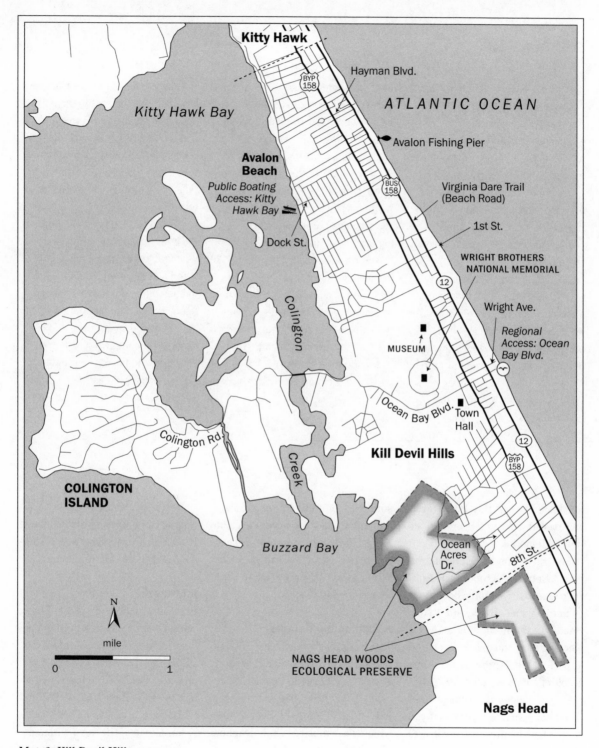

Kitty Hawk

Hayman Blvd.

Kitty Hawk Bay

BYP 158

ATLANTIC OCEAN

Avalon Fishing Pier

Avalon Beach

BUS 158

Public Boating Access: Kitty Hawk Bay

Virginia Dare Trail (Beach Road)

Dock St.

1st St.

WRIGHT BROTHERS NATIONAL MEMORIAL

Colington

Wright Ave.

MUSEUM

Regional Access: Ocean Bay Blvd.

12

Ocean Bay Blvd.

Town Hall

Kill Devil Hills

Colington Rd.

Creek

12

BYP 158

COLINGTON ISLAND

Buzzard Bay

Ocean Acres Dr.

8th St.

N

mile

0   1

NAGS HEAD WOODS ECOLOGICAL PRESERVE

Nags Head

Map 6. Kill Devil Hills

Roll Tide Roll

Several years ago, I watched a lunar eclipse at the beach. I felt like the magical spell of the full moon was pulling me toward the water, as well I should. After all, the moon moves oceans—why not people?

The moon commits gravity on the high seas; by another name, it is the tide. It's wild to think that molecule by molecule, the sun and moon move the sea. Each molecule/droplet moves on cue. The sea crawls up and back, shifting to a heavenly metronome. This is done with cunning not muscle. What moves the waters is not the mass of the sun but the proximity of the moon.

You have to hang around the coast to appreciate this daily dance. The moon sleeps late, rising later each day by an average of 50 minutes. So does the tide. The full tidal cycle is 24 hours and 50.4 minutes. As the moon passes through its phases, waning from full to new then waxing to full again, the tidal rise corresponds; it's highest on the full and new.

The big tides, called spring tides, come when the moon, earth, and sun are aligned during the full and new moons. On these syzygies, the combined gravitational pull of the sun and moon summons the oceans to their greatest flood, usually 20 percent greater than normal.

In addition, the moon's elliptical orbit carries it closest to the earth once every revolution. If this minimal orbital distance coincides with the time of a new or full moon, then the result is the perigean spring tides—the highest of the cyclical tidal flows.

The lowest tides occur during the quarter phases of the moon. When the gravitational pull of the moon and sun are perpendicular to each other, the lowest, or neap, tides occur. There are fourteen days between spring tides and neap tides, corresponding to the time between full and new moons.

So much for the astral mechanism behind the tides, but as with

ton Road (Ocean Bay Boulevard), just past the Wright Brothers National Memorial.

Several ramps serve off-road vehicles. Between October 1 and April 30, you may drive on the beach.

The Hayman Boulevard Estuarine Access on the sound has a pier, gazebo, and picnic area and is perfect for fishing or first-time crabbing. It is a quiet spot with the hope of beautiful sunset. Take along some insect repellent if you are going to be there for any length of time.

The North Carolina Wildlife Resources Commission maintains a fishing and boating access area on Kitty Hawk Bay at Avalon Beach, $1/2$ mile west of US 158 on Dock Street. Parking is available, and there is no launch fee.

Handicapped Access

The neighborhood access site at Second Street has a dune crossover and deck accessible for the handicapped, as does the Ocean Bay Boulevard regional access site, which is completely handicapped accessible with handicapped parking spaces.

Beach wheelchairs may be arranged by contacting the Kill Devil Hills Fire Department at 252-480-4060. Advance calling is best.

Information

For information, contact Outer Banks Visitors Bureau, One Visitors Center Circle, Manteo, NC 27954, 252-473-2138, 877-629-4386; or Outer Banks Chamber of Commerce, P.O. Box 1757, Kill Devil Hills, NC 27948, 252-441-8144.

For a map of the town with a description of municipal services and important information for visi-

almost everything about the ocean, the tidal picture is not so simply completed. On a jigsawed coast like North Carolina's, there are local fluctuations in tide times. It's never high tide everywhere at once (no, that would be too neat). It's different because the shape of the shoreline modifies the effect of the tides.

When, as Ocracokers say, it is "hoigh toid on the sound soid," it is not high tide on the mainland at Swan Quarter. The tides are different in the shifting inlets of the Outer Banks, affected by the slope of the ocean or sound basin, the width of an inlet, and the depth of a channel. The tide has to move through inlets; the greater the distance from open ocean, the later the tide.

The U.S. Coast and Geodetic Survey is armed with all these local differences and can predict the time and approximate height of the tide at any given location. Commerce at the coast moves on this information.

North Carolina's semidiurnal tidal rhythm—two high tides and two low tides each day—is normal for the Atlantic coast. The highs and lows are very similar, covering or failing to cover approximately the same amount of beach as the previous pair in the tidal cycle. Not so on the Pacific coast, where a high high tide then a low low tide are followed by a lower high tide and a higher low tide.

Along the Gulf coast, tidal change is minimal during a given day—one swelling for a high and one exhalation for a low. Since these different tidal patterns cannot be attributed to changes in the moon and sun, other factors must govern this rhythm—factors that are tremendously complex.

I prefer to keep my tidal management simple: low tides are for clamming and shelling, high tides are for fishing and inlet travel, but I won't lose sleep over either extreme. This is, after all, the beach.

tors, contact the Office of the Town Clerk, P.O. Box 1719, Kill Devil Hills, NC 27948.

Web addresses: <www.kdhnc.com>; <www.outerbanks.org>; <www.outerbankschamber.com>; <www.nccoastalmanagement.net/Access/sites.htm>

Wright Brothers National Memorial

A century later, the accomplishments of Orville and Wilbur Wright seem more remarkable, improbable, and amazing than before. The First Flight Centennial Celebration in December 2003 underscored the "miracle of flight" when, after several years and millions of dollars, an exact reproduction of the Wright's first motorized plane did not have the day on the runway that a proper reenactment deserved. Instead, bad weather and engine miscues orchestrated a duplicate of the Wright Brothers' first *public* flight on May 23, 1904, when the original flyer bumped along and would not leave earth. The effort leading to the reenactment was hardly for naught, however, because the craftsmen of the Wright Experience, who actually built two full-scale working replicas of the 1903 flyer, shared their hands-on learning with the world. They learned and admiringly demonstrated that the Wright Brothers were both very, very smart and very, very lucky. Most important of all perhaps, they didn't know what they couldn't do.

Although the reenactment flight lacked loft, the weeklong celebration rejuvenated appreciation for everything about this national historic site and the story it memorializes. The celebration brought additional permanent exhibits to the site, the most important of which is the full-scale flight-capable replica of the 1903 flyer, known as the Harry Combs Flyer in honor of the donor who paid its million-dollar construction cost. It is on display with a replica of the 1902 glider in the Flight Room auditorium of the memorial. (The replica used in the reenactment was funded by the Ford Foundation and, following the centennial celebration, went on display in Dearborn, Michigan.)

The new permanent exhibits in the pavilion also include a replica 1901 glider, as well as video footage of successful flights of both the replica glider and the replica flyer.

If anything, the Wright Brothers National Memorial is more of a "must-see" destination than ever before. Part of the story that unfolds is that this corner of Kill Devil Hills did not look anything like it does today.

Imagine the surrounding landscape barren of trees and Kill Devil Hills every bit as bald as nearby Jockey's Ridge. It is tough to do, but that was the case until the Great Depression. In 1928 the U.S. Army Corps of Engineers stabilized Big Kill Devil Hill by planting grass (by then it was more than 400 feet southwest from its location on the day of the Wright Brothers' flight). In the post–First Flight Centennial Celebration calm, it will be the 60-foot pylon atop 90-foot-tall Big Kill Devil Hill that catches the eye. The pylon, composed of

Mount Airy, North Carolina, granite, was built between 1928 and 1932, and its cornerstone was set on the twenty-fifth anniversary of the Wrights' December 17, 1903, flight. (Initially, the pylon was to serve as an additional lighthouse and, until several years ago, visitors could climb the narrow stairs inside.) After its completion, builders imagined it would be a landmark for pilots during competitive cross-country flights. These races often used Kill Devil Hills as a terminus, demonstrating aviation's progress since December 17, 1903. Big Kill Devil Hill dominates the west horizon of the community and provides a grand overview of the Kill Devil Hills oceanfront.

On the south side of the monument is a new full-scale sculpture by Stephen H. Smith depicting the moment of the first flight and its photography by surfman John T. Daniels of the Kill Devil Hills Life-Saving Station. Daniels and other members of the life-saving crew were among the few witnesses to the repeated trials conducted over a three-year period. (The original Kill Devil Hills Life-Saving Station was removed to Corolla in 1984 by realtor Doug Twiddy, who restored it and uses the building as an office. The office is filled with first-flight and Life-Saving Service memorabilia, and the public is welcome to visit and admire the artifacts.)

Atop the hill at the pylon's base, the other noticeable element in this historical composition is the nearly continual wind. If it had not been

for this wind, the pylon might be in another state, perhaps Ohio.

One tip: Shoes are a must if you walk to the monument, and stay on the paved paths. Kill Devil Hill and the field of the memorial grounds are covered with prickly pear cactus and sand spurs.

Access

The Wright Brothers National Memorial is open 9 A.M. to 5 P.M. (7 P.M. in summer), and there is an admission charge of $3 per car or $1 per person, which is good for seven days. You may visit the interior of the monument from June 16 to Labor Day, 3 P.M. to 4:30 P.M., if weather permits.

Handicapped Access

The visitors center is handicapped accessible, although some assistance may be needed on the back patio. Wheelchairs are available in the center.

Information

For information, contact Wright Brothers National Memorial, c/o Cape Hatteras Group, Route 1, Box 675, Manteo, NC 27954, 252-441-7430.

Web addresses: <www.nps.gov/wrbr>; <www.wrightexperience.com>

Nags Head Woods Ecological Preserve

Nags Head Woods, which lies within both Kill Devil Hills and Nags Head, is a surviving example of a once-prevalent maritime eco-system of the mid-Atlantic coast. This unusual hardwood forest developed in the salt-spray sheltered lee side of the massive sand dunes that form the central mid-rib to the peninsula. Development threatened its sanctity as unaltered woodland until the Nature Conservancy initiated an active campaign to help preserve it. Today, the Nature Conservancy manages more than 1,100 acres of the forest and uses it as a teaching and research site. This unique preserve is open for limited visitation.

Nags Head Woods predates its companion in the North Carolina Coastal Reserve, Kitty Hawk Woods, but the two share much in common. Both are not just woods, but complex pieces of the Outer Banks. Nags Head Woods has 300–500-year-old trees (southern red oaks) and freshwater ponds with rare aquatic plants. There are nesting sites of several threatened and endangered birds, among them the osprey and pileated woodpecker, and plants that are at the extremes of their geographic range, such as woolly beach heather, a tough, diminutive, dune-field plant that has not been found farther south than Nags Head Woods.

Two great sand dunes, Run Hill and Jockey's Ridge, that deflect salty winds shelter the dunes sufficiently for the forest to perpetuate its unusual mix of vegetation. Some of the plants would be familiar and unremarkable to visitors from Piedmont locations where they naturally occur. In this place,

however, these plants are very unusual, which makes the niche they live unique and remarkable.

The Nature Conservancy purchased an initial 420-acre tract of land in 1978, most of which is in Kill Devil Hills. In 1984 the town of Nags Head bought 300 acres of similar woods within the town limits immediately south of the original Nature Conservancy land and agreed to let the conservancy manage the parcel. In October 1991 the town of Nags Head and the Nature Conservancy jointly purchased an additional 389-acre tract, immediately south of the 1984 Nags Head tract. The conservancy manages this as well.

Trails through the woods originate from a visitors center on the Nature Conservancy land. The center has parking and provides interpretive material that helps explain the significance of Nags Head Woods.

The greatest pleasure in Nags Head Woods is its silence, the hush of a distant forest cove. One of the more interesting trails that provides access to the woods is the sand Old Nags Head Woods Road.

There is a sign directing you to the visitors center from US 158 at Ocean Acres Drive, just before milepost 10. Turn west at McDonald's restaurant onto Ocean Acres Drive and continue toward the sound. The road in the preserve is not paved.

Access

The center is open to Nature Conservancy members Monday–Friday during daylight hours and on Saturdays between Memorial Day and Labor Day. Nonmembers may visit weekdays 10 A.M. to 3 P.M. You must register in the center before hiking the trails.

Handicapped Access

At present, the trails are not wheelchair accessible, but there is a ramp to the observation deck of the visitors center, and there are accessible restrooms in the center.

Information

For information, contact Nags Head Woods Ecological Preserve, Visitors Center, 701 West Ocean Acres Drive, Nags Head, NC 27948, 252-441-2525.

Web address:

Nags Head

Nags Head carries a cachet that is rooted in its undisputable heritage as the oldest resort community on the Dare County oceanfront. There are approximately 11 miles of beachfront in this very narrow community (the greatest width, slightly more than a mile, is near Kill Devil Hills). Except for Jockey's Ridge State Park and parts of Nags Head Woods, the northern half of Nags Head, from Kill Devil Hills south to Whalebone Junction where US 64 begins (or ends), is a scramble of commercial and residential development from all eras and fashions. In this length, there is every kind

	Fee	Parking	Restrooms	Lifeguard	Camping	Showers	Beach Access	Hiking	Trail	Handicapped	Boating	ORV Access	Fishing	Programs	Historic	Sand Beach	Dunes	Upland	Wetland
Nags Head	•	•	•			•				•			•		•	•	•	•	•
Regional Access: Old Nags Header	•	•	•		•	•				•			•			•	•		
Regional Access: Epstein South	•	•	•				•			•			•			•	•		
Jockey's Ridge State Park	•	•							•					•	•		•	•	•

of accommodation and a variety of dining, shopping, and recreation. At the junction, Beach Road (Virginia Dare Trail) veers right and Old Oregon Inlet Road continues south through 5 miles of residential development that backs against the maritime shrub and marsh habitat of the Cape Hatteras National Seashore to the west.

Nags Head visitors will find a community with a fine beach and excellent access, but with an oceanfront that is in a state of transition from modest, more-than-adequate accommodations that nestle by the sea, to larger, massive structures, lavishly styled and appointed, that loom over the oceanfront. Because of Nags Head's resort history, the contrast between newer and established buildings seems more acute here.

Summering on the banks in Nags Head began on the soundside of the community well before the Civil War. This evolution began in similar fashion to other sea island getaways, such as Pawleys Island, South Carolina, as a refuge from the "miasma"—heat, humidity, and mosquitoes—of mainland planter communities.

Author David Stick writes that a planter from Perquimans County, North Carolina, purchased 200 acres in the soundside woods and built a house in 1838. He then sold lots to others. A hotel followed soon thereafter, midway between sound and sea. Visitation increased but was hindered by an arduous walk to the beach—1/2 mile through sand—and too shallow water that limited direct docking by passenger schooners. An extended pier for docking and a "railroad" for mule carts for bathers solved these two problems, and antebellum Nags Head was a social gathering spot during the "miasma months," July and August.

A road south of Jockey's Ridge State Park angles back to the vicinity of the old village center—the sand dune itself has covered some home sites. While a few older houses can be seen, there is little evidence of the resort's soundside birthplace.

The Civil War interrupted these happy times, ultimately dismantling the economy that supported such leisure, but by the late 1870s Nags Head bustled again. In this new wave of summering, a family built a house on the oceanfront approximately 300 yards away from the breakers. By 1885, there were thirteen cottages rowed on the ocean's edge slightly north of the once lonely Nags Head Life-Saving Station.

The resort "officially" went seaside in the 1930s, following the construction of the Wright Memorial Bridge, which brought US 158 to the banks, and the paving of the first 18 miles of what would become NC 12. Shortly thereafter, the post office moved east and the development of the Nags Head oceanfront began in earnest.

In the early decades of the twentieth century, the beachfront houses evolved a distinctive, environmentally adaptive style attributed by architectural historian Catherine Bisher to the remodeling and construction handiwork of

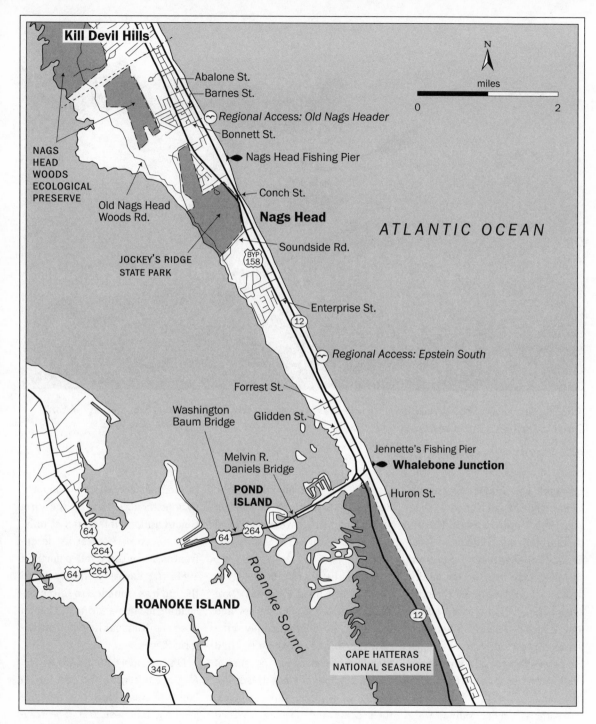

Map 7. Nags Head

Kayakers on a natural history interpretive tour on the soundside at Jockey's Ridge State Park. Courtesy of North Carolina Division of Parks and Recreation.

Elizabeth City builder Stephen J. Twine, who did much of his work in a one-mile length of beach. Known popularly as the "Unpainted Aristocracy," the cottages set a transcending tone for the community that is acknowledged by their inclusion in the "Nags Head Cottage Row Historic District." The peculiar district includes sixty cottages (and two shipwrecks!); nine of the original thirteen houses from 1885 still stand.

Weathered cedar siding, wide porches with lean-out seating, and characteristic green shutters are hallmarks of these stately, simple

retreats. Perched on pilings, the houses were made to be moved, and in fact, some have been moved at least three times since construction.

To see the district, drive slowly along Beach Road (Virginia Dare Trail) between Conch Street and Small Street (approximately milepost 12.5 to 13.5). Personally, I find the old cottages a good measure of the civic pulse of Nags Head. For nearly a century, these homes, their scale and spacing, defined the visual quality of the Nags Head oceanfront. The genteel quality of their purpose, simple shelter by

the sea, set a stylistic tone adopted by guesthouses such as the First Colony Inn, a vintage inn at milepost 16. Threatened at its oceanfront location three miles north in 1988, the Lawrence family saved the inn by sawing it into thirds, relocating it, and restoring it. The inn is on the National Register of Historic Places.

On November 24, 1877, the USS *Huron* sank with the loss of all hands at Nags Head just offshore at about milepost 11.5. The tragedy spurred the deployment of the Life-Saving Service as a year-round, professional rescue organization. The wreck lies in 20 feet of water, approximately even with the end of the Nags Head Pier. On the 114th anniversary of the sinking, the wreck became the first North Carolina Historic Shipwreck Preserve. A display with details of the wreck is in a gazebo at the beach access parking area at the east end of Bladen Street.

Early on, Nags Head named its east-west streets ingeniously by giving all streets within a given mile a name beginning with the same letter of the alphabet, progressing in alphabetical order from north to south. For example, at the northern city limits at milepost 10, all east-west street names once began with the letter "A"—Abalone, Albatross, etc; at milepost 11, with the letter "B," and so on. Unfortunately, the quaint scheme was not consistently followed. Still, it is useful to remember that Whalebone Junction (and Jennette's Fishing Pier) is at Gulfstream Lane—in the "G"s. Generally speaking, if you are lost, but know a cross street, you can follow the alphabet up or down (north or south) to find your way.

There are other classic and enduring enterprises in Nags Head that bridge eras. Owens' Restaurant at milepost 16.5 on Beach Road is the longest-running family restaurant on the beach. Local seafood in Outer Banks style is the specialty on a first-come, first-served basis. The restaurant, modeled in the style of the old lifesaving stations, has a lobby filled with local and family memorabilia.

In addition to this longtime favorite, Kelly's Outer Banks Restaurant and Tavern on the west side of US 158 at milepost 10.5 features southeastern seafood in a comfortable setting infused with local pictures and memorabilia so that you eat well and learn a lot, too.

On the causeway to Manteo is Basnight's Lone Cedar Café, where folks come early for the waterside setting and fresh seafood that is purchased and cleaned daily at the restaurant—emphasis on local and fresh. Early dining guarantees the daily specials will be available.

Access

There are currently more than 30 signed access sites of various sizes within the town limits and abundant parking. There is a regional facility with 60 parking spaces, restrooms, showers, and summer lifeguards at the Old Nags Header site at Bonnett Street along Virginia Dare Trail (Beach Road) between mileposts 10 and 11. Another similarly sized regional access site known as Epstein South is off of Virginia Dare Trail at about milepost 15.25, just north of the tennis courts at the Village Beach and Tennis Club. This site also has restrooms, showers, and a dune crossover ramp. There is a third regional access with a bathhouse at Hargrove Street in South Nags Head.

All access areas are signed from Virginia Dare Trail. If you are in a hurry, remember that many east-west streets terminate in public access locations. Along the nearly 10 miles of shoreline, there are access sites about every $1/2$ mile,

even closer near the northern city limits.

Other major neighborhood sites with improved spaces are provided at the eastern terminus of each of the following streets: Abalone, Bainbridge, Barnes, Bittern, Blackman, Bladen, Conch, Enterprise, Epstein Midway, Epstein North, Forrest, Glidden (with off-road-vehicle access), Governor, Gulfstream, Gull, Hargrove, Holden, Hollowell, Huron, Juncos, and Town Hall.

Estuarine access locations are at the west end of Danube Street, at the Causeway site, and the Little Bridge site.

Handicapped Access

The two regional access sites are fully handicapped accessible.

There are also handicapped facilities at the sites at Enterprise Street, Epstein Midway, and Gulfstream Street.

The town of Nags Head will loan beach wheelchairs by advance reservation. Contact the fire department at 252-441-5909.

Information

For information, contact Outer Banks Visitors Bureau, One Visitors Center Circle, Manteo, NC 27954, 252-473-2138, 877-629-4386; or Outer Banks Chamber of Commerce, P.O. Box 1757, Kill Devil Hills, NC 27948, 252-441-8144.

Web addresses: <www.townof nagshead.net>; <www.outerbanks. org>; <www.outerbankschamber. com>; <www.nccoastalmanage ment.net/Access/sites.htm>

Jockey's Ridge
State Park

In mid-July 2004 my nephew and I slogged to the top of Jockey's Ridge, which was, give or take, 92 feet above sea level and by far and away the best free vista on the Outer Banks. It was 90 degrees, and we angled west to a more gradual climb that picked up the hint of breeze pushing across the summit.

"This is the Sahara," declared young Jack Boyle and to a kid from New York, it might as well have been. It was a weekday and family hour on top, with regularly staged races down the steeply angled scarp of the northeast face.

With a stick he collected on the way, Jack wrote his name across the great dune's forehead, and a lively protest followed when I accused him of graffiti. Jockey's Ridge inspires such silliness as sandboarding, rolling or racing down the face of the dune, or with the help of nearby Kitty Hawk Kites, hang gliding or flying the kite of your choice.

Jockey's Ridge is the tallest sand dune on the East Coast and the central feature of a 420-acre state park where you can walk just about anywhere your sand-filled shoes can take you. In 1971 bulldozers began to flatten the dune for a subdivision when they were single-handedly stopped by a single-minded resident, Carolista Baum, who formed a committee to save what

had always been a historic playground. With the help of the Nature Conservancy, the main dune was saved, and subsequent purchases have tried to buy their way around the massive pile, which has shifted more than 1,000 feet southwest since the 1970s.

Not only has it moved, the dune has shortened; it once scaled a full 20 feet taller than it does today. The dune does what the wind tells it to do, as did other historic sand hills on the Outer Banks, including Run Hill, Engagement Hill, Pin Hill, and Seven Sisters. The prevailing wind moves Jockey's Ridge slightly southwest, but each year other winds push it back northeast. Seasonal changes in breezes roll the sand from one side to the other. Thousands of visitors climb it each year, and of course, memory or perhaps a photograph is the only record of their visit. Stroll the southwest edge of the dune, and you can see what it is up to, which is to gradually engulf the forest on its southwest border. (Historically, other dunes played havoc with the first homes built on their shoulders in Nags Head's early soundside settlement.)

In the early 1980s I wrote a short magazine article about a miniature golf course on the southeast side of the park, right by US 158. Each spring, the absentee owner, returning to prepare for the season, dutifully swept (and shoveled) the winter spindrift off the course. Sometime between then and now, Jockey's Ridge won.

In July 2004 the castle turret of that miniature golf course rose like a fantasy out of the great dune, fenced off for safety reasons. I suspect everything else about that once prosperous corner, including the parking lot, lies beneath the sand. I cannot help but wonder what lies beneath it elsewhere on the 420 acres.

While the geological origin of the dunes is disputed, its historical presence is not; explorers noticed it and mapped it as early as 1775. Despite its "mobility," historical aerial photographs show that the dune has not altered radically in size or configuration since 1949.

There is no bad time to be there, but the view from the top at sunset is especially magnificent. Climbing is more comfortable in the early or later hours of the day, and the park stays open until 9:00 P.M. June–August for just that reason. Shoes are always a good idea, particularly for children. On very windy days, sunglasses or other eye protection is recommended. Leave the dune if a thunderstorm is imminent; it is the highest location around and a frequent target of lightning strikes. As you might expect, the very fine wind-driven sand clings persistently to skin and clothing. Brush off as best you can, but you will always take a little of Jockey's Ridge with you.

As my intrepid companion discovered, one of the rewards of climbing to the top is the bounding footrace down. And so we did as thousands do, great bounding

Hang gliders soar at Jockey's Ridge. Courtesy of Outer Banks Visitors Bureau.

leaps down the steep northeast scarp, flailing our arms for balance. When we reached bottom, Jack Boyle climbed it—two steps up, one slide back—and ran down it again, and then there was "one more time."

Access

Parking and restroom facilities are located off of the US 158 bypass. Park hours coincide with daylight throughout the year (but how do you close a dune?).

For alternative recreation, pick up the park flyer, "Tracks in the Sand." It is the guide to a 1.5-mile nature walk along the backside of the dune with keyed drawings of the tracks of animals that live on the dune or in the nearby maritime forest. It takes about $1^1/_2$ hours to complete the walk.

Jockey's Ridge State Park also has a sound access site and a soundside overlook accessible from Soundside Drive.

Handicapped Access

The ranger's headquarters, restrooms, and some of the picnic shelters and pathways near the restrooms are accessible to the handicapped. There is a handicapped accessible boardwalk to an overlook of the main ridge. The soundside access is handicapped accessible.

Information

For information, contact Jockey's Ridge State Park, P.O. Box 592, Nags Head, NC 27959, 252-441-7132.

Web address: <www.ncsparks. net/jori.html>

Whalebone Junction

On the Outer Banks, all roads lead to Whalebone Junction, the place where routes US 158, US 64/264, and NC 12 convene to go their enumerated ways. It is not a destination, just a landmark that has the best nickname in the state for an intersection, hands down.

The origin of the name comes from a service station that was once located at the intersection that closed around the time the US 158 bypass was built. It displayed whalebones from a beached leviathan.

The intersection carries a high volume of traffic, and drivers should use caution before entering the intersection, paying particular attention to southbound traffic on US 158.

When driving north from Whalebone Junction, note that signs for NC 12 indicate that it is named the Marc Basnight Highway. Postal addresses will refer to NC 12 by its older name, Virginia Dare Trail, and in conversation, the route is known locally as Beach Road.

Washington Baum Bridge

A new highway leads west from Whalebone Junction, crossing a causeway that connects Cedar Island and Pond Island en route to Roanoke Island by way of the highrise Washington Baum Bridge. This 1990 four-lane bridge greatly improves travel across Roanoke

Sound, and the high, smooth arc of the structure offers a great view of the marsh-fringed sound. Evening travelers can also catch the telltale flashing of the Bodie Island Lighthouse.

Starting in the mid-1920s, Washington Baum, the bridge's namesake, pushed for the construction of a bridge and causeway connecting Roanoke Island to the barrier beaches. He got the job done, too, although the idea was not well received at the time because the toll ($1 per car) drawbridge and causeway seemed kind of steep when the only paved road in the region ran between Manteo and Wanchese. The original bridge, however, turned out to be the proverbial domino because by 1930, another private group had built the toll bridge across Currituck Sound to Kitty Hawk, and within two more years the state had paved a road along the beach.

The current bridge replaces a swing bridge that would have to open for passing boat traffic on Roanoke Sound, obviously delaying automobile traffic.

The causeway has become a little busier than being just a mere passage. Marinas and boat ramps extend from the road into the estuary. Crabbing and fishing are permitted in traffic-safe locations along the route, including on the Melvin R. Daniels Bridge, east of the Washington Baum Bridge. There are also several fine restaurants along the passage, each of which offers its own soundside vista for dining.

South of the Washington Baum

Bridge on Roanoke Island is an access pull-off that has a boat-launching ramp. Local fishermen began coming to the site almost immediately after the opening of the bridge because of the elbow room. They also like the quietness caused by the fact that the bridge elevates the highway sounds.

Access

The town of Nags Head maintains two estuarine access locations with parking. Both are on the south side of the causeway. The first, Little Bridge, is by the west end of the Melvin Daniels Bridge at Pond Island. The second is just east of Basnight's Lone Cedar Café on the same side of the causeway.

Roanoke Island

Roanoke Island sits in the shelter of the Dare County resort beaches joined by the causeway and bridge that cross shallow Roanoke Sound. On the island's western side, slightly deeper Croatan Sound is the watery barrier to mainland Dare County, now spanned by two bridges that touch at opposite ends of Manns Harbor. The island is small, 11 miles long and 2.5 miles wide, but it stands large in history because it is here that English-speaking people made their first attempt to colonize the New World. The two main communities, Manteo and Wanchese, are namesakes of the two Native Americans who returned to England with members of the pioneering 1584 expedition.

While the outcome was not a good one for the would-be colonists who came here, Roanoke Island would, in time, become a home for generations that was solidly anchored in a maritime way of life. It became a safe harbor for the self-sufficient who were happy living within the limits of its early isolation. Manteo, the Dare County seat, is more tourism-oriented than Wanchese, which still has the easygoing, down-to-earth character of a traditional fishing community.

Solidity permeates Roanoke Island. One cannot help but think that it must have appeared as an oasis to the first sea-weary voyagers who disembarked on its forested shores. The tree cover alone makes it a wonderful visual contrast to the nearby oceanfront, and then there is the different mood and pace, which is much more small town than beach resort (do not think that you will hurry local drivers). A day trip there becomes a bit of comparatively cool relief from the heated setting of the sun-bleached beaches. As a visitor during high summer heat remarked, "Going there after being on the beach is like sitting under a great green beach umbrella."

I put the island on the top of the list of coastal places to visit for at least a day. It gets high marks all the way around on my upscale entertainment index—an informal gauge for rating how a destination feeds the insatiably curious. A visit has the potential to be akin to picking fruit from a learning tree. The broad appeal of specific events and venues and the island at large guarantees something for anybody who is conscious. Only in the last two decades has the full force of Roanoke Island's appeal and personality become approachable and accessible.

Until bridges closed the watery gaps and opened up the Outer Banks in the 1930s, there was no reason to visit and no easy way to do so. This relative isolation was just a fact of life on Roanoke Island, and whatever happened here took some time to make its way to population centers. Today's strong push toward tourism displays the island's history and charm for all to see.

Archaeologists and historians have busily filled in the details on several compelling threads of the island's past. One of these is the Civil War. Roanoke Island fell to Union forces in 1862 when an attack led by General Ambrose Burnside routed, then captured, Confederate troops occupying Fort Huger, now submerged 300 yards off of the island's north end. Union control made Roanoke Island a haven for runaway slaves, and the population quickly soared to more than 1,000. Union troops eventually established the Freedmen's Colony of Roanoke Island that grew into a village of more than 3,000 people and 600 homes. The colony was disbanded in 1866 after the federal government reversed a decision that had granted ownership of the houses to the freedmen. Many left the island, yet some remained to live and work here. An interpretive display at Weir Point at the east end of the William B. Umstead Bridge details this history.

Richard Etheridge was one of the Roanoke Island freedmen who made history in the U.S. Life-Saving Service when he was appointed the first African American captain of a station at Pea Island. Etheridge eventually commanded an all–African American crew who served with distinction and bravery. An exhibit at the North Carolina Aquarium provides additional details. (One of Etheridge's handwritten rescue reports is displayed at the Centennial Pavilion of the Wright Brothers National Memorial.)

For centuries—at least two—most Roanoke Islanders made all or most of their livelihood from the waters of sounds or sea. One local nineteenth-century boatbuilder, Washington Creef, developed and built wooden workboats that were unsurpassed for working local waters. Creef's sturdy, low-gunneled, wide-bottomed shadboat, which he designed and built in a boat shop in Manteo, is the official wooden boat of North Carolina. A reconstruction of his son's 1940s-era Manteo boat shop is an adjunct of the North Carolina Maritime Museum in Beaufort and is open as both museum and working boat shop.

The island's attractions and natural attractiveness suffered for many years because of the press of traffic-routing to the beaches. The Virginia Dare Memorial Bridge, which routes traffic in a direct flow from Manns Harbor to the Washington Baum Bridge, has made lo-

	Fee	Parking	Restrooms	Lifeguard	Camping	Showers	Beach Access	Hiking	Trail	Handicapped	Boating	ORV Access	Fishing	Programs	Historic	Sand Beach	Dunes	Upland	Wetland
Washington Baum Bridge		•						•			•		•						•
Roanoke Island		•	•		•			•		•	•		•	•	•			•	•
Roanoke Island Festival Park	•	•	•					•		•				•	•			•	•
Public Boating Access: Manteo		•									•							•	•
Fort Raleigh National Historic Site		•	•					•	•	•				•	•			•	
North Carolina Aquarium, Roanoke Island	•	•	•							•				•	•			•	
Dare Co. Airport Recreation Area		•									•		•						•
Public Boating Access: Wanchese		•									•		•						•
Outer Banks Welcome Center		•	•						•		•							•	•

cal traffic on the island more, well, local. The Outer Banks Welcome Center at the east end of the Virginia Dare Memorial Bridge is a great first stop before exploring Roanoke Island and the rest of the Outer Banks. Pick up a welcome packet, which includes an "Outer Banks Vacation Guide" that provides an excellent listing of places and services. Enjoy the introductory video as well.

Among the attractions you should plan to visit are the *Elizabeth II* State Historic Site; the North Carolina Aquarium; and the Fort Raleigh National Historic Site, nestled on the north end of the island along with the Lindsay Warren Visitors Center and the adjacent Elizabethan Gardens. During the summer, these attractions stay extremely busy, particularly the aquarium, so arrive early.

Access

Dare County maintains boating access locations on Roanoke Island and within the town limits of Manteo and Wanchese.

There is a boat ramp at Dare County Airport Recreation Area, south of the North Carolina Aquarium at the end of Airport Road.

There are plans for a boat ramp, basin, and public parking south of the Emergency Medical Service Center west of US 64 on Bowsertown Road.

Handicapped Access

The individual federal, state, and municipal attractions have accommodations for handicapped travelers.

Information

For information, contact Outer Banks Visitors Bureau, One Visitors Center Circle, Manteo, NC 27954, 252-473-2138, 877-629-4386; or Outer Banks Chamber of Commerce, P.O. Box 1757, Kill Devil Hills, NC 27948, 252-441-8144.

Web addresses: <www.outer banks.org>; <www.outerbanks chamber.com>; <www.nccoastal management.net/Access/sites. htm>

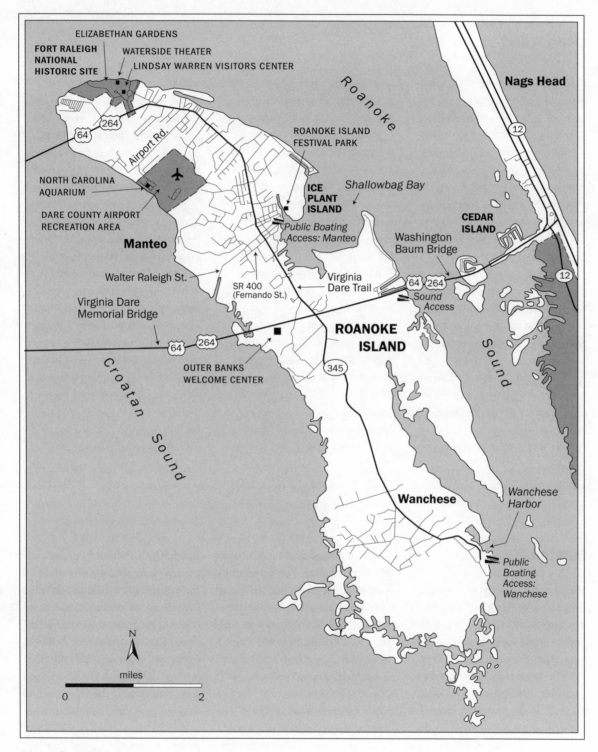

ELIZABETHAN GARDENS

FORT RALEIGH
NATIONAL
HISTORIC SITE

WATERSIDE THEATER

LINDSAY WARREN VISITORS CENTER

Roanoke

Nags Head

264

64

Airport Rd.

ROANOKE ISLAND
FESTIVAL PARK

NORTH CAROLINA
AQUARIUM

DARE COUNTY AIRPORT
RECREATION AREA

Manteo

ICE
PLANT
ISLAND

Shallowbag Bay

CEDAR
ISLAND

Public Boating
Access: Manteo

Washington
Baum Bridge

Walter Raleigh St.

SR 400
(Fernando St.)

Virginia
Dare Trail

64 264
Sound
Access

Sound

Virginia Dare
Memorial Bridge

64 264

ROANOKE
ISLAND

OUTER BANKS
WELCOME CENTER

345

12

12

Croatan Sound

Wanchese

Wanchese
Harbor

Public
Boating
Access:
Wanchese

N

miles

0   2

Map 8. Roanoke Island

Good Wood

Put yourself in a waterman's boots eighty years ago—fishing, a little farming, and maybe guiding for sportsmen. You are tied to the water like a boat to a dock. There's a lot of wood in your life: your boats, docks, and decoys; your siding, shingles, fences, and posts; your whittling, if you have time.

There are no big box house stores; there are no wood preservatives. So pick a tree, waterman—you've got repairs to make. Which wood is good wood?

It must be durable and able to withstand winter ice and torpid summer heat. It must not rot or at least rot slowly enough to make it worth spending time felling, hauling, barking, splitting, and shaping. Once fashioned, it will be in contact with water and air and the

fungi and little animals that seem to eat things you value. It will be tested.

It must be buoyant, lightweight, smooth-grained, and splinter-free; sandable, workable, and easily shaped and turned with the boatbuilder's tools and the carver's knife. It would be nice if it were aromatic; the shavings might sweeten the air.

It must be nearby, it must be plentiful, and it must be free or close to it.

There was such a tree once: Atlantic white cedar, known botanically as *Chamaecyparis thyoides*. Watermen called it juniper, a misnomer that was derived from its resemblance to eastern red cedar, a *Juniperus* species. Atlantic white cedar is a wetland species

with a native range extending between Maine and Florida. The Great Dismal Swamp and the peninsula between Albemarle and Pamlico Sounds once sheltered some of the largest stands of this soggy-ground evergreen within its range.

It became the waterman's tree and, subsequently, one of the most valuable commercial species in the East. Beginning in the late nineteenth century, railroads and drainage ditches siphoned away the swamp's protective bogginess, leaving pure stands of juniper open for harvest. By the time of the Great Depression, most of the virgin stands were gone. How much timber was cut? At one time juniper stands may have covered some 62,000 to 112,000 acres within the Great Dismal Swamp alone.

Manteo

Manteo, the county seat of Dare County, carried on quietly for years as tourists and tourism sped past (figuratively speaking) in a headlong charge to the Outer Banks. Civic leaders took note, however, and since the 1980s have undertaken one improvement after another to enhance Manteo's appeal to tourists without destroying its inherent charm. It is a case in point

of how one good thing leads to another good thing. The community is capitalizing on its historical and natural assets, and today Manteo is well past the tipping point of curiosity. It is delightful, itself a rightful destination, and it has the simple appeal that invites sharing with special friends.

My favorite way to reach the heart of Manteo is by slowly driving NC 400, Fernando Street from its intersection with US 64 Business. It is

a pleasant transition from the commercial buzz of island traffic and the engagingly distracting Manteo waterfront. Fernando Street eases under trees, past the inviting gardens of the Roanoke Inn, and then along the shrubby edge of Shallowbag Bay, past a small overlook park, and then by the old renovated wooden boat shop that houses the North Carolina Maritime Museum to move into the closer quarters of the village. At the Queen Eliza-

Today, between 6,000 and 7,000 acres of juniper remain.

In fact, Atlantic white cedar may grow on only 10 percent of its original acreage in North Carolina. This deficiency is probably a direct result of land management in the timbered regions. The land was drained, the timber harvested, and then came the plow. What is considered old-growth timber today is second-growth timber from natural reforestation.

Commercial harvesting of this secondary growth boomed again in the mid-1970s. The ditch digging and road building in use today is altering the groundwater characteristics of the soil where the juniper grows. It loves wet feet, and the yet unanswered question is, will juniper reseed and return?

Unlike other trees that are commercially lumbered, there has been no large-scale replanting. Atlantic white cedar needs assistance to recover from cutting; seedlings must have direct sunlight. It is thought that firing the clear-cut area to remove growth and debris may help—after all, the stands recovered somewhat from the initial harvest of nearly 100 years ago. However, in those early days, the swamp remained a swamp, even after the timber was felled. Today the swamps are being drained.

The tree is not in danger of extinction, but the reduction in habitat jeopardizes other components of its unique environmental niche. Also, an important component of maritime heritage is threatened. Juniper skiffs, boats, and decoys *are*

indispensable to the eastern North Carolina waterman's story.

Fortunately, some handsome stands are now protected. The Emily and Richardson Preyer Buckridge Preserve protects a 5,000-acre juniper forest, which is half the acreage of this unusual forest type remaining in the state. There are also juniper stands in the Alligator River National Wildlife Refuge.

Reforestation efforts are under way in the Great Dismal Swamp. If you want to see the wood in action, visit the *Elizabeth II* at Roanoke Island Festival Park in Manteo harbor. This sturdy replica is planked with juniper. It's good wood—everything a waterman could ask for; let's hope there's more someday.

beth Street intersection, buildings snug up to the road, and the town unfolds unpretentiously. I prefer to park three blocks north at the foot of the Cora Mae Basnight Bridge and walk the town from there, but any parking place will do. Manteo rewards time spent walking, window shopping, and chatting up 450-year-old sailors at Roanoke Island Festival Park.

In 1984 Manteo drew back the curtain on a waterfront renovation timed to celebrate the 400th anniversary of the first attempt by English-speaking people to colonize the New World. The still spiffy development brought a mix of uses to the waterfront by stacking residential property atop ground-level shopping and dinning in a bid to create a new economic anchor downtown. Coupling this with a municipal boardwalk along the harbor that has more than fifty boat slips cemented the appeal to casual passersby. The waterfront offers a glimpse at the docked *Elizabeth II* at Roanoke Island Festival Park across the harbor. The ship was actually built at the south end of the waterfront. It is a full-scale reconstruction of a sixteenth-century sailing vessel. Continue strolling south to see a replica of the Roanoke Marsh Light, the type of navigation light historically used in Croatan Sound and a reminder of the island's nautical heritage.

Manteo's foresight is paying off today. The Waterfront Shops and Centennial Plaza have a seasonal bustle that pulls people to the waterfront, and an adjoining four-square-block area has been invigorated with restaurants and specialty shops. A sterling hostelry, Tranquil House Inn, a spirited revival of vernacular architecture, anchors the other end of the waterfront adjacent to a municipal parking lot. The inn also features an outstanding restaurant, 1587, where the cuisine and the artistry of the presentation have few equals. Reservations are recommended.

One of the best local vendors (if you are a reader) is Manteo Booksellers on Sir Walter Raleigh Street, a comfy spot for any bibliophile, which has expanded sections for North Carolina fiction and Outer Banks history. Across the street—by design, not providence—The Coffeehouse on Roanoke Island, with espresso, house blends, delicious fresh pastries, smoothies, and milkshakes, is a great place to start a morning or take a break when vacation overwhelms you.

The continued development and expansion of Roanoke Island Festival Park on Ice Plant Island is also fueling Manteo's appeal as a destination. The Cora Mae Basnight Bridge to Festival Park serves literally as the jumping-off place for local kids to splash into the basin below. This childhood exuberance fits right in with the town.

Take the time to wander side streets such as John Borden Street or Devon Street, moving through the residential areas of the town, working your way to head north on Winginia Street. It's serene and calming under some of the largest, loveliest loblolly pines you are likely to see, and flowers abound in private gardens. Manteo is a homey-looking town, and it feels that way, too.

Access

Manteo provides a public dock along Fernando Street with several parking places. There is paid municipal parking along Queen Elizabeth Street.

Also, the Manteo Public Boat Landing is at the east end of Ananias Dare Street, adjacent to the Cora Mae Basnight Bridge. There is public parking there as well.

Handicapped Access

Handicapped parking spaces are provided in the off-street parking lot next to the Tranquil House Inn on the waterfront.

The municipal boardwalk and public dock are handicapped accessible from a small parking area on Fernando Street, across from the Roanoke Inn.

Information

For information, contact Outer Banks Visitors Bureau, One Visitors Center Circle, Manteo, NC 27954, 252-473-2138, 877-629-4386; or Outer Banks Chamber of Commerce, P.O. Box 1757, Kill Devil Hills, NC 27948, 252-441-8144.

Web addresses: <www.outer banks.org>; <www.outerbanks chamber.com>; <www.manteo. govoffice.com>

North Carolina Maritime Museum

What appears to be a modest-sized weathered building at 104 Fernando Street in Manteo is the restored boat shop of George Washington Creef Jr. There has been a Creef family boat shop on this site since 1880. In 1939 a fire destroyed the buildings along Manteo's waterfront. The following year, George Washington Creef Jr. built the present boathouse to ply his trade. He built new working craft and would also repair the shadboats invented and built years earlier by his father.

The shop is now an adjunct of the North Carolina Maritime Museum at Beaufort, and it is actively dedicated to North Carolina's place in boatbuilding history. Staff and volunteers are busy restoring and rebuilding wooden boats. Exhibits inside detail local boatbuilding history. On display are a variety of small sailing skiffs and an actual 1883 Washington Creef shadboat, the boat invented by George Washington Creef Sr. and since declared the North Carolina state boat. Visitors may watch a media presentation that details the construction of the *Elizabeth II*, which was built on this site.

Access

The North Carolina Maritime Museum is open Tuesday through Saturday, 10 A.M. to 6 P.M. in summer, and 9 A.M. to 5 P.M. fall, winter, and spring. There is public parking near the museum.

Handicapped Access

The museum is accessible to the handicapped.

Information

For information, contact North Carolina Maritime Museum at Roanoke Island, 104 Fernando Street, Manteo, NC 27954, 252-475-1500.

Web address:

Roanoke Island Festival Park

The Cora Mae Basnight Bridge is the passage into Roanoke Island's niche in history offered in the multiple media venues of Roanoke Island Festival Park. Taken as a whole, Festival Park is a full-fledged interpretive experience. There is a feature film, *The Legend of Two Path*, the interactive Roanoke Adventure Museum, and two distinct, but obviously related living history interpretive sites, the *Elizabeth II* and the Settlement Site. The emphasis throughout is on enjoyable learning; and it is set up so that the greater your participation, the richer the experience, so show up with plenty of curiosity and, at one venue at least, a (wooden) boatload of questions.

While the separate sites can be visited in any order, I recommend first going to the auditorium to see *The Legend of Two Path*, the docudrama that explores the relationships among Native Americans and the changes effected by the first European contacts. The original story, developed by the North Carolina School of the Arts, is compelling; importantly, it puts a different frame of reference around the First Colony. The fact that the *Elizabeth II* appears in the film should be your cue for the next stop.

The *Elizabeth II* is the full-scale reconstruction of a sixteenth-century sailing vessel that is manned by interpreters in Elizabethan dress. The 69-foot-long, 17-foot-wide ship, which was built in Manteo for the 400th anniversary of the first English-speaking settlement in the New World, is fully seaworthy by sail (with motorized backup). The seasonal interpreters are fully tourist-worthy too, but if you walk by and never speak to them, you will miss the best part of the show and some wonderful speech.

Ask how many made the journey to "Vir-gineeyah." Where did they sleep? How many crew does it take to haul the main? To weigh anchor? What is a spar? What did they eat on the crossing? Assuredly, you will come away from such a chat with a better appreciation of the English language, the spirit of adventure, and the consummate craftsmanship of the shipwrights who built her.

Carry the same attitude to the nearby first settlement, where there is sure to be at least one soldier standing guard. Ask what the colonists expected to find in the New World. What riches did they seek? Did they feel safe? Try on a soldier's helmet.

The Roanoke Adventure Museum nicely finishes a visit by exploring the natural aspects of the island as well as cultural themes that are more recent historically. Take note of the sturdy, workable, wooden shadboat built by Washington Creef that is on display. This is North Carolina's official state boat, and it originated on Roanoke Island.

The Outer Banks History Center is next to the visitors center at the park. It's a treasure trove of information on the Outer Banks that is maintained by the North Carolina Division of Archives and History for historical research on topics concerning the Outer Banks. Author David Stick initiated the establishment of the center in the late 1980s by contributing his extensive personal collection of Outer Banks reference material, as well as original paintings and illustrations by his father, Frank Stick. Today, the center includes nearly 35,000 photographs and a large collection of historic maps, some of which are more than 400 years old. It is the starting point for research on the Outer Banks, but on a casual note, it often exhibits historic photography of the area.

Not everything at the park is tied to history. During the summer months, there are children's programs such as magic shows and performing artists scheduled for mid-morning in the theater. The Pavilion Outdoor Theatre is the site for concerts and "moonlight movies" throughout the year; the Museum Store offers distinctive books and gifts; and the Festival Park Art Gallery has changing monthly exhibits.

Access

Admission is $7 for adults, $1.50 for children, and $2 for senior citizens. The visitors center is open April–August 15, 10 A.M. to 7 P.M. daily; August 16–October 10 A.M. to 6 P.M. daily; and November–March, Tuesday–Sunday, 10 A.M. to 5 P.M. The last tour is at 3 P.M.

Handicapped Access

The *Elizabeth II* Visitors Center, settlement site, auditorium, adventure museum, restrooms, and picnic area are fully accessible for the handicapped. The ship is not easily accessible for the handicapped.

Information

For information, contact Roanoke Island Festival Park, 1 Festival Park, Manteo, NC 27954, 252-475-1500 or 252-475-1506 for a 24-hour events line; or Outer Banks History Center, 1 Festival Park, Manteo, NC 27954, 252-473-2655.

Web addresses: <www.roanoke island.com>; <www.ah.dcr.state. nc.us/archives/obhc>

North Carolina Aquarium, Roanoke Island

The North Carolina Aquarium on Roanoke Island is a place of high-pitched excitement and muttering awe, a splendid peek-below-the-surface coastal education. This extraordinary facility reopened in May 2000 after an extensive redesign to present living vignettes of aquatic life from the brackish waters of the sound estuaries to the pulsing near shore of the "Graveyard of the Atlantic." It is a great place to see with whom or what you share the sea!

"Wetlands on the Edge," an atrium exhibit, recreates a typical river environment that drains into the sounds where river otters swim playfully and an alligator obligingly floats within touching distance. Coastal vegetation reaches overhead. The familiar cooters and sliders (turtles) and the not nearly so bowfins and gars swim in the "Coastal Freshwaters" exhibit.

The shallow tanks of the "Close Encounters" allow visitors to choose their moment to touch a skate as it glides effortlessly across the wide pool. Hermit crabs and sea urchins are among the other creatures there.

Ever wonder what is like to live through a storm on the Outer Banks? At the "Hurricane/Northeaster" exhibit, residents narrate videos of the perilous storms that have swept these low islands. The historic background is the memorable Ash Wednesday storm of 1962 that washed over and washed out Dare's resort communities.

The big show, however, is the silent swirl of sea creatures in the two-story, 285,000-gallon "Graveyard of the Atlantic" exhibit. The central feature is a $1/3$-scale model of the upended shipwreck of the USS *Monitor*, but the stars are the finny actors that swim in stratified swaths throughout. A sand tiger shark menacingly moves through the water and around it swim the game fish and the purely beautiful fish of the high-energy Outer Banks ocean.

Announcements of lectures and special programs resonate through the halls; the aquarium staff constantly presents a variety of programs and special events. The place fairly jumps with ecological educational opportunities, including one where you can generate a sample of the voltage that could come from an electric eel, an exhibit with an unusually quick learning curve.

There is always a crowd, but be warned: do not save it for a rainy day—that is when everybody goes. Lunchtime and mid-afternoon typically find crowds waning, as does first thing in the morning.

Access

The facility is open daily 9 A.M. to 5 P.M. during the summer; hours are shortened in the off-season. Admission is $6 for adults, reduced for seniors and military personnel, and $4 for children.

Dare County maintains a boat-launching ramp next to the aquarium.

Handicapped Access

The aquarium and restroom facilities are accessible to handicapped travelers.

Information

For information, contact the North Carolina Aquarium on Roanoke Island, Airport Road, Manteo, NC 27954-0967. For a recorded listing of programs at the aquarium, call 252-473-3493. To schedule group visits, call 252-473-3494.

Web address: <www.ncaquariums.com>

Fort Raleigh National Historic Site

Fort Raleigh National Historic Site honors nothing less than the birthplace of English-speaking settlement in North America. The heart of the complex is the disarmingly simple but accurately restored earthwork moat and "fort" originally constructed to protect the members of the Ralph Lane colony in 1585. The ramparts were reconstructed in 1950 by the National Park Service based on what remained of the original fortifications, which were uncovered during archaeological investigations in 1936 and 1948.

It is an austere exhibit. Fortunately, the history of these brave attempts to settle the New World is better known than the park service can present on the ground. While site historians and archaeologists feel reasonably certain that the location of the settlement that the earthworks defended is within site boundaries (some of it might have been lost to erosion), this has yet to be documented by additional archaeological investigations.

Until then, these simple earthworks and the artifacts recovered from the site during the original excavations are the only tangible remains of what was, of course, a failure compounded by mystery. Able park interpreters of the site fill in the narrative voids surrounding the physical artifacts with insight and humor. By the orientation of the earthwork ramparts, speculation is that the builders feared an overland attack by Native Americans more than an attack by sea, which would have come from England's New World rival, Spain.

In summer, frequently scheduled guided walks flesh out the history, putting emotions, motives, and personality to the figures behind this attempt. Self-guided visiting is also possible, but the interpretive walks are far more rewarding.

Stop at the Lindsay Warren Visitors Center first for an introduction into the colonial history of the New World by means of a video that describes colonization efforts during the sixteenth century. Adjacent to the theater is an actual Elizabethan-era reading room. Dismantled and reassembled here, it provides some flavor about the "money behind the mission," the aristocracy who invested in the colonization venture in the hopes of returns from gold, silver, and other precious metals. Displays show original artifacts, such as a wrought-iron sickle, that were uncovered here and compare the cultures that ultimately collided in the early years.

Between the visitors center and the fort is a monument commemorating the christening of Virginia Dare, the first child born to English-speaking people in the New World. Beyond the fort is the Thomas Hariot Nature Trail, named after the scientist who wrote reports on the explorations of the Lane colonists in the New World. Hariot's words provide the narration on this self-guided tour that winds you through both time and the natural woodlands.

Next to the historic site is the famed Waterside Theater, which is the site of the nation's first and longest-running outdoor drama, *The Lost Colony* by Paul Green. Referred to as a "symphonic outdoor drama" for its orchestration and musical influence, the opulent play recounts the story of the first English settlers sent here by Sir Walter Raleigh in 1585. Interpretations change a bit from year to year reflecting the personality imparted by a director's staging. The script is tight, easily followed, and wonderfully enjoyable. Professional actors play the leads, but many locals have grown up through the ranks of the cast. All seats are excellent, but those in the "Producers Circle" (with a slight premium) offer the most balanced viewing, as much action occurs at the wings of the main stage. Reservations are advised and sooner rather than later; the play is very popular. A note: It can be chilly, and mosquitoes can be vicious; a sweater and repellent are a good idea, as is emergency rain gear.

The Elizabethan Gardens, a 10-acre formal garden, is also accessible from the Lindsay Warren Visitors Center (though it has a separate parking area as well). Created by the Garden Club of North Carolina in 1960, the gardens rival any formal gardens in the state for their design authenticity and the extensive collection of plant materials. The plant selection obviously cannot duplicate sixteenth-century English gardening because of the coastal climate, but it is faithful to the styles of the Elizabethan era. True to form, it functions as a controlled retreat for strolling in the heart of the wilderness, a theme appropriate to the settlement of the New World. It is designed to have year-round appeal as well as seasonal highlighting. It is exquisite in any season but especially in summer, when annual plantings come to the fore. The centerpiece of the garden is a sunken parterre with statuary and a central, tiered fountain, a geometry of clipped hedges, and annual color. Secreted within is the proclaimed 1859 Virginia Dare statue, a romantic interpretation of the legend that the first child born in the New World to English parents grew to womanhood among Native Americans.

One of the best treats of the summer is to time your garden visit to coincide with that of Elizabeth I, who holds court in the garden weekly in a performance of *Elizabeth R*, a one-hour, one-act play. You will learn much about the likes and dislikes of this powerful monarch.

Access

Fort Raleigh National Historic Site is open 9 A.M. to 8 P.M. Monday–Saturday, 9 A.M. to 6 P.M. Sunday, during the summer drama season; 9 A.M. to 5 P.M. during the rest of the year. The Lindsay Warren Visitors Center is open 9 A.M. to 5 P.M. Performances of *The Lost Colony* are usually staged from mid-June through August and begin at 8:30 P.M., Monday–Saturday; admission is $10 for adults, $5 for children under 12. The Elizabethan Gardens are open all year from 9 A.M. to 5 P.M. (8 P.M. in summer), except Saturdays and Sundays during January and February. Admission is $2.50 for adults; children under 12 are admitted free.

Handicapped Access

Most of the facilities at the fort are handicapped accessible or negotiable for wheelchair travelers with minimal assistance. Access to the auditorium in the visitors center is restricted because of a narrow doorway and steep slope. New restrooms are planned to provide accessible facilities.

The Waterside Theater is accessible. Wheelchairs are available at the theater, and wheelchair spaces are provided. Restrooms are accessible with some assistance.

The Elizabethan Gardens are negotiable by wheelchair with assistance.

Information

For information about Fort Raleigh National Historic Site, call 252-473-2111. For information about performances of *The Lost Colony*, call 252-473-3414. For information about the Elizabethan Gardens, call 252-473-3234.

For further information, contact Outer Banks Visitors Bureau, One Visitors Center Circle, Manteo, NC 27954, 252-473-2138, 877-629-4386; or Outer Banks Chamber of Commerce, P.O. Box 1757, Kill Devil Hills, NC 27948, 252-441-8144.

Web addresses: <www.nps.gov/fora/raleigh.htm>; <www.thelost colony.org>; <www.outerbanks-nc. com/elizabethangardens>

Wanchese

I have always liked Wanchese (locals pronounce it "Won-cheese") for its hardworking honesty as a fishing and boatbuilding village that it wears on its sleeve. Named after the Native American who accompanied his chief Manteo to England on the 1584 return voyage of colonists Amadas and Barlowe, Wanchese is on the south end of Roanoke Island.

It is sleepy by contrast to Manteo, and it is both understated and understood that the village keeps older, more traditional rhythms of work and life than the nearby county seat. In many respects, the few miles between them are symbolic of many, many decades. Fishing boats leave before sunrise, and cicadas buzz from the treetops in summer.

Everybody I've ever met from Wanchese—young adults who are waiting tables or working in family businesses—enthusiastically endorsed growing up here—and I know why. We were dining harborside at the Fisherman's Wharf restaurant when a small boat motored in from the sound driven by a crew of three kids, one on the bow, one at the wheel, one at the deck—suntanned, no shirts, cut-offs, average age thirteen, maybe. As they passed the restaurant, the smallest kid jumped up on the bow and pushed the largest right into the drink. It was a page out of *Boy's Life*.

The first inkling of the Wanchese community is the white siding of Bethany Methodist Church at a fork on Old Wharf Road, which winds around and connects with other streets, eventually looping back to the main road. You can go either way at the fork, but if you go left, you'll reach the seafood packers quicker.

The boats bring in steady catches daily. Seafood vendors at Wanchese usually have low prices on fresh seafood, certainly worth the side trip to fill up a cooler before returning inland. If you don't have a cooler or ice, they sell those, too. The Fisherman's Wharf restaurant, a family restaurant serving tradition local seafood, overlooks the harbor. The pungent breezes you would expect from fishermen's wharves scent the air.

Residents offer crafts, services, and bed-and-breakfasts out of their homes. Folks are friendly and easy-going, so drive friendly. Watch out for horses and children in the streets—this is a village not used to through traffic.

Access

Dare County maintains a public boat ramp and dock on Mill Creek in Wanchese, just south of the Wanchese Fish Company building.

Information

For information, contact Outer Banks Visitors Bureau, One Visitors Center Circle, Manteo, NC 27954, 252-473-2138, 877-629-4386; or Outer Banks Chamber of Commerce, P.O. Box 1757, Kill Devil Hills, NC 27948, 252-441-8144.

Web addresses: <www.outer banks.org>; <www.roanokeisland. com>

West by Southwest: US 264 from Manteo

If you are not in a roaring hurry to head west from Manteo, then turn southwest on US 264 from Manns Harbor. It's an excellent highway through country less traveled and eventually links back with US 64 at Rocky Mount. Out of the way, possibly; worth the wandering, absolutely. Here are a few of things you might see along the way.

Alligator River National Wildlife Refuge

The junction of US 64/264 is well within this huge refuge. At 152,000 acres, it is one of the largest and newest sanctuaries in the country. If you have a North Carolina road map, the refuge is the peninsula between the Alligator River on the west and Croatan and Pamlico Sound on the east and south.

The refuge was built around the largest single private land donation ever recorded at the time, 120,000 acres. The Nature Conservancy assisted in the 1984 transfer from the Prudential Insurance Corporation and an agricultural subsidiary, Prudlo Farms, to the U.S. Department of the Interior. Since then, the refuge has grown to its present size.

Most of the refuge is pine pocosin (an elevated swamp), but the preserve contains extensive virgin stands of Atlantic white cedar, the traditional waterman's wood for boatbuilding and decoy carving. Several streams are sufficiently pure that the American sturgeon spawns here, and the refuge has nearly 1,000 miles of estuarine shoreline.

While the refuge supports a substantial number of wintering waterfowl, deer, and black bear, the big story of these big, damp woods is the successful reintroduction of the red wolf, once native to the coast. There are more than 100 of these shy, nocturnal hunters roaming Alligator River and the lands of the enclosed outparcel, the Dare County Bombing Range. The wolf likes the marshy upland and thick forest habitat of Alligator River. There is every indication that the population is active and breeding. Refuge personnel also schedule regular Red Wolf Howling Safaris between April and October.

One of the treats driving US 264 in spring or midsummer is the fragrance from wildflowers. Sweetbay magnolia, which blooms in spring, and loblolly bay, a late-summer flowering tree, crowd the refuge edge. Both have very conspicuous white flowers and a sweet fragrance, aromatic at any speed.

Caution: Red Wolves are night hunters, and cars are their biggest threat. Drive carefully through the refuge at night. If you spot a red wolf or a seemingly large dog, please report the sighting by calling the headquarters at 252-473-1131.

Web addresses: <http://alligator-river.fws.gov>; <www.outer-banks.com/alligator-river>

Stumpy Point

Stumpy Point is a commercial fishing community on Stumpy Point Bay, an area hit hard by Hurricane Isabel. Turn east on SR 1100, which skirts the bay and eventually follows a small tidal creek that serves as a commercial boat basin. This end of the community is known as Drain Point. There is a fishing and boating access area with parking at the end. The view to the east is across Pamlico Sound to the Pea Island National Wildlife Refuge.

The vastness and low relief of the landscape features are nearly overwhelming here. On calm days, the slack, glassy waters of Stumpy Point Bay are serene, excellent waters for blue crabs. Most of the fishing boats working out of the boat basin are crabbers.

Sometimes through here, you will hear the shriek of military aircraft. Inland from Stumpy Point is a joint military command bombing range, the Dare County Bombing Range. It is off-limits to unauthorized personnel.

Engelhard

Engelhard is a compact, rural community, where you can buy hand-scooped ice cream cones at a service station on its outskirts. There's a small roadside park that is an attractive mini-garden, where visitors can get information about Hyde County attractions. The town sits in a location that marks a transition in the local economy from forest and timber management to large-scale agriculture. The shift provides a pleasant change of view from the earlier miles of coastal plain forests.

You can't tell it from town, but Engelhard is on Far Creek, which feeds into Pamlico Sound, and five miles west is Lake Mattamuskeet, North Carolina's largest natural lake.

Lake Landing
Historic District

US 264 comes to Farrow's Fork, an intersection with SR 1114, slightly north of Amity, one of the older communities in Hyde County. It marks the entrance to one of the state's most unusual historic areas, the 13,400-acre Lake Landing Historic District, which is on the National Register of Historic Places.

It is a purely agricultural historic district that features twenty-five houses and structures along a 15-mile loop tour. From Farrow's Fork, the route goes south to Middletown connecting on SR 1108 to White Plains. It then intersects with SR 1110 to reach the town of Nebraska. From Nebraska, the loop returns via SR 1114 to US 264 at Lake Landing, just south of Lake Mattamuskeet. Six homes along US 264 west of Lake Landing are also on the tour.

However, it does not take a marked tour to make you aware of the historical interest of the structures. It is exquisite planter architecture—Greek Revival, Federal, Georgian, Queen Anne—example follows example of fine homes and outbuildings in excellent condition. One of the most celebrated is the curious Octagon House, which dates from 1857. It is fully restored and open for visits.

Most of the houses sit the same distance back from the highway with "backyards" between $1/4$- and $1/2$-mile in length, beautiful fields reaching to the woods of Gum Swamp.

In the early eighteenth century, these lands belonged to the Mattamuskeet Indian Reservation. By the late 1720s, Europeans had purchased or received patents for the land from the Native Americans and began farming. The district is a superb example of rural architectural and agricultural heritage.

There is a historic pamphlet available to guide your tour. Copies are usually available at the roadside park in Engelhard or in the Hyde County Courthouse in Swan Quarter.

Web address: <www.hydecounty.org>

Mattamuskeet National Wildlife Refuge

Lake Mattamuskeet would be enticing even if were not the heart of a 50,180-acre preserve. It is the state's largest natural lake, more than 18 miles long and 6 miles wide. It is nearly 3 feet below sea level with an average depth of 3 feet, and no one is certain about its origin. Since 1934, 40,000 acres of lake, 6,500 acres of adjoining marshland, 3,000 acres of pine and hardwood forest, and nearly 300 acres of cropland have been a refuge for migratory waterfowl, principally whistling swans, Canada geese, and dabbling ducks such as pintail, black ducks, and mallards.

Many, many other species have been sighted, too.

Mattamuskeet's big story begins at the turn of the century when investors purchased the lake to drain it and farm the bottomland. They built the world's largest pumping station, Mattamuskeet Lodge near New Holland, which flushed the water out the Grand Canal, crossed by US 264 at New Holland. They farmed the lake for a time, but nature soon made it a lake again. The refuge soon followed.

NC 94 bisects the lake, and US 264 swings along its southern borders. A network of county roads circumvents the eastern, northern, and western boundaries of the refuge.

There is an excellent observation tower at the refuge headquarters at New Holland and ample bird-watching at any point around the lake. Fishing and hunting are permitted in accordance with refuge regulations. Hunting visits are limited to assigned blinds, determined by lottery, which overlook the water at the southern edge of the property.

For information, contact Matta-muskeet National Wildlife Refuge, 38 Mattamuskeet Road, Swan Quarter, NC 27855, 252-926-4021.

Web address: <http://matta muskeet.fws.gov>

Swan Quarter National Wildlife Refuge

The ferry from Ocracoke passes through Swan Quarter National Wildlife Refuge just offshore from the village of Swan Quarter. It's a sprawling, migratory waterfowl refuge that includes 16,441 acres of Pamlico Sound saltwater marshland. Marquee visitors also include wintering bald eagles and a northernmost population of American alligator.

Trails are open for daylight hiking, and there is a 1,000-foot fishing pier for use as well. Hunting is permitted in designated areas. An additional 24,450 acres of the sound adjoining the refuge have been closed to hunting by presidential proclamation.

For information, contact Swan Quarter National Wildlife Refuge, c/o Mattamuskeet National Wildlife Refuge, 38 Mattamuskeet Road, Swan Quarter, NC 27855, 252-926-4021.

Web address: <mattamuskeet. fws.gov/swanquarter>

Gull Rock Game Land

The North Carolina Wildlife Resources Commission manages an 18,856-acre game land between the Mattamuskeet and Swan Quarter refuges. These lands are open to hunting subject to federal regulations. Unpaved SR 1164 leads 7 miles south from New Holland to a boat ramp at East Bluff Bay. The ramp is open year-round.

Swan Quarter

US 264 does not go directly through Swan Quarter, but you can easily detour through the community. Hurricane Isabel dished Swan Quarter hard with extensive flooding. It's a quaint, rural town that is the county seat of Hyde County.

Belhaven

This is possibly one of the most peaceful detours you will ever take, so do so. Belhaven is a small harbor town on the Pungo River, reached by turning onto NC 92 from US 264.

The River Forest Manor, a country inn in an old plantation house, is set up to serve the traffic on the Intracoastal Waterway. There is also the Belhaven Memorial Museum upstairs in the town hall, an eclectic compilation of the late Eva Blount Way.

Web address: <www.beaufort-county.com/Belhaven/museum>

Bath

This historic town was the first colonial port of entry. Founded in 1705, Bath is the oldest town in the state. Bath perches on a bluff overlooking the Pamlico River, and as the evolving colony became more commercially inclined, the safe harbor played an increasingly important role in trade and mercantile development.

Named for the Earl of Bath, one of the original eight Lords Proprietors of the English colony that became North Carolina, the small community, while becoming tremendously important, never became more substantial than it is. The town's size has changed little in its almost 300 years of existence.

It is a jewel of a city and has benefited handsomely from restoration and conservation efforts. The state has sought to ensure that visitors understand the importance of this small community by staffing a full-time visitors center at the Historic Bath State Historic Site. The center is open 9 A.M. to 5 P.M. Tuesday–Saturday, 1 P.M. to 5 P.M. Sunday. A 35-minute film depicts the history of the state's oldest city.

Several restored buildings may be toured for a nominal fee. One notable attraction is St. Thomas Episcopal Church, erected in 1734, the oldest church in continuous use in North Carolina.

For information, contact Historic Bath State Historic Site, 207 Carteret Street, Bath, NC 27808, 252-923-3971.

Web address: <www.ah.dcr.state.nc.us/sections/hs/bath/bath.htm>

Goose Creek State Park

Goose Creek State Park is a 1,200-acre park located 7 miles east of Bath and south of NC 92 and US 264 on SR 1334. The park includes sandy beaches along the Pamlico River and has a boat ramp for fishing access to the waters of Pamlico Sound. River swimming, as well as primitive camping, are also permitted.

Web address: <www.ncsparks.net/gocr.html>

Pamlico River Free Ferry

East of Bayview, NC 306 leads to a free ferry that crosses the Pamlico River. There are ten departures daily north and south. This is very out of the way and will carry you past the fossil-rich Texas Gulf Phosphate mine and to the town of Aurora, once the potato capital of North Carolina, now home of the Aurora Fossil Museum, an astonishingly rich collection of the fossil finds of the mines.

Web address: <www.ncferry.org>

Cape Hatteras National Seashore

Whalebone Junction marks the northern boundary of Cape Hatteras National Seashore. It is where NC 12 leaves behind the traffic and hubbub of the resort beaches to begin a solitary 75-mile-long route through a 30,000-acre preserve that is at once wild and tenuous, awesome and serene. On a map, it is a $2^{1}/_{2}$-hour drive that can easily become a lifelong enchantment. The difference between the two is the time invested in discovering the seashore on its own terms.

The windshield view is a picturesque, contemplative trip: three islands, three lighthouses, one bridge, one wildlife refuge, two counties, eight communities, one ferry ride, and nearly three centuries of settlement and culture. But getting to know the place means accepting that it will never be the same. Because of this, the trip *is* the destination, and it takes more than one visit to take the measure of this place.

A magnificent yet fragile corner of ground, Cape Hatteras National Seashore has a simple appeal —miles of unfettered barrier island. There is, however, an underlying edginess. The highway, the vital artery that sustains the several islands, tiptoes along a bed of sand between the Atlantic Ocean and Pamlico Sound. The horizons along it are immense, and except for the communities, the highway route is naturally austere. In some locations, the road barely gets by the water continuing over new pavement. The road has been rebuilt and so have the adjoining dunes.

Sooner or later, there comes the realization about the seashore's storm-tossed history and its wary local culture. Then it is abundantly clear what Outer Banks means—it means miles away from safe, solid ground.

Sand, sea, vegetation, and people struggle in a shaky war of attrition along the Outer Banks. People who live here have a particular mind-set, appreciation tempered by acceptance. Water laps at the boundaries of their existence and can move the islands around like dust on a shelf. Mostly, it swallows land whole.

It helps to have a personal memory of how things used to look to gain an understanding of the Outer Banks. These vivid recollections can register how quickly and often Cape Hatteras National Seashore changes, which is really the essence of the place. Names linger on here even after the geography changes—Bodie Island and Pea Island are islands no more; New Inlet is filled but pilings of the old crossing are visible. The names honor periods of mappable stability; that they persist beyond their defining conditions is one way of keeping in touch with underlying nature of the Outer Banks. Simply put, no two visits to the seashore are ever the same since the beach is never the same.

The three islands of the national seashore—nearly nine miles of Bodie Island, the crooked arm of Hatteras, and the exclamation point of Ocracoke—have been breached and battered by the ocean countless times. In September 2003 Hurricane Isabel severed Hatteras Island south of Frisco, opening a 300-yard breach. It crushed Durant's Station, a vintage U.S. Life-Saving Station more than a century old in Hatteras Village, shoaled Hatteras Inlet, adding 20 minutes to the Ocracoke crossing, and removed five miles of dunes and road from Ocracoke's north end. As always, the seashore recovers, rebuilds, and readies for the certainty of the next storm.

In spite of this natural tumult, there are some expected constants that seemingly never change. There are the lighthouses, the villages, the infinity of utility poles marking passage along NC 12. Even the artificial dune line constructed by the Civilian Conservation Corps in the 1930s, which brought a bit of stability to miles of seashore and which has been repeatedly whacked by storms, is an expected feature. These comparatively "permanent" features have become benchmarks for measuring change. In this regard, the relocation of the Cape Hatteras Lighthouse causes the most jarring adjustment to my personal Outer Banks geography.

This is the nation's first national seashore, dating from the first acquisitions in 1935 around Buxton and continuing through the 1950s, when the boundaries were completed. It was officially authorized as a national seashore in 1953.

Legend and lore have literally washed ashore here, as the offshore waters were a mariner's nightmare instead of the landsman's vacation spot it is today. Even through the middle of the twentieth century, the seashore was better known for disaster than for pleasure. Hundreds of oceangoing vessels have run aground on the ever-varying shoals, and thousands of tons of shipping were torpedoed by German U-boats during World War II. Less than a hundred years ago, twelve stations of the U.S. Life-Saving Service, the forerunner of the U.S. Coast Guard, and three lighthouses stood watch over the "Graveyard of the Atlantic," where more than 400 ships have met their final port, among them the Civil War ironclad, USS *Monitor*, which has since been partially salvaged. Occasionally, the ocean will pull back the shrouding sands to reveal a piece of long-lost vessel. Meanwhile, on land, the restored Chicamacomico Life-Saving Station, the Little Kinnakeet Station, the three lighthouses, and the Graveyard of the Atlantic Museum offer glimpses into those earlier times.

Cape Hatteras National Seashore encompasses a broad swath of nature, from fore dunes to forest to salt marsh. Traveling south from Whalebone Junction, you drive a lovely, winding passage through a maritime shrub thicket feathering to brackish marsh to the west. To the east are the rooftops of the private beach cottages of South Nags Head; to the south, the Bodie Island Lighthouse peeks from behind a slash pine forest bordering its entry drive.

Crossing the Herbert C. Bonner Bridge over Oregon Inlet, NC 12 follows the narrow spine of the banks that turns due south at Rodanthe, continuing to a narrow passage just north of Buxton. At Buxton, the seashore encompasses an extensive natural dune field and a stable maritime hardwood forest, Buxton Woods. Beyond Frisco, the seashore again narrows precariously before flaring to make the wider base for Hatteras Village.

Southwest by ferry, Ocracoke is long, flat, and sparsely vegetated, the most isolated island of the accessible seashore. Ocracoke Island is the charm on the sand bracelet, accessible by ferry only. This is the quietest place on the seashore, a place with a character far different from any other place along the Outer Banks. Regardless of whether you are heading north from Cedar Island or Swan Quarter or coming from Hatteras, Ocracoke is a stopover not to be missed. It still epitomizes the independent, yet nature-dependent, character of the Outer Banks.

Here are some suggestions to make your visit smoother and more rewarding:

— Pick up a copy of "In the Park," a free publication available at all park service and Outer Banks visitors centers. It lists important information about the seashore as well as a schedule of lectures, walks, and interpretive programs.
— Confirm a room reservation for summer weekends and fall fishing weekends before you go.
— Make and/or confirm departing ferry reservations for the Ocracoke/Swan Quarter or Ocracoke/Cedar Island crossings before going to the island. Call the Ocracoke reservation line, 800-345-1665.
— Double-check the park service campground vacancy listings posted at the Whalebone Junction Information Center.
— Driving on the beach is permitted but regulated. Pick up a copy of the pamphlet "Off-Road Driving," which provides the rules and regulations governing beach driving. It also shows beach ramp locations. Always carry a shovel and a tow rope or chain.
— Obey restricted area prohibitions. Shorebird nesting may close some beach areas; people, pets, and vehicles are forbidden entry.
— Pets must be leashed at all times.
— Swim at lifeguarded or populated beaches. Rip tides are common on the national seashore beaches. It is safer to swim with a crowd.
— If a tropical storm or hurricane is approaching, head for the mainland. Unexpected flooding can wash out the road or kill car engines.

Access

Cape Hatteras National Seashore and its southern sibling, Cape Lookout National Seashore, exist to protect and "to conserve the natural and historic objects and the wildlife therein and to provide for the enjoyment of the same in such manner and by such means as will leave them unimpaired for the enjoyment of future generations," according to the National Park Service Organic Act of August 25, 1916. The practical interpretation means miles of ocean and sound access. As more people travel to these treasures, the numbers of visitors can overwhelm the delicate balance between preservation and use. The park service controls and sometimes restricts access to protect the fragile seashore ecosystem.

Nevertheless, it is almost always possible, if not necessarily easy, to visit the entire 75-mile length of the national seashore. You must park only at the numerous designated parking areas and use the designated ramps. Both are good ideas since these are safer.

If you are looking for a stretch of beach all to yourself, count the number of cars at the parking pullovers. Few will be vacant during the summer, but once you reach the beach, your privacy is limited only by how far you want to walk. A cooler with something to drink and eat is all you need to be self-sufficient and solitary within the boundaries of the seashore.

Dune crossover ramps are numbered, and there is parking at most crossover locations. The numbering is a useful reference for surf fishermen and law enforcement personnel. The numbering does not mean that the ramps are spaced at regular intervals.

The park service also maintains several major access facilities with bathhouses and lifeguarded beaches. These are described below in the discussions of specific locations within the seashore.

Certain portions of the seashore may be closed to protect the nesting areas of rare species of birds or animals, such as the least tern or pelagic turtles. The closed portions of the beach will be clearly marked. In addition, you cannot drive on the beach within the boundaries of Pea Island National Wildlife Refuge (extending approximately from the old Oregon Inlet Coast Guard Station to just north of Rodanthe) since the U.S. Fish and Wildlife Service, which manages the refuge, forbids driving in it. Camping is permitted on a first-come, first-served basis at the campgrounds at Oregon Inlet, Cape Point, and Frisco. You may make reservations for the Ocracoke Campground. The campgrounds are open mid-spring to mid-fall, generally. Ocracoke, Oregon Inlet, and Frisco will close in mid-October; Cape Point closes in early September. There is usually a staff person on duty by 7 A.M., and you may arrive as late as 11:30 P.M. to set up, provided that space is available.

The park service does not take telephone inquiries directly at the campgrounds. Reservations for the Ocracoke Campground may be secured in person at the campground, by mail at the national seashore headquarters, or through Biospherics, Inc., by calling 1-800-365-CAMP (<http://reservations.nps.gov>). There is a $20 fee for Ocracoke per night per campsite; Visa and MasterCard are accepted. Each campsite has cold showers, restrooms, drinking water, picnic tables, and outdoor grills. There are no utility hookups. The park service provides garbage-dumping stations near the Oregon Inlet, Cape Point, and Ocracoke Campgrounds. One practical tip: If you are camping in a tent, use long stakes; it's windy out there, and the sand does not provide much purchase.

Bicycle trips here are best taken in fall or spring. During the summer months when traffic is heavy, NC 12 is dangerous, and there is not enough road to compensate for any error. The road seems big enough on paper, but a slow-moving camper behind a bicycle makes traffic back up, and drivers can do crazy things.

Winters on the seashore can vary from bluebird days to bone-chilling cold. Wave energy increases, tourists decrease, and seashelling is wonderful. Winter visits give you a chance to come face-to-face with the residents and the isolation. If you ever want to feel as though you own an island, visit the seashore in late February.

	Fee	Parking	Restrooms	Lifeguard	Camping	Showers	Beach Access	Hiking	Trail	Handicapped	Boating	ORV Access	Fishing	Programs	Historic	Sand Beach	Dunes	Upland	Wetland
Whalebone Junction Information Center		•	•																
Coquina Beach		•	•	•		•	•			•				•	•	•	•		
Bodie Island Lighthouse and Visitors Center		•	•					•	•	•				•	•			•	•
Oregon Inlet Campground	•	•	•		•	•	•						•			•	•		•
Oregon Inlet ORV Access		•										•	•			•	•		•
Oregon Inlet Fishing Center		•	•								•		•						
Herbert C. Bonner Bridge		•	•					•	•				•			•	•		

Handicapped Access

Generally speaking, most of the structures and all of the visitors centers in the national seashore that are managed by the National Park Service are accessible to the handicapped. This includes restrooms, such as those at the Whalebone Junction Information Center, the Bodie Island Visitors Center, the Hatteras Island Visitors Center, and the Ocracoke Island Visitors Center.

Special wheelchairs for use in the sand can be arranged by contacting the various visitors centers in advance.

Cape Point and Oregon Inlet Campgrounds each have at least one bathhouse that accommodates handicapped travelers. Although reservations are only accepted at the Ocracoke Campground, the park service attempts to assign handicapped travelers a campsite close to an adapted bathhouse.

Dune crossover ramps or decks that are accessible to the handicapped are available at Sandy Bay Oceanside Access (south of Frisco), at Ramp 55 near the Hatteras ferry docks, and at Ramp 70 at Ocracoke Beach.

Handicapped parking spaces are provided at the visitors centers and the lighthouses.

Information

For information, contact Superintendent, Cape Hatteras National Seashore, 1401 National Park Drive, Manteo, NC 27954, 252-473-2111.

For campsite availability, call the Bodie Island Visitors Center at 252-441-5711.

Emergency numbers: in case of life-threatening emergencies, call 911; for other types of emergencies, call 252-441-4134 (north of Oregon Inlet), 252-986-2144 (south of Oregon Inlet), 252-928-4831 (fire or medical emergencies in Ocracoke), or 252-928-7301 (Ocracoke sheriff's office).

Web addresses: <www.nps.gov/caha/index.htm>; <http://reservations.nps.gov>

Whalebone Junction Information Center

The Whalebone Junction Information Center is the first pullover in the Cape Hatteras National Seashore. It is generally staffed during the summer months; staffing during the rest of the year can vary. Pick up a copy of "In the Park" and any other information that can make your trip more enjoyable (whether or not the Cape Hatteras

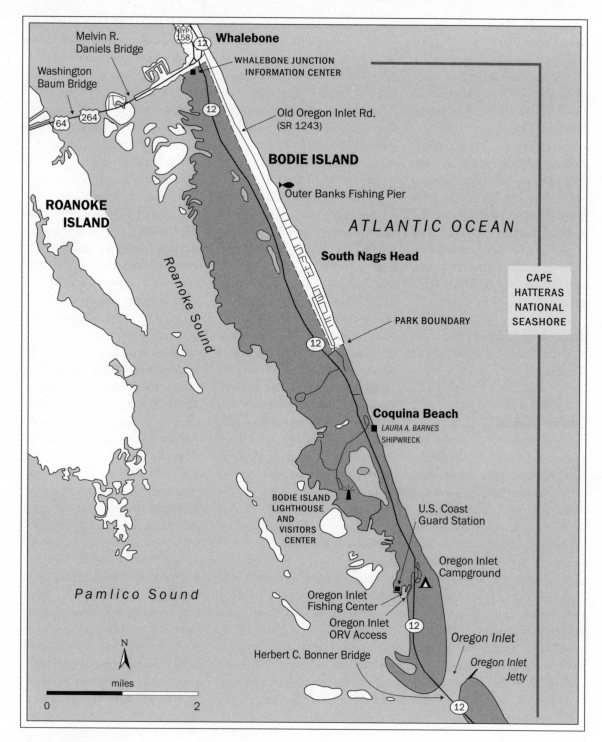

Map 9. Whalebone Junction to Oregon Inlet

Lighthouse is open for climbing, for example).

It is also a good place to gauge campsite availability farther south. Although campground information is posted here, there is a disclaimer about its being current. Nevertheless, you can estimate your odds at securing a vacant space in the first-come, first-served system, and you can also double-check the ferry schedule to Ocracoke. In a perfect world with light traffic and no stops, you are slightly more than one hour away from the Ocracoke ferry. There are also restrooms here.

Handicapped Access

The restrooms are handicapped accessible.

Bodie Island

As you drive south from the Whalebone Junction Information Center, you are on Bodie (pronounced "body") Island. Don't look for an inlet at the northern end of the "island," it's gone—Roanoke Inlet shoaled-in near present-day Nags Head. Today, the southern end is Oregon Inlet, which opened in 1846, but the name "Bodie Island" has been around since 1770s, when its southern boundary was an inlet much farther south. The name generally refers to the peninsula south of Whalebone Junction.

Bodie Island provides a serene introduction to the Cape Hatteras National Seashore. The first 5 miles is a causeway that winds through wax myrtle thickets, by freshwater ponds, and beside the grassy meadows of the low-profile island. The drive is a study in summer greens, created by the jungle-dense vegetation that crowds the road. In fall the wild grape vines turn yellow, threading through the durable olive of the wax myrtle, and sumac plumes reach red for the sky.

The road winds in such a curious fashion that it plays tricks on your mind. The only landmark plainly visible, the Bodie Island Lighthouse, seems to move around, changing from one side of the road to the other. You may stop at several small, two-car capacity pullovers with elevated observation platforms placed advantageously for bird-watching, usually best in winter. Eventually, the horizon widens as the maritime shrub thicket pulls back from the road, and the lighthouse stays put on the west side of NC 12. At sunset, the lighthouse provides a beautiful setting for a photograph.

Coquina Beach

Coquina Beach is the first public beach access site when traveling south on NC 12 after entering the seashore. It is on the east side of the road, about 5.5 miles south of Whalebone Junction.

This is a must-stop for bathers, one of the widest, nicest beaches along the entire seashore with excellent facilities and lifeguards. The beach width above the high-water mark varies between 75 and 100 yards of sand. It is a vulnerable stretch, however, and has been reconstructed several times, most recently in the early 1990s.

The name of the beach honors the brightly colored bivalve creature —the coquina clam—that digs into the sand with each return of the swash. Tidal pools, great for children, occur regularly here, particularly during the early summer, and the shelling is moderately good, although the high wave energy of nearby Oregon Inlet damages the shells quickly. Fishing is usually good, especially to the south of the parking area toward the inlet.

There are several picnic shelters and a public bathhouse. It is a soft-sand slog from the end of the boardwalk to the water's edge after passing the dune line that protects the parking area. The sand is hot; shoes or sandals are necessary. As mentioned, the park service provides lifeguards.

In July 2004 I went searching for a longtime landmark, the shipwreck *Laura A. Barnes*, displayed at Coquina Beach. Part of the hull and keel is all that remains of the schooner that ran aground in a sudden squall on June 1, 1921. Buried then unearthed by a storm, it had become quite a feature. Slightly more than a decade ago, the *Laura A. Barnes* sat behind roped bollards in the median between two parking areas, but in the winter of 1992–93, storms knifed into this beach, shaved the sand away, and wrecked the existing picnic shelters and parking area. The park service retreated to safer ground and built the much-improved, fully accessible bathhouse of today. I found the *Laura A. Barnes* about ten yards past the end of the boardwalk, still behind the bollards, but slowly being covered with sand once again.

During the summer, park rangers host a regular schedule of interpretive programs on barrier island ecology here. Check the schedules at the Whalebone Junction Information Center or consult a copy of "In the Park," the park service publication that will have the summer schedules.

Access

The area is open during daylight hours only. Parking and picnic tables are on a first-come, first-served basis.

Off-road-vehicle access is periodically restricted depending on the width of the beach.

Handicapped Access

Coquina Beach is handicapped accessible. The seashore will provide a beach wheelchair on advance notice. Call 252-473-2111.

Bodie Island Lighthouse and Visitors Center

The horizontally striped Bodie Island Lighthouse has served mariners and Oregon Inlet since 1872. It is one of the four "great lighthouses" along North Carolina's coast dating from the nineteenth century, so-called because of the first-order Fresnel lens that ampli-

fies the lamp and projects the beam so far at sea, in this case, 19 miles. The top of the focal plane of the lens is 156 feet high, and the light blinks in a repeating sequence of 2.5 seconds on, 2.5 seconds off, 2.5 seconds on, and 22.5 seconds off, with two cycles every minute. The light can also be seen from Wanchese and the causeway between Manteo and Nags Head.

In July 2000 the U.S. Coast Guard turned the lighthouse tower and oil house over to the National Park Service, but it maintains the light as a navigation aid. (The Coast Guard changes the lamp every six months.) Since 1992, the park service has had the keeper's quarters open as the Bodie Island Visitors Center, and the static displays inside offer a primer on lighthouse operations.

Restoration efforts to the tower are proceeding in stages. In the spring of 2004 it was repainted in its hallmark banding. Future restoration efforts are pointing toward opening the tower for climbing by 2007. All things considered, the tower is in excellent shape, but when it was built, the engineers did not plan for the heavy use that public access to the 214 steps will certainly bring. Take the time to enter the tower and look up into the diminishing spiral of the stairs; it is a memorable way to remember the lighthouse. Note also the marble cornerstone that gives the precise latitude and longitude of the beacon.

This particular tower is the successful, third effort to build

a lighthouse as a marker for this stretch of coastline. Both the first and second lighthouses were built on the south side of Oregon Inlet, which opened in 1846. The first lighthouse was destroyed because of poor construction and deterioration; the second by the retreating Confederate army. The present site was selected to avoid the migration of the inlet. This natural inlet migration explains why the lighthouse is so distant from the inlet today.

During the summer, the Bodie Island Visitors Center is the site for several interpretive programs and general information about activities in the seashore. Be sure to ask for the publication, "In the Park," which details the summer schedule of interpretive programs for all age groups along the entire length of the seashore. There are also restrooms at the center.

Two trails begin at the visitors center: one leads to the sound, and another is longer, a 1¹/₂-mile loop, the Dike Trail, which details the history of the lighthouse property from the days of the Bodie Island Hunt Club that created the impoundment adjoining the tower for waterfowl hunting. Today, it is superb location for waterfowl-watching.

Access

The visitors center is open during daylight hours, 9 A.M. to 6 P.M., during summer months, with reduced hours in winter. If you plan to take the soundside trail after hours bring plenty of insect repellent.

Handicapped Access

There is a paved path to the visitors center and a sandy walkway leading to the soundside trail.

The restrooms at the visitors center are handicapped accessible.

Information

For information, call the Bodie Island Visitors Center at 252-441-5711.

Oregon Inlet Campground

The oceanside Oregon Inlet Campground remains one of the most popular of the four campgrounds the National Park Service maintains in the seashore. It is a preferred location for anglers, but swimmers should be extremely careful because the currents of Oregon Inlet are treacherous. It is usually open from mid-April to mid-October. There are 120 campsites available on a first-come, first-served basis for a nightly fee of $20 (2004). The campground usually rents close to its capacity.

Better fishing, cooler temperatures, and reduced insects make prime camping times in the spring and fall. The popularity of fall surf fishing causes a campground rush, and weekend space through the October closing can be difficult to get. There are no utility hookups, but there are restrooms, cold showers, drinking water, picnic tables, and outdoor grills. Because of the sandy location, the park service recommends longer and wider tent stakes and mosquito repellent and netting during the warmer times of year.

Access

The campground opens at 7 A.M., and you may arrive as late as 11:30 P.M. to set up.

Handicapped Access

There are presently no handicapped facilities, but there are plans to upgrade the site. Contact the National Park Service for specific information.

Information

For information, stop by the Bodie Island Visitors Center or call 252-441-5711.

Web address: <http://reservations.nps.gov>

Ramp 4: Oregon Inlet Off-Road-Vehicle Access

An unpaved off-road-vehicle access ramp on the east side of NC 12 just before the Herbert C. Bonner Bridge serves the north shore of Oregon Inlet. Oregon Inlet is a dynamic location, and vehicle access makes it easy to take advantage of its shifting configuration. Only four-wheel-drive vehicles or vehicles modified to drive on soft sand should attempt the drive to the inlet. This is an excellent starting place for first-time beach drivers since the sand paths are plainly marked, heavily traveled, and when, not if, you get stuck, there is a high likelihood of someone to ease the embarrassment.

The park service may restrict travel north of the inlet depending on the width of the beach, the number of visitors in the Cape Hatteras National Seashore, or wildlife nesting seasons.

Access

Access is year-round unless restrictions are posted.

Oregon Inlet Fishing Center

A large marina and convenience store, known as the Oregon Inlet Fishing Center, are privately operated concessions licensed by the National Park Service. With the food-rich waters of the Gulf Stream a mere 35 miles to the east, the center does a bustling charter fishing business, even if the inlet is sometimes tricky. All necessary fishing gear, baits, and food supplies are available at the store, which also has a small eating area and grill, especially popular around breakfast time with the fishermen. Dioramas of mounted game fish of the type frequently caught in the local waters fill several display cabinets.

Fishermen and cars swarm across the pavement like crabs on the beach. By mid-June it is easy to tell who is crew and who is visitor by the tan lines.

You may also launch your own craft at a public boat ramp that has five ramps and ample parking for vehicles with trailers.

The U.S. Coast Guard completed a new multimission station on land adjacent to the marina in 1991. The station was established to replace the smaller building on the north end of Pea Island that was no longer serviceable due to shoaling of the boat slip used by the Coast Guard rescue vessels. The new building is not only large but also exceptionally handsome, drawing from the architectural heritage of the lifesaving and U.S. Coast Guard stations of the Outer Banks.

Access

The center is on the west side of NC 12 immediately before the Herbert C. Bonner Bridge as you head south. The store and marina open very early, usually closing around dusk. Hours vary with the season —and with the fishing.

Handicapped Access

Ramps serve the store and restaurant, and there are restrooms that accommodate handicapped travelers.

Information

For information on charter fishing, contact the Oregon Inlet Fishing Center, P.O. Box 533, Manteo, NC 27954, 252-441-6301.

The Oregon Inlet Coast Guard Station may be called at 252-987-2311.

Herbert C. Bonner Bridge

The Herbert C. Bonner Bridge has always been one of my favorite segments of an Outer Banks trip because Oregon Inlet, which it crosses, is constantly shifting, and the bridge-crossing provides physical evidence of the unstable nature of barrier islands. The bridge is the essential link to and from the remainder of the Cape Hatteras National Seashore and the private communities to the south. Finished in December 1963, it honors the memory of North Carolina congressman Herbert C. Bonner, who worked ambitiously for its construction.

The importance of this connector cannot be underestimated. When it replaced ferry service, it jump-started tremendous growth and change on the seashore.

Today, the reliability of the bridge is bumping heads with both time and Mother Nature. In fact, it is nearing the end of its life span—engineer speak for al-

Where Does the Sand Go?

One gusty day two decades ago, I took my two-year-old daughter with me to walk along the north shore of Pea Island National Wildlife Refuge, on the south bank of Oregon Inlet. The tide was ebbing, and the wind, driving from the northwest, pushed the water against our sandy beach. (This was before the rocky terminal wall there now.) No one was fishing; the channel current was a sluice, too strong to bother.

As my daughter wandered near the water, I grabbed her arm just as the beach edge crumbled nearly from beneath her feet. That same wind-driven, strengthened, and directed tidal current sliced sand off Pea Island just as smoothly as a woodworker would plane a plank. We watched as Pea Island shortened by 10 feet in about 2 hours.

Nature incessantly shapes the beaches of the barrier islands, stealing sand here, dropping it off there. The waves running out on the sandy apron must recede, and, sliding seaward, they drag particles of beach with them. Wave action in the surf zone suspends loose sand in a churning froth, and most of this sand moves parallel to the beach in a littoral current, a process known as longshore transport of sand. Wave direction determines longshore currents. Most longshore transport along North Carolina's barrier beaches runs from north to south.

The Herbert C. Bonner Bridge crossing Oregon Inlet is a terrific vantage point for seeing the effects of longshore transport and sand deposition. There is a wide sandy beach curling under the bridge and fanning out into the sound west of it. This grand recreational beach, covered with fishermen whenever you cross, did not exist when the bridge opened in 1964. In fact, much of the bridge appears to be crossing above stable land that arrived via longshore transport from beaches to the north.

While the south end of Bodie though it is still safe to cross until it is closed, it needs to be replaced. The facts are that Oregon Inlet continues to shoal and shift south and the bridge is approaching its life expectancy and is increasingly vulnerable to storm damage. None of this is unexpected. A storm originally blasted open the inlet (named for the side-wheeler *Oregon*, the first ship to pass through) in 1846. Since the bridge opened, the inlet has been migrating steadily southward at the rate of 75–125 feet per year, independent of storm-powered alterations. (The original location of the inlet was more approximately 3 miles north.) As Oregon Inlet moves south, sand deposits beneath the northern end of the bridge, while the ocean gnaws at the north end of Pea Island. A substantial length of the bridge is now above the sandy beach of Bodie Island. At present, the inlet gives every indication of trying to close and continue south, jeopardizing the Pea Island terminus. A rock groin was built to arrest the erosion of Pea Island and buy some time for the Bonner bridge.

The North Carolina Department of Transportation has penciled in beginning a replacement bridge in 2006 and finishing by 2010. Several proposals have been considered. One is a 17.5-mile-long elevated highway from Wanchese to a point south of Pea Island National Wildlife Refuge that would effectively bypass the troubled inlet. Although this is the most expensive proposal, the new highway would be out of harm's way and avoid any conflicts with Pea Island National Wildlife Refuge (south of the inlet), which must agree to the project. It would also bypass a troubled

Island gains sand, the north end of Pea Island eroded rapidly as the inlet shifted south until the 1991 installation of the terminal rock groin or jetty. The north end of Pea Island now cannot shift naturally, but if it could, it would cost the south end of the bridge. For engineers, Herbert C. Bonner is the bridge over troubling waters.

As the ocean shears sand from the headland, longshore currents move it parallel to the Outer Banks, depositing much of it farther south at Cape Point and in the treacherous fan of submerged sand known as Diamond Shoals, east of the Cape Hatteras Lighthouse. Deposition occurs where currents spread out or otherwise lose velocity and the particles drop to the bottom, at inlets and flattened bottom profiles like Cape Point.

The direction of wave and storm attack hits the beaches from Virginia south to Cape Hatteras hardest. The waves strike obliquely, eroding and transporting sand southward. Rarely does it return. Between Cape Hatteras and Cape Lookout, waves take a smaller bite. Farther south at Sunset Beach, deposition from longshore transport has shoaled Mad Inlet and added nearly $1/8$ mile of sand to the beach.

Longshore transport is part of the natural equilibrium of barrier islands. The sand must and will move. The same system that carries sand away from any given beach is likely to be bringing sand to the same location from elsewhere—so long as sand is available. When sand is dredged from a shipping channel and stored on an artificial island, it is taken out of the system, theoretically "missing" from a beach down current.

Watch the sand in the surf someday when waves slant in on an angle. See if the foam and sand doesn't slide sideways on return. It is on the move to another length of beach, pausing now and again in its longshore journey. It's visiting, too, just as you are.

stretch of NC 12 on northern Pea Island that storms repeatedly overwash. (Between 1987 and 1999, the North Carolina Department of Transportation estimated that $50 million was spent on bridge and road maintenance and repair.)

In the summer of 2004 the North Carolina Department of Transportation, which once favored this lengthier project, proposed a shorter bridge design west of the present bridge as another option. The shorter proposed bridge would parallel the existing bridge but would connect with existing NC 12 farther south in Pea Island National Wildlife Refuge. As a condition of consideration, the North Carolina Department of Transportation must consider the cost of maintaining NC 12 south of the new bridge junction for fifty years.

This shorter alternative would impact the quality of the refuge and disrupt its mission and mandate. The debate may eventually require congressional action to resolve.

On October 6, 1990, a "nor'easter" tore a dredge, the *Northerly Isle*, free of its moorings in the inlet and slammed it into the Bonner bridge, sending 370 feet of the roadway into the channel and plunging Hatteras into a time warp—no access, interrupted utilities, and no truck-delivered supplies. Panic spread among the 3,110 vehicle owners who were visiting Hatteras Island, and it took five days to clear them from the islands via the southern ferries.

Meanwhile, daily commuters to Nags Head from Rodanthe had to start their days much earlier to reach work on alternate routes. Finally, electrical power was restored on November 2, and by early De-

	Fee	Parking	Restrooms	Lifeguard	Camping	Showers	Beach Access	Hiking	Trail	Handicapped	Boating	ORV Access	Fishing	Programs	Historic	Sand Beach	Dunes	Upland	Wetland
Pea Island, North End	•	•					•						•			•	•		
Old Coast Guard Station	•						•						•		•	•	•		
Pea Island National Wildlife Refuge	•	•					•	•	•	•			•			•	•	•	•
Pea Island N.W.R. Canoe Launch	•	•									•		•						•
Rodanthe	•	•										•	•		•	•	•	•	•
Chicamacomico Life-Saving Station	•	•													•	•			

cember, ferry service across the inlet had moved into full swing. By February 1991, workers had repaired and reopened the bridge, a job initially estimated to take six months.

The temporary loss of the bridge reaffirmed the dependency of the Outer Banks economy on year-round tourism and on the bridge as well. Memories had shortened considerably, it turned out, and the good old days weren't quite so good.

There is a catwalk on the east side of the south end of the bridge that is used by fishermen to bottom-fish the inlet waters. A parking area at that end provides access to the catwalk.

Caution: Currents are very strong in Oregon Inlet when the tide is running; extreme care should be exercised when boating or fishing in the inlet. Swimming in or near the inlet is not advisable under any circumstances.

Oregon Inlet Jetty

Oregon Inlet is one of the most fickle of the sound-to-sea passageways on the Outer Banks. It is constantly shoaling, and the passage through it is so precarious that only shallow-draft vessels and good skippers try it. This unpredictability has nearly strangled commercial fishing in Wanchese and has caused the loss of several, very expensive fishing trawlers. In response to the crisis, a controversial proposal was made to construct jetties to secure the inlet.

The debate over the proposal was furious. Proponents of the plan argued that it would protect the bridge from erosion, as well as secure the channel for commercial fishing; opponents countered that the jetties would only secure the inlet at the expense of down-current locations, which would very likely suffer erosion as a result. The compromise is the $13.5 million, 244,000-ton, 9-foot-tall, $1/2$-mile-long curving granite "terminal wall" on the north end of Pea Island, the south side of the inlet.

Almost immediately, after the North Carolina Department of Transportation completed construction of the jetty in January 1991, sand began to accumulate on the landward side, part of its original purpose. It seemed to be working—so far. It also provided a fine fishing spot to landlocked anglers, who parked at the old Coast Guard station nearby to lug fishing gear nearly a half a mile across soft sand to reach the jetty.

The Department of Transportation subsequently posted "No Tres-

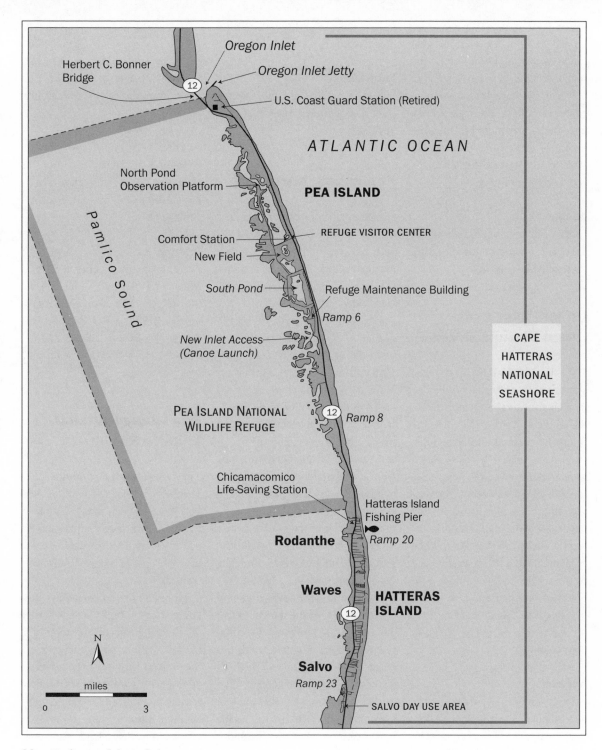

Map 10. Oregon Inlet to Salvo

passing" signs along the sandy approach to the jetty, warning that the area was dangerous since the rocks are slippery when wet. So far, however, the state doesn't seem inclined to enforce the measure. In fact, the Department of Transportation does not have enforcement staff, so a cold war of turned heads is the order of the day.

Access

As there is no public access to the jetty, the people you see fishing there must be a mirage.

Oregon Inlet Coast Guard Station (Retired)

The original 1923 U.S. Coast Guard station on the north end of Pea Island is the weather-beaten building on the east side of NC 12 as the bridge makes landfall. All the functions once served by this station were transferred to the new multi-mission station adjacent to the Oregon Inlet Fishing Center on the north side of the inlet. This original location had to be abandoned when erosion shoaled the boat slip used by the service's rescue vessel. Visible from the road and bridge, the building is on the National Register of Historic Places, but sadly, it is in poor condition.

Access

After crossing the Herbert C. Bonner Bridge, take the second left-hand turn to reach the station. The station is closed, but the old road is used for access parking. Be careful of soft sand.

Information

For information, call the Oregon Inlet Coast Guard Station at 252-987-2311.

Pea Island, North End

At the north end of Pea Island is a small access area next to NC 12 with parking and portable toilets for day visitors. This area is under the jurisdiction of the Pea Island National Wildlife Refuge.

Less than twenty years ago, the remnants of several paved roads were visible on the east side of NC 12 (south of the jetty), all that remained of extensive recreational facilities destroyed by past storms. In fact, there was a loop drive leading to a picnic area, and the ocean was nearly $1/2$ mile north and east from the abandoned Coast Guard station. Today, any hike to the ocean skirts the south edge of the jetty and is far shorter indeed. Still, there are quiet waters beyond the pull of the inlet currents after Pea Island turns back to the south.

Swimming is not advised, except far to the east of the parking area, away from the Oregon Inlet channel. Shelling is only fair, partly because of the turbulence of the inlet waters. The beach widens and the dune line created by the Civilian Conservation Corps in the 1930s becomes more stable as the shore arcs south.

Before the jetty was completed, northwest winds and outgoing tides sometimes combined to shave as much as 10 feet of shoreline per hour from the north end of Pea Island.

Access

Parking is at the south end of the Herbert C. Bonner Bridge. There are portable toilets and litter receptacles.

Information

For information, contact Refuge Manager, Pea Island National Wildlife Refuge, P.O. Box 1969, Manteo, NC 27954, or P.O. Box 150, Rodanthe, NC 27968, 252-987-2394.

Web address: <http://peaisland. fws.gov/>

Pea Island National Wildlife Refuge

The refuge occupies the northern 13 miles of the island south of Oregon Inlet and is a jewel of a place to visit. The primary purpose is to provide habitat and forage for wildlife, but people are certainly welcome as guests.

More and more people have discovered the serenity and isolation of the refuge beach, prompting a casual attitude about driving on the beach, keeping pets leashed, and wearing clothes. In 2004, in response to complaints, refuge management posted signs reminding visitors that Pea Island is for daylight use only and to keep cars on

Bird-watching near Bodie Island Lighthouse. Courtesy of Outer Banks Visitors Bureau.

the road, pets on the leash, and shirts (or swimsuits) on their backs. The refuge also has a full-time, permanent law enforcement officer to enforce all refuge regulations.

This shouldn't cramp anybody's style. Pea Island National Wildlife Refuge is one of the best features of the Outer Banks that offers something for every season. The most popular time for waterfowl-watching is during the fall and winter months when Canada geese and snow geese join approximately twenty-five species of ducks here. Several trails and dikes crossing the freshwater ponds provide locations for stealthily viewing the inhabitants. The refuge bird list includes more than 365 species, along with the 25 species of mammals and 24 species of reptiles that make the refuge their home. Endangered species recorded on the refuge include the peregrine falcon, the loggerhead turtle, and piping plover.

The refuge dates from May 1937, when 5,834 acres of barrier sand dunes, ocean beaches, salt marshes, and tidal creeks were set aside. There are also 25,700 acres of "proclamation" waters—added by presidential proclamation—in adjacent Pamlico Sound that provide forage and habitat. Before the refuge, the area was a prime hunting ground for commercial-market hunters. The area also supported commercial fishing, farming, and grazing of livestock. The principal recipient of this long-term protection has been the greater snow goose, whose numbers were severely depleted at the time the refuge was established but have now significantly recovered from that ebb.

The Plight of the Piping Plover

One creature's nursery is another's playground, and the two different uses do not mix very well.

A small shorebird, nearly invisible against the dry sand of the dunes, is buying time against extinction on not-nearly-lonely-enough segments of the barrier beaches. The piping plover, named for its "piping" song, is one of several species that nest at the base of the dunes, in the same sands where people walk or drive on the beach. In January 10, 1986, biologists placed it on the federal endangered species list, primarily because of loss of habitat due to increased construction and people in places where the bird wanted to nest. Fortunately, this small shorebird is finding refuge in the existing preserves along the Outer Banks. People could give this sand-nesting species a big boost simply by sticking to the trails and minding the signs.

April and May are the critical times to mind your dune-climbing manners on the isolated beaches of Cape Hatteras and Cape Lookout National Seashores. These are the months when the nesting season begins for this plover and other birds that leave their eggs in simple depressions in the warm sands. Similar nesters include the least tern, the gull-billed tern, the common tern, and skimmers.

Adult piping plovers will feign an injured wing to draw you away from an unseen nest. This behavior may be the only clue you will receive that you are walking where you should not be. Unlike the plovers, common terns, which nest in colonies, will attack and aggressively defend their nests.

The plover and the least tern are the two species of most concern. By some counts, the population of the petite plover is nearly 1,400 pairs along the eastern seaboard where it migrates. The beaches of such places as Pea Island, Cape Hatteras Bight, Ocracoke Island, and much of Cape Lookout are prime nesting habitat. When there were few visitors, the plovers and other birds could leave their camouflaged eggs in the open to hatch, threatened only by the pillaging of either raccoons or larger birds that steal chicks. Today, loss of suitable, undisturbed beach, human disruption, and unleashed pets that disturb or destroy nests pose the biggest threats to successful nesting.

In the summer of 2004, National Park Service biologists had flagged $1^1/_2$ miles of oceanfront due north of Ocracoke's beach with yellow crossing tape. It marked a restricted nesting area, but the closure still left many miles of oceanfront free.

Please stay out of flagged portions of the national wildlife refuges and national seashores. Plover eggs are extraordinarily difficult to see, and you might step on them, probably the only way you'll know that you've found a nest.

If you find a nest of chicks (most likely in midsummer) in an unprotected area, notify the appropriate personnel so that confirmation of the sighting can be made. The U.S. Fish and Wildlife Service is in charge of the protection program for the piping plover, but other National Park Service and state parks personnel will relay the information to them.

Web address: <www.fws.gov>

In particular, a system of dikes and freshwater ponds were constructed to provide habitat and to enable refuge personnel to grow certain types of grasses and other food plants for the migratory waterfowl. The dikes provide the primary locations for viewing wildlife.

Approximately 4.5 miles south of Oregon Inlet is the visitors center with parking, a comfort station, and access to the North Pond Trail. This loop trail is about 4 miles long and passes around the North Pond. Should you go for a hike around the North Pond, wear a long-sleeved shirt and long pants and carry plenty of insect repellent, particularly in summer. (The refuge teems with deer flies, or green flies, persistent and vicious pests.)

Cross NC 12 from the visitors center parking lot and look beyond the breakers. What is visible is the partially submerged boiler of the Federal steamer *Oriental*, wrecked in the ocean during the Civil War.

One memorable feature of the refuge is the once continuous barrier dune seaward from NC 12. Civilian Conservation Corps workers bulldozed the sandy ridge and planted it in the 1930s. The dune barrier may only be crossed at designated parking areas where the route is well established. The dune line has been severely hurt by storms, and the road has been washed out several times between the visitors center and Oregon Inlet. Previously, NC 12 was moved west because the protective dune line was destroyed between the visitors center and the maintenance buildings at the New Inlet access area at milepost 7.5.

Old pilings are visible in the tidal creek to the west of the New Inlet access parking. These are the remains of the old New Inlet Bridge (the inlet closed in 1945). The interpretive displays east of NC 12 at New Inlet tell the story of the famed Pea Island Life-Saving Station, made famous by the heroism of its all-black crew. In 1995, after the persuasive arguments of four young historians who researched the Pea Island station, the U.S. Coast Guard awarded the gold life-saving medal to members of the 1896 crew for their part in the res-

cue of all passengers and personnel of the schooner *E. S. Newman*. Cross the highway and take a short walk north on the beach, and you may see the foundations of the station. When the station was deactivated, the building was auctioned and removed to the community of Salvo where it is privately owned.

The beaches of Pea Island are open for swimming and fishing (permit required) year-round. It's a good bet you will find a serene beach, but you will have to do without restrooms or conveniences. If you do not see another car at a turnout, you are not likely to see anyone else on the beach.

The refuge closes some access areas during the nesting of certain shorebirds to prevent visitors from disturbing the birds. For this reason, there are no trails around the New Field and the South Pond. The North Pond trails, however, are always open.

Camping, campfires, hunting, guns, driving on the beach, and unleashed dogs are prohibited. Dogs are not allowed on the pond sides of NC 12, and you cannot fish in the ponds.

While interpretive programs are provided during the summer, the refuge comes alive every fall. Every year in the first week of November, the refuge hosts the "Wings over Water" celebration of wildlife and habitats on the Outer Banks in conjunction with the National Park Service, the Carolina Bird Club, and the Coastal Wildlife Refuge Society.

Access

Volunteers staff the refuge office between April and October, 8 A.M. to 4 P.M. weekdays.

There are eight parking areas serving the refuge, all plainly visible from NC 12. There is a soundside parking area and canoe launch just south of the refuge office at New Inlet, an excellent location for crabbing and fishing. Restrooms are also provided there.

Handicapped Access

The comfort station at North Pond is accessible. The trail over the dike and between the ponds and the restrooms at the parking area, part of the North Pond Trail, is negotiable by wheelchair. Renovations to the refuge may improve facilities for handicapped travelers.

Information

For information, contact Refuge Manager, Pea Island National Wildlife Refuge, P.O. Box 1969, Manteo, NC 27954, or P.O. Box 150, Rodanthe, NC 27968, 252-473-1131 (office), 252-987-2394 (visitors center).

Web address: <http://peaisland. fws.gov/>

Rodanthe

Rodanthe is the first of the "private" communities surrounded by the Cape Hatteras National Seashore, often referred to as part of a trilogy: Rodanthe, Waves, and Salvo. Pronounced "Ro-dan'-theh," the name is somewhat easier to say than the original community name, Chicamacomico Banks. The name change came in 1874 with the U.S. Post Office (interestingly, the U.S. Life-Saving Service selected the original community name for its station, also established in 1874). More than likely, federal postal officials rejected Chicamacomico because of its length, and then mysteriously substituted Rodanthe. While it could be a family name, it is quite possible the new name originated with an obscure "everlasting" flower, *Rhodanthe manglesii*, an attractive daisy-like flower. That this species is native to Australia deepens the intrigue.

Pea Island National Wildlife Refuge ends and Rodanthe begins at a point where the island thins to the width of a sneeze. It looks tenuous and is. If your dashboard had a circa 1876 coastal map, it would show that you had just driven through Loggerhead Inlet, right at the northern edge of Rodanthe.

Look past the precarious circumstances of individual houses as you enter Rodanthe and note the name of the development, Mirlo Beach. It is a name riveted in local history. The *Mirlo* was a British vessel destroyed by either a German mine or torpedo in 1918. The crew of the Chicamacomico Life-Saving Station, which is restored and a superb place to visit, rescued most of the stricken sailors from the flaming vessel offshore.

When it was built, Mirlo Beach made an eye-opening gateway to Rodanthe because of its themed architecture. The development was the vanguard of the Outer Banks real estate boom just gaining traction on these once-isolated sands. At the time of construction, the houses east of NC 12 were safely tucked behind sand dunes, but a series of storms, launched by Hurricane Dennis in 1999, left them mercilessly exposed.

NC 12 takes time to meander through Rodanthe, in a lazy sequence of bends. If you have a car compass, you may note as you weave through the three communities that just past Waves, the compass heading swings due south. Rodanthe is most likely built on the end of a prehistoric island that extended into the sea beyond the present-day oceanfront, similarly aligned as Pea Island. In 1611 the remnants of the island were charted as Cape Kendrick, east of present-day Salvo. Cape Kendrick disappeared sometime in the seventeenth or eighteenth century, and the remnants of the submerged spit are now known as Wimble Shoals.

The crook in the banks and the shoals offshore made for hazardous navigation, and so the U.S. Life-Saving Station came to the village of Chicamacomico in 1874. The station adopted the local name and became an anchor for the community. As it prospered, so did Rodanthe.

While tourism has taken hold in Rodanthe, it still has the salt-scoured veneer of a self-contained village. There is a boat basin still used by commercial fishermen as a public harbor, even though the land around the basin is privately owned. There are vendors for water sports equipment and outings.

All in all, Rodanthe is still a slower place in the vacation-charged traffic stream streaking along NC 12, more of an eddy than a rapid. Vacation rental real estate is making inroads, and the side streets intersecting NC 12 offer glimpses of the juxtaposition of local resident and rental property. This community, along with Waves and Salvo, has a more basic, play-in-the-water appeal than the polished facade of northern beaches.

The Hatteras Island Fishing Pier, at Atlantic Drive and Ocean Drive, is the center of oceanfront activity. You can bet either the fishing or the waves will be up, and both bring visitors to the beach.

By way of extreme local color, Rodanthe and surrounds remain one of the few locations that still celebrate "Old Christmas" on January 6 (the Twelfth Day of Christmas or Epiphany), a vestige of the Julian calendar, replaced by the Gregorian calendar in the mid-eighteenth century. Perhaps the information about the updated calendar took a long time to reach these isolated residents, and when it did, they saw little reason to change a joyous community occasion.

Rodanthe offers numerous places for overnight and lengthier stays, from cottages to motel rooms. With its sister communities, it has become a camping center of sorts.

The three towns offer more than 700 campsites with utility hookups, and many with direct beach access. One of the striking images in Rodanthe is the open land and well-groomed look of the large campgrounds on the ocean and sound, even when chock-full.

Access

There are no designated public beach access sites in Rodanthe. In the past there has been some limited public parking at one large lot near the Hatteras Island Fishing Pier, which was rebuilt in 2000 after severe storm damage. The parking is provided through the courtesy of the adjacent Hatteras Island Resort. The pier charges a fee, both for fishing and sightseeing. There is off-road-vehicle access at the pier parking lot, but it is closed between May 15 and Labor Day.

Handicapped Access

There are no public handicapped facilities here. Some of the private resorts and campgrounds may have accommodations for handicapped travelers.

Information

For information, contact Outer Banks Visitors Bureau, One Visitors Center Circle, Manteo, NC 27954, 252-473-2138, 877-629-4386; or Outer Banks Chamber of Commerce, P.O. Box 1757, Kill Devil Hills, NC 27948, 252-441-8144.

Web addresses: <www.outerbanks.org>; <www.outerbanks chamber.com>

Chicamacomico Life-Saving Station

Every time that I have passed the Chicamacomico Life-Saving Station since the 1980s, it has looked better than it did before. Some days it was open; on others, closed, but even when all I could do was survey from the driveway, the improvements were evident. It is now shipshape and open for inspection. Any stop, however brief, is akin to throwing open a window on the Outer Banks past.

There are two great private restoration successes on the Outer Banks, the Currituck Beach Lighthouse and Lightkeeper's Quarters and the Chicamacomico Life-Saving Station. In both locations, impassioned volunteers leveraged elbows and enthusiasm to restore the signature buildings of their communities. In 1974 the indefatigable Carolista Baum, who previously marshaled preservationists to save Jockey's Ridge in Nags Head, spearheaded the efforts of the recently formed Chicamacomico Historical Association. This group is responsible for the artful, accurate, and elegant compound that is open to visitors today.

There's something to learn with every stride or step at Chicamacomico. For example, climb the narrow stairs to the observation tower atop the 1911 station, and you experience the identical 8.5-mile horizon of a surfman on watch. Out in the front of the station, which faces

east, is where the old sand road serving the Outer Banks routed. Inside the 1874 station, which later became the boathouse, is the very same self-righting/self-bailing surfboat used in the 1918 rescue of the crew of the *Mirlo*. The boathouse has a vintage life car, too. Invented in 1848, it was the scariest means of escape from a sinking ship that never failed to bring a passenger to solid ground safely. The station even has the salvaged lookout cupola of Durant Station—all that remains of that landmark after Hurricane Isabel in 2003.

The Chicamacomico Life-Saving Station first came into service in 1874, one of the seven original stations on the Outer Banks and the first built and manned. It maintained an active vigil over the nearby coast until the U.S. Coast Guard closed it in 1954. Since the station housed heroes, it is fitting that it should now be the subject of heroism of a different kind—and that would be the volunteers of the Chicamacomico Historical Association. This private, nonprofit group didn't simply take over the maintenance of the complex, which was in disrepair in the late 1970s; they turned it into the historical tour de force of the Outer Banks. Both stations, the 1874 boathouse (the original station) and the hipped-porch 1911 building, are classic examples of the indigenous institutional architecture that the U.S. Life-Saving Service and its successor, the U.S. Coast Guard, adopted for their Outer Banks stations. The cottage-

The meticulously restored historic Chicamacomico Life-Saving Station in Rodanthe is open to visitors as a historic site. Courtesy of Outer Banks Visitors Bureau.

like complex was both office and home for the station keeper and crew. The buildings were all constructed for the single purpose of housing crews and equipment to save the lives of the shipwrecked.

During the station's heyday, between 1874 and the end of World War II, life was spartan and demanding for the crew members. The crew stood at the ready to go out at the first sign of a ship in distress. While no less was true of every station along the Outer Banks, the valor shown by the Chicamacomico crew became legendary in the history of the service.

It was from that 1874 boathouse, in August 1918, that crew members launched the boats to rescue the survivors of the British tanker *Mirlo*. The oil carrier had been ripped apart by either a German mine or torpedo while sailing in the shipping lanes east of Rodanthe. Secondary explosions set the water on fire, and the British crew were scattered around the burning vessel. Most were saved. The feat had been accomplished under the determined direction of J. A. Midgett, one of the many members of the local Midgett family who served in the U.S. Life-Saving Service.

The rescue gained international celebrity, and the British government was so moved and grateful that it created the King George Gold Medal for Valor and awarded them to the surfboat crew. The heroic episode became known as the greatest rescue of World War I.

In 1930 the Coast Guard also recognized the heroism of the *Mirlo* rescue, awarding each member of the six-man crew the Grand Cross of the American Cross of Honor; five of those brave crew members were Midgetts.

The restored quarters are open to the public and showcase exhibits highlighting historic moments and rescues. During the summer, volunteers hold mock life-saving drills to demonstrate the rescue techniques that were standard among all the crews from Virginia Beach to Ocracoke. Once you see the effort needed to merely stage a rescue for an audience on a sunny day, you can let your imagination picture a rescue on a stormy, moonless night.

Access

The station is open mid-April–December 23, Tuesday–Saturday, 9 A.M. to 5 P.M. Beach Apparatus Drills are held during the summer months on Thursdays at 2 P.M. There is also a gift shop that features items tied to the nautical history of the Outer Banks.

Information

For information on how to participate in the restoration effort, contact Chicamacomico Historical Association, Inc., P.O. Box 5, Rodanthe, NC 27968.

Web address: <www.chicamaco mico.org>

Waves and Salvo

Waves and Salvo follow Rodanthe on the southward journey. Both are small; Waves, once known as South Rodanthe, seems gone before you get there. In response to the growing number of summer visitors who either camp or rent homes, Waves has become a center for wind/water sports, as has adjoining Salvo.

There is an eye-catching change in the island's appearance, however; large cedar trees give this length of island a nestled-in look. Some of the homes and churches along the highway peek out from behind their evergreen sentinels, which are the first to be seen in the seashore to this point. NC 12 scoots through Waves and then curves back toward the center of the island, entering Salvo.

The border between the two is not distinct—save for the Salvo sign (Waves signs tend to be stolen) —and the communities blend into one another. In a conversation some years back, a resident expressed the local laissez-faire attitude about civic lines, saying, "There's supposed to be a boundary here somewhere, but folks don't seem too sure about it."

Salvo has experienced a good deal of growth. New homes are filling the low grassy flats to the east of the highway, well behind a dune line that is substantial. At present, Salvo is blessed because the offshore configuration of Wimble Shoals is causing sand to be deposited on its oceanfront. One result is the reappearance of the artificial Civilian Conservation Corps dune line that has been washed away in Rodanthe and the expansion of that dune field because of the accumulation of new sand on the beach.

Even though there are many new homes, the sky seems bigger and the horizon more spread out on the south side of Salvo. It is as though you have passed through a gate. A few trees grow along the

soundside, but it seems as though the road passes through a meadow. There once was a National Park Service campground south of Salvo that is now converted to a day use area. There is sense of serenity in this particular place. If you stop at the day use area, you'll learn about one of the first (if not only) captures of a Union ship by a ship from the Confederate navy, which occurred in Pamlico Sound offshore.

Likewise, the southern approach to Salvo is one of the gentlest visual transitions along the entire Outer Banks. First, there are the grassy flats, then some maritime shrubs, and slowly the punctuation of houses, churches, and trees appears, and you have slipped right into a community. Your speed slows to the pace of local drivers. The highway hugs the soundside of the island, and the houses and stores are clustered along its route.

Perhaps an apocryphal tale, supposedly the name Salvo originates from an incident during the Civil War. After a Union naval officer commanded his sailors to "give it a salvo" or broadside of cannon fire, the name "Salvo" was entered into the records and superseded the original name of Clarksville.

My favorite anecdote about Salvo involves its once famously small and portable post office, for many years the smallest in the world. The little white building with blue trim was mounted on rails so that it could be easily moved as the postmaster changed. In 1992 arsonists torched it. The community moved quickly to rebuild but was rebuffed

	Fee	Parking	Restrooms	Lifeguard	Camping	Showers	Beach Access	Hiking	Trail	Handicapped	Boating	ORV Access	Fishing	Programs	Historic	Sand Beach	Dunes	Upland	Wetland
Salvo Day Use Area	•	•				•	•	•		•		•				•	•		•
Public Boating Access: Avon		•									•	•							•
Haulover Day Use Area	•	•				•	•				•	•	•			•	•		•

by the U.S. Post Office in Washington, D.C., because the old post office failed to meet disability standards. Nevertheless, the town rebuilt the old post office as a memorial and collects their mail from a characterless brick structure that could use a bit of romance or local flavor, but will never achieve the star qualities of its predecessor.

Access

Beach access is primarily by rental of a private cottage or a campsite at one of the many large private campgrounds.

The National Park Service operates a day use area south of Salvo that is designated for wind- and kitesurfing, but of course, anyone is welcome. There are live oak trees that make kitesurfing a bit problematic (I saw a kite that had been flown into a tree as the rider came in from the sound). Also, this day use area is a good location to park to carefully cross NC 12 to the beaches beyond the dunes.

Handicapped Access

Salvo Realty will loan a beach wheelchair by advance notice. Call 252-987-2766.

There are no other public handicapped facilities in Waves or Salvo, but some of the private resorts and campgrounds may have accommodations for handicapped travelers.

Information

For information, contact Outer Banks Visitors Bureau, One Visitors Center Circle, Manteo, NC 27954, 252-473-2138, 877-629-4386; or Outer Banks Chamber of Commerce, P.O. Box 1757, Kill Devil Hills, NC 27948, 252-441-8144.

Web addresses: <www.outer banks.org>; <www.outerbanks chamber.com>

Salvo to Avon

NC 12 between Salvo and Avon is one of the most evocative lengths of island on the Outer Banks. It is where you can be alone with your thoughts, a ribbon of roadway for mind and solace. It is also

where your mind may drift freely and, except for the ease of driving on paved road, develop a sense of what the Outer Banks were like so many years ago. The scenery is wondrously constant: a sinuous dune line, mounding masses of evergreen foliage, the slate-green of the sound waters beyond the thickets of shrubbery, the hypnotic march of the utility poles, the cinema of the sky. I find this length of coast magical for its solitude. Take advantage of the invitation to pull into one of the parking lots and trek to look over the dunes.

The Little Kinnakeet Life-Saving Station stands in isolation ten miles south of Salvo. Both the 1874 original station and the 1904 expanded station sit right beside NC 12. As in all the stations, the crews lived here—the middle of nowhere—waiting for disaster and paid to risk their lives. The historic 1904 building with its hipped roofs attached to square tower is one of the two architectural styles adapted for the life-saving stations on the south Atlantic seaboard, but especially in North Carolina. The

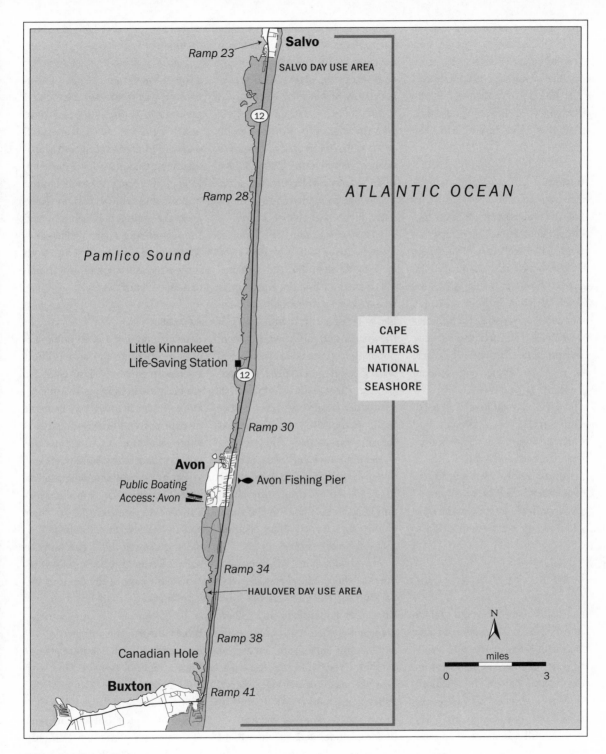

Map 11. Salvo to Buxton

other prototype is Chicamacomico. The Little Kinnakeet Station is currently a National Park Service property, and restoration is underway.

At Ramp 27 north of Avon, the schooner *G. A. Kohler*, which sank in August 1933, is visible on the beach.

Access

The National Park Service maintains several parking turnouts and off-road-vehicle access ramps between Salvo and Avon. The ramps are numbered, and Ramps 23, 28, and 30 have large parking lots. Beach driving is recommended only for four-wheel-drive vehicles or vehicles modified to negotiate the soft sands between the parking area and the packed wet sand beach.

At least six soundside off-road-vehicle trails give fishermen and others access to the sound waters between Salvo and Avon.

Web addresses: <www.nps.gov/caha/index.htm>; <www.cr.nps.gov/nr/twhp/wwwlps/lessons/57kinnakeet/57kinnakeet.htm>

Avon

Avon was once a small village served by a small basin for fishing boats, but it has grown into one of the more popular summer destinations in this part of the seashore. New "mega-homes" are intruding on the old shingled Avon. While there is still a soundside community that is home to traditional livelihoods, since the 1980s, de-velopment has reached a density surpassing that of any village south of Oregon Inlet. Avon has a modest strip shopping center with a grocery store and several commercial blocks housing multiple services. Now that it has grown beyond much of the isolated idiosyncrasies previously common to the Outer Banks, Avon has a resort rhythm and look, a sea change in character from its early days as Kinnakeet.

Not every tradition here changed, though. Avon still belongs to the surf fishermen, for the beaches north and south of the community remain hot spots for saltwater anglers. During the fishing runs of the spring and fall, when the local population returns to residential status, local enterprises and anglers stay in constant radio contact with other fishermen. The point of being on the wire is to hear urgent information—what is biting where. Depending how business is on a given day, surf-fishing locals have been known to drop everything and head to the beach if the radio chatter says game fish are feeding furiously in the surf.

Avon has a private fishing pier, open to the public for a fee, with parking for the pier. This is a serious pier for serious pier fishermen, somewhat renowned in the surf-fishing subculture for record catches of red drum, also known as channel bass. Red drum is diehard fishermen's fishing, sometimes in the worst of weather because of their "shoulder season" movement that follows the migrations of bait fish such as menhaden. Avon was where a world-record 94-pound red drum was caught.

I always seem to pass through Avon around lunchtime. Fortunately, I was steered to the Pickled Steamer in Hatteras Plaza ("right next to the Food Lion"). It is a small deli with limited seating and is usually busy, though quite unhurried, kind of New Age in attitude. It is not a place that will be rushed. However, the waitstaff is friendly, and the astounding menu yields sandwiches and salads that are both innovative and copious (the lunch salads will stuff two).

Access

Avon has no designated public access locations to the beach, but it is easy to find a parking spot for sunbathing, fishing, or swimming. Once you leave town, you are back on the Cape Hatteras National Seashore, and the access ramps are spaced about every 3 miles.

Ramp 34, south of Avon, is a traditional fishing hot spot for bluefish or for red drum during their spring and fall runs. Ramp 38 provides access to the ocean and the sound. Ramp 41 provides beach access just north of the Buxton Village limits.

Information

For information, contact Outer Banks Visitors Bureau, One Visitors Center Circle, Manteo, NC 27954, 252-473-2138, 877-629-4386; or Outer Banks Chamber of Commerce, P.O. Box 1757, Kill Devil Hills, NC 27948, 252-441-8144.

Windsurfing at Canadian Hole, near Avon. Courtesy of Outer Banks Visitors Bureau.

Web addresses: <www.outer banks.org>; <www.outerbanks chamber.com>

Canadian Hole

There may be only a few who remember the early years of windsurfing when word of the easy access, steady prevailing winds, and shallow and *warm* (by comparison) waters of Pamlico Sound spread among Canadian enthusiasts. The result was a steady influx of our neighbors from the north who migrated to a little-used access lo-

cation $1/2$ mile north of Buxton. These sound waters earned their nickname from the prevalence of Canadian license plates on cars initially pulled over on the shoulder of the road. After a while everyone knew where the Canadians came to windsurf, and its reputation spread as one of the finest windsurfing locations in the United States. For a Canadian who prefers to be on water instead of ice during the fall and winter, Pamlico Sound is a reasonable trek—sixteen-plus hours or so —to stay on top of the windsurfing game.

Pamlico Sound is generally shal-

low, but offshore in this location, the bottom was dredged for replacement fill after a storm blew out the dunes and road. The dredging deepened the sound, improving the conditions for windsurfing.

The National Park Service responded to the demand by building the first parking area to serve the site in 1988. That filled up and so they enlarged it in 1990, and it stays full. It is called "The Haulover" day use area, and the name recalls a past when local fishermen would haul over their boats from the sea to the sound or vice versa.

You cannot miss the soundside

Wild Rides on the Soundside

There is a new use for the Wrights' stuff on the Outer Banks. The constant steady winds that brought the brothers and their lofty dreams here now power more down-to-earth dreams—windsurfers and kite boarders. These adventuresome athletes who harness wind for water play are cutting a wake in some of the breeziest sports around.

Dolphin-quick and butterfly-bright, these sailing surfers may have found their mecca on Hatteras Island. While the ocean here has long attracted surfers after its wind-ginned waves, the slacker sound waters now have their sports-on-a-board as well. Fastening a sail to a surfboard—or a surfer to a kite in the case of wind kiting—has brought new activity to the waters between Buxton and Avon. Pamlico Sound is coming into its own as *the* place not to be bored with a board.

One particular confluence of steady wind and shallow smooth water has an international reputation—welcome to Canadian Hole. It's a proud nickname that recognizes the pioneering windsurfers from our neighbor to the north who put this place on the windsurfing map.

Stop at the Haulover Access north of Buxton and check out the license plates; there is typically a continental flair, especially in fall and early spring, when the water is chilly, but Canada is frozen.

Those in the know rate Canadian Hole one of the best rides in the nation. Interest is booming; there are surf shops at Rodanthe, Avon, and Buxton that have the gear and the know-how for hire as well. Although entry-level equipment can cost nearly $1,000, individual lessons can get you wet and hooked for about $50. But what a ride!

Unlike a surfer who is dependent on waves, a windsurfer fears only becalming. Soundside or surfside, windsurfers ride as long as the wind blows or their arms tire, whichever comes first. Riders use their body weight to balance against the force of the wind on the sail; the stronger the wind, the greater the lean the rider needs to balance that force. Steady, unvarying winds make for ideal long runs. As you might imagine, gusty winds present problems, as does a sudden becalming on the run out from shore.

Canadian Hole has no lock on

ideal conditions. In fact, the prevalence of sound waters all along the North Carolina coast ensures that any location that is a haven for sailing will soon be a hot spot for windsurfing. Duck and Corolla are busy hubs, too. When wind and waves come together, there is usually more sailable wind than surfable waves, making windsurfing one of the faster growing water sports.

Kite boarders reach all new heights of high-wire activism, tethered to a parasail with a surfboard that is mounted much like a snowboard. The rider gets power and loft from the wind-driven kite that pulls him or her across the water. Unlike a windsurfer who can tack like a sailboat, the return trip of a kiter is more problematic.

Windsurfers and kitesurfers are more than passengers. They join with board and sail, fused by the dream of flight before the wind and above the water. Advocates call it the ride of a lifetime; watching their brilliant-hued, buoyant-hulled fins flitter across the sound, it's easy to see why.

Web address: <www.outerbanks. org>

access—there are more than 100 spaces, showers, telephone, and trash cans. Also, the soundside beach here is significantly wider than other locations because of past overwash, which makes the spot ideal for setting up a windsurfing base and taking to the water. Kitesurfers or kite boarders, the new way to harness wind for water recreation, are joining the windsurfing crowd at the Haulover. They tend to spread out a bit more so as not to interfere with the windsurfers. Plan to arrive early if you want a parking place. Folks that windsurf are passionate about it and easily spend the entire day on the water.

There are surf shops in Rodanthe, Avon, and Buxton that have windsurfing equipment for sale or rent. Buxton is steadily developing an international flavor, and the new guests add a wonderful patois to the music of traditional speech. Windsurfing, kitesurfing, and "O Canada" are here to stay. C'est bon!

Access

The parking is on a first-come, first-served basis. There are restrooms, showers, and other conveniences. Overnight stays are not permitted, so don't plan to camp in your car.

Information

The park service occasionally schedules interpretive programs at the site. Inquire at the Hatteras Island Visitors Center, beside the lighthouse, for specific times and programs, or call 252-995-4474.

Web address: <www.nps.gov/caha/index.htm>

Buxton

A vivid memory about the drive from Avon to Buxton is that from the road all lines converged on the Cape Hatteras Lighthouse. The edges of the road, the painted lane divider, and the endless procession of utility poles seemed to point at the great tower as if to underscore its mission as a landmark. In July 1999 this perspective on Buxton changed dramatically when a team of specialists jacked up the tower and moved it southwest. It is still visible from the highway, of course, but it no longer has the same verve as an exclamation point to Outer Banks travel. Nevertheless, the Cape Hatteras Lighthouse still signals arrival.

Buxton is the figurative heart of the Outer Banks and the first glimpse of its famed barber-pole-striped beacon is one of the most exhilarating sights along the entire island chain. What framing for a lighthouse: grassy flats and dunes to the east, the grass feathering west to maritime shrubs, black needle rush in the marshy flats, and the great gray-blue pond of Pamlico Sound. If possible, arrive at Buxton at dusk as the light begins its nightly work. It is an assuring, transfixing spectacle, and nearly every car that comes to town makes the turn to the lighthouse before checking in at a motel or continuing on its journey. Now, after the turn off NC 12, the lighthouse is on your right, and not on your left.

Although the village of Hatteras is actually southwest, Buxton is the town that means "Hatteras" to many visitors. The confusion lingers because of Buxton's proximity to Cape Hatteras, the tip of which is Cape Point, the sandy spit of land southeast of the Cape Hatteras Lighthouse that is the visible portion of the "corner" of shoals and shallows that all north-south ocean travelers, fish or vessel, must nego-tiate. This is where the action is: waves, wind, water, and winding reels. When people say, "Going to Hatteras, fishing," they mean they are going to the point, give or take a mile or five, where there will be a jam of anglers crowded together hoping for the Big One.

The southwest bend in the island occurring at the Cape Point elbow changes the effect of prevailing winds and waves on the land. Large sand dune ridges have formed, and you can see a sample of these as you drive south along NC 12 through the village. These dune ridges shelter inland interdune spaces from salt spray. In the lee of those breezes grows an extensive maritime forest.

The combination of island width, wooded protection, and high ground has sheltered a community here since the earliest days of European settlement. Prior to that, Buxton was the site of a Native American village, a story told at the small Native American Museum in neighboring Frisco.

Buxton is still heavily wooded. The maritime forest that covers the widest portion of the island gives the community a noticeably different appearance from the towns to the north. After entering the village at the closest point—the most precarious point—in the entire community to the ocean, the road moves closer to the sound with the maritime forest between the community and the Atlantic Ocean. There's a softball field on the northern edge of town, and after passing that, the road carries you into the

	Fee	Parking	Restrooms	Lifeguard	Camping	Showers	Beach Access	Hiking	Trail	Handicapped	Boating	ORV Access	Fishing	Programs	Historic	Sand Beach	Dunes	Upland	Wetland
Buxton		•	•		•		•	•	•	•		•	•		•	•	•	•	•
Hatteras Island Visitors Center/ Cape Hatteras Lighthouse	•	•	•	•			•	•	•	•				•	•	•	•		
Buxton Woods Nature Trail		•						•	•					•				•	•
Buxton Woods Coastal Reserve								•	•									•	•
Cape Point Campground	•	•	•		•	•	•			•		•	•			•	•		
Cape Point Beach		•	•	•			•					•	•		•	•	•		
Frisco Campground	•	•	•		•	•	•	•				•	•			•	•	•	
Frisco Day Use Area		•	•			•	•			•			•			•	•		
Sandy Bay Access		•					•			•			•			•	•		•
Hatteras Island Access (Ramp 55)		•					•			•		•	•			•	•		
Hatteras Ferry	•	•	•																
Graveyard of the Atlantic Museum		•	•												•				

surprisingly hilly and forested village center. Businesses and homes appear as commercial and residential notches in the thicket of the maritime forest.

Buxton organizes itself along NC 12 in a slightly hapless fashion. Individual enterprises stand side by side with older houses, and there is an inherent utilitarianism about most of the stores because they remain open all year. Some of the restaurants could but do not. It is really not the place to come looking for souvenir tee shirts though doubtless some are available; the point here being that tourism shopping has not become part of local culture yet. Buxton doesn't have to entice visitors; they come anyway, and because of fishing and water sports, the season is longer than strictly the summer. As far as driving to a particular store or restaurant goes, ask for a landmark when getting directions. Then keep an eye out while driving; things appear suddenly around the wooded bends in the highway.

It is easy to become comfortable here, especially if you are less inclined to crowded places. There is all the civilization you could want, including very early breakfasts and baked goods at superb locations like the constant and constantly pleasing Orange Blossom Café and Bakery (underscore bakery).

Buxton has been a bit of a secret, but not the kind that is easily kept. After all, the lighthouse and the chance to climb it are a heck of a draw. The greatest evidence of Buxton's popularity is the summer traffic, a stream of vehicles moving steadily to go to the Cape Hatteras National Seashore facilities.

Cape Point has made Buxton the mecca of surf fishing, particularly in fall and spring. Fishing season brings an older and friskier group

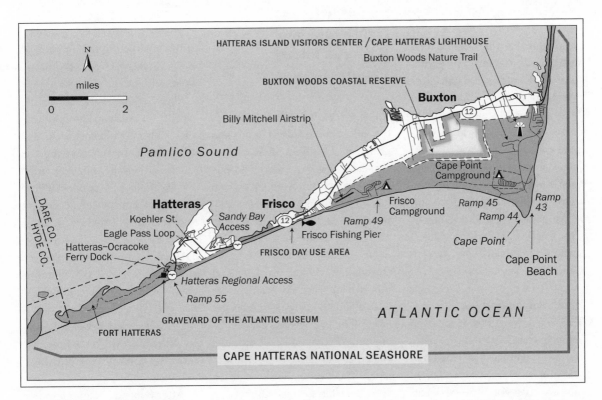

Map 12. Buxton to Hatteras Inlet

of children to Buxton, as friendly a group as will ever tow you out of deep sand. When the fish are running, it's a grand time to visit. Buxton hosts the exclusive Outer Banks Invitational Fishing Tournament. The organizers have limited the numbers of teams because it is such a popular event. Finding a place to stay during the tournament may be far more difficult than catching a fish.

People who fish from the surf have a certain mind-set about their pursuit. If you don't fish this way, then the phrase "going to Hatteras" will never have the rich, full,

expansive meaning that it does to those who wait endlessly through inclement weather, beside thundering surf, for a fish that probably won't show and are still able to call it a good day. "Going to Hatteras" is less an exact direction than it is a shift in consciousness. Once you go there and drive out to Cape Point, where the diehards have their lines in the water, you'll understand that there is a whole lot more to Buxton than can ever be easily explained.

Access

The motels and cottages you see as you enter the community are the

closest accommodations to the water. Unless you stay in one of these, plan to commute by car or bicycle to the waterfront. If you have a bicycle with you, then you will find it much easier to gain access to the beach.

The park service controls beach access and provides designated parking areas and off-road-vehicle ramps. To reach the access sites, turn south at the sign for the Cape Hatteras Lighthouse and Hatteras Island Visitors Center. Follow the wooded drive until the left turn leading to the lighthouse, where there is limited parking. You may also turn right and follow the signs to the campground and a larger parking area farther south at Cape Point Beach. You may also park on the shoulder of the road unless otherwise posted.

Avoid the mistake of turning east on Old Lighthouse Road, which dead-ends at an old naval facility. It has been turned over to the Coast Guard and has, in the past, been used by retired military personnel, active personnel, and dependents. The Coast Guard is considering turning the property over to Dare County.

Handicapped Access

The best access location for handicapped travelers is at the Cape Hatteras Lighthouse and the Lightkeeper's Quarters, where all buildings are accessible. There is a path to the beach from the parking lot that has a firm surface. Arrive early to secure a parking place.

Information

For information, contact Outer Banks Visitors Bureau, One Visitors Center Circle, Manteo, NC 27954, 252-473-2138, 877-629-4386; or Outer Banks Chamber of Commerce, P.O. Box 1757, Kill Devil Hills, NC 27948, 252-441-8144.

For information about campsite availability at the nearby Cape Hatteras and Frisco Campgrounds, inquire at the Hatteras Island Visitors Center, beside the lighthouse, or call 252-995-4474.

Web addresses: <www.outer banks.org>; <www.outerbanks chamber.com>

Cape Hatteras Lighthouse and Hatteras Island Visitors Center

The Cape Hatteras Lighthouse is the tallest in the United States and probably the tallest in the world that has ever been moved in one piece. It is certainly one of the enduring maritime symbols worldwide. The 208-foot-tall light casts a revolving beam visible 20 miles out at sea, alerting mariners to the treacherous waters of Diamond Shoals, which are east-southeast of Cape Point and have claimed many a ship. The two beacons each make one full rotation every 15 seconds, visible as one flash every 7.5 seconds. The National Park Service is responsible for maintaining the barber-pole-striped light tower, while the U.S. Coast Guard operates the actual light.

The park service has made the lighthouse the central feature of a redesigned Hatteras Island Visitors Center. The complex of buildings is officially the Cape Hatteras Lighthouse Historic District. It is a fine place to take a break from the road. Parking is more than adequate; there are vending machines and new, expansive restrooms. The main show here is the lighthouse, which added an intriguing chapter to its history when it retreated from the sea.

In 1999 this was also one of the most endangered structures along the coast. When first lighted in 1871, the edge of the sea was more than 1,500 feet away, but by February 1999, the ocean had gnawed to within 150 feet of the lighthouse's base. Choices were stark: move it or lose it.

The National Park Service decided to move both the tower and the double lightkeeper's quarters adjoining it. In February the contractors literally tunneled under the lighthouse, separated it from its foundation, placed a platform with rollers beneath it, jacked it up, and put it on tracks. The tracks led to the new foundation 2,899.57 feet to the southwest, 1,600 feet away from the Atlantic Ocean. On July 9, 1999, 23 days after actual moving began, the journey was over. By November 13, 1999, Cape Hatteras Lighthouse was relit in its new location.

After relocation and renovation, the National Park Service policy allows visitors to climb to the catwalk at the top of the tower. They restrict the numbers to approximately 30 climbers every 10 minutes. The fee is $6, and when the ticket is purchased, the time of the permitted ascent will be stamped on the ticket.

Having climbed the lighthouse long ago in its previous location, I returned on a hot July morning to try it again. Too hot, in fact. The lighthouse was closed because the heat index inside was above 105 degrees.

"When this hot outside, it acts like a chimney," explained a ranger. As the tower fills up with people, it doesn't get any cooler. The takeaway from all of this is, arrive early in the day (ascents begin at 9:00 A.M.) or try and squeeze in at the end of the day before the tower is closed to new climbers (at 5:50 P.M.).

The double lightkeeper's quarters serves as both a museum and the Hatteras Island Visitors Center. This building is located in the exact same position (to within 1/4 inch) relative to the lighthouse as in its original location. Exhibits detail the history of the lighthouse as well as the exploits of the U.S. Life-Saving Service, which operated along the length of the Outer Banks from the 1870s through World War II. Interpretive programs are regularly scheduled during the summer: Outer Banks history is a topic given twice daily at the visitors center.

The waves break disarmingly close to the site of the old lighthouse, which is worth the short drive (or 2,900-foot walk). The park service has a unique memorial there: granite blocks with the names and dates of service of all the lighthouse keepers form the shape of the lighthouse base on the spot where it used to stand.

Access

There is a large parking lot at the new visitors center, eliminating the squeeze that plagued the lighthouse at its old location. While the lot can be close to full, the visitors center and tower can absorb a lot of patrons. There are restrooms at the parking area.

Parking for the lifeguarded beach is located off the access road to the old lighthouse site.

The park is officially closed at dusk.

Handicapped Access

The Hatteras Island Visitors Center is accessible.

A path to the beach has a firm surface leading to the dune line.

Information

For information, call the Cape Hatteras Lighthouse and Hatteras Island Visitors Center at 252-995-4474.

Web address: <www.nps.gov/caha/index.htm>

Buxton Woods Nature Trail

The Buxton Woods Nature Trail, maintained by the National Park Service, is one of the easiest ways to see the extensive hardwood forest that is the heart of Buxton. Though only a small portion of this ecosystem is within the boundaries of the national seashore, it adjoins the 970-acre Buxton Woods Coastal Reserve managed by the state. The trail is easily accessible, easily hiked, and quite a surprise. It showcases what naturally happens to swales between old dune ridges that become sheltered from salt spray—they become magnificent forests of a special type.

The short loop trail departs from a picnic area that is beside the road to the Cape Point Campground. Compacted sand trails wind through the dense and varied canopy of a thriving forest that ex-

ists because it occurs on sequential ridges of sand parallel to the ocean. This ridge-and-swale pattern protects the forest canopy from the "shearing effects" of salt-laden wind.

The self-guided trail has interpretive markers that detail the natural history of the woods and the curiosities the trail passes. Large pines, with hickories, oaks, and even beech trees in the interior, dominate the woods. Although the woods themselves are not particularly memorable, the forest is significant because, with the freshwater ponds and specialized herbaceous plants, it occurs on the Holocene dunes of a sandy island. The many familiar species of plants here may not seem particularly extraordinary either, but again context is everything. One marker along the trail calls attention to a large flowering dogwood, quite remarkable on the barrier islands. You may also see the sharp, spreading fronds of the dwarf palmetto, a species common in South Carolina but at its extreme northern range in Buxton Woods.

The trails also lead to several freshwater ponds where freshwater bass once lived, the only known population to ever live on the Outer Banks. The presence of the water underscores the perhaps little-understood role that the woods play in the maintenance of groundwater replenishment for the aquifer that is the sole source of drinking water in Buxton. Elsewhere in Buxton, unprotected portions of the woods are being subdivided into lots for permanent and second homes. Though the long-term effect of developing the woods is unknown, the potential threat to the groundwater from the additional septic systems and wells and the elimination of the filtering and percolation provided by the woods could be irreversible.

These issues are a part of the story of the fragile and interlocking nature of life on Hatteras Island. It is difficult to think of Buxton Woods as anything other than a rumply jungle, tangled with vines and sometimes visited by snakes. However, just being "the woods" may be the highest and best use of the land. Fortunately, many acres of Buxton Woods adjacent to the national seashore have been set aside and protected in the North Carolina Coastal Reserve. Hiking trails link the two parcels.

Access

Continue straight past the turnoff to the Hatteras Island Visitors Center to reach the trailhead and picnic area. Parking is available at the site. It's a good idea to wear long-sleeved clothing or to have effective insect repellent in order to enjoy the walk. The first 50 yards of trail, as you move out of the cedar thicket and into the shelter of the first dune line, is a seasonal deer fly paradise. After your walk, check carefully for ticks.

Handicapped Access

Although the trail is compacted, it is probably not sufficiently compacted for someone in a wheelchair

to make the complete loop without assistance.

Information

For information, stop at the Hatteras Island Visitors Center, beside the lighthouse, or call 252-995-4474.

Web address: <www.nps.gov/caha/index.htm>

Cape Point Campground and Cape Point Beach

The Cape Point Campground is at the southern end of the main road serving the Cape Hatteras Lighthouse and Hatteras Island Visitors Center. The campground is open from mid-April through the first week in September, which picks up some very nice fishing times. Modern restrooms, cold showers, and a fish-cleaning station are provided at the campground. Campsites are available on a first-come, first-served basis. Extra-long tent stakes and mosquito repellent are recommended for tent campers. Although it is possible to walk to Cape Point from the campground, it is heavy slogging in soft sand. It is better to drive to the parking lot at Cape Point Beach (although it is smaller by half because of erosion), and bring a cooler so that once you get to the beach you can stay there.

Access

Turn right off the entrance drive and continue past the lighthouse to

reach the campground. Continue on the main drive just past the turnoff to the campground, and you will see the ramp leading to Cape Point Beach, a large fish-cleaning station with running water, and trash cans. To your left or the north, past this station, is a large parking lot serving the curving spit of sand closest to Cape Point. Early arrivals are more likely to get parking places —figure 10 A.M. during the summer or on weekends to get a parking space, especially since the area is smaller.

The campground is open from mid-April to the first of September. A ranger is usually there by 7 A.M. You may arrive as late as 11:30 P.M., but spaces are first-come, first-served. Ramp 45 provides beach access from the campground.

Handicapped Access

There is one campsite reserved for the handicapped, which includes a cut-out picnic table. The bathhouse at the campground includes a handicapped accessible shower with a ramp but no fold-down seat.

There is a boardwalk over the dunes from the parking area at Cape Point Beach, but there are no handicapped accessible restrooms.

Information

For information, stop by the Hatteras Island Visitors Center, beside the lighthouse, or call 252-995-4474.

Web address: <www.nps.gov/caha/index.htm>

Cape Point

Cape Point is the pinnacle of surf-fishing locations on the Outer Banks—a narrow salient of sand heading almost due east from the Hatteras Island elbow. It can be ridiculously crowded at times for the simple reason that fish swimming along the shore have to turn the corner. The point moves like a skate tail, whipping through the compass points, varying nearly 180 degrees in orientation, as the waves and currents that swirl offshore roll into the land. A storm in October 1991 sliced it cleanly away, but in some form or another, the waves reform it, building it anew.

Charged waves, steered by currents from north and south, meet at Cape Point. You can stand at the point on a day with an onshore wind and watch waves breaking from two directions simultaneously. This unexpected phenomenon occurs because waves, driven by winds from out in the ocean and moving toward land, refract or bend, trying, as all waves do, to break nearly parallel to the shore. At Cape Point, a wave starts to "bend around" the submerged extension of the point beyond the visible beach. By the time it reaches breaking depth, it has nearly folded in half. The collision is explosive and underscores oceanographers' contention that the beach energy at Cape Hatteras is the highest on the East Coast.

Cape Point has always been southeast of the Cape Hatteras Lighthouse (and still is, even after the relocation of the tower), but the ocean decides the exact bearing. It changes almost daily as waves refashion the point. Visit the point over several years and the ability of the waves to move it around relative to the Cape Hatteras Lighthouse becomes amazingly evident.

This is the location where the compass bearing of the Outer Banks makes a pronounced shift from a slightly west of south to a decidedly south of west orientation. Instead of the almost frontal assault that the ocean makes on beaches north of Cape Point, waves driven by northeast winds slice obliquely at the sands (and islands) south of the point. The waves and prevailing winds slide sand sideways along the face of the beach; and, generally speaking, the barrier islands south of Cape Point have a characteristically long, low profile instead of the abrupt (and artificial) dune line to the north of the point, which prevailing winds have more or less been able to sustain for nearly three-quarters of a century.

As mentioned, the place where the islands shift direction makes an ideal fishing location since any northern or southern migration of fish following the Outer Banks must "turn the corner" at Cape Point. Red drum (or channel bass) and bluefish are two popular game species that circumnavigate Cape Point during their spring and fall migrations, moving through the breaking waves. Fishermen are also predominately seasonal creatures and populate the point in the greatest numbers when the fish are passing on their semiannual journeys, but some are there at any time of day, any day of the year.

When the fish come to the point, so do the people. A bluefish blitz in Buxton is a four-alarm event. If you've been there at such a time, you know how nearly comic it is when hundreds of people are standing shoulder to shoulder trying to fish in the same spot. Even if you don't fish, go to the point to watch, and try to figure out why, all other things being equal, one person is catching fish but no one else is. Of course, each empty-handed angler knows his or her turn is next . . . .

Access

Beach closings are clearly posted. Cape Point can be reached by walking from the parking lot at Cape Point Beach, but the lengthy trek through soft sand and sometimes water-covered flats is difficult. Instead, if you have a four-wheel-drive vehicle, drive to Ramps 43 and 44 where you can cross over the dunes to reach Cape Point. Follow the numerous vehicle tracks that indicate crossable sand leading to the point. Even four-wheel-drive vehicles can become mired in the sand, but rarely is anybody stranded; the location is too popular for someone not to pass by in a short period of time to help first then laugh afterward. If you don't have a four-wheel-drive vehicle, stick out your thumb and somebody will pick you up.

Information

For information, stop by the Hatteras Island Visitors Center, beside the lighthouse, or call 252-995-4474.

Web address: <www.nps.gov/caha/index.htm>

Buxton Woods Coastal Reserve

The Buxton Woods component of the North Carolina Coastal Reserve is now a stout 970 acres that backs up to the north border of the Cape Hatteras National Seashore with a front boundary along NC 12, approximately halfway between Buxton and Frisco. It is a continuation of the same forest of parallel dune ridges and swales that have been stabilized by a mix of maritime evergreen trees and shrubs. There are also seasonally flooded and permanent freshwater marshes, with a mix of cattails, sawgrass, wild rice, and various rushes.

The forest provides important habitat for wildlife. More than 360 species of birds, including bald eagles and peregrine falcons, have been sighted within. Common mammals include gray fox, mink, river otter, and white-tail deer. There are two rare butterflies, the Northern Hairstreak and the Giant Swallowtail, that have sustainable populations.

Important, too, may be the role of the woods in the recharging of the local aquifer simply by being woods and not an impermeable surface (see Buxton Woods Nature Trail).

Equally important is that Buxton-Frisco has always been heavily for-

ested, and the protection provided by inclusion in the Coastal Reserve system assures that a greater portion of the island than simply the seashore will remain in a natural state.

Currently, the state intends to maintain the woods as a research preserve, which means that it will remain undeveloped. There are no plans at present to open the property for additional access or to build interpretive facilities. The Buxton Woods site is accessible by either Old Doctors Road off of NC 12 in Buxton or Water Association Road off of NC 12 in Frisco.

Information

For information, contact Northern Sites Manager, North Carolina Coastal Reserve, 983 West Kitty Hawk Road, Kitty Hawk, NC 27949, 252-261-8891; or Education Office, North Carolina Coastal Reserve, 135 Duke Marine Lab Road, Beaufort, NC 28516, 252-728-2170.

Web address: <www.ncnerr.org/pubsiteinfo/siteinfo/buxton/buxton.html>

Frisco

Frisco straddles the winding course of NC 12 from Buxton south and west nearly to Hatteras. It includes a post office and a small village, but the buildings do not cluster at the center of the community. Frisco is a collection of independent businesses and residents that lines the roadway beneath the shade of the pines and hardwoods

near the waters of Pamlico Sound. Some homes hug the highway, and in a few places, houses are burrowed into the island's interior or perch above Pamlico Sound, barricaded from traffic by the maritime forest.

Explore Frisco by car or bicycle. It is linear and level. In contrast to Buxton, Frisco is sleepy. The comparative bustle—all relative—of commercial activity and traffic in Buxton levels off here dramatically. If you get the feeling that life, like NC 12, is winding down from a hard straight run, you are right. Want not, worry not in Frisco.

Frisco is a soundside traditional village. Several marinas and private boat slips along NC 12 have restaurants, seafood retailers, and exquisite long, quiet creeks leading to open water. The oceanfront is miles away by car but just over the sand dunes and through the woods by crow. At the west end of town, you sense the oceanfront again as you reenter the Cape Hatteras National Seashore on the way to Hatteras. Only when you reach the extreme southwest corner of the community does the road curl out of the forest with a view of the primary dunes.

Frisco is also the location of the 3,000-foot Billy Mitchell Airstrip and airport, approximately one mile west of Frisco center. From this field, General Mitchell of the U.S. Army Air Corps took off on the historic bombing demonstration directly offshore from Frisco that would eventually result in the complete rethinking of naval battle tactics and strategic planning. In 1923 he and his squadron sank a battleship with bombs dropped from the planes. Surprisingly, even after this demonstration, the military establishment remained reluctant to accept the capabilities of air power in naval warfare for years afterward.

The road that leads to the airport winds past some monumental dunes ending at the National Park Service campground. Even if you aren't interested in camping, this campground is worth driving through to see the commanding view of the undulating grass-covered dune field, as well as to experience the delightful breezes. It is one of the most beautiful spots on the seashore, with a dramatic view of the ocean from the upper campsites. The beach here lies in the curve of the Cape Hatteras Bight, the protected bay south of Cape Point, and frequently has calmer water than the beachfront north of Cape Point. Parking is adequate, and the walk from the campground to the beach is no more than 1/4 mile.

At the southwest limit of the town is the Cape Hatteras Pier, or Frisco Pier as it is locally known, which extends some 600 feet into the ocean. The pier is open 24 hours a day between April 1 and November 30, and situated as it is in the sheltered waters of Cape Hatteras Bight, it is a hot spot for summer mackerel fishing. There is parking at the base of the pier, and the pier charges admission for sightseers as well as fishermen.

South of the pier stretch several miles of comparatively unvisited beach with a steep, narrow profile. Driving is prohibited here. Also, several private campgrounds on the western edge of Frisco offer sites. Most are close to the pier, with reasonable ocean access.

Access

The park service provides several access ramps, public parking areas, and the campground. The campground is a short ride east from NC 12 at Frisco. It is open from mid-June to early September, and spaces are first-come, first-served. It is sequestered between parallel dune lines and adjacent to an extensive high-dune maritime forest. Cold showers and restrooms are provided. A splendid and isolated stretch of beach with lifeguards during the summer is available for campground users. Ramp 49 is near the campground; from there, a wonderful wandering trail leads across the interdune flats and then over the primary dunes to the beach. Shoes are recommended for this hike. Driving on the beach southwest of the campground is restricted due to the nesting of loggerhead turtles and the narrow beachfront. Cape Hatteras airstrip is adjacent to the campground entry drive.

South of Frisco is the Sandy Bay Oceanside Access with parking and a bathhouse. The parking is very close to the primary dune line because the island narrows. Prior to Hurricane Isabel, there was a parking area on the north side of

NC 12, but that is gone, and at present, there are no plans to reconstruct or replace it.

The last ramp, number 55, is near the ferry docks at the village of Hatteras.

Handicapped Access

The Sandy Bay Oceanside Access area has handicapped restrooms and also has outside showers. Sandy Bay Oceanside Access and Ramp 55 have ramps and boardwalks that are handicapped accessible leading to an observation deck overlooking the dunes.

Individual businesses and campgrounds may have facilities for handicapped travelers.

Information

For information, contact Outer Banks Visitors Bureau, One Visitors Center Circle, Manteo, NC 27954, 252-473-2138, 877-629-4386; or Outer Banks Chamber of Commerce, P.O. Box 1757, Kill Devil Hills, NC 27948, 252-441-8144.

Web addresses: <www.outer banks.org>; www.outerbanks chamber.com>

Frisco Day Use Area

On the oceanside, just south of the fishing pier in Frisco, is the Frisco Day Use Area. This site is plainly visible just after the road curves back behind the primary dunes along one of the narrowest lengths of Hatteras Island. The access site is reserved for daytime use and provides a means to reach the sheltered waters of the Cape Hatteras Bight.

Approximately one mile south on the north side of NC 12 is the Sandy Bay Oceanside Access.

Access

The Frisco Day Use Area has paved parking, full restrooms, cold showers, and a dune crossover ramp. There is parking at the Sandy Bay Oceanside Access.

Handicapped Access

Frisco Day Use Area is fully handicapped accessible.

Diamond Shoals

Offshore of Cape Hatteras is a sweep of ocean that has shaped the history of the islands you visit today. These are the waters of Diamond Shoals, and they have made the passage around Cape Hatteras a mariner's nightmare.

Extending approximately 12 miles to the southeast from Cape Point, the shoals are covered by shallow waters of varying depth. The essential terror of the place is not only that the waters are shallow, but that they are unpredictably so, especially true for deeper draft vessels such as oceangoing freighters. Navigation charts of the shoals are covered with disclaimers and danger signs.

Diamond Shoals is the great mixing bowl where the warm waters of the Gulf Stream collide with the cooler, slow-moving, closer-to-land flowing remnants of the

Labrador Current, creating turbulence and danger. This mingling of nutrient-rich waters that originated in such disparate locations creates a rich breeding ground for fish at all levels of the ocean food chain.

There are three separate shoals, the innermost being Hatteras Shoals, then Inner Diamond Shoals, followed by Outer Diamond Shoals. Channels pass between the three—Hatteras Slough separates Hatteras and Inner Diamond Shoals and Diamond Slough between Inner and Outer Diamond Shoals—but they are ever-changing and unreliable. In addition to the Cape Hatteras light, a Diamond Shoals light tower stands at the extreme eastern edge of the hazard. When the tower was erected in 1967, it replaced a lightship that had been on duty for more than fifty years.

This extensive, shifting, and shoaling navigation hazard has claimed countless commercial and pleasure craft. Indeed, so numerous are the recorded shipwrecks around the waters of Cape Point that they have earned the nickname "Graveyard of the Atlantic." According to one estimate, 1,500 vessels have been lost in the passage from Cape Henry, Virginia, to Cape Fear. Diamond Shoals in particular tempted mariners in the days of sail. To avoid extensive delays, north- or southbound maritime traffic would try to skirt these waters as closely as possible. However, cutting this corner is dangerous, and some have paid dearly for attempting it.

During World War II, the shoals provided a natural pinching point that made freighters especially vulnerable to predatory German submarines. The U-boats simply waited for the inevitable maritime traffic to attempt to navigate Diamond Shoals. The German submariners sent more than 80 vessels to the bottom of the sea in and around Cape Hatteras, earning it the notorious nickname "Torpedo Junction."

Hatteras

The village of Hatteras is at the southwest end of the island, a few miles south of Frisco. The road squeezes between marsh and dunes along this narrow pinch of the island, and if you look closely, you will notice that the pavement is very new.

On September 18, 2003, Hatteras became an island again. Hurricane Isabel slammed the village directly and added insult to the devastation by cutting the town from the northern beaches. The hurricane chewed through the dunes, the roadbed, and soundside marsh to open a 300-yard gash in the barrier beach. In doing so, it unearthed old pilings that had been part of a bridge spanning a similar gap that had opened early in the twentieth century.

This was the first direct hurricane hit within memory for Hatteras, and it was devastating. The storm devoured the dune line that provided protection for the ocean-

The Albatross III *entering the harbor at Hatteras Village. Courtesy of Tom Carlson.*

front houses on the south side of the village, and then it went after the houses with a wind-driven storm surge. One of the landmarks it claimed was the more than century-old life-saving outpost known as Durant's Station.

The new breach in the island began acting like an inlet immediately—with tidal waters moving freely through it. This set off a lively debate not only on what to do—whether to fill it or plan for a new ferry—but on what to call it

—breach or inlet. The former was chosen as it sounded less permanent, and the state moved quickly to hire a dredge to close the yawning "breach." Meanwhile, Hatteras residents, most of whom had stayed on the island during the storm, began pulling their lives back together without benefit of electricity, gasoline, roads, and a reliable water supply.

Hatteras is bruised, a bit weather-beaten, and not quite as comfortable in its place as it was

before Isabel. The loss of trees and their natural soft and cool look gives the village a starker appearance. It's coming around, though, and is still a place to anticipate as it is the last easily accessible outpost on the barrier islands—figuratively and somewhat literally, the end of the road at the edge of the water.

Hatteras, along with Wanchese, is one of two major fishing centers on the Outer Banks. Commercial fishing is not the economic engine it once was here; instead, sportfishing and charter- and head-boat fishing trips for recreational anglers are assuming a greater importance in the local economy. Ocean access through Hatteras Inlet has been far more stable than that through Oregon Inlet, leading to the local boom. All types of sound, open water, and half- and full-day fishing trips are available. In the last twenty years, the word has spread that the waters offshore of Hatteras are one of the great fall and winter aggregation points for game fish, and surprisingly, giant bluefin tuna. This discovery has extended the charter fishing season greatly. (If surf fishing is your pleasure, you might want to know that local fishermen will take the ferry to Ocracoke to surf fish.)

One type of tourism sometimes begets another, and Hatteras became a desirable spot for second-home construction, which began filling in the vacant lots in the village. This, in turn, has sparked a slight shift in the merchandise and foods that appear in the Burrus Red and White Grocery, the village grocery store that is a local institution and dates from 1866. New merchants and less utilitarian merchandise are deftly weaving into the town without displacing its essential small-town character.

If you have time to leave the road and look around, it is evident that Hatteras living is simple and for the most part unadorned. What strikes me is that somehow, though, there always seems to be time for flowers, particularly in front of the small houses along Koehler Street,

SR 1237, which meets NC 12 beside the Burrus Red and White. This is the old heart of the village and where the land use would make a city planner cringe—houses next to offices next to marinas, cemeteries separate houses, and so on. It is a wonderful portrait of how life in Hatteras evolved—portraying life as it evolved at the time.

This unpredictability means there are just more things to be discovered—a private fishing club, a pony pen, and an old homestead site overlooking the marsh, even abandoned earthworks. The sense of discovery can extend right down to the architecture. There are bungalows, traditional frame farmhouses, colonnaded facades, and chimney-buttressed houses that radiate durability. One of the prized houses is the restored weather station, reputed to be the first official building constructed by the U.S. Weather Bureau. The National Register building is in the heart of the village and is managed by the Cape Hatteras National Seashore. The sturdy bungalow has survived some of the worst storms to come ashore in North Carolina.

Most visitors to Hatteras are passing through on the way to or from Ocracoke. NC 12 traffic pulses with the gorging and disgorging of the Ocracoke ferryboats. If you are coming from Buxton and in a hurry to reach the ferry, turn left on Eagle Pass Loop, which winds through a residential section of the village and delivers you to the ferry dock slightly quicker than the main route. But if you have more time,

park your car and walk through the village. You'll learn a lot about the fabric of existence on the Outer Banks.

If you like driving on the beach, the National Park Service bans vehicles from driving on the beaches between Hatteras and Buxton between May 15 and September 15 due to sea turtle and sea bird nesting. There is a soundside off-road-vehicle trail on Hatteras.

Access

The park service maintains two beach access locations with parking and dune crossovers. The first is the Sandy Bay Oceanside Access, just north of the town limits. There are lifeguards here in the summer. The Sandy Bay Sound Access is on the north side of NC 12. The second is a large access area with parking for about 25 cars at the Ocracoke ferry dock. A wooden ramp slightly more than 100 yards long leads over the primary dune line to the wide beach. The road to the access area also leads to the Hatteras Coast Guard Station and a ramp that provides four-wheel-drive access to the South Beach area, the point of land to the north side of Hatteras Inlet that is gradually curling southwest into the inlet. The point is easily 2 miles from the ramp. If you can reach it, there's a lot of very nice beach and good surf fishing as well.

Dare County maintains one boat slip and two parking spaces for unloading at the Harbor Seafood Marina on the west side of NC 12. There is a 4-hour limit on the use of the slip. The public slip is available at the private marina because the U.S. Army Corps of Engineers maintains the channel between the sound and the basin.

Handicapped Access

Both the Sandy Bay Oceanside and Sound Access sites have handicapped restrooms. Sandy Bay Oceanside has an accessible observation deck overlooking the dunes.

The access area at the ferry dock is accessible to handicapped travelers, and a boardwalk extends to a deck at the crest of the primary dunes.

The ferry landing has restrooms accessible to handicapped travelers.

Information

For information, contact Outer Banks Visitors Bureau, One Visitors Center Circle, Manteo, NC 27954, 252-473-2138, 877-629-4386; or Outer Banks Chamber of Commerce, P.O. Box 1757, Kill Devil Hills, NC 27948, 252-441-8144.

Web addresses: <www.outer banks.org>; <www.outerbanks chamber.com>; <www.hatteras onmymind.com> (a local website with Hurricane Isabel photographs by residents)

Graveyard of the Atlantic Museum

With unique architecture evocative of the ribs of a ship, the Graveyard of the Atlantic Museum is a new facility dedicated to interpreting the compelling story of the maritime history of the Outer Banks. It is just becoming established—collections and displays are being assembled—but it already promises to be a must-stop for return visits. Every year will bring new additions, and the history it commemorates—the often tragic story of navigation along the Outer Banks —will never cease to be engaging.

As of July 2004, there were exhibits on the wreck of the USS *Huron* on November 24, 1874, at Nags Head, where ninety-eight died because the life-saving stations were not manned during the winter months. This pivotal tragedy spurred the development of the U.S. Life-Saving Service to become a year-round professional service.

There is a desk from the *G. A. Kohler*, wrecked on August 23, 1933 (and sometimes visible from Ramp 24 north of Avon), as well a charming exhibit of local interest on the mail boat *Aleta*, which was the only means of reaching Ocracoke until the mid-1950s.

Here, too, visitors can learn much more on the entire saga of maverick General Billy Mitchell and his successful bombing of the decommissioned battleships *New Jersey* and *Virginia* on September 5, 1923. Mitchell and his squadron took flight from nearby Frisco airfield in an epic demonstration that changed naval warfare forever.

One of the keynote exhibits in the future will be the story of the sinking and recovery of the Union ironclad *Monitor*, sunk nearly due east from this point in a storm in 1862 while being towed following its historic sea battle with the Confederate ship *Merrimac* at Hampton Roads, Virginia.

The museum has a gift shop with an emphasis on maritime history.

Access

To reach the museum, stay in the left lane as you approach the Hatteras ferry docks and follow the signs to the U.S. Coast Guard and Beaches, instead of the signs to the ferry docks.

Be advised that leaving the museum to return to the ferry queue may be difficult, depending on traffic bound for Ocracoke.

Handicapped Access

The museum is fully accessible for handicapped travelers.

Information

For information, contact the Graveyard of the Atlantic Museum, 59158 Coast Guard Road, Hatteras, NC 27943, 252-986-2995.

Web address: <www.graveyard oftheatlantic.com>

Fort Hatteras

At the very south end of Hatteras Island, approximately 2 miles south from the Ocracoke ferry dock, are the earthwork remains of a Confederate fort constructed to facilitate raiding on the Union traffic through the inlets. The Confederate soldiers were driven out of their positions in 1861 as the Union secured the sea-lanes and inlets of

It's a short, easy trip by free ferry from Hatteras Village to Ocracoke Island. Courtesy of Outer Banks Visitors Bureau.

the Outer Banks to prevent the southerners from receiving supplies by sea.

Access

Access to the fort is by foot or off-road vehicle from the National Park Service ramp, which is obviously signed.

Hatteras Ferry

The free ferry from Hatteras Island to Ocracoke is a ride worth waiting for—how long you wait depends on both the time of day and time of year. It was only a fifteen-minute wait late Thursday afternoon in July 2004, the week after the Fourth. The day was blistering, and the ferry service employed three vessels to handle the traffic. When we arrived at Ocracoke, we saw why—the line of departing vehicles was one-quarter mile long, and there is no shady place to wait on Ocracoke's north end.

The ride is a wonderful passage for children. Gulls and terns follow the ferry looking for an easy feed. If you choose to feed the gulls—which some drivers dislike because of unwanted bird deposits—do so at the back of the ferry. Some of the gulls are tame and adept enough to ma-neuver with the ferry and take food from your fingertips.

Hurricane Isabel rerouted the ferry channel, which now follows a serpentine route close in to Hatteras Island before skipping across the inlet to curl back east to the sheltered ferry dock on Ocracoke Island. The new routing has increased the length and time of the passage. The hurricane shoaled the channel, making navigation clearly challenging, as noted by the ferry's drop in speed, in some places.

Part of Isabel's legacy to Hatteras Inlet is a substantial shoal that in July 2004 looked like an island in the making. Also, as the ferry approaches Ocracoke, the pilings from two previous ferry docks are visible at the edge of the island's north end.

Expect ferry traffic to be especially intense around holiday weekends and during the summer. Waiting in line to go to Ocracoke is not so bad, a case of the end justifying the means, which happen to be zero —the crossing is free. Play the waiting game: walk to the dock, look for the ferry, walk back, throw a Frisbee, play some cards. Don't be so smug about self-discipline that you slip over to the Hatteras Landing shopping center to idle some of that time away. More than one would-be traveler has shopped their way out of a place in line. Expect no mercy from the drivers behind your abandoned car in the ferry line.

The ferry service schedules departures every 30 minutes during daylight hours from April 15 to October 15, and during winter, every hour on the hour, 5 A.M. to 5 P.M., as well as at 7, 9, and 11 P.M. Throughout the summer season, as many as six vessels may be in service to handle the large numbers of visitors continuing their trip to Ocracoke. Placement on the ferries is on a first-come, first-served basis, and the personnel who direct traffic onto the ferries are very astute at delaying those who they think have jumped in line.

Information

For information, call the North Carolina Ferry Division at 252-726-6446, or the Hatteras ferry dock at 252-928-3841.

Web address: <www.ncferry.org>

Hatteras Inlet

Hatteras Inlet has been a primary passage between Pamlico Sound and the Atlantic Ocean since a hurricane split the barrier island in 1846, also opening Oregon Inlet. Maps prior to 1760–70 show an inlet closer to Ocracoke Village, which would have isolated the higher, more stable portions of the island where the village was established.

The inlet for the most part has been fairly stable as a navigable channel between Pamlico Sound and the Atlantic Ocean. Hurricane Isabel moved the channel alignment around and shoaled the channel sufficiently so that at low tide sand seems visible where none was before. The reliability of Hatteras Inlet presents an alternate outlet to commercial fishermen of Wanchese who must fight the constant shoaling of Oregon Inlet. However, a glance at a map will show that churning to Hatteras Inlet from Wanchese is not cost-efficient since it adds to the fuel consumption as well as to the time that a vessel is not fishing. Trawlers are not geared for speed or cruising, but the long ride is better than running aground.

For all its relative stability, however, Hatteras is an inlet on the move. In 1954 a storm and erosion took away an abandoned U.S. Coast Guard Station at the north end of Ocracoke in the inlet.

The Houses of Heroes

The architectural style of recent Outer Banks vacation homes, characterized by wide dormers, hip-roof towers, shingled siding, and carpenter Gothic ornamentation, draws from the historic buildings of the U.S. Life-Saving Service. One of the forerunners of the U.S. Coast Guard, the Life-Saving Service became a legendary institution on the North Carolina coast. Starting with the first seven stations established in 1873, the service's presence grew to twenty-nine stations on the state's barrier islands.

The federal Life-Saving Service was modeled after the all-volunteer system of the Massachusetts Humane Society, but it struggled for more than two decades, overwhelmed by need and plagued by inconsistency. It floundered until 1871, when Sumner Increase Kimball, a Maine lawyer, took charge as chief of the Treasury Department's Revenue Marine Division.

Politically gifted and blessed with excellent organizational abilities, Kimball completely remade the service, building new stations and establishing six-man boat crews and a keeper or captain (who had to be able to read and write) at each outpost. Kimball standardized the equipment, rescue techniques, and station routines. By 1874, North Carolina had its first outposts up, running, and in service.

The treacherous waters nicknamed "Graveyard of the Atlantic" brought the stations. The stations in turn each provided steady employment for six crew members at $120 a year and $200 a year for the station keeper. The crew's families became the nucleus of towns; the buildings became community landmarks; some were often the only building visible along the lonely, empty, sand-swept shoreline.

The business of the U.S. Life-Saving Service was heroism. The job description was simple, the demands incredible: walk the beach every night for eight months a year, and if a ship wrecks near the station, rescue everyone they can, regardless—regardless of sea conditions, regardless of their own safety.

The North Carolina stations made their contribution to the lore of the service and the legends of the Outer Banks. Best known perhaps is the Chicamacomico station at Rodanthe and the rescue by its crew of the survivors of the tanker *Mirlo* in World War I, a story well documented at the restored station today.

Keeper Patrick Ethridge of the Creed's Hill station (near present-day Frisco) on North Carolina's Outer Banks became symbolic of the dedication expected of crewmembers. A crewmember reported a ship stranded on Diamond Shoals off Cape Hatteras in a terrible storm, and Ethridge commanded the lifeboat out. One of the crew shouted that they might get there but might not make it back. Ethridge looked at him and said, "The Blue Book says we've got to go out, and it doesn't say a damn thing about having to come back."

Between 1871 and 1915, its glory years, the Life-Saving Service could boast these statistics: "28,121 vessels and 178,141 persons became involved with its services." Only 1,465 people were lost during rescue and recovery operations. Particularly heroic efforts, like that of Rasmus Midgett, were recognized with the Gold Life-Saving Medal.

At 3:00 A.M. on August 18, 1899, surfman Rasmus Midgett of the Gull Shoals station (south of Salvo) on North Carolina's Outer Banks came upon the barkentine *Priscilla* shipwrecked 100 yards offshore. He heard cries for help, but his station was three round-trip hours away—time, the *Priscilla* crew did not have. Midgett followed a receding wave toward the ship and yelled for the crew to jump overboard one at a time, and he would help them. He did this seven times, leaving three incapacitated men on board. Undeterred, Midgett struggled to the wreck and brought each one back. He had single-handedly saved ten men.

The stations were buildings of distinction, pure and simple. The first stations were simple boathouses; some of the crew bunked upstairs. Larger, more substantial buildings followed later. The boathouse was a single large room like a garage, usually with three bays for the high-prow surfboats. The quarters were sometimes over the boathouse. Some stations had distinctive watchtowers capping the main building.

All were wood, and many, particularly the Currituck Beach Lighthouse lightkeeper's quarters, were prefabricated and shipped to their locations. The siding and roof were cedar shakes. An extensive guttering system carried rainwater to a cistern for storage. The stations were constructed with a Victorian carpenter Gothic flair, and it is their decorative brackets that adorned end gables and paneling used as trim that have been creatively adapted for use in new houses.

In 1915 the U.S. Life-Saving Service became the U.S. Coast Guard, a change that meant little in the day-to-day operation of the lonely Outer Banks stations. But by the 1930s, the need for the stations had declined, and the Coast Guard began to decommission them, only to reactivate them during World War II. Following the war, the stations were decommissioned and sold. The last on active duty, at Ocracoke, has been retired and given to the state of North Carolina.

The remainder are neither gone nor forgotten. Many wear different hats, and if you know what to look for, you can spot them and enjoy these treasures of a bygone era. By far and away, Chicamacomico Historic Life-Saving Station in Rodanthe is the single best place to see two generations of stations fully restored and open for visitors. Here are a few more to look for.

The retired Wash Woods station is a private residence within the boundaries of the Currituck

National Wildlife Refuge, north of Corolla.

Twiddy and Company Real Estate maintains offices in the restored 1896 Kill Devil Hills station, which Twiddy moved to Corolla. Visitors are welcome.

The Sanderling Restaurant and Bar in Sanderling is the former Caffey's Inlet Life-Saving Station, which is on the National Register of Historic Places. The original sign is at Owens' Restaurant at Whalebone Junction in Nags Head, which is modeled after that station.

The Black Pelican restaurant at milepost 4.5 on Beach Road (NC 12) in Kitty Hawk is in one of the more ornate Gothic station buildings that survives from 1874, although it has been moved back from the oceanfront. Slightly south and on the west side of Beach Road stands the old Kitty Hawk Coast Guard Station, now privately owned.

Owens' Restaurant echoes many of the architectural traits of the former station at Whalebone Junction. The bar is appropriately called the Station Keeper's Lounge.

On the north end of Pea Island, the weathered Oregon Inlet station is barely holding on. A new multimission station has been constructed next to the Oregon Inlet Fishing Center.

At the Pea Island National Wildlife Refuge maintenance building at the south end of the refuge are the foundations of the old Pea Island station. It housed the only all-black crew in the history of the Life-Saving Service.

Chicamacomico at Rodanthe is on the National Register of Historic Places and is currently operated by the private Chicamacomico Historical Association. This is the station made famous by the Midgett family, six of whom lived and served here. Seven Midgetts have won the Coast Guard Gold Medal and three the silver, an unmatched family accomplishment. The station is restored and open for visitation and interpretive programs.

South of Avon is Little Kinnakeet station, one of the original life-saving stations constructed along the Outer Banks. Its isolated location best captures the severity of being in the service. The National Park Service began restoration work in the summer of 1991; it is still ongoing.

Hurricane Isabel struck Hatteras Village and destroyed the historic Durant Station, which had been converted as part of a hotel. The building cupola is now on display at Chicamacomico.

The Portsmouth Island station was also damaged by Hurricane Isabel, but it will be restored as funding becomes available.

The Cape Lookout station is used as a headquarters for ecology tours by the North Carolina Maritime Museum.

Even in their new uses, the buildings have a distinctive look. Today, that distinction is a part of the architectural vernacular of the Outer Banks.

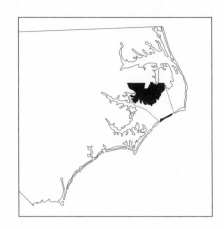

Hyde County

At some point before it docks on Ocracoke Island, the ferry from Hatteras crosses into Hyde County. The Dare County border, established in 1870 when Dare County was cobbled together from Currituck, Tyrrell, and Hyde Counties, most likely split Hatteras Inlet, which opened in 1846. The line's real world location—the inlet has shifted—is a moot question because both headlands are in Cape Hatteras National Seashore. The county question is germane for the community of Ocracoke, for it is not in the national seashore and is a salient of mainland Hyde County. Swan Quarter, the Hyde County seat, is approximately 2 hours northwest by a toll ferry. This separation is more than a matter of miles and water, however.

Mainland Hyde County remains below the radar for most coastal North Carolina travelers, yet it includes some of the state's most magnificent and accessible coastal plain features. US 264, the primary highway through the county, slips through its southern third, routing around the south border of Mattamuskeet National Wildlife Refuge, a 40,000-acre natural lake that is the largest in the state. A shallow basin, barely 6 feet deep at some points, the lake is prime waterfowl habitat and has a long tradition of being a superlative hunting area. NC 94 spans the lake and improved roads circumnavigate it, affording access to boat docks and the permitted hunting blinds.

North of Lake Mattamuskeet is Alligator Lake or New Lake, a 6-foot deep, 6,000-acre body of water that, with adjoining wetlands and fields, is a part of Pocosin Lakes National Wildlife Refuge. Hunters or bird-watchers better know the routes to these destinations, and there is an abundance of opportunities for each along this route.

A substantial portion of the county is high swamp or pocosin, a term that literally means "swamp on a hill." This is not to be confused with high ground. The county seat, itself on the perimeter of Swan Quarter National Wildlife Refuge, is barely 10 feet above sea level. In fact, Swan Quarter and the Hyde County mainland were among the hardest hit areas in the state by Hurricane Isabel, which flooded the several coastal villages. Four feet of water filled the county courthouse, and many, many homeowners lost everything. The damage was not widely reported because the area is isolated and lightly populated. The life and lifestyles that dominate on the mainland are the straightforward and traditional means of making a living from the earth, and these folks tend to take care of their own when disaster strikes.

Agriculture, including huge timber plantations, forms the economic base of the mainland. This is big agriculture; the farms and plantings are vast, horizon to horizon in some places. It is no exaggeration to say that some of the homes along US 264 south of Lake Mattamuskeet have backyard "gardens"—tilled and planted with cash crops—that are 1/2 mile long, stretching from the back door to dense woods beyond. A tour de force of the county's history is captured in the Lake Landing National Register Historic District, so designated for its archetypical settlement patterns of family farms, churches, and commercial buildings. It comprises 13,400 acres and has only twenty-five buildings.

A necklace of traditional fishing villages laces the Pamlico Sound waters, and commercial fishing —particularly commercial crabbing—is an industry with a lot of small practitioners in the county. While this might seem obvious for Ocracoke, it is the crab fisheries of the Hyde County mainland at Stumpy Point, Engelhard, and Swan Quarter that are more substantial.

The Intracoastal Waterway skews across the county from a neck of the Alligator River in a southwest line north of Lake Mattamuskeet until it reaches the waters of the Pungo River. The passage is 20 miles long, the longest inland traverse of the waterway.

Tourism, mostly in the form of hunting and fishing, does play an increasing part in the mainland economy. It struggles somewhat because the county's attractions, fascinating local historic sites and four magnificent wildlife refuges, lack a broad-based marketing appeal. The county is somewhat off the beaten path, and there are no centers of population much larger than a village. In the classic chicken-and-egg dilemma, there are not a lot of restaurants and accommodations because there are not enough tourists, who may not visit because there are not a lot of restaurants and accommodations.

So how does Ocracoke Island fit with the rest of the county? Consider this: There are 634 square miles of land in Hyde County; Ocracoke may have 10 square miles. Ocracoke is both outnumbered and out of the way, but not out of mind. Ocracoke Village is one of the largest permanent communities in the county and accounts for nearly all of the county's tourism revenues.

Though always marching to its own beat, Ocracoke has more in common with the resort communities north of it than it does with the mainland. It is a natural and cultural extension of the barrier island chain, and the fundamental differences between island and mainland are a cause for civic strain. In recent years, Ocracoke has expressed the desire to leave Hyde County (it once was in Carteret County) and to join Dare County, which is not only physically closer but much more similar in character and economic base. In fact, Ocracoke receives marketing assistance from Dare County–based organizations (as well as Hyde County) for the simple reason that their customers perceive Ocracoke as part of the same tourism experience. This is logical both on a map and on the road.

Access

The National Park Service provides access on Ocracoke Island.

Handicapped Access

The Cape Hatteras National Seashore will loan a beach wheelchair. Contact the Ocracoke Visitors Center at 252-928-4531.

Information

For information, contact Greater Hyde County Chamber of Commerce, P.O. Box 178, Swan Quarter, NC 27855-0178, 252-926-9171, 888-493-3826; Mattamuskeet National Wildlife Refuge, 38 Mattamuskeet Road, Swan Quarter, NC 27855, 252-926-4021.

Web addresses: <www.hyde county.org>; <www.ocracoke island.com>; <www.outerbanks. org>; <http://mattamuskeet.fws. gov/>

Ocracoke Island

Ocracoke evokes both nostalgia and a sense of possession among those who have known the island for a number of years. I think it is because Ocracoke is fundamentally a simple place, seemingly naive to the guile, cunning, and commercialism that sometimes tarnish oceanfront destinations. The island is easy to comprehend, and it only asks (never outright, islanders are too polite) civility from its guests because that is the indispensable trait that enables a society to thrive for centuries in such an intimate setting.

Ocracoke's easygoing, tolerant personality is infectious. While the island presents a charming first impression, longer stays sharpen the focus on the local "quirks," such as goods or services assumed, but not available, the idiosyncratic power supply, and isolation from the world beyond the inlets. All these things add up to life on Ocracoke, which is different from everywhere else, and folks do just fine, thank you very much.

"It's like being at summer camp with lots of free time," said one visitor; "You can walk anywhere, do lots of things, and it's safe. All the pressure comes off when you're here."

How about that?

Summer camp memories can have a fierce hold on feelings about a place, so that when Ocracoke, like the barrier island itself, changes and adapts in order to survive, it is not always well received. There are folks who lament this inevitable alteration in the Ocracoke of their memory. They decry the improved access, discovery, and tourism. There are more specific complaints about new, nontraditional buildings, commercial enterprises catering to tourism, and traffic. The heart of the matter is edginess about the homogenization of Ocracoke Island, the sanding of its distinguishing elements to make it smooth and more convenient.

It will never become too smooth. The power will still go out arbitrarily, and it is possible to walk everywhere and let your children ride their bikes all over the island.

Or in the words of another first-time visitor, "it's like Key West without the weird."

The village remains an appealing counterpoint to the more driven beachfront communities to the north, but the number of tourists coming to this 16-mile-long spit of sand and wooded village creates a bit of tension. I confess a bit of wistful stir, a sense of loss about something that is not mine to lose.

The island includes 775 acres of private land surrounded by the Cape Hatteras National Seashore. The condemnation of land for the seashore did not go down well; however, it has probably been the central reason the island's character has remained intact.

Because there is little private land, the island is exclusive; because the island's ability to provide fresh water and dispose of waste is limited, it is likely to remain small and charming. Ocracoke will always be a distinctive village. More shops and hotels will probably come, the population will steadily grow, and some of the wonderful, insular, traditional ways of life may be tempered by the next generations, but the changes will occur on island time.

If this is your first visit, I suggest you arrive without any preconceived notions or schedules. Let the island unfold to you as you drive south, looking over your shoulder at the sea as it gnaws at the north end of the island, threatening the road. Let antsy drivers pass you, and look at what they miss. Cruise between the grassy flats and the

	Fee	Parking	Restrooms	Lifeguard	Camping	Showers	Beach Access	Hiking	Trail	Handicapped	Boating	ORV Access	Fishing	Programs	Historic	Sand Beach	Dunes	Upland	Wetland
Ocracoke Island		•	•	•	•	•	•	•	•	•	•	•	•	•	•	•	•	•	•
Ocracoke North End		•					•									•			
Ocracoke Pony Pen		•								•				•	•			•	•
Ocracoke Campground	•	•	•		•	•	•	•	•			•	•			•	•		
Ocracoke Day Use Area		•	•	•			•					•	•			•	•		
Southpoint Rd.												•	•			•	•		

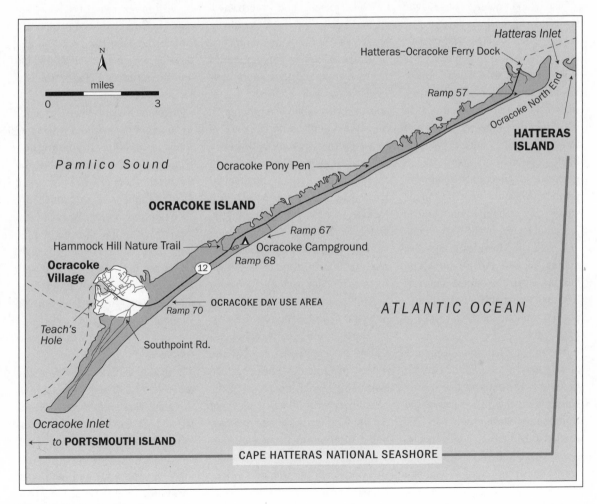

Map 13. Ocracoke Island

low overwash dune field, marking your passage by utility poles and occasional osprey nests.

Stop at the pony pen, cross the small creek at Six-Mile Hammock (6 miles from the village), and then drive slowly into town. Make your first visit a time to walk around to talk with residents. Talk about the weather, ask which fish are running and the best bait to buy, and listen to the wonderful islander pronunciation. You will pick up the richness quickly.

The island encompasses a wide prairielike grassland where the famed ponies once ran freely, gnarly live oak trees, and Teach's Hole, where Blackbeard died. There is the Ocracoke Lighthouse, the Coast Guard station, the British Sailors' Cemetery, the new Ocracoke trolley, and the old, reliable Community Store. There is the post office, the wonderful, rambling Island Inn, the magic woods of Springers Point, and a few patches where the old cement-and-shell road buckles. There are Scotch bonnets on the north end and mullet in the sound. There is first and foremost Howard Street, a place to walk along the dirt lane of bygone days.

No one can paint you a picture of what to expect at Ocracoke, for there is really nothing like it elsewhere. Visit the post office or the Community Store, walk past the wonderfully tended family cemeteries that snuggle in the middle of residential streets. When you step onto the island, you step into a community; you can experience

it, or you can look at the postcard views and read the guidebooks as you drive through.

Stephen P. Leatherman, director of Florida International University's Laboratory for Coastal Research, also known as "Dr. Beach," pegged Ocracoke third in the 2004 rankings of best beaches in the nation. I haven't seen the rest of them, but I will vouch for the wonderfully wide, all-natural apron of sand at the lifeguarded beach maintained by the park service. It is gorgeous.

Wide, clean, and uncrowded, for more than a mile to the north, there was nothing but footprints and a restricted-access shorebird nesting area, and then more, gorgeous open beach. To the south, was the off-road-vehicle beach with an astonishingly orderly crowd of beachgoers. Everyone in this ORV set parked at the same angle with their tailgates to the water, opened the back of their mobile beach tackle/swim/surf shop, and hit the water. From the pedestrian-beach vantage point, the cars looked so neat the beach might as well have been striped for parking.

At Ocracoke, the beach holds only the sky, dunes, and sea and, of course, communal beachgoers. There are no houses behind the dunes, no motels with seaside swimming pools, no streetlights. The beach is the beach, and except for the lifeguards, no one makes a living directly on the oceanfront. The village, in the wooded soundside portion of the island, is where people live and work. The separation brings home the fact that,

fundamentally, Ocracoke is an island of simple pleasures, mingled, to some extent, with history and a colorful personality.

Ocracoke is probably one of the most written-about locations in the state, beginning with Carl Goerch's *Ocracoke*, published in 1956, a descriptive and delightfully anecdotal book that is considered one of the classic works about the island at the beginning of the present era. *Ocracokers*, by Alton Ballance, unintentionally reads as a follow-up volume, bringing the story left dated in Goerch into contemporary times. Between the two, you can develop a rich feel for the island and the intimacy between the residents and the place.

It is not wise to visit Ocracoke in the summer without a ferry or room reservation. If you are day-tripping from Hatteras, note the ferry schedules and allow yourself plenty of time to line up for the return crossing. Remember also that the departure line may be $1/2$ mile long and in full sun while you wait. Of course, arrive too late, and well, the ferry dock is not the coolest place to sleep in summer, but you wouldn't be the first.

Access

The National Park Service maintains several beach access locations on Ocracoke. Ramps 59, 68, 70, and 72 provide vehicle access for the wet sand beach. There is a parking area at the ferry dock serving the north end and additional parking at Ramp 68 at the Ocracoke Campground. About 3 miles south is Ramp 70 at the Ocracoke airstrip (you'll know it by the wind sock). The beach between the two is closed to vehicles from Memorial Day to Labor Day. Lifeguards staff the swimming area at Ramp 70 during the summer months. From this ramp, it is about a 4.5-mile walk to the south end of the island and Ocracoke Inlet. The entire seashore is open to the public, but you are strongly advised to park only at designated parking spots or on a paved or hardened surface.

Handicapped Access

The Ocracoke Pony Pen has a parking turnout that is accessible to handicapped travelers.

The Ocracoke Island Visitors Center is accessible for handicapped travelers. The Ocracoke Beach turnout, Ramp 70, has a boardwalk leading over the primary dunes to an observation deck. Various private facilities have handicapped accommodations.

Information

I highly recommend that you do not plan to go to Ocracoke without either a hotel reservation for the night or a ferry reservation off the island.

For information about accommodations, contact Greater Hyde County Chamber of Commerce, P.O. Box 178, Swan Quarter, NC 27855-0178, 252-926-9171; Ocracoke Civic Club, P.O. Box 456, Ocracoke, NC 27960, 252-928-6711; Outer Banks Visitors Bureau, One Visitors Center Circle, Manteo, NC 27954, 252-473-2138, 877-629-4386; or Outer Banks Chamber

of Commerce, P.O. Box 1757, Kill Devil Hills, NC 27948, 252-441-8144.

For additional information, call the Ocracoke Island Visitors Center at 252-928-4531 or contact Superintendent, Cape Hatteras National Seashore, 1401 National Park Drive, Manteo, NC 27954, 252-473-2111.

Emergency numbers on Ocracoke Island: 252-928-4831 (fire and medical emergencies), 252-928-7301 (sheriff's office).

Web addresses: <www.hyde county.org>; <www.ocracoke island.com>; <www.outerbanks. org>; <www.nps.gov/caha/index. htm>; <http://reservations.nps. gov> (campground reservations)

Ocracoke North End

In September 2003 Hurricane Isabel washed over Ocracoke's north end, erased the dunes, and destroyed approximately two miles of highway. The road was quickly repaved, but the flattening of the protective dune line changed the landscape dramatically, and the drive south from the ferry dock seems eerily exposed. Even a year later, there was little more than a gentle rise in the sand between the highway and the ocean.

Because it is so distant from the village and close to the inlet, the north end of Ocracoke is a shelling hot spot, particularly following less severe storms than hurricanes that push shells higher on the beach. If it is possible to pull off

the road, do so and glean this less-walked beach. There is also an access area, Ramp 59 slightly south of the ferry dock, that gets you onto this beach that is also a good bet for fishing and bird-watching.

This end of the island stays wide, low, and flat, and in stormy weather the waves surge over the sandy spit and deposit shells from offshore and the intertidal zone. Here you are likely to find different species of mollusks than those found on Hatteras Island beaches. Angel wings, turkey wings, razor clams, and even some helmet-shell species turn up more frequently here. The state shell, the Scotch bonnet, begins to appear in profusion along Ocracoke's strand.

The island's latitude, orientation, and proximity to the Gulf Stream account for the shift to warmer-water molluscan species. The low-energy nature of the ocean, a generally gentle wave action, does not grind the shells up as severely as the ocean does north of Cape Hatteras. Early risers following storms get the best pick of shells, and you will certainly have much better luck in the winter months when there are fewer visitors competing for the same treasures.

Be sure to respect any roped-off areas set aside for shorebird nesting.

Access

Parking is available at the ferry docks, or you may park along the side of the road about 200 yards south of the ferry dock—the place is obvious.

The high-energy Outer Banks beaches churn up a superb mix of shells. Isolated beaches in winter provide the best shelling because fewer people are around. Courtesy of the author.

Seashell Serendipity

Shelling has nothing to do with looking and everything to do with just being there, pretending you're not looking, strolling the beach, casual-like. You successfully stalk the perfect sand dollar or the pristine Scotch bonnet not when you're looking for one but when it's your turn to find one. Shelling is a sport out of your control; all you can do is go to the court and hope someone shows up with the ball.

It is serendipity; it is half-buried treasure. This is why we all do it, this and the fact that it is without a doubt one of the few glorious, free, money-back-guaranteed things left to do.

Shelling is especially fine between Cape Hatteras and Cape Lookout for two reasons: there is a confluence of currents that brings together a large number of different shell fauna that normally do not live in the same waters, and most important, there's more beach with fewer people.

On the first reason: The cold waters of the Labrador Current slink down the eastern seaboard. As they do, they bring along a drift of cold-water fauna such as the surf clam, the quahog, and the knobbed whelk, its left-handed look-alike, the lightning whelk, and their smooth cousin, the channel whelk. Shellers find these regularly between the Virginia border and Cape Hatteras.

Hop the ferry to Ocracoke, and you may pick up some southern fauna such as the angel wings, the giant murex, the heavily armored helmet shell, the giant tun, and of course, the Scotch bonnet, the official seashell of North Carolina. (I ran into a Scotch bonnet bonanza one winter's day at the north end of Ocracoke!) These shells and others are rare finds farther north.

The shell fauna mixing bowl is off of the North Carolina capes. Colliding currents that originated in different latitudes bring their resident seafloor life with them. The Labrador Current brings seafloor "snowbirds" south, while the Gulf Stream ushers semitropical-water shells north. Everybody meets and mixes at the salient of Cape Hatteras. If you think it is a tough corner for ships, try it underwater at a snail's pace, so to speak. Hatteras is where shelling fortunes, not shells, make the turn.

Nearly 1,300 species of mollusk have left their calling cards along the Outer Banks, so you are likely to discover a personal-first find on any hard-working, shelling trip—unless you have been shelling for a long time. Almost any foray on the beach, particularly in winter, is going to bring an unusual discovery.

Why winter? Mainly because the typically stormy seas during that season deposit more shells where you may find them. Also, fewer people visit the beach this time of year to pick over the shells. Pick an isolated stretch of beach following a February storm, and not only is it all yours, but the shelling can be phenomenal.

Summer tactics have to be different, except for the timing—after a storm is still best. The best shelling is where there are the least people or where there is no easy access. The north end of Ocracoke is probably the most easily accessible bountiful location, year in and year out, for the mix of shells from north and south. If the surf's edge fails to yield a prize, glean the sand-blown overwash flats landward of the surf zone. The more adventuresome you are, the richer the reward. Hire a boat in Ocracoke to guide you to Portsmouth Island, just across Ocracoke Inlet. This scarcely visited part of Cape Lookout National Seashore is one of the undersearched areas for shells or other flotsam. Farther south, Core and Shackleford Banks, also part of Cape Lookout, offer the greatest likelihood of successful shelling because of fewer visitors. But shelling following a storm has one disadvantage—wave damage. The systems that beach so many shells in these locations beat them up pretty badly as well. You'll find a shelling bounty on Core Banks, but you'll turn over many a shattered part while looking for the select whole shell.

Other locations that should reward an off-season look are Hammocks Beach State Park near Swansboro, Masonboro Island south of Wrightsville Beach, and Fort Fisher State Recreation Area south of Kure Beach. As you move closer to Cape Fear along the barrier islands, the possibility of finding the delicate sand dollars, sea biscuits, and keyhole urchins increases, primarily due to the comparatively gentle slope of the beach and the generally lower wave energy, which allows these shells to wash up intact.

The North Carolina Aquariums at Roanoke Island, Pine Knoll Shores, and Fort Fisher have representative shells (both occupied and empty) on display. *Seashells of North Carolina*, a guidebook, is available from the University of North Carolina Sea Grant Program, 105 1911 Building, North Carolina State University, Raleigh, NC 27650. The booklet may also be obtained from the North Carolina Maritime Museum in Beaufort.

Web address: <www.ncseagrant. org>

Ocracoke Pony Pen

Unlike their cousins north of Corolla, the Ocracoke ponies live in a fenced pasture, which prevents them from wandering across the highway. The National Park Service feeds them daily and sees that a veterinarian is called when needed, something that was impossible when the animals roamed wild in the late 1950s and early 1960s.

The ponies are direct descendants of Spanish mustangs and are anatomically distinct—having a different number of vertebrae—from horses that came from English-speaking countries. Given the turbulent nature of the Outer Banks ocean passage, it seems likely that a shipwreck brought the first ponies to the island, but it is not known when this occurred. The ponies thrived. At one time, there were several hundred roaming free on the island, and each year there was a pony penning and auction.

Islanders have long used the ponies. The U.S. Life-Saving Service trained them to haul boats on the beach, and some ponies were harnessed to buggies. In the 1950s there was even a mounted Boy Scout troop on the island that lassoed, trained, and cared for their horses.

Small, lithe, and durable, the ponies roam free within the confines of their enclosure, which secures several miles of rich grassland and freshwater sources. A marker at the pen, which is located on the west side of NC 12, details what is known about their origin and remarkable physiology.

Hurricane Isabel caused the death of one pony and severely damaged the outbuildings and the enclosure. As of 2004, there are twenty-four ponies, which is within the carrying capacity of the management plan.

Access
There is parking at the pen. The horses are fed daily at approximately 8:30 A.M. and 6 P.M., which you are invited to watch.

Handicapped Access
The parking area at the pen accommodates handicapped travelers.

Information
For information, call the Ocracoke Island Visitors Center at 252-928-4531; or contact Superintendent, Cape Hatteras National Seashore, 1401 National Park Drive, Manteo, NC 27954, 252-473-2111.

Ocracoke Campground

Ocracoke Campground is on the east side of NC 12, 3 miles north of the village of Ocracoke. It is the only National Park Service campground that will take reservations. There is a $20 fee per night per campsite, and the campgrounds are open mid-spring to mid-fall. There are 130 tent and trailer spaces but no utility hookups. The campground has a bathhouse with cold showers, restrooms, drinking water, and a dumping station. The campsites are windy and bare, and there is no shade. Long tent stakes are advised, since Ocracoke can be the windiest of the campgrounds.

The campground offers ample access to the wide sandy beaches of the island. In the past, the beach had a lifeguard, but now lifeguards are on duty during the summer only at the beach at Ramp 70 farther south. Ramp 68 provides access to the beach here, but the beach south from this ramp is closed to vehicular traffic from Memorial Day to Labor Day. There is also a self-guided nature trail that leads through an ecological cross section of the island.

Access

Check-in time is noon. If you reserve a campsite, the park service will hold it until 8 A.M. the next day. Better call if you will miss the 8 A.M. deadline.

This is a good place to hit the beach, but it is more or less set aside for campers.

Information

For additional information, call the Ocracoke Island Visitors Center at 252-928-4531; or contact Superintendent, Cape Hatteras National Seashore, 1401 National Park Drive, Manteo, NC 27954, 252-473-2111.

Web addresses: <www.nps.gov/caha/index.htm>; <http://reservations.nps.gov>

Ocracoke Beach

Ocracoke Beach is the main public beach maintained by the National Park Service. The paved parking area is on the left, plainly signed as you approach the outskirts of the village.

This is tip-top beach, with a beautiful sand berm and a gently sloping gradient into the water. It is also long. From the parking area the walk southwest to Ocracoke Inlet is approximately 5 miles; Hatteras Inlet is about 10 miles to the northeast. If you are willing to hike, there is plenty of room for isolation, but not much for privacy since the dune field (in 2004) was at least 100 yards from the water's edge.

On hot summer days, the clean fine sand can be extremely hot, so bring shoes or beach sandals.

There is a bathhouse and showers. The National Park Service provides lifeguards at the beach during the summer. The parking lot is closed at night.

Beach rules are posted at the parking area, but a reminder of the most important: no fires on the beach; pets must be kept on leashes; and stay out of the areas clearly marked for shorebird nesting. Oh, and keep your swimsuit on.

Ramp 70 Access Area

Slightly north of Ocracoke Village, you will find Ramp 70, also known as the airport ramp since the Ocracoke airstrip is nearby. The parking lot is in a low area known as the plains. It is open year-round and is the only convenient crossing if you want to spend the day at Ocracoke Inlet. The inlet is approximately 5 miles south of the ramp, accessible by foot or four-wheel-drive vehicle.

The beachfront to the south is isolated, and bathers or shellers seldom visit. Keep your clothes on though. The south beach has a well-deserved reputation for nude sunbathing—it's common knowledge, accepted by residents of this live and let live island. The park service used to look the other way, so to speak, but enforcement priorities have changed, and nude sunbathers could get burned more ways than one.

The south beaches are sometimes the location for nesting sites of pelagic turtles, as well as certain bird species that lay their eggs in shallow depressions in the sand, such as the piping plover or the least tern. During such times, the beach is posted, and you must confine your vehicle to the wet sand beach. There is often excellent fishing on the spit of sand that curls into Ocracoke Inlet at the south end.

Access
Parking is first-come, first-served.

Handicapped Access
This parking turnout allows you to drive as close to the water as any location on Ocracoke. There is a boardwalk leading over the primary dunes to an observation deck.

Information
For information, call the Ocracoke Island Visitors Center at 252-928-4531; or contact Superintendent, Cape Hatteras National Seashore, 1401 National Park Drive, Manteo, NC 27954, 252-473-2111.

Southpoint Road

South of the turn for the Ocracoke airstrip and nearly opposite the Café Atlantic Restaurant and Bar is Southpoint Road, the sand road leading to the southern point of the island. Also known as Ramp 72, this 3-mile route is suitable for four-wheel-drive vehicles only.

The southern point at Ocracoke Inlet is a terrific location for shelling and fishing, and there are usually fewer people there. Pack a cooler and picnic lunch and go explore wildest, remotest Ocracoke.

Ocracoke Village

A bend in the highway, the flag of the post office, and $1/2$ mile of restaurants, hotels, and other businesses announce Ocracoke Village. The speed limit is reduced to 25 miles per hour at the outskirts of town; the landmark to look for is the sheriff's office and post office on the left side of the highway. Mind the speed reduction immediately; the road is busy and so are the sheriff and his deputies.

This commercial spillover from the village core has been inevitable, and the businesses stay quite busy serving the increasing numbers of visitors to the island. Several of the establishments, True Value Hardware, Ocracoke Variety Store, Jason's Restaurant, and Howard's Pub, are busy all year. Ocracoke Village proper is on the soundside of the island, at the highest location above sea level, rimming the basin known to locals as "the Creek" and to others as Silver Lake. While the village is on "high" ground, it does not take a lot of imagination to understand how this is a relative term. The most telling observation about permanent residency on Ocracoke is that very few buildings are on ground level. The restaurants and hotels on the outskirts of town are at least $1/2$ story above ground. This is true of many of the older homes on the island.

(In the summer of 2004, Hurricane Alexis brushed past the island and sent three feet of water surging inland from Pamlico Sound. More than 300 vehicles belonging to vacationers were flooded; many were ruined and had to be abandoned when a mandatory evacuation of nonresidents followed the storm's passing.)

The village is bicycle-size and if you do not bring your own, most hotels have them for hire. It is easier to explore the island on a bike because many of the narrow streets are private residential lanes that end at a residence, and generally, parking spaces are at a premium. In fact, on summer evenings, put your car key in your pocket. After dinner, pedestrians and cyclists take over Silver Lake Road and Irvin Garrish Highway (NC 12), strolling/riding around the lake, walking the winding streets to the ferry dock and back. At this time of night, cars are an exercise in self-frustration; too big a pain to bother with. It's far more fun and friendlier to walk and watch the "Dingbatters," a traditional (long before the 1970s sitcom *All in the Family*) Ocracoke term for people who do something sublimely oblivious, such as riding their bike in the middle of the highway as traffic piles behind them. On summer evenings, Dingbatters flock to the roads like moths to a light, and so it is easier to join them or walk well to the side of the road for that after-dinner ice cream.

NC 12 loops at the dock where ferries serve Swan Quarter and Cedar Island. In the center of the large loop of pavement at the ferry dock

	Fee	Parking	Restrooms	Lifeguard	Camping	Showers	Beach Access	Hiking	Trail	Handicapped	Boating	ORV Access	Fishing	Programs	Historic	Sand Beach	Dunes	Upland	Wetland
Ocracoke Village	•	•						•		•	•		•		•			•	•
Ocracoke Lighthouse		•								•				•	•			•	
British Sailors' Cemetery		•													•				
Ocracoke Island Visitors Center		•	•							•	•			•	•				
Ocracoke Ferry		•	•																

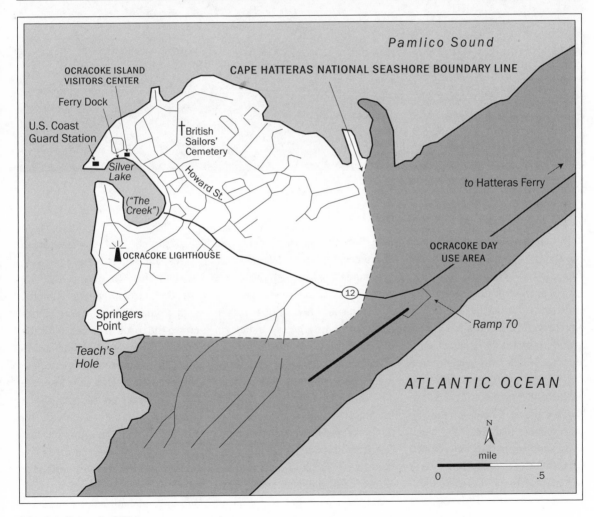

Map 14. Ocracoke Village

Ocracoke Village. Courtesy of North Carolina Travel and Tourism.

is the National Park Service Office and Interpretive Center for the Cape Hatteras National Seashore, a small picnic area in a lovely grove of cedar trees, and an old family cemetery. Adjacent the ferry dock is the retired U.S. Coast Guard Station, which was constructed in 1934 and which is now used by the state of North Carolina as the North Carolina Center for the Advancement of Teaching.

On your way to the loop, you will pass the Community Store, one of two year-round bread-and-butter stops of the island (the other is the Ocracoke Variety Store), various specialty retailers, and dock-side shops that serve as fishing and charter centers for the island. There are numerous intriguing shops, eateries, and places to stay. At present, Ocracoke shows a healthy balance in its retail and restaurant offerings between those serving a traditional economy and those more closely aligned with tourism. The shops are interesting; the homogenization of merchandise at the lowest common denominator of beach retail is not happening. (Yes, there are Ocracoke-appropriate tee shirts, kites, and useful things like folding beach umbrellas.)

Off the main roads, the side streets are more like winding paths that thread past homes, small stores, and family cemeteries side by side, where they happened long ago. Cedar trees, live oaks, yaupon, and grape-tangled young pines crowd the roads in places, partially screening the modest homes behind their evergreen drapery. The salt spray shears the tops from the few large trees on the island—the largest live oaks seem to be on Howard Street—and the gnarled and wild limbs seem to press the houses down into the soft gray sand with an effect both mysterious and enchanting. In summer, the houses are bright with flowers. The side streets lead to places like

Albert Styron's General Store on Lighthouse Drive, a building disassembled and moved here. It is now on the National Register of Historic Places and still has the atmosphere of a 1920s general store. Across the island is Ocracoke Coffee on Back Road, the place for starting your day with a pastry and a cup of wake up. Ocracoke Coffee is one of the new wave of ventures that is meeting a need while fitting in with the independent spirit of Ocracoke.

A bike is not mandatory because the village is easily walked and lovely for that, whether in the morning to find coffee or at dusk to catch sunset beyond Silver Lake. Mosquitoes might keep you company at night, but they are not unbearable. A dab of insect repellent will serve well.

Settlers first arrived at Ocracoke in the early eighteenth century, when Silver Lake was indeed a creek. Ocracoke Inlet to the south has been continuously open since recorded history, longer in fact than any other in the state. The town's early commerce swelled with the maritime, mercantile economy that passed through the inlet to mainland ports. Deep-draft oceangoing ships could not sail very far into Pamlico Sound, and so they would anchor to unload their cargo to shallow-draft ships that then continued to mainland ports, a process called "lightering," as in making the vessel lighter. In the nineteenth century, when Ocracoke received designation as a port with a permanent crew of pilots, the village began its steady growth. In fact, the town was originally called Pilot Town. Not all pilots lived here, however. Some lived in Hatteras and, according to Outer Banks historian David Stick, would walk to work (before Hatteras Inlet opened, of course).

Ocracoke Inlet, by the way, is dependable but not deep, certainly not deep enough to hide a submarine as Tom Clancy suggests in *The Hunt for Red October.*

The Ocracoke Lighthouse is the most visible reminder of this early mercantile era, and its longevity matches that of the inlet, having been in continuous use longer than any other on the coast. Other major players in the village history were the U.S. Life-Saving Service in the late nineteenth century, followed by the U.S. Coast Guard. In fact, in one way or another, government has always been prominent here. During World War II, the navy dredged the creek and created the ferry dock and transportation system, and following the military's departure, the park service became the largest landholder on the island in the 1950s.

Today, tourism, real estate, and fishing are the big businesses in the village. Tourism is not new, but it is building, and more islanders rely on it. The restaurants are staffed with island college-age kids who go off to school, glad to get away, but knowing they will likely come back. A bustling restaurant business thrives around the lake and on the main road into town. Howard's Pub is a landmark, celebrated because it never closes, regardless of the weather (it has its own generator). Across the street is Jason's, which has outstanding pizza and a flair for local fresh fish. The best breakfast on the island is the Pony Island Restaurant, next to, but not associated with, The Pony Island Motel. It has first-come, first-served seating, and if you sleep until 8:30 A.M., you will be waiting in line to have breakfast there.

Ocracoke has always been a tight little island (permanent population of approximately 700), but now it is much tighter in summer.

Access

The closest beach access is Ocracoke Beach on the outskirts of town.

You may park at the lot next to the Ocracoke Island Visitors Center, and there is limited pullover parking on the island, which you may use as long as you do not block travel lanes or access to boat slips or launches.

The park service maintains Silver Lake Marina, 400 feet of dock space at the park service headquarters. There is no dockage fee. If you find a place open, simply tie up. There is a 14-day limit during the summer months.

Handicapped Access

The Boyette House and the Silver Lake Motel are the only accommodations that advertise handicapped facilities. Some of the rental cottages accommodate handicapped travelers.

Information

For information about accommodations, contact Greater Hyde County Chamber of Commerce, P.O. Box 178, Swan Quarter, NC 27855, 252-926-9171; Ocracoke Civic Club, P.O. Box 456, Ocracoke, NC 27960, 252-928-6711; Outer Banks Visitors Bureau, One Visitors Center Circle, Manteo, NC 27954, 252-473-2138, 877-629-4386; or Outer Banks Chamber of Commerce, P.O. Box 1757, Kill Devil Hills, NC 27948, 252-441-8144.

The Ocracoke Civic Club publishes a directory and map with excellent listings of accommodations and features; the club also maintains an answering machine to take incoming calls.

For information about park programs, call the Ocracoke Island Visitors Center at 252-928-4531; or contact Superintendent, Cape Hatteras National Seashore, 1401 National Park Drive, Manteo, NC 27954, 252-473-2111.

Web addresses: <www.hyde county.org>; <www.ocracoke island.com>; <www.outerbanks. org>

Ocracoke Lighthouse

The Ocracoke Lighthouse has been in operation since 1823, making it the oldest continually operating lighthouse in North Carolina and, after the Sandy Hook Lighthouse in New Jersey, the second oldest in the United States. To reach the Ocracoke Lighthouse, turn off of NC 12 onto the road that passes in front of the Island Inn. A little over $1/4$ mile down the road, you will come to the lighthouse, surrounded by a picket fence nearly as famous as the lighthouse itself.

The squat white tower is modest by the standards of the other lighthouses on the Outer Banks. A mere 75 feet tall, with 5-foot-thick walls, the focal plane of the light is at 65 feet. Its steady white beacon is visible 14 miles at sea, signaling safe harbor. It was one of four lighthouses authorized by Congress in the late eighteenth century, along with Cape Hatteras, Cape Lookout, and the Baldhead light at the mouth of the Cape Fear River. The purchase for the original one-acre lot was voided because the construction did not begin before 1801, as specified in the contract of sale. The existing two-acre site was purchased in 1822 for $50 from Jacob Gaskill, a member of a family still prominent on the island today, and this time construction proceeded immediately.

At the time of construction, the light guided mariners to the entrance to the only reliable inlet north of Cape Lookout. The reach of Diamond Shoals at Hatteras made the Ocracoke light doubly important. A ship sailing north around the Outer Banks that could see the light at Ocracoke would know it was on a collision course with the shoals. It could then tack to the east, riding the Gulf Stream current north as it makes its natural curl around Cape Hatteras.

The lightkeeper's quarters, constructed at the same time as the light, is currently in use as the residence of a National Park Service ranger.

Access

The lighthouse is presently undergoing renovation and is not open to the public, but the grounds are. The restoration is expected to take several years.

Handicapped Access

The lighthouse grounds are negotiable by handicapped travelers.

Information

For information, call the Ocracoke Island Visitors Center at 252-928-4531; or contact Superintendent, Cape Hatteras National Seashore, 1401 National Park Drive, Manteo, NC 27954, 252-473-2111.

Silver Lake

One of the most scenic basins you are likely to see as you travel this coast or any other, Silver Lake is the tidal basin and harbor of Ocracoke, the central body of water that serves the town. Natives refer to it as "the Creek." If you arrive by ferry, you pass the former U.S. Coast Guard Station on the north side of the entrance, a shrubby spoils area, and some private residences on the south. Before you, nearly dead center at the east end of the basin, is the shingled roof of the Island Inn, one block away. The

Ocracoke Lighthouse peeks above the trees to the southeast.

Arriving by car from Hatteras, you first see Silver Lake through a framing of small dock houses, trees, and private homes on the southwest horizon. It is an approach that is best timed for sunset.

The dredged and bulwarked entrance to the basin, the only way in and out, is deep enough to serve the ferries and Coast Guard vessels. Before World War II, the Creek was a very shallow tidal basin, according to some accounts about the same size but not more than 4–5 feet deep. The navy, which had an extensive base on the island to monitor German submarine activity in nearby "Torpedo Junction," dredged the basin during World War II. The bulwarks were added because the larger vessels that use the Creek create a wake that causes erosion.

If you awaken early, before the sun rises high, and stroll around the basin, or do the same at sunset, you will see gulls on pilings, mullet and menhaden skipping over the water, and the low-gunnel, high-prow wooden fishing boats designed to ride the sound waters safely while their captains work—photographs waiting to be taken against the backdrop of waterside buildings.

Nobody will tell you not to wade in Silver Lake, and nobody will mind you taking your children crabbing or fishing here either.

There are several marinas here; private docks are plainly marked.

British Sailors' Cemetery

One part of Ocracoke Island, the British Sailors' Cemetery, is not privately held nor does it belong to the Cape Hatteras National Seashore. It belongs to the United Kingdom, a legacy of the war that shattered these peaceful shores during the 1940s.

In 1942 German submarines operated practically unchecked off of the Outer Banks, and by the end of April 1942, they had sent sixty-six vessels rounding the point at Cape Hatteras to the bottom. The region became known as Torpedo Junction. Unprepared for submarine warfare, the United States suffered tremendous losses as the U-boats operated with impunity.

The United Kingdom responded by sending experienced crews and antisubmarine vessels to the Outer Banks. One of the ships was the HMS *Bedfordshire*, a 170-foot-long converted commercial fishing vessel. The *Bedfordshire* reported at Ocracoke with four officers and thirty-three crewmembers and began patrolling east of the island.

On May 11, 1942, in the ship's second full month of patrol, the *Bedfordshire* was torpedoed, and all crew members were lost. Within three days, two bodies washed ashore and were identified by islanders as British sailors Thomas Cunningham and Stanly Craig. The Williams family donated the land adjacent to their family cemetery as a burial site for the two

men. A week later, two more bodies, dressed in similar clothes but not identifiable, came ashore and were placed in the same cemetery.

The small cemetery is beside British Cemetery Road about one block beyond the west end of Howard Street. Back Road also intersects with British Cemetery Road. You may visit the cemetery any time. The British War Graves Commission and the U.S. Coast Guard maintain the graves. The flag of the United Kingdom, the Union Jack, flies above the graves. The British government sends a new flag each year. Every spring a memorial service is held to commemorate the loss of these and other sailors during World War II.

A plaque on the cemetery fence quotes Rupert Brooke's poem, "The Soldier": "If I should die, think only this of me: / That there's some corner of a foreign field / That is forever England."

A repeating broadcast detailing the history of the events leading up to the interment and the cemetery may be heard by tuning an AM radio to frequency 1590.

Teach's Hole

The dense maritime forest on Ocracoke Island's east side, Springers Point, faces a shallow indentation and navigable channel known as Teach's Hole, the snug harbor of the infamous Edward Teach, or Blackbeard, during the early eighteenth century.

Virginia's royal governor Alexander Spotswood, perceiving Blackbeard and his fellow pirates as a threat, sent Lieutenant Robert Maynard and two sloops south to trap Teach in his current port of call, Ocracoke. They found Teach in this very haven, and Teach was beheaded during hand-to-hand combat by Maynard's boarding party. Several of Maynard's men were killed in the costly fight, but all of the pirate's band were killed or captured and hanged later. Legend has it that Teach's body circled his grounded ship seven times before it sank. Teach's head made one last sailing trip, mounted on the bowsprit of Maynard's sloop, as it returned to the mainland as confirmation of his death. Apparently, the secret of the location of the hiding place of Teach's buried plunder died with him. It is allegedly still on the island.

In a great underwater archaeological coup, the wreck of Edward Teach's flagship, *The Queen Anne's Revenge*, has been discovered and confirmed just outside Beaufort Inlet. The ship was sailed there following Blackbeard's death. The North Carolina Maritime Museum exhibits several artifacts from the ship and future archaeological dives are bound to yield more that will be put on display at the museum.

Access

You can reach Teach's Hole by boat or by a long walk along the sound beach from the south jetty of the cut. You have to cross private property to reach the wooded portion of the island overlooking Teach's Hole. Request permission before you do.

Ocracoke Island Visitors Center

The Ocracoke Island Visitors Center is opposite the toll ferry dock and provides information about the Cape Hatteras National Seashore and the village of Ocracoke. During the summer season, the center bustles with activity. If you disembark the ferry with little or no idea of what to do, then go to the center. The helpful staff will give you information about attractions and locations on the island or elsewhere in the seashore.

Most important, the visitors center and its small outdoor amphitheater are the hub for many of the interpretive programs about Ocracoke. A full schedule of events is posted for these activities, which usually begin in mid-June and continue until Labor Day. Programs target various ages, and children usually find most of them enjoyable. In past years, the programs have included morning bird walks, cast net fishing demonstrations, exhibitions on pirates, and historical presentations on Ocracoke. Participants in certain limited programs such as soundside snorkeling are chosen by drawing names out of a hat.

The center also provides maps and various materials on both Cape Hatteras and Cape Lookout National Seashore. Information on the availability of campsites is also provided upon request. There are also restrooms at the center.

Access

The center is open during the summer from 9 A.M. to 6 P.M. daily. After Labor Day, the schedule varies. There is parking at the center.

Handicapped Access

The center is accessible to handicapped travelers.

Information

For information, call the visitors center at 252-928-4531; or contact the Superintendent, Cape Hatteras National Seashore, 1401 National Park Drive, Manteo, NC 27954, 252-473-2111.

Ocracoke Preservation Society Museum

For a quicker take on the island, visit the Ocracoke Preservation Society Museum next to the ferry dock parking lot. The renovated house of U.S. Coast Guard captain David Williams, circa 1900, houses the museum. The building itself is a preservation case in point, having been moved from its original site where the Anchorage Inn now stands.

The museum seeks to preserve elements of Ocracoke's traditional way of life, including the remarkable "Ocracoke brogue" reminiscent of dialects spoken in the south and west of England—300 years ago. By far and away, one of the more enjoyable and entertaining exhibits is a repeating video, "The Ocracoke Brogue," the outgrowth of a ten-year-long linguistics study involving nearly 100 island residents from ages 10 to 91. It is a joy to watch and probably one of the best chances to hear one of the island's treasures, which is its manner of speech. "O'cokers," as residents call themselves, are more inclined to free and easy traditional speech between each other than in front of guests. The video captures some delightful exchanges that need a careful listening to understand. Some of the takeaways from the video include "Dingbatter," generally a nonnative who is oblivious or lacking in commonsense; "quamish," meaning sick to the stomach; and "meehonkey," a form of hide and seek.

There is also a reference library upstairs.

The museum staff is delightful. I witnessed a humorous exchange between the docent and a breathless tourist who "needed directions to the airport."

The docent politely told her to "take the highway, and the airport will be on your right."

"Which way do I turn on the highway?" the tourist asked.

"Well it only goes one way," said the docent, adding, "it dead ends to the right." (The museum is adjacent to the ferry dock loading area.)

"I'm not from around here," said the tourist, a bit chippy.

The docent smiled a "Do tell" smile and reaffirmed directions

to what she later called Ocracoke International.

Access

The museum is open from Easter to November. Summer hours are Monday–Friday, 10 A.M. to 5 P.M.; Saturday and Sunday, 11 A.M. to 4 P.M. Admission is free.

Handicapped Access

The museum is not easily accessible for handicapped travelers.

Information

For information, contact the Ocracoke Preservation Society, P.O. Box 491, Ocracoke Island, NC 27960, 252-928-7375.

Web address: <www.ocracoke museum.org>

Ocracoke to Portsmouth Island

Across Ocracoke Inlet lies Portsmouth Island, part of North Core Banks, which is in the Cape Lookout National Seashore. Ocracoke is the closest point of departure for visiting what is rightfully called "the only ghost town on the East Coast," the historic, restored village of Portsmouth (see Portsmouth Island in the next chapter). Visiting Portsmouth is a unique outing because, more than any other trip that can be made on the Outer Banks, it offers the most accurate duplication of living on the Outer Banks before the modern era. It is an unmatchable day trip, not necessarily one of creature comfort

because the environment—heat, humidity, and insects—can be absolutely daunting, nearly hostile. Yet this is the way people lived on Portsmouth.

The National Park Service licenses individuals and businesses to operate ferry services to the island. The Ocracoke Island Visitors Center will have information on the options for making the trip to Portsmouth. One local option offers a slice of Outer Banks life. For many years, the Austin family has ferried visitors to Portsmouth in their sturdy boats, dropped them off for several hours of exploration, and returned them across the inlet. Captain Rudy Austin carries on the tradition, running daily round-trips in the summer and by appointment in the off-season. Call at least one day in advance for reservations, 252-928-4361 or 252-928-5431. Portsmouth Island ATV Excursions, 252-928-4484, provides guided tours of the island and Portsmouth Village on ATVs from April through November.

Both of these vendors are official National Park Service concessionaires in accordance with U.S. Coast Guard regulations for providing public transportation to the island. Be sure to take insect repellent, sunscreen, and something to drink with you. If you are going fishing, take plenty of everything, including comfortable shoes. You will walk a fair distance when you reach Portsmouth.

Information

For information on local ferry services, stop by the Ocracoke Island Visitors Center or call the center at 252-928-4531.

Ocracoke Toll Ferry

The North Carolina Department of Transportation operates two ferry routes connecting Ocracoke Island to the mainland. One route crosses northwest across Pamlico Sound to the village of Swan Quarter, the county seat of Hyde County, Ocracoke's parent county. The other route crosses southwest to Cedar Island in Carteret County; various connections then lead to the beaches of Cape Lookout National Seashore, as well as to Carteret County's resort beaches. Both rides will transport you to new and different types of exploration of North Carolina's coast.

Disembarking from the Cedar Island ferry is the beginning of the Outer Banks travel experience for many travelers (which means you'll have to read this book backward); others arrive at the ferry at Ocracoke as the southern terminus of their vacation.

The Ocracoke–Swan Quarter ferry primarily serves traffic to the seat of county government. Accordingly, the schedule is more constant during the year. Between May 25 and September 6, there are three departures from Ocracoke daily, at 6:30 A.M., 12:30 P.M., and 4:00 P.M. Departures from Swan Quarter to Ocracoke are at 7:00 A.M., 9:30 A.M., and 4:00 P.M. From September 7 until May 23, there are two departures daily from Ocracoke at 6:30 A.M. and 12:30 P.M. and two from Swan Quarter at 9:30 A.M. and 4:00 P.M. The ride takes approximately 2½ hours. Reservations are always best.

The Cedar Island ferry operates a seasonal schedule. Between May 25 and September 27, there are nine daily departures each from Ocracoke and Cedar Island, beginning at 7:00 A.M., with the final daily departure at 8:30 P.M. From April 6 through May 24 and September 28 through November 8, there are only six daily departures from each dock, beginning at 7:00 A.M. and ending at 8:30 P.M. From November 9 through April 5 there are four daily departures from each port, beginning at 7:00 A.M. and ending at 4:00 P.M. The ride takes 2¼ hours.

The name of the driver and the license plate number of the vehicle making the crossing must be given when making reservations. Reservations must be claimed at least 30 minutes prior to departure and are not transferable. It is strongly advised to be on time for all departures. The cost is $15 for a passenger car under 20 feet long, $30 for larger vehicles or combinations, $3 for bicyclists, and $1 for pedestrians.

Information

Do not go to Ocracoke without either a hotel reservation or a ferry reservation off the island. This cannot be stressed enough. Reservations may be made up to one year in advance by calling the Swan Quarter terminal at 800-773-1094 or 252-926-1111, or the Cedar Island terminal at 800-856-0343 or 252-225-3551. The telephone number at the Ocracoke terminal is 800-345-1665 or 252-928-3841. For general information on all ferries, locations, and departures call 800-BY-FERRY (800-293-3779).

Web address: <www.ncferry.org>

Swan Quarter

A ferry from Ocracoke transports you to Swan Quarter, the historic seat of Hyde County. Swan Quarter is one of the finest stops you can make with an empty cooler and a taste for fresh seafood. It is a commercial fishing village that is practically surrounded by Swan Quarter National Wildlife Refuge, and just a few miles northeast is the magnificent Mattamuskeet National Wildlife Refuge. The departure from the ferry sends you through a forested, then agricultural setting to bring you into downtown Swan Quarter. Turn south and the road will take you to where the shrimping and crabbing fleets dock. The folks will gladly sell to anyone with an empty cooler to fill for the ride home.

The road from the ferry dock leads into Swan Quarter sideways. The town is small and dignified and will be a long time recovering from the assault of Hurricane Isabel. At the corner of NC 45 and SR 1129, the main street of the small town, stands the Hyde County Courthouse, listed in the National Register of Historic Places. Handsome, modest homes line the streets of this residential community, many of them elevated dramatically since Isabel's visit. One of the most striking features is the massive loblolly pines on the north side of the community, along SR 1129, which leads northeast to US 264.

Several churches front SR 1129, including Providence United Methodist Church, located at the corner of Main and Church Streets. Known locally as the "church moved by the hand of God," this church is the subject of one of the more intriguing legends of the area. The story has it that after the congregation's offer to purchase a building site was refused by a landowner, they built a wood frame church on brick piers elsewhere. On the day of the building's dedication, a terrible flood struck Swan Quarter (which is only 10 feet above sea level) and lifted the church from its piers, floated it down the street and around a corner, and dropped it smack in the middle of the lot originally selected. The previously reluctant owner took the hint and deeded the land to the congregation. The church, however, is struggling to remain open and may in fact be abandoned.

Swan Quarter was first settled in early 1836 when it became the county seat. It is believed that the town is named for Samuel Swann and was originally called Swann's Quarter, where "quarter" referred to a division of land. It was incorporated in 1903 but repealed the charter in 1929.

Information

For information, contact Greater Hyde County Chamber of Commerce, P.O. Box 178, Swan Quarter, NC 27855-0178, 252-926-9171, 888-493-3826.

Web addresses: <www.hyde county.org>; <www.ocracoke island.com>

A Slice of Island Life

North Carolina's barrier islands are neither all one place nor all alike. There can be several different environments on any island, and each is the home for its own group of dwellers. Not all islands have all possible barrier island environments or have them in the same proportion as a percentage of the total island.

If there were such a thing as a "typical" North Carolina barrier island and you walked from sea to sound, you would probably see the following environments and might see what makes a home there.

Beach

There are two parts to a beach, the foreshore, which is the beach covered by the tides, and the backshore, beyond the reach of the tides but not part of the dunes. You spread your towel on the backshore and splash in the foreshore.

The foreshore is a high-energy environment (for animals and children), where the tides rearrange the sands daily. Wave action makes for a challenging environment, so only a few creatures call the foreshore home. Two of my favorites are the brightly colored coquina clam and the mole crab. Each brings a smile to my face. The coquina lives in large colonies, and each shell is brightly colored with individual markings. It spends its day being exposed by waves, then upending and rapidly burying into the sand as the revealing wave recedes. For my money, synchronized swimmers have nothing on coquina clams.

Mole crabs are those adorable, streamlined, retro-looking crustaceans that tunnel backward into the sand as waves recede, leaving little antennae waving above their hidey-hole. Mole crabs happen to be prime bait for red drum and other game fish.

The backshore is the sand that sears bare feet, unrelentingly hot, and few things grow there or choose to live there. The champion of this environment is the nocturnal, sideways-stalking ghost crab. These swift-moving creatures tunnel deeply into the sands to remain cool, scooting out only to feed and wet their gills in order to breathe, mostly in the evening.

By far and away, the most celebrated users of the backshore are the great pelagic turtles—the loggerhead, green, Kemp's-Ridley, and leatherback. Loggerheads are the most numerous, and, as do the others, they come on land in early summer to crawl to the backshore to excavate their nests and lay eggs, which hatch slightly more than two months later. While the turtles are rarely seen, their nesting is easily recognized by the noticeable "crawl" marks above the high-water mark.

Dunes

Dunes develop where the wind can pile sand into mounds and vegetation is able to take root anchoring the sand. Dunes serve as the storm shock absorber for the island. The dunes closest to the ocean are known as frontal or primary dunes. This is a harsh environment, battered by ocean storm surge and whipped by salt-filled wind, baked by the sun.

It takes a tough, salt-tolerant plant to live on and anchor a dune. Sea oats, easily recognized by their tall "flags" of seeds in late summer, are the most elegant (and photographed) of all beach plants and are well adapted to dune life. So too, is the tender, fleshy sea elder, a plant with succulent-like leaves that also can tolerate this hot spot.

One function of a primary dune field is to deflect this salt spray–laden wind upward, thus sheltering inland locations and, in turn, allowing more tender plants to grow. In undisturbed locations, there can be parallel dunes separated by a trough. Usually on the lee side of secondary dunes (the back dunes) is the first growth of woody shrubs. While tolerant of the arid conditions, these plants are frequently salt-sculpted, sheared at the height of the dunes that shelter them.

Few creatures live in the dunes, but several species of shorebirds, like the endangered least tern and piping plover, along with royal terns, nest in shallow depressions or flats at the base of the dune zone.

Medanos

If wind piles sand high enough and the dune can remain free of vegetation, it becomes a medano, a sand dune on the move. Such dunes are active and naturally wig and wag with the push of the wind. If these move over adjoining maritime thickets and forests, as is happening on the southwest side of Jockey's Ridge State Park, they will engulf and suffocate the plants. Jockey's Ridge is the best-known medano, but there are others, including nearby Run Hill and the now stabilized Big Kill Devil Hill.

Barrier Flats

Occasionally behind the primary dunes are flat, grass-covered plains, where water may stand after a hard rain. Usually such areas are behind a relatively low dune line, and the plants that thrive there can survive periodic inundation. Currituck National Wildlife Refuge, Ocracoke Island, and Portsmouth Island have such locations. I tend to avoid them because they are also home to mosquitoes in indescribable numbers and the deer fly.

Thickets

In the lee of the dunes grows the maritime shrub thicket—push through it if you can. It develops naturally where the land is sheltered from oceanic influence by a combi-

nation of distance and dune height. The woody plants of this pioneering zone, southern wax myrtle, yaupon, bayberry, and red cedar, are sturdy. As they mature, they reach for height and become glorious sculptural mounds, rounded and leaning by prevailing winds.

Thickets are a sign of stability, harboring many creatures, including rabbits, raccoons, opossums, mice, and sometimes snakes. Mockingbirds and catbirds also seem to thrive in the thickets among the berry-producing trees and shrubs.

Maritime Forest

Thickets are the leading edge of a maritime forest that needs shelter or distance from salt-laden wind to thrive. Mature maritime forests such as Kitty Hawk, Nags Head, and Buxton Woods are nearly indistinguishable from inland forests. Forests are usually on the highest and safest part of a barrier island and offer the best growing conditions for plants and shelter and food for wildlife.

The live oak is the dominant hardwood tree in the maritime forest. At the limit of its range on the northern islands, it grows in a gnarled and weathered form, lacking a grace that it attains farther south. There are pioneering pines, American and yaupon holly, and other hardwoods such as bald cypress. In Nags Head Woods Ecological Preserve, the mix of species (which includes hicko-

ries) is normally found far west on the mainland, making this forest extraordinary for a barrier island.

The Outer Banks maritime forests support populations of fox and white-tailed deer in addition to the mammals of the maritime thickets.

Salt Marsh

Invariably, you step out of the forest and into the muck, sinking ankle-deep or more into the salt marsh. This is the soggy, grassy habitat influenced by tidal waters on the soundside of the island. The forest and thicket shrubbery, hard-pressed to withstand a salty environment, fades, and black needle rush occupies the highest marshy ground, terrain that is intermittently flooded and characteristically above the normal tide line.

The more pervasive the tidal influence, the more abundant is salt marsh cordgrass or spartina. Spartina forms the shimmering expanses of marsh that sweep across the horizon, growing in soil that is inundated daily. Without a doubt, this is the most productive habitat of the many that you can find along the coast. It is the nursery for many species of animals that inhabit the waters adjacent to the barrier islands, and the decaying spartina becomes the food at the base of the food web that ultimately can sustain all creatures that inhabit the coast, including humans.

Cape Lookout National Seashore

On the south side of Ocracoke Inlet is Portsmouth Island, the northern portion of the lengthy Core Banks and the first link in the 55-mile-long chain that is the Cape Lookout National Seashore. Authorized in 1966, Cape Lookout is the younger, wilder sibling of the Cape Hatteras National Seashore. The major difference between the two is evident immediately: there are no bridges to Cape Lookout National Seashore.

You will find Cape Lookout as serene as Hatteras is energizing, as solitary as the other is social, and powerfully, desolately beautiful. Cape Lookout National Seashore is "the edge of the sea," in the words of one of the most insightful observers of this coastline, Rachel Carson.

The two seashores are paired opposites. Cape Hatteras National Seashore, wonderfully storied and saturated with historical interest, has pods of intensive development, is managed for convenient access for visitation, and accommodates many visitors. In contrast, Cape Lookout figures more in local and regional history, is wholly undeveloped and nearly pristine, exists in a calm appreciation of its benefit as a habitat for its wildlife, and receives only the more intrepid visitors. Cape Lookout National Seashore is no less rich than Cape Hatteras, but it is fundamentally different.

Consider this question: If a hurricane strikes an island head-on, and no one lives there, does it make the news?

The answer is, not so much.

Hurricane Isabel blew right over Cape Lookout, crossing in the vicinity of Drum Inlet as a Category II storm, continuing northwest to pile its somewhat diminished storm surge into the mainland communities fronting Pamlico Sound. There was statewide and national anxiety about the damage inflicted on Cape Hatteras and the beach communities of Dare County, but there was little concern over Cape Lookout. It, too, took a hit. The storm surge on North Core Banks was approximately 8 feet; on South Core Banks, it reached 6 feet, which just about tops everything on this low-lying strand. There was nothing unexpected here: the waves washed over the islands, rushing to the sound, dissipating their energy. Sand was taken from the dunes and the southeast-facing beaches and spread on the northwest side of the islands, rolling the islands imperceptibly toward the mainland.

Portsmouth Village flooded badly, but this was after the storm passed over the island, and the reversed winds of the hurricane's southwest quadrant began piling the sound waters into the village, damaging the George Dixon House and the old life-saving station (the volunteers who live in the village evacuated prior to the storm). In the words of a park official, "everything got wet and muddied." The combination of waves and water performed some badly needed weeding on the low islands of the seashore, clearing vegetation to improve the habitat for some species of birds.

The lighthouse area faired fairly well at first, as the initial storm surge was a mere 3–4 feet. The story changed, however, when the hurricane crossed the island, and the winds reversed. Then, the winds, sliding along the face of Shackleford Banks, piled the waters of the Cape Lookout Bight against the lighthouse, surrounding it, but not flooding the visitors center in the old lightkeeper's quarters.

Very few reports made the press because there were very few structures and people on the islands (the hurricane did destroy approximately one-half of the concession cabins, which are owned by the National Park Service, on Core Banks). What happened is what should happen—the island adjusted to meet the demands of the storm. In fact, the cabins on North Core Banks, which were elevated 5 feet in a rebuild prompted by Hurricane Gordon, are now within 2 feet of the ground because of the sand washed underneath them by Isabel. The park service will restore or replace the destroyed cabins.

The unfortunate concessionaires, who risk the furnishings of the primitive cabins (an uninsurable risk), will refurbish as the cabins are rebuilt (I do not mean to minimize or marginalize their hardship). Without being callous, the storm's impact on Cape Lookout is what it was meant to be; there was not much property damage because there was not much property. The island's interaction with a hurricane is part of the system; it is neither bad nor good, it is just what happens. Following the storm, the island began to rebuild as it had after an October 1991 "nor'easter" that badly roiled both seashores.

This is the best lens through which to look at Cape Lookout: It is a living laboratory, protected and preserved so that barrier islands in their natural state may be studied and enjoyed. It happens to be one of 260 Biosphere Reserves worldwide, an outgrowth of the Biosphere Program established by the United Nations in 1971. In its capacity as Cape Lookout National Seashore South Atlantic Biosphere Reserve, the seashore serves as a research "constant," managed for conservation purposes. The islands, offshore locations, and the water above them are all included in the reserve. The participation of the seashore in the Biosphere Program strongly influences the management plans of the National Park Service and decreases the likelihood of human encroachment. There is not a single road or readily available source of water on the Cape Lookout barrier islands. Except for park service volunteers, there are no residents. What the seashore does have are miles of beach and marsh, singularly outstanding fishing, terrific bird-watching, and some of the finest shelling in North Carolina.

North to South from Ocracoke Inlet to Cape Lookout, the component islands are known by the single name, Core Banks. This is the longest barrier complex in the seashore. The artificial opening of a new Drum Inlet, east of the town of Atlantic and south of where sand had filled in an old inlet long ago, thwarted the natural process that was creating a single barrier island and divides the lengthy stretch into North and South Core Banks.

These two stretch their sandy lengths northeast to southwest, shielding the coast and creating Core Sound. The barriers have a low, almost flat, island profile, void of any significant dunes. Core Banks is for the most part a narrow, thinly vegetated barrier, little more than a spit of sand. If you have visited the north end of Ocracoke or the narrow beach between Avon and Buxton without its artificial dunes, then you have an image of Core Banks. The wind will not let the sand lie, and there is hardly a dune or shelter of any kind for any creature. The shrubby growth of the mid-island flats with its few brushy tangles and nearly indistinguishable hummocks of beach grass thwarts any desire to pause. Extensive marshes fringe the backside of the banks like the lacing of a doily, creating the rich productive fisheries that support commercial crabbing and clamming and offer fine flounder fishing.

At Cape Lookout the coast makes another severe shift in direction, and the barrier islands after Core Banks align fully east and west. One such island, the next in the chain, is the last component of the seashore and the wildest of the islands, Shackleford Banks. On Shackleford Banks, the shift in orientation allows the prevailing winds to pile sand in immense dunes that spill into the only maritime forest of any significance in the seashore. Shackleford Banks once supported several small villages, and the largest village, Diamond City, was the whaling center of the North Carolina coast during the eighteenth and nineteenth centuries. Today, the island is closed to motorized traffic and has been under consideration for wilderness designation.

The "ghost" village of Portsmouth, once the largest community on the Outer Banks, is on North Core Banks. It has been vacant since 1971 except for seasonal volunteer employees. On South Core Banks stands the distinctive diamond-patterned Cape Lookout Lighthouse, first illuminated on November 1, 1859, and the only major lighthouse that operates during the day. The Coast Guard maintains the fully automated light, which serves as a major navigational aid for mariners circumventing the treacherous Frying Pan Shoals southeast of the lighthouse. In June 2003 the Coast Guard turned over the tower to the National Park Service. The light is also a prime guide to the entrance of Beaufort Inlet to the east.

One of the four great lighthouses on the Outer Banks, Cape Lookout Lighthouse has two rotating airport beacons that make a complete revolution every 30 seconds, appearing as a flashing beacon every 15 seconds, with a focal height of 150 feet, visible more than 12 miles out at sea. The curiously painted lighthouse invokes a diamond shape, hence seemingly more appropriate for Diamond Shoals farther north. But when the Light House Board authorized the painting of the four towers for daytime identification on April 17, 1873, it decreed, "Cape Lookout Tower will be checkered, the checkers being painted alternately black and white."

The old lightkeeper's quarters are used by the park service as a residence for a volunteer ranger

Paddlers enjoy the waters near Cape Lookout Lighthouse. Courtesy of Crystal Coast Tourism Development Authority.

who lives on the island. The U.S. Coast Guard once maintained a station on Cape Lookout south of the lightkeeper's quarters, which is now used by the North Carolina Maritime Museum in Beaufort for programs.

The Cape Lookout Hook is the sandy promontory to the southwest of the lighthouse that curls north. Cape Lookout and the sandy ocean beaches offer some of the finest shelling and fishing within the seashore. The water is shallow here, and currents are mild.

Cape Lookout National Seashore came about in an unusual manner. Beginning in the 1960s, the state of North Carolina condemned and then purchased Core Banks, north and south, and deeded it to the federal government for use as a national seashore, and the federal government condemned Shackleford. Property owners from that period still hold leases on the islands, and some hunting clubs retained twenty-five-year leases. Through the mid-1970s, there were fishing shacks clustered in various locations along Core Banks, used as overnight shelters. Such areas were called "shack towns" by leaseholders, and the owners of the shacks were officially squatters, with no title to the property. The area has since been razed and returned to nature. Over many years, island users had moved nearly junkable vehicles to the island and drove them across the sand until they sank or died, abandoning them where they stopped. The park service had the vehicles removed, a process that took several years.

Historically, the villages notwithstanding, the islands of the seashore have served as seasonal outposts for hunting and fishing, activities still allowed within the boundaries when conducted according to state laws. Ring-necked pheasant, an oriental bird species, were introduced to Core Banks by hunters and have flourished in the past. As little as two decades ago, there were substantial populations of bobwhite quail, and some hunting was allowed.

People have not changed the natural state of the islands much. Park service personnel note only three significant intrusions: the artificial opening of Drum Inlet, the jetty at the Cape Lookout Hook, and the state-mandated opening of Barden Inlet between Cape Lookout and the east end of Shackleford. None of the buildings within the seashore interfere with the natural processes of the island.

The Cape Lookout allure is that of unreachable, untamed islands. It does not matter where you start—Ocracoke, Cedar Island, or one of the "downeast" villages of Carteret County, the parent county of the seashore—when you reach the seashore, it is remote and without conveniences. Frankly, it is not for everybody, since you have to arrange transportation and carry everything needed for however long you intend to stay.

The only thing provided is 55 miles of beach, enough room for all comers. One ranger reported that one July 4 several years ago, he counted only 12 visitors in 25 miles of beach. In fact, the busiest season is between Labor Day and mid-December, when the fish are moving.

Rental cabins are available for overnight stays on North and South Core Banks, the only improved facilities open to the public on the islands, and they are considered primitive (hot and cold running water; gas stoves and ovens; a few are wired for generators, if you have one). Essentially, though, the Cape Lookout experience is a wild one, for the hardy beachgoer and nature lover who revels in solitude and the sound of the sea.

The Cape Lookout National Seashore Visitors Center is at Shell Point on Harkers Island, which is in sound waters north of the bend of Cape Lookout—just high enough above the sound it seems. It is a gorgeous, windswept site, at the end of the main road of the island. The islands of the seashore are on the horizon to the east and south, appearing as a continuous thread of land from this distance. The lighthouse and the tree line of Shackleford Banks stand above anything else that you can see from the visitors center parking lot.

Access

Access to locations within the seashore is by boat only. The usual routes are across Ocracoke Inlet from Ocracoke, across Core Sound from the mainland villages of Atlantic and Davis, or across Back Sound from Harkers Island or Beaufort. If you have your own boat, there are no restrictions on landings.

There are numerous marinas and boat-launching ramps that serve the seashore. The North Carolina Wildlife Resources Commission maintains a boat-launching ramp near Beaufort that provides access to Taylor Creek. To reach it, follow US 70 east from Beaufort, turn south on SR 1310 (Lennoxville Road), follow 1.5 miles, and then turn right on SR 1312, and the ramp is 100 yards ahead on the left.

If you do not have a boat, the

No bridges carry vehicles to "the Point" of Cape Lookout National Seashore, unlike its look-alike sibling to the north. Anglers must hire concession ferries to transport their vehicles to reach prime fishing spots. Courtesy of Crystal Coast Tourism Development Authority.

park service authorizes individuals who meet certain stringent requirements to operate ferry services. Amazingly, a round-trip lift to one of the islands is still priced as low as $12 per person. However, it is a complicated business, and operators change frequently.

Ferry operators at Davis and Atlantic are equipped to transport vehicles. All vehicles must have a Cape Lookout vehicle permit, which may be obtained at the ferry dock or at the Harkers Island Ranger Station. You may drive in the seashore on a system of ap-

proved inland sand roads and along the beach where it is not posted as closed. However, no vehicles are permitted on Shackleford Banks.

You should plan to be completely self-sufficient during your visit, whether you are camping or day-tripping, since there are virtually no facilities for visitors. Cape Lookout Lighthouse has a restroom, and park service volunteers live at Portsmouth Village and in the lightkeeper's quarters. Here's a minimum checklist of items to take: food, drinking water (at least 2 quarts per person per day), pro-

tective clothing from sun and rain, a hat, sunglasses, sunscreen lotion, insect repellent, and shoes suitable for walking in hot sand. If you are going fishing at Cape Lookout, you can take a cooler since a shuttle will take you round-trip from the ferry dock at the lighthouse to the point for $6. Otherwise, you would have to carry the cooler and your fishing gear the 1.5 miles through soft sand to the point.

Camping is primitive since there are no developed campsites. Insect repellent and long tent stakes are advised. Mosquito netting helps tremendously for a good night's sleep. Bring plenty of water for cooking and drinking, and the rangers suggest that you bring lots of food. You will eat more here than you usually do.

The local regulations of the North Carolina Marine Fisheries apply to size limitations on some saltwater species and on any shell-fishing for clams, crabs, or oysters in the sound waters. As long as you are not in closed waters, regulations allow recreational clamming (up to 100 per day for personal use) and crabbing, by drop line.

Hunters must meet all state and federal game standards and licensing requirements.

Information

For information, call the Cape Lookout National Seashore Visitors Center at 252-728-2250, 8 A.M. to 4:30 P.M. daily, or contact Superintendent, Cape Lookout National Seashore, 131 Charles Street, Harkers Island, NC 28531, 252-728-2250.

Web addresses: <www.nps.gov/calo/home.htm>; <www.portsmouthisland.com> (North Core Banks); <www.drumwagon.com/awfc/default.htm> (South Core Banks)

Cape Lookout National Seashore Concession Ferries and Cabins

The following ferry operators meet National Park Service and U.S. Coast Guard regulations and have been listed as providers of transportation to Cape Lookout National Seashore. You must make your reservations directly with them and verify the rates as well as the schedules. Some operators also have rental cabins or beach transportation within the seashore.

Portsmouth Village: Trips to Portsmouth Village depart from Ocracoke. The Austin family provides transportation, and they request at least a one-day advance notice for reservations by calling 252-928-4361 or 252-928-5431. Also, Portsmouth Island ATV Excursions, 252-928-4484, provides guided tours of the island and Portsmouth Village on ATVs from April through November. For additional operators during the summer months, call the Ocracoke Island Visitors Center at 252-928-4531.

North Core Banks: Long Point–Morris Marina, Kabin Kamps, and Ferry Service operates a ferry that leaves from a dock north of Atlantic, which is on US 70 at the northeastern tip of Carteret County, and docks about 7 miles north of Drum Inlet and 16 miles south of Portsmouth Village. The ferry ride is $13 per person round-trip. The four-car ferry will take your vehicle (less than 18.5 feet) over for $65 round-trip (larger vehicles and trailers cost more). The Morris family also rents 25 cabins in the Long Point Cabin Area between April and November for $65–$150 a night, depending on the season and the size. The smallest sleeps four, the largest twelve. Cabins have safe water for drinking, hot and cold water in showers, gas stoves, and indoor toilets, but no electricity. Pets are permitted on leash, but confirm this before arriving. Contact Morris Marina, Kabin Kamps, and Ferry Service, 1000 Morris Marina Road, Atlantic, NC 28511, 252-225-4261.

Web address: <www.portsmouthisland.com>

South Core Banks: Great Island–Alger G. Willis Fishing Camps operates a ferry service to the Great Island Cabin Area, 7 miles south of Drum Inlet and approximately 14 miles north of Cape Point. The ferry departs from the community of Davis, on US 70, and can transport vehicles. The fee is approximately $13 per person round-trip and $65 round-trip for a vehicle. There are approximately 25 cabins available from April to November for $28–$120 a night. Pets are permitted on leash, but confirm this before arriving. Contact Alger Willis Fishing Camps, P.O. Box 234, Davis, NC 28524, 252-729-2791.

Web address: <www.drumwagon.com/awfc/default.htm>

South Core Banks: New Drum Inlet. Passenger ferry. Pets permitted on leash, but confirm in advance. Contact Core Sound Ferry, Sea Level, NC, 252-728-4595.

Cape Lookout / Shackleford Banks: Check with the Cape Lookout National Seashore Visitors Center for a listing of current operators by calling 252-728-2250. Here is a partial listing by departure port. These are passenger ferries only. Pets are permitted on leash, but check in advance.

Beaufort to Cape Lookout Lighthouse and Shackleford Banks: contact Island Ferry Adventures, Beaufort, NC, 252-342-7555; Mystery Tours, Beaufort, NC, 252-728-7827; or Outer Banks Ferry Service, Beaufort, NC, 252-728-4129.

Harkers Island to Cape Lookout Lighthouse and Shackleford Banks: contact Calico Jacks Ferry, Harkers Island, NC, 252-728-3575; Harkers Island Fishing Center, Harkers Island, NC, 252-728-3907; Local Yokel Ferry and Tours, Harkers Island, NC, 252-342-2759.

Morehead City to Shackleford Banks only: These ferries are for passengers only; confirm pets in advance. Contact Anderson Maritime, Morehead City, NC, 252-728-3988; or Waterfront Ferry Service, Morehead City, NC, 252-726-7678.

Portsmouth Island

Portsmouth Island is the name given to the northeast end of the low barrier island known as North Core Banks, the northernmost section of the 55-mile-long Cape Lookout National Seashore. Swash Inlet, an intermittently flooding breach where wind tides may flood the flats behind the dune line, separates Portsmouth Island from the rest of North Core Banks. While the flooded flats are common on Portsmouth, the island is one of the historic locations sufficiently high above sea level for permanent settlement to persist.

It is also one of the most rewarding places to visit, but it is not for those that are expecting a cushy

getaway. In summer, Portsmouth can be searingly hot. There is little shade, and the beaches, the prime shelling locations, are about a mile from the village beyond often-flooded flats. It is a hot hike, and there are few services on the island. Pack your water in and pack your bottles out.

Then there are the mosquitoes. If you catch them following a hatch, they are beyond language, that is, Standard English fails in its ability to describe their density and voraciousness. Of course, a breeze can kick up and blow them clean away, and shoulder-season trips avoid much of the mayhem. The visit to this remarkably preserved community more than rewards the possible annoyances. After all, there is no other place like it on the East Coast.

The "ghost" village of Portsmouth, established by an act of the North Carolina General Assembly in 1753 and a location of national historic significance, sits on the northwest corner of the island, the most habitable acreage of the few in Cape Lookout National Seashore.

Hurricane Isabel tested that notion severely. An 8-foot storm surge powered over much of the island to the south, but it was the storm's backwash after it crossed over the island that flooded the restored village from the sound. Isabel caused severe damage to several buildings, among them the Dixon House and the old Coast Guard station, where it popped the floorboards loose from underneath.

The storm put 3 feet of water into

the elevated primitive cabins south of Swash Inlet, cabins that had been rebuilt 5 feet off the ground after flooding from Hurricane Gordon earlier.

There are no permanent residents in Portsmouth today. In 1971 the last two residents moved to the mainland, ending the continuous occupancy of the village since the early 1700s. The twenty-one surviving structures of the village, including a church, a Coast Guard (life-saving) station, and the island's schoolhouse, still stand proudly but beaten up on the highest ground available, which is not always high enough though. The freshly painted yellow houses and the blue and white Methodist church are the centerpieces in a 250-acre historic district that is on the National Register of Historic Places. The Dixon/Salter House serves as a visitors center, and the church is also open to the public.

During its heyday in the eighteenth century, Portsmouth was a major port of call for all shipping into North Carolina, eventually becoming the state's busiest seaport. Oceangoing vessels would put in at Portsmouth to transfer their cargo to smaller craft for the continuation of the journey across shallow Pamlico Sound to Bath or Washington, a practice known as "lightering." Portsmouth was sufficiently important to North Carolina's economy that British troops seized and occupied the port along with the port of Ocracoke during the War of 1812. Portsmouth thrived until a storm carved Hatteras and Oregon Inlets

	Fee	Parking	Restrooms	Lifeguard	Camping	Showers	Beach Access	Hiking	Trail	Handicapped	Boating	ORV Access	Fishing	Programs	Historic	Sand Beach	Dunes	Upland	Wetland
Cape Lookout National Seashore	•	•			•		•	•	•		•	•	•	•	•	•	•	•	•
Portsmouth Island			•		•			•	•		•	•	•	•	•	•	•	•	•
North Core Banks			•		•	•	•	•	•		•	•	•		•	•	•	•	•
Cedar Island	•	•								•									•
Public Boating Access: Lola		•									•		•						•
Cedar Island National Wildlife Refuge		•						•	•		•		•					•	•
Public Boating Access: Thorofare Bay		•									•		•						•
Atlantic		•	•								•		•					•	•

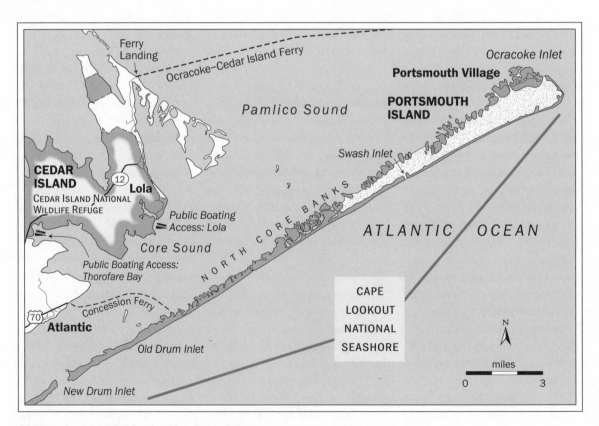

Map 15. Portsmouth Island to New Drum Inlet

in 1846, after which Ocracoke Inlet soon shoaled, and Portsmouth's commercial days were over.

One of the more poignant stories of Portsmouth is that of Henry Pigott, an African American who was the last male to live in the village. Henry Pigott was born May 5, 1896, of descendants of slaves brought to the island who decided to stay after emancipation. As the economy waned in Portsmouth, he continued to fish to support himself. In 1967 he sold his house on Doctor's Creek to the state of North Carolina and retained a life estate to the house. He fell ill and died on January 5, 1971, and is buried in the cemetery near the Methodist church. Shortly after his death, Elma Dixon and Marion Babb, the remaining two inhabitants of Portsmouth, moved to the mainland, and the community that was known as Portsmouth ceased to exist.

There are several private holdings on Portsmouth Island, some leases authorized by the park service, as well as cemeteries still visited and tended by descendants. The park service requests that visitors to the island respect private property.

Although the National Park Service maintains a ranger station in the village (frequently staffed by resident volunteers who contract to stay for several months), the island has no facilities or concessions of any kind. You should take everything you will need during your visit. Overnight stays are permitted, but make sure to bring supplies, especially water and insect repellent.

The flats of the island are substantial—wide areas of sand, sometimes dry and sometimes covered with nearly 2 feet of water. Winds from the north can pile the water onto the island and build a moat between you and the beach. If you are hiking to the beach from the village, be prepared for a walk of about a mile, not all of it easy, not always dry, and none of it insect-free.

For day-trippers, Portsmouth is one of the shelling hot spots on the Outer Banks. Storms frequently scatter thousands of shells on the wide flat beach, and the competition for shells is limited. If you go in late winter or early spring, you have your pick of the flotsam and jetsam and most likely an almost guaranteed shelling success. Fishing is also unsurpassed on Portsmouth. For both, however, you have to walk around the island, so take sunscreen lotion, drinking water, insect repellent, and comfortable walking shoes.

On your way to Portsmouth from Ocracoke, it may still be possible to see remnants of Beacon Island and Shell Castle Island in the waters north and west of the inlet. Approximately 400 yards long, Beacon Island was named for the presence of two beacons used by pilots to navigate Ocracoke Channel. The south end was fortified in 1794–95 by an act of Congress because of the importance of the shipping channel. Shell Castle Island was the site where John Gray Blount and John Wallace launched a speculative venture to expand the island in order to make a more favorable "lightering dock" for oceangoing vessels. In the 1800s Shell Castle Island supported a lumberyard, tavern, dwelling house, and notary public's office. Hurricanes sweeping through the inlet sealed the fate of both islands, however.

Access

Trips to Portsmouth Village depart from Ocracoke. The Austin family provides transportation, and they request at least a one-day advance notice; for reservations, call 252-928-4361 or 252-928-5431. Also, Portsmouth Island ATV Excursions, 252-928-4484, provides guided tours of the island and Portsmouth Village on ATVs from April through November. For additional operators during the summer months, call the Ocracoke Island Visitors Center at 252-928-4531.

Information

For information, call the Cape Lookout National Seashore Visitors Center at 252-728-2250, 8 A.M. to 4:30 P.M. daily, or contact Superintendent, Cape Lookout National Seashore, 131 Charles Street, Harkers Island, NC 28531, 252-728-2250.

The Coastal Constant Is Change

Coastal geologists describe the relationship of natural forces such as the wind and sea level to barrier islands as a system having "dynamic equilibrium." A loose definition is that the system has a moving balance, like a person riding a unicycle. The rider stays upright, so long as there are no restrictions on movement.

The dynamic equilibrium of the coast is analogous but more complex. To survive as islands, barrier beaches must be able to shift and reshape freely when shoved about by wind and waves. Each individual island is part of a system that includes other islands. Restrictions on a single island's ability to respond naturally to wind and wave introduce a "wild card" that may play havoc elsewhere—perhaps on an adjacent island. There's no certainty about when or where or even if it will happen.

The system is not unlike an unbreakable balloon filled with water —the force you exert on it will squeeze out in an unexpected place. Similarly, if we interfere and try to keep a part of an island (usually sand) from moving where nature directs it (by constructing a jetty to trap sand, for example), we rob the replenishment material from other beaches. Erosion is not really stopped; it's just directed elsewhere.

There's a lot to be learned from unrestricted barrier islands such as those of Cape Lookout National Seashore. The islands constantly shift and reshape responding to wind and wave action throughout the system. In fact, the whole system stays fairly constant; coastal geologists have established that the total amount of sand in the system changes little, but how and where the sand is piled changes constantly. When Hurricane Isabel rolled over Core Banks, it didn't destroy the sand that formed the dunes or the beach, it just moved it.

You could characterize the response of barrier islands to wind and waves as a form of coastal aikido—they literally roll and rearrange with the punches. They are malleable; they do not actively resist the forces, and in so doing they "survive" as a system.

Back to an earlier point, islands retain the total mass of sand within the barrier island chain. In some places, the beach is eroding; at others, it is accreting or growing. Some inlets are more or less stable; others are on the move. Within the big overall picture, the sand remains constant.

The greatest force at work on North Carolina's barrier islands is the rising sea. It is elevating at the rate of one foot per century. It is widely accepted that barrier islands respond to this chronic pressure (as opposed to the acute attack of storms) by deliberate, strategic retreat, moving landward, up hill on the coastal plain shelf, at the press of the ocean. This is an orderly retreat with a sequence of steps.

First, sand fills the marsh behind the island, and vegetation secures this new sand. Then, the entire vegetation and land pattern of the island shifts toward the mainland. The stable ground of the island inches steadily away from the ocean.

"Wash Woods" in Currituck, where tree stumps emerge from the wet sand beach, provides vivid evidence of this landward island march.

The rate of retreat—how far an island will move each year—is determined by the slope of the offshore bottom (which is not constant along the coast) and can be computed. The ballpark range is that for every inch in sea-level rise, the coastline retreats somewhere between 10 feet and 100 feet. (In 2004 Duke University researchers estimated that a one-foot rise in sea level could flood 770 *square miles* of coastal North Carolina.)

If the coastal system is moving (geologically speaking), then permanent structures are at an inherent risk. The operative question about artificial structures on nearly every barrier island is *when* they will be threatened, not *if* they will be threatened (although the time period could be quite lengthy—Ocracoke and Portsmouth Villages have been around for more than 200 years).

It is difficult for us to think this way, but storms do not threaten the islands themselves—the island is not permanent but a movable part of a system that is permanent. Storms threaten humans and their "permanent" possessions. Put another way, you do not own land on the barrier islands, you rent. Some leases are longer than others, depending primarily on their location and elevation above sea level.

The changes along our coast are severe enough to be noticed from season to season because there are many benchmarks—homes and businesses mostly—marking the advance of the sea. Some of these may not survive, but there will always be an island.

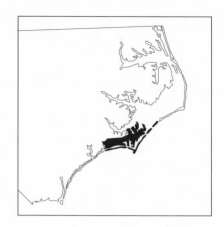

Carteret County

If Dare County flings the Outer Banks to its seaward salient, Carteret County gradually reels the island necklace back in. The county claims 75 miles of barrier islands, and except for distant, lonely Portsmouth Island, the beaches of the other four islands are less than 4 miles from the mainland. Too close to land, I suppose, to be considered "outer," but banks nonetheless.

Cape Lookout is one of three "elbows" in the alignment of barrier islands in the state. This is where the generally southwest string of barrier beaches alters direction to a nearly compass-perfect run due west. West of Cape Lookout, the barrier islands align end to end in a great concave arc sweeping inland to a midpoint on Topsail Island before bending back again to the promontory of Cape Fear. The two horns of land, Capes Lookout and Fear, enclose a great area of water known as Onslow Bay. This crescentic pattern is a repeat of that to the north between Capes Hatteras and Lookout, which encompass the waters of Raleigh Bay. Yet, this similar large-scale pattern of arcing islands and embraced bays yields no similarity in the character of the islands. Instead, the orientation of the island chains to prevailing winds is responsible for their differences.

Portsmouth Island and Core Banks, the eastern barrier islands in Carteret County, align with the northeast-southwest orientation of the prevailing winds. Accordingly, there is no steady landward breeze to push sand higher on the beach; instead, the wind tends to stream sand along the beach in stinging, ankle-high sheets parallel to the line of the water. The wind-driven sand on Core Banks can be annoying on dry, hot sunny days. I have spread a towel in such conditions, and within 45 minutes I was eroding on my leeward side and becoming a dune on the windward. Sand stuck wherever sunblock was applied, and those grains were about the only ones to slow down sufficiently to fall or stick to something. There is not much refuge because the dunes are few, distant, low, and well away from the beach; the only practical solution was building a windscreen from the beach sand.

The bigger picture is that because the winds give these islands a low, flat profile and minimal fore dunes, there is no shelter to permit forests to develop: salt spray shears vegetation, and the elements combine to keep it diminished and stressed. The absence of dunes makes these islands vulnerable to flooding during storms, which is exactly what happened during Hurricane Isabel. The storm rolled right over the island, dissipating much of its damaging force before striking the mainland. Nothing happened to these islands that wasn't supposed to happen; however, the concession rental units added by man did not fare so well.

Portsmouth Island and Core Banks contrast mightily with the east-west oriented companion islands, Shackleford Banks and Bogue Banks. These islands are "around the elbow" of Cape Lookout in southern Carteret County and face south.

The high dune profile that graces these islands results from a steady supply of sand driven and piled into dunes by onshore winds and waves. The relatively stable dunes—some are quite large— behind the surf zone deflect salt spray up, which allows vegetation to thrive inland from the dune line. As it grows and dies, it decays creating topsoil; more plants take hold; and eventually, an island maritime forest in balance with the elements thrives. Shackleford Banks features one of the few remnant stands of maritime forest in this particular section of coastline; residential development fills the substantial corresponding forest on Bogue Banks.

Carteret County's barrier beaches are every bit as marvelous as their counterparts in the northern tier of barrier islands, but there are some distinguishing differences from those of the Outer Banks. The 55 miles of undeveloped barrier islands of the Cape Lookout National Seashore are far more pristine (and therefore primitive) than their counterparts in Cape Hatteras National Seashore, and the resort communities of Bogue Banks, which are a seamless stream of residential subdivisions, developed from a strong statewide loyalty and "local tradition" as travel destinations. The inherent appeal here, the one that keeps people returning, is the simple, predictable pleasure of going to the beach—renting a place near the water and staying and playing.

Because of a generally flattened near-shore profile, Carteret County beaches tend to have gentle surf. Average wave action is not nearly as dramatic or energized as it is north of Cape Hatteras, where the fetch of the wave-generating wind can be lengthy. On Bogue Banks, the primary recreational beach, the waves laze, lap, and plop across the sands. There can be red-flag days of high surf and strong undertow as at any beach, but by far and away the summer waters are benign and inviting, and for many years, the wet sand beach has been wide and flat. In recent years, some popular beaches on Bogue Banks have been reduced by erosion, rebuilt by nourishing, reduced and rebuilt again. The practice has sharpened the debate about permanent oceanfront development and beach nourishment in particular. People readily stipulate that on Bogue Banks, at least, an attractive, useable beach is everything to the local economy; the disagreement is on drawing and maintaining the line in the sand.

There are many other features, primarily of statewide or regional interest that draw folks to the Crystal Coast, as residents refer to it. In 1934 the 12,000 acres of the northeastern tip of the county, a region of tidal marsh and low grassland and some upland, were preserved as the Cedar Island National Wildlife Refuge, a location that nearly adjoins the Cape Lookout National Seashore. Audubon North Carolina helps manage nearby Wainwright and Beacon Islands as rookeries for sea birds. Harkers Island is host to Cape Lookout National Seashore headquarters and the most reasonable jumping-off point for a day trip to the Cape Lookout Lighthouse or Shackleford Banks.

The Rachel Carson component of the National Estuarine Research Reserve program, comprised of Horse Island and Bird Shoal across Taylor Creek from historic Beaufort, completes the conservation packet that is immediate to the oceanfront. (There are also four federal wilderness areas in northwest Carteret County.)

In Beaufort, a National Register Historic District guards the remnants of the state's third-oldest town and one of the liveliest historic communities you'll ever visit. It is also home to the North Carolina Maritime Museum. Morehead City is a bustling dining, fishing, and diving center; the waterfront is an enjoyable site for an after-dinner stroll. The brick earthworks of Fort Macon State Park dominate the eastern end of Bogue Banks, and the resort community of Pine Knoll Shores is the site of one of North Carolina's three state aquariums.

Last, and so obvious that it is often overlooked, is the fact that there is a lot of accessible waterfront land in the county. Increasing numbers of folks are building homes to take advantage of the boating, fishing, and waterfront living possibilities, particularly east of Beaufort, an area that is big, water-logged, and served by only one major road.

There is one important footnote to the Carteret County beach story: while some beaches are easy to reach, the majority of oceanfront mileage is not. For practical traveling purposes, this bifurcation occurs at Beaufort Inlet: west of the inlet, you can reach the vibrant, tourist-friendly beaches of the county in the family car; east of the inlet, you need a boat (or to pay a fee to ride a boat) to reach the limited access beaches of the Cape Lookout National Seashore.

This division mirrors the different nature of the county on opposite sides of the inlet. The villages east of Beaufort are locally referred to as "downeast," and their inhabitants are "downeasters." Agriculture and a unique maritime way of life, a story wonderfully told in Beaufort's North Carolina Maritime Museum, shape this corner of the county.

Downeast is rural, and if US 70, the main highway connecting commerce and social life, is not crossing a creek or embayment, it is passing through farmland and remnant upland forests. The communities serve local needs; conveniences and services are few. Harkers Island, which has the Cape Lookout National Seashore headquarters and several concessionaires who cater to seashore visitors, has better adapted to the tourism economy. The rest of the downeast communities, Marshallberg, Sea Level, Davis, and Atlantic, are traditional maritime and fishing villages "protected" from the Atlantic Ocean by the barrier island of Core Banks. Hurricane Isabel jumped that fence, blowing right across Core Banks to carry a storm surge ashore on the mainland, which had not happened in recent memory. Places that had weathered other storms could not dodge this near-direct hit, and the damage was wide and substantial, far more significant than that on the Outer Banks—with the exception of Hatteras. The storm claimed nearly half of the rustic concession cabins on Core Banks that provided a means of experiencing Cape Lookout National Seashore.

Hurricane Isabel gave residents and eager second-home property seekers reason to pause because what had once been a statistical possibility had become a hard-hitting reality. Previously, limitations on waste management and available water had provided the only natural "brake" on downeast real estate development. Typically, the landfall of a hurricane sets in a corresponding period of wariness that eventually wanes. With water access so abundant, this will likely be the case downeast, and the traditional farms and forests will gradually yield to increasing numbers of vacation homes.

Visitors who arrive in Carteret County on the ferry from Ocracoke enter downeast at Cedar Island, but they are the exception. The main routes to Carteret County enter on the north and west, approaches that funnel traffic to the two high-rise bridges that span Bogue Sound at Morehead City and Cape Carteret. The primary routes, US 70 on the northeast and NC 58 and 24 on the west and south, skirt a vast area of Croatan National Forest in western Carteret and Pamlico Counties. The area is not inviting, but it is outstanding from an environmental perspective, and it is also untouched. In fact, nearly 30,000 acres of the forest have been set aside in four National Wilderness Areas.

Except for NC 24, the primary coastal road between Morehead City and Jacksonville, the routes to the coast in Carteret County are rural. Commercial development intensifies as the distance to Bogue Sound diminishes.

US 70 parallels the North Carolina Railroad line to Morehead City, and that rail, the project of nineteenth-century governor John Motley Morehead, a Greensboro resident, is the reason for the city. Morehead pushed for the development of another deep-water harbor in North Carolina (the Cape Fear River is the only dependable natural deep-water port), linked by rail to the industrial Piedmont. The railroad made the oceanfront more accessible, and as leisure time became more available during the early twentieth century, Morehead City's evolution as a vacation destination gained momentum even as it grew modestly as a commercial deep-water port. The neighboring island of Bogue Banks followed as a matter of course to become the foundation of local tourism.

Access

The individual municipalities and management agencies in Carteret County provide beach access locations. It is a daunting task, and considering the growing numbers of people that come to the region, primarily to Bogue Banks, it is a task that will be unending and perhaps never complete.

Generally speaking, access is a problem at the popular resort beaches on Bogue Banks only for those visitors who come for the day. Between Memorial Day and Labor Day, parking, particularly on weekends, is available only for early birds. Weekend parking can become difficult as soon as Easter vacation. The separate descriptions of the locations on Bogue Banks below detail specific access sites.

The most visited state park in North Carolina is Fort Macon on Bogue Banks. Part of the attraction is two very large parking lots, one at a regional access area and the other at the fort. These provide direct beach access to the eastern end of Bogue Banks. Atlantic Beach maintains several regional oceanfront access sites. There is a smaller neighborhood access site in Indian Beach. Carteret County maintains a major regional access site in Salter Path on 22 acres of land donated, in part, by the heirs of Theodore Roosevelt. This fully developed site stays full, and if you want one of the 65 parking spaces any time between Memorial and Labor Day, you must arrive early. Emerald Isle maintains one regional access site.

Renting a cottage or staying in a motel simply is the best avenue for Bogue Banks. During the busy time of the year, both parking and access are difficult, and the closer you can sleep to the water, the more you will eliminate the stress of trying to find a location to park your car.

The county also maintains a soundside access on the Newport River at the north side of US 70 and a recreational fishing dock beside the bridge to Harkers Island.

The Cape Lookout National Seashore presents an altogether different access problem, which is addressed in the preceding chapter on the seashore.

Web addresses: <www.nc coastalmanagement.net/Access/sites.htm>; <www.protectthe beach.com/parking.html>

Handicapped Access

Cape Lookout National Seashore, Fort Macon State Park, and the communities of Emerald Isle and Atlantic Beach will loan beach wheelchairs with advance notice.

The regional access areas at Fort Macon and Salter Path are fully handicapped accessible. Both have designated parking places and dune crossover ramps to the oceanfront.

The regional access sites in Atlantic Beach and Emerald Isle are accessible to handicapped travelers.

Web address: <www.nccoastal management.net/Access/sites. htm>

Information

For information on accommodations, contact Crystal Coast Tourism Authority, 3409 Arendell Street, Morehead City, NC 28557, 800-SUNNYNC (800-786-6962), 252-726-8148; or the Carteret County Chamber of Commerce, 801 Arendell Street, Morehead City, NC 28557, 252-726-6350.

The National Park Service Visitors Center on Harkers Island can field most of your questions about access to Cape Lookout National Seashore. You may reach the station daily at 252-728-2250, 8 A.M. to 4:30 P.M. For additional information, contact Superintendent, Cape Lookout National Seashore, 131 Charles Street, Harkers Island, NC 28531, 252-728-2250.

Web addresses: <www.sunnync. com>; <www.nccoastchamber. com>; <www.nps.gov/calo/home. htm>

Cedar Island

The Ocracoke–Cedar Island ferry docks at the slice of land named Cedar Island. Ferry riders approaching the dock see an island in miniature—some small dunes, a layer of shrubs, and trees sheared by salt spray. Occasionally, one can see livestock ranging into the waters east of the jetties that protect the ferry dock. There's a small community beside NC 12 inland from the docks with some houses, a church, and family graveyards. It is remote, and if you are departing the ferry, NC 12 moves into the forested

"high ground" of the island, with a surprise in store, a winding, unhurried passage through the marshes of Cedar Island National Wildlife Refuge. If you are heading to the ferry, after a few enticing and disorienting glimpses of water, NC 12 comes to an abrupt end at the ferry dock.

Access

There is a large parking lot at the ferry dock where you may leave your car while you take the ferry to Ocracoke. An improved private boat ramp is available for a fee. The Driftwood Motel, Restaurant, and Campground offers food and accommodations of all kinds here; call 252-225-4861. They do a fair business with travelers waiting for the ferry or hunters and fishermen who hire the local guides.

Reservations for the ferry are a must and can be made by calling 800-856-0343 or 252-225-3551. You may reserve a space up to one year in advance. Your name and the vehicle license number are required when making the reservation. Be at the ferry terminal at least 30 minutes prior to leaving to claim your reservation.

The Ocracoke ferry operates a seasonal schedule. Between May 25 and September 27, there are nine daily departures each from Ocracoke and Cedar Island, beginning at 7:00 A.M. with the final daily departure at 8:30 P.M. From April 6 through May 24 and September 28 through November 8, there are only six daily departures from each dock, beginning at 7:00 A.M. and ending at 8:30 P.M. From November 9 through April 5 there are four daily departures from each port, beginning at 7:00 A.M. and ending at 4:00 P.M. The ride takes 2 1/4 hours.

Cedar Island National Wildlife Refuge

At the eastern end of Carteret County, NC 12 knifes through the middle of the 14,480-acre Cedar Island National Wildlife Refuge. The U.S. Fish and Wildlife Service describes the refuge as 11,000 acres of irregularly flooded brackish marsh and 3,480 acres of forested wetlands. It is a classic marsh, dense with shimmering needle rush and cordgrass in summer, that encloses the view from NC 12 as the grasses mature with the season's growth. The passage through the Cedar Island marsh rivals the exquisite winding of Princess Anne Road onto Knotts Island in Currituck County and is one of the finest such drives anywhere.

Established in 1964, Cedar Island National Wildlife Refuge offers a rare crossing often exquisite in the warmer light of the lower-angled sun of a waning year, when the grasses waver bleached against the horizon. High ground—the forested wetlands are hummocks supporting loblolly, long-needle, and pond pines, wax myrtle and gallberry, and even occasional live oak—punctuate the plains of pale threads. Without question, it is the expanse of marsh, mostly black needle rush, spreading endlessly

to either side, that makes the lasting impression.

Nearly 270 species of birds can be seen here each year. December and January are the peak season for waterfowl, and the predominant species are redhead ducks, lesser scaup, and a few black ducks. During the summer season, even on a quick drive-through, you will likely see some of the permanent populations of wading shorebirds.

As an undeveloped wildlife refuge, Cedar Island offers little access to vehicles, and there are few public facilities. Hunting and fishing are permitted. The road crosses a high-rise bridge over the 40-foot-wide slough linking Thorofare Bay on the east side of Cedar Island to West Thorofare Bay on the west side of NC 12. Drive slowly if you can—the elevation of the bridge provides one of the best changes in perspective for viewing the marsh. All lands west of NC 12 are in the refuge; the land on the southeast side of the slough is not. There is a boat-launching ramp at this location frequently used by fishermen and hunters.

The headquarters of the Cedar Island National Wildlife Refuge are at the south end of Cedar Island on SR 1388, known locally as Lola Road. Inside you may obtain information and maps of the refuge.

Access

Cedar Island National Wildlife Refuge is open during daylight hours all year.

There is an improved boat-launching ramp at the refuge head-

quarters on Lewis Creek south of Lola Road and a boat-launching ramp on the southwest side of NC 12 at the Thorofare Bay Bridge.

Information

For information, contact Cedar Island National Wildlife Refuge, c/o Mattamuskeet National Wildlife Refuge, 38 Mattamuskeet Road, Swan Quarter, NC 27885, 252-926-4021; or Cedar Island Shop, 252-225-2511. Office hours are 7:30 A.M. to 4:30 P.M.

Web address:

Atlantic

Surprisingly, Atlantic is home to nearly 1,000 people, but many more know it as the departure point for one of the concessionaires that provides ferry service to the North Core Banks in Cape Lookout National Seashore. This is also the eastern terminus of US 70 that tails out at an intersection with Salter Drive. SR 1387 connects to NC 12 some miles north of town, and if you approach from Cedar Island, SR 1387 is a lovely winding approach to the community that comes to an intersection with Morris Marina Road. Turn east to go to the marina; turn west to go toward town.

Atlantic can fairly be called a traditional downeast fishing village, and the houses are as tight and neat as a coil of rope. I think a telltale element of the town is the street names: Morris, Willis,

	Fee	Parking	Restrooms	Lifeguard	Camping	Showers	Beach Access	Hiking	Trail	Handicapped	Boating	ORV Access	Fishing	Programs	Historic	Sand Beach	Dunes	Upland	Wetland
Davis	•	•			•													•	•
South Core Banks					•		•	•	•		•	•	•		•	•	•	•	•
Cape Lookout Lighthouse			•				•	•	•		•	•	•	•	•	•	•	•	•
Cape Lookout N.S. Visitors Center	•	•								•	•		•	•	•				•

Fulcher, and Bullock among others, a who's who of downeast surnames. Then there is School Road, Core Sound Road, and Air Base Road—folks make it easy to know where you are or where you are going in Atlantic.

It is a handsome, tidy town, and obviously, by the shrimpers or fishing boats tied at their moorings, many who live here are dependent on the ocean for their living.

One key to their economy is a reliable passage to the open ocean, currently New Drum Inlet.

The closing of the first Drum Inlet sometime during the eighteenth century made the passage to the ocean arduous. A new inlet was dynamited in the early 1970s nearly due east of Atlantic. Already, the inlet shoals heavily, and from Core Banks, Drum Inlet almost seems to be a crossing that could be made on foot at low tide.

The lack of reliable access to the open ocean throttles commercial fishing from the small community. However, Atlantic is becoming a sailing and fishing center since the shallower drafts of smaller boats allow sportsmen to pass through Drum Inlet.

The Morris family, who once owned nearly 1,000 acres of land on Core Banks, operates the ferry concession, Morris Marina, Kabin Kamps, and Ferry Service. The ferry is equipped to carry four four-wheel-drive vehicles and disembarks passengers at a dock on North Core Banks, north of Drum Inlet.

Access

As charming as the town may seem, it is not yet set up for tourism. Restaurants and accommodations, if any, are limited.

Morris Marina, Kabin Kamps, and Ferry Service, 1000 Morris Marina Road, Atlantic, NC 28511, 252-225-4261, offers ferry service and cabin rentals on North Core Banks.

Web address: <www.ports mouthisland.com>

There are several private marinas with launching ramps in Atlantic that provide access to Core Sound for a launch fee. The North Carolina Wildlife Resources Commission maintains a fishing and boating access area at Salters Creek, at the northeast end of the high-rise bridge crossing Nelson Bay, south of Atlantic on US 70. From Beaufort, follow US 70 east until you reach Nelson Bay, approximately 7 miles from Atlantic. Parking is available, and there is no launch fee.

Information

For information on accommodations, contact Crystal Coast Tourism Authority, 3409 Arendell Street, Morehead City, NC 28557, 800-SUNNYNC (800-786-6962), 252-726-8148.

For further information, call the Cape Lookout National Seashore Visitors Center at 252-728-2250, 8 A.M. to 4:30 P.M. daily, or contact Superintendent, Cape Lookout National Seashore, 131 Charles Street, Harkers Island, NC 28531, 252-728-2250.

Web addresses: <www.nps. gov/calo/home.htm>; <www.

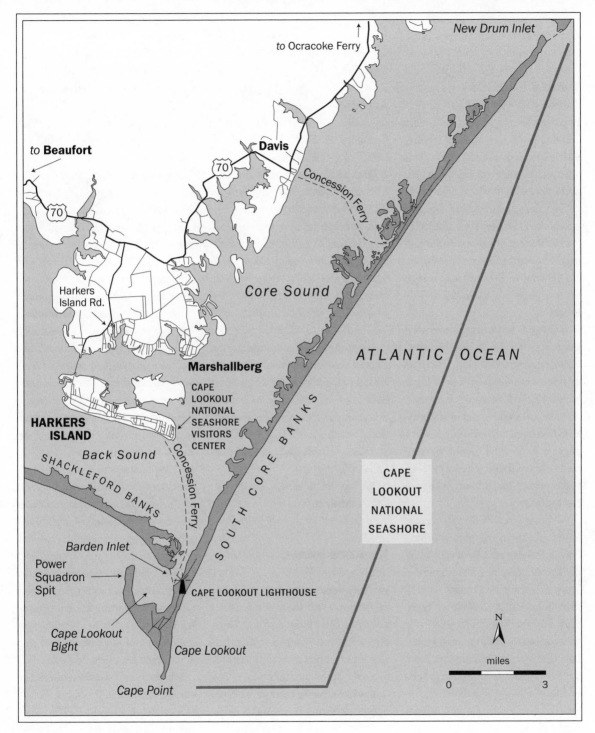

Map 16. New Drum Inlet to Cape Lookout

sunnync.com>; <www.nccoast chamber.com>

Davis

Ferry access is provided to Core Banks from Davis, an even smaller village than Atlantic. There is a sharp right turn on US 70, which comes in a length where prim white houses line the roadway and the shade trees hover over the lanes just a bit, that signals the community. The rest of Davis strings along US 70 west of the turn and sleeps out of sight down several small side roads.

Davis is a favored launching point for fishermen and hunters crossing to Core Banks. There is a small campground here. Alger Willis Fishing Camps is a concessionaire for Cape Lookout National Seashore and operates the ferry service to South Core Banks and rents cabins there. The ferry dock is due east of the right-angle turn in the highway.

Visitors using this ferry access, which docks on the barrier island less than 600 yards from the Atlantic Ocean, may see the structure known as the Core Banks Club, a private club that existed for more than fifty years on the island. After the national seashore was established, the club maintained a lease for fishing and hunting privileges in the seashore. The building, intended for use by Cape Lookout National Seashore, is falling behind in the war with the elements. The substantial landholdings of the Core Banks Club were purchased by the state of North Carolina and turned over to the National Park Service in 1976.

Access

Contact Alger Willis Fishing Camps, P.O. Box 234, Davis, NC 28524, 252-729-2791.

Web address: <www.drum wagon.com/awfc/default.htm>

Information

For information on accommodations, contact Crystal Coast Tourism Authority, 3409 Arendell Street, Morehead City, NC 28557, 800-SUNNYNC (800-786-6962), 252-726-8148.

For further information, call the Cape Lookout National Seashore Visitors Center at 252-728-2250, 8 A.M. to 4:30 P.M. daily, or contact Superintendent, Cape Lookout National Seashore, 131 Charles Street, Harkers Island, NC 28531, 252-728-2250.

Web address: <www.nps.gov/ calo/home.htm>

Harkers Island

Harkers Island stands alone. You must aim to go there since it lies inside of the elbow of Cape Lookout, well off the beaten track. It is likely that a fair number of people discover it by mistake since National Park Service rangers report being asked numerous times every year for the dock location of the Ocracoke ferry. Under less pressing circumstances, arriving on Harkers Island would be a fortuitous wrong turn.

The island community is decidedly "downeast." Literally and figuratively, it is out of the ordinary tourist loop, even though Cape Lookout National Seashore Visitors Center is at Shell Point, the end of the road on Harkers Island. Harkers Island attracts those who enjoy its genuineness and who go to visit the national seashore.

Fronting on Back Sound and protected from the Atlantic Ocean by Shackleford Banks, Harkers Island is a launching point for water sports—fishing, sailing, kayaking, canoeing, and windsurfing. The island has a tradition of building sturdy wooden working boats and is still peopled with artisans who can look at a stack of lumber and envision how to rearrange it for safe sailing. It's not unusual to see such a boat in progress beneath the shade of one of the island's sculpted cedar trees, an opportunity to glean peeks at the art of the specialized construction of "flared bow" boats that are suited for heavy work in shallow sound waters.

Harkers Island (along with other downeast communities) also has a strong tradition of decoy carving, which local residents did either for supplemental income or for personal use. An effort to revive and celebrate this tradition led to the establishment of the Core Sound Decoy Guild in 1987. The Core Sound Decoy Festival followed, and the interest burgeoned sufficiently to enable the construction

Core Sound Waterfowl Museum at Harkers Island. Courtesy of Crystal Coast Tourism Development Authority.

of the Core Sound Waterfowl Museum in 2003 nearly at the end of the road on Harkers Island. (Anyone can find the end of the road on Harkers Island.)

The museum is bigger than just decoys: it embraces the range of traditional water-related working arts peculiar to downeast, including with decoy carving, boatbuilding, storytelling, and hunting and fishing practices. The museum is open Monday–Saturday, 10 A.M. to 5 P.M., Sunday 2–5 P.M., 252-728-1500.

Within easy reach, by boat of course, are the Cape Lookout Lighthouse area of Core Banks and Shackleford Banks. Several ferry operators serve the seashore from Harkers, in addition to commercial charter fishing services. The island lives on the water in more ways than one.

Harkers Island is aligned on the same east-west arc as Shackleford Banks, visible to the south across the very shallow waters of Back Sound. The shelter of Core and Shackleford Banks exact a price

in the form of sometimes precarious channels that web outward to reach the inlets. This clearly does not stop residents from traversing the waters, however, since there are four marinas on the island.

You cross to the island by a causeway and two bridges, one of which is a low, fixed-span bridge and the other a swing bridge over local waters known as "the Straits." The crossing connects the forested mainland to the wind-sheared low island, a difference you see almost immediately. A local dock filled with stout working boats beside the road as you reach the island signals that you are going to a waterman's island, not a playground.

Harkers feathers into the shallow, greenish sound waters with ruffles of marsh and armies of pilings, legions of piers and docks, old boats, boats under construction, and salt-sheared cedar trees, modest homes, a school, and limited services. The main street is not lined but framed by the live oaks of adjoining yards. It feels like a neighborhood, not a thoroughfare.

Today, because of the excellent docking facilities and the proximity of two popular portions of the Cape Lookout National Seashore, the island is a launching point for day-tripping and camping at the edge of the sea, on the islands of the horizon. But you can get away here as well. In a pleasant, languorous way, Harkers Island is a respite with a hardened, working edge. I once watched in near terror and complete awe as an electrical storm danced across the Shackleford and Core Banks in a stroboscopic nightmare of charged exchanges, the kind of storm that melts sand. Every flash painted the wavering, uneven line of the islands on the horizon, and the ever-steady flash of the Cape Lookout Lighthouse seemed comic in comparison. It was a wild night, full of ozone and the silhouettes of the fishing fleet out of my window. Harkers Island became welded into my memory then.

But memory-fixing experiences are probably the exception rather than the rule here, possibly because the island is one large neighborhood surrounded by water. When you drive to the end of the island, you have seen it all (unless you visit the Cape Lookout National Seashore Visitors Center and the Core Sound Waterfowl Museum).

There are several places to stay, which is a boon to anglers and hunters since fishing trips depart very early, and taking a room the night before is a big help. Two major marinas on the island offer rooms, boat rentals, and docking services.

At Shell Point, at the end of SR 1335, you might see at least one or two cars drive to the dead end and turn around. It is not people looking for the Ocracoke ferry; it is the locals following a tradition, noted in an island cookbook: If you're a true islander you have to drive down to Shell Point at least once a day. They do it, too.

Access

The Cape Lookout National Seashore Visitors Center includes a large parking lot and picnic area at Shell Point, at the end of SR 1335. You may inquire about ferry schedules and operators to reach Cape Lookout National Seashore at this location.

There are four private marinas on Harkers that offer access for boaters for a fee.

On the east side of the fixed bridge to the island, Carteret County has constructed a small T-shaped wooden accessway for fishing or crabbing near the north bridge. There is ample parking.

Handicapped Access

The national seashore will loan visitors a beach wheelchair with advance notice. Call Cape Lookout National Seashore Visitors Center at 252-728-2250, 8 A.M. to 4:30 P.M. daily.

The visitors center is accessible to handicapped travelers. Access at private enterprises on the remainder of the island varies by establishment.

Information

For information on accommodations, contact Crystal Coast Tourism Authority, 3409 Arendell Street, Morehead City, NC 28557, 800-SUNNYNC (800-786-6962), 252-726-8148; or the Carteret County Chamber of Commerce, 801 Arendell Street, Morehead City, NC 28557, 252-726-6350.

For further information, call the Cape Lookout National Seashore Visitors Center at 252-728-2250, 8 A.M. to 4:30 P.M. daily, or contact Superintendent, Cape Lookout National Seashore, 131 Charles Street, Harkers Island, NC 28531, 252-728-2250.

Web addresses: <www.sunnync.com>; <www.nccoastchamber.com>; <www.nps.gov/calo/home.htm>

Shackleford Banks

Shackleford Banks is currently under review as a possible wilderness area, a curious, ironic legacy of a late nineteenth-century hurricane season. By federal standards for in-

	Fee	Parking	Restrooms	Lifeguard	Camping	Showers	Beach Access	Hiking	Trail	Handicapped	Boating	ORV Access	Fishing	Programs	Historic	Sand Beach	Dunes	Upland	Wetland
Shackleford Banks			•		•		•	•	•		•		•		•	•	•	•	•

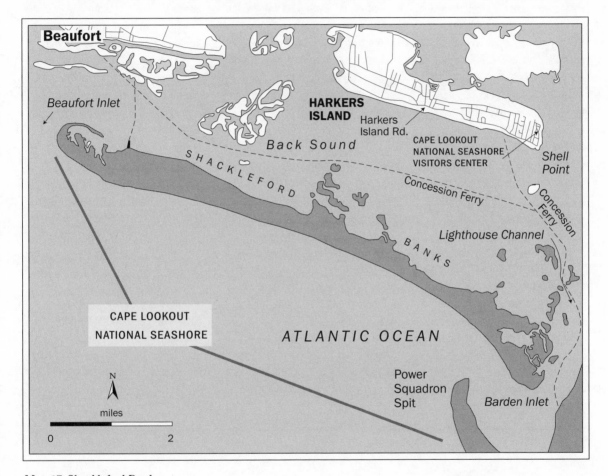

Map 17. Shackleford Banks

clusion in the wilderness system, this 7-mile-long, 2,500-acre barrier island qualifies since there is no development, few artificial structures, and no roads; the island is unaltered and federally owned and managed. The irony of its possible designation as a wilderness area is that in the nineteenth century as many as 600 people lived and fished from here. The island once supported two thriving whaling communities, Diamond City at the east end and Wade's Shore on the west, but the series of hurricanes that pummeled the island beginning in the 1890s and continuing into the early twentieth century destroyed the maritime forest and many of the houses that were in it.

The livelihoods, houses, and

The Shapes of Islands

Although all southeastern states have barrier islands, they differ in form and alignment. The differences are the result of sand responding to the differing coastal influences from one state to another. Where islands look alike, the coastal environments are much alike.

North Carolina's barrier islands are long and narrow, typical of barrier islands shaped by wind, wind-generated waves, and strong currents. Texas has similar islands; Padre Island National Seashore is virtually a mirror image of North Carolina's barrier preserves (but closer to mainland).

Along coasts where tidal forces predominate and the source of new material are inland rivers, such as South Carolina and Georgia, barrier islands tend to be short, wide, and drumstick-shaped.

Island configuration varies within North Carolina, though not so much in shape as in cross section. This variety is most evident at Cape Lookout National Seashore. The Cape Lookout Lighthouse is on South Core Banks, the southernmost lengthy northeast-to-southwest trending island of the seashore. Next to it, across Bardon Inlet, is Shackleford Banks, the first of the islands on the east-west arc of Onslow Bay.

What a contrast! Core is low with sparse vegetation and barely any dunes; Shackleford has extensive dunes and behind them thickly forested sections. Accounting for their difference is the islands' response to the prevailing winds that seasonally come from the northeast or southwest. On Core Banks, the wind moves sand in stinging, wispy streams along the beach, parallel to the ocean. This makes dune formation difficult. That same wind, though, moves sand perpendicular to the long axis of Shackleford Banks. Over time, this results in the widening of the island and the piling of sand into higher dunes.

This pattern of dune formation repeats periodically along the coast as the orientation of the barrier islands shifts between north-south and east-west. At three locations, Cape Hatteras, Cape Lookout, and Cape Fear, the compass orientation of the islands changes abruptly. Each increasingly westward bend of the islands changes the effects that prevailing winds have on the sand available to beaches. While in theory it might seem that *all* islands trending east-west would typically have higher dunes, sheltered forests, and higher elevations, it is not exactly so. Too many other factors come into play—such as sand supply and the underlying geological history, to mention two. In other words, it is not possible to cover all beach profiles with a blanket declaration about their origins.

---

communities were either beaten to pieces or lifted from their foundations. Several people were killed, and eventually the survivors abandoned what had been a village of at least 500 people at Diamond City, leaving only grave markers and some livestock behind. Some moved to Harkers Island, others sailed to what is now Salter Path on Bogue Banks, and a third group settled in a section of Morehead City described by one resident as the "Promise Land." For many years, the only inhabitants of Shackleford Banks were a thriving feral animal population.

With no fences, all animals were free to roam the island. The National Park Service removed the sheep because their grazing method, which consumes roots of the pioneering grass plants, was harmful to the island's natural systems. Horses are not as damaging, however, and have been allowed to remain.

The horses are one of the great attractions of Shackleford Banks because there are so few places on the East Coast where wild horses roam free. The horses come from noteworthy stock, carrying genetic markers that tie them to horse populations descended from Spanish stock more than 400 years ago. The peculiar genetic marker has also been typed in Paso Fino horses of Puerto Rico and the Prior Mountain Mustangs of Montana.

The exact origins are uncertain, however, but there was more than ample opportunity for either English or Spanish vessels carrying livestock to have landed or shipwrecked nearby, allowing horses to escape. The horses are small and lithe, averaging 12 hands (4 inches per hand) in height at the withers. The herd today numbers about 100 and is organized into approximately 25 harems and 7 bachelor bands. Dominant "alpha" stallions guard the harems.

D. I. Rubenstein, Ph.D., of Princeton University, who has studied the horses for nearly two decades, documents a territorial behavior by these stallions that does not usually occur in wild horse populations. The herd is managed to maintain genetic diversity by using immunocontraception selectively and periodically removing horses from the herd for private adoption. This keeps both the herd and island healthy.

Horse-watching on the island is popular, and the best advice is to bring binoculars and study from a distance. These animals are wild and should not be approached.

Shackleford's maritime forest is still recovering from the damage of hurricanes and several generations of occupancy. Most of the rejuvenating forest is along the western third of the island, behind the extensive dune ridge that in some locations is more than 40 feet above sea level. The eastern end of the island, the closest to Cape Lookout, is low and flat, resembling neighboring Core Banks in its physical appearance. One can imagine how little protection these sands would have offered from the force of a hurricane surging over them.

Shackleford Banks is perhaps the least known of the barrier islands, a function of its comparative inaccessibility. However, you can go there by ferry or private boat, and in recent years, it has become an increasingly popular spot for residents of Beaufort and Morehead City who have boats. When you step off of the ferry onto the island, near the jetty at the northwest end, you are entering a sanctuary of natural systems. You are very much a guest, and virtually everything on the island is protected. The restrictions may seem severe, but they protect an island in a dynamic balance with the sea and change. Following these rules is a small price to pay for what the island offers—7 miles of shelling or fishing and generally very little competition for either.

If you visit Shackleford, take plenty of water and food. As you make preparations for the visit, particularly if you're going fishing, remember that you will be carrying everything you bring. There is a water pump and restrooms near the jetty on the island's west end.

The park service places the following restrictions on your visit in order to protect the island's resources:

- All wildlife is protected. Since endangered species nest in the area, look out for posted areas. Hurricane Isabel created some superb nesting habitat for shorebirds such as the skimmer, and these areas may be closed during their summer nesting season.
- All vegetation is protected and should not be disturbed.
- Fires are allowed only below the high-water mark.
- Walk only at the lowest part of the dunes.
- Shelling is limited to two gallons of uninhabited shells per person per day.
- Metal detectors are prohibited.
- Carry your trash off the island.
- Pets must be leashed.

Access

Cape Lookout/Shackleford Banks: Check with the Cape Lookout National Seashore Visitors Center for a listing of current ferry operators by calling 252-728-2250, 8 A.M. to 4:30 P.M. daily. Here is a partial listing by departure port. These are passenger ferries only. Pets are permitted on leash, but check in advance with the ferry operator.

Beaufort to Cape Lookout Lighthouse and Shackleford Banks: contact Island Ferry Adventures,

Beaufort, NC, 252-342-7555; Mystery Tours, Beaufort, NC, 252-728-7827; or Outer Banks Ferry Service, Beaufort, NC 252-728-4129.

Harkers Island to Cape Lookout Lighthouse and Shackleford Banks: contact Calico Jacks Ferry, Harkers Island, NC, 252-728-3575; Harkers Island Fishing Center, Harkers Island, NC, 252-728-3907; Local Yokel Ferry and Tours, Harkers Island, NC, 252-342-2759.

Morehead City to Shackleford Banks only: These ferries are for passengers only; confirm pets in advance. Contact Anderson Maritime, Morehead City, NC, 252-728-3988; or Waterfront Ferry Service, Morehead City, NC, 252-726-7678.

You may also take your own boat, and there are no restrictions on where you may land, save one —you cannot tie up at the jetty, but you may unload there.

Information

The National Park Service Visitors Center on Harkers Island can field most of your questions about access to Cape Lookout National Seashore. You may reach the station daily at 252-728-2250, 8 A.M. to 4:30 P.M. For additional information, contact Superintendent, Cape Lookout National Seashore, 131 Charles Street, Harkers Island, NC 28531, 252-728-2250.

Web address: <www.nps.gov/calo/home.htm>

Beaufort

I am continually amazed at the ability of Beaufort to maintain its artfully balanced personality and the dapper appearance that attracts increasing numbers of visitors to its colonial streets. I suspect this delightful port and county seat stays Beaufort by the same persevering spirit that has enabled it to become the third-oldest town in the state. It does not appear that Beaufort, singly or collectively, wants or needs to be anything other than what it is—a three-century-old waterfront town, once serving industry, now serving hospitality, history, good food, and a real easy attitude.

It is as consistent as the tides.

Appearances speak volumes, and by this standard Beaufort has the civic backbone and good sense to say no to things that do not fit in. Sometime early in the historical preservation debate, Beaufort squarely came down as a place preferring renovation instead of renewal and reconstruction. It may have been a natural choice because the town weathered hard economic times with most of its buildings occupied. People stayed here, and as the town rejuvenated by growing a tourism economic base, historic preservation was more of a proven economic fact than a fashion. It became doctrine here, and fitting into the fabric and the feeling of its salt-swept history became the right thing to do. The result is a viable old town that is sparklingly sound.

It is also true that Beaufort has

a lot of character that it has come by honestly—and is still a heckuva lot nicer than most places that have been so close to saltwater for so long. Walking the town lets you absorb the wonderfully cockeyed architecture of this former fishing, really truly, fishing village. Everything seems slightly askew, and the cants and tilts of age are the proudly worn badges that are confirmed by the shields on the facades that bear the date of construction.

The soul of the town is the National Register Historic District, which encompasses most of the town from Broad Street south to Taylor Creek (the waterfront) and Live Oak Street to the east to the water of Beaufort Channel. There are more than 100 carefully restored buildings from the eighteenth and nineteenth centuries, stately behind the tree-shaded sidewalks. It is not the age per se that makes the district so attractive to stroll; it is the sense of proportion and scale of house and lot, trees and street. These blocks are made for walking.

The historic elements grant Beaufort a special status among coastal towns. If Ocracoke is the quintessential living-history village, where both the village appearance and way of life persevere in the face of tourism, then Beaufort is more the Mystic Seaport of North Carolina. The town is more carefully set as a museum display than as a working village. People can live in Beaufort and work elsewhere, earning the funds nec-

	Fee	Parking	Restrooms	Lifeguard	Camping	Showers	Beach Access	Hiking	Trail	Handicapped	Boating	ORV Access	Fishing	Programs	Historic	Sand Beach	Dunes	Upland	Wetland
Public Boating Access: Taylor Creek		•									•		•						•
Beaufort		•	•							•	•		•	•	•				
North Carolina Maritime Museum		•	•								•			•	•				
Public Boating Access: West Beaufort Road		•									•		•						•
Carrot Island and Bird Shoal								•	•		•		•	•		•			•
Radio Island		•											•						•
Regional Access: Newport River		•	•				•			•			•						•
Carteret County Museum of History		•	•								•			•	•				
Morehead City Municipal Park		•	•							•	•		•						•

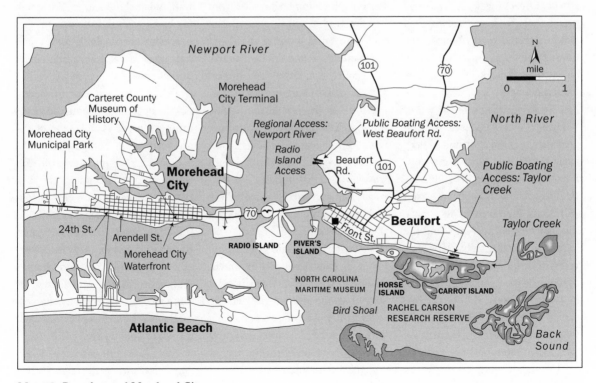

Map 18. Beaufort and Morehead City

essary to afford the historical ambience. Prices of buildings in the historic district are stellar.

The historic homes make a marvelous gateway. You must pass through the eighteenth-century portals of the district that occupy 15–20 blocks of the town to reach the Front Street, the main business street. The most direct route is to turn south at the light at the intersection of US 70 and Turner Street.

On the left will be the distinctive red-brick Carteret County Courthouse, commanding a square bounded by Cedar and Broad Streets to the north and south and Turner and Craven Streets to the west and east, respectively. Almost immediately after crossing Broad Street (over the railroad tracks that arc through town), you will be greeted by the homes, columned porches, and full-width balustrades that seem to smile, grinning side by side with a colonial air of dominion over the water.

Turner Street passes several parking lots, and unless it is very early in the day, don't press your luck—drop the car. Beaufort is built for boat or bike, but walking will cover the territory at a pace that permits sightseeing—and the buildings are the sights. Besides, you will be quicker on foot during the summer season than you will be on four wheels. To take the historical plunge full tilt, stop at the Beaufort Historical Association Welcome Center, on Turner Street, and arrange a guided tour of the eight-building complex known as

Old Beaufort by the Sea, which is open all year. There are some fine sights within the buildings, and the tour sets the tone of the town. Four sites include the Carteret County Courthouse of 1796, an 1859 apothecary shop, and the 1829 Carteret County jail. The Beaufort Historical Association is responsible for the significant preservation of the sites.

This historic wrapping of the town's past gives way to the bustling waterfront of its present. Today, Beaufort may, in fact, be busier as a port of call than ever before, with one major change—the boats that dock here unload people, not fish, according to the wishes of the community. As soon as you reach Front Street, it is evident that Beaufort is capitalizing on its waterfront history, trading on its past as the means to build a future. Beaufort completed an ambitious, nearly audacious, waterfront restoration smack in the heart of this seafaring town in the late 1970s. It was the step that jump-started an economic shift because it made the waterfront useable and attractive to travelers on the Intracoastal Waterway. They carried the word of this ambitious community up and down the eastern seaboard.

After all was said and done, Front Street, the heart of town, remained the heart of town. The street has one foot on land and the other in Taylor Creek. What is new is the shine that gleams from the brass fittings on cruising yachts and pleasure sailboats instead of the shine that glinted from older

tin-roof fish shacks. Beaufort is a prime and happening transient harbor for the sailing and power-cruising set.

The waterfront restoration created a two-sided downtown, approachable and appealing from both water and land. The restoration removed some older buildings—one resident remembers them as "fish houses" serving local trade—that blocked the view of the water. Taylor Creek became the feature of the community, framed by renovated, useable buildings. The dockmaster's office sits like a control tower centrally located between two parking lots. It overlooks the waterfront promenade adjacent to the Beaufort Docks, the name for the boat slips. A summertime walk along the docks is like strolling into a yachting showroom. The boat slips are available for a nominal nightly amount on a first-come, first-served basis.

Taylor Creek, out of the channel, is open water, and the backdrop is Carrot Island, part of the Rachel Carson component of the National Estuarine Research Reserve system. At dusk, the setting sun casts a golden glow across the marsh grasses and myrtles on the island and warms the waterfront with a sunset glow. Occasionally, the small herd of feral horses that roam on Carrot Island slips into view, emboldened by the separation Taylor Creek provides from the waterfront bustle.

The boardwalk and Front Street stay busy with pedestrian traffic. The central building with the har-

Wild horses on Carrot Island, part of the Rachel Carson National Estuarine Research Reserve. The Beaufort waterfront is the backdrop. Courtesy of Crystal Coast Tourism Development Authority.

bormaster's office also has a restaurant. If ever there were a place to prop your feet up and watch the world sail by, it would be this one. This small harbor is as inviting as any I have ever visited.

Beside Beaufort Docks is a small commercial cluster known as Somerset Square, almost directly at the end of Turner Street. Several restaurants line the 300 block of Front Street, and at the end of Orange Street, the beginning of the 200 block of Front Street, is the dock serving the Shackleford and Carrot Island ferry. This spot, where

Orange Street "tees" into Front Street, provides one of the richest, all-encompassing views of the town and its surrounds. The west extension of Front Street is residential, and the homes look toward the waterfront. The five adjacent houses in the 100 block have both first- and second-story porches that seem to have been built to a single chalk line. As you look along the length of Front Street, the porches nicely frame the view of Piver's Island and the Duke University Marine Laboratories.

Beaufort unfolds best block by

block, and each block is a variation of an evolved mix of houses and businesses side by side. Turner Street, close to the waterfront has a busy mix of shops. One of Beaufort's better-known restaurants, the Net House, is across the street from the Beaufort Historic Site. It features local seafood cooked with a light touch. It is steady and reliable, low-key but good local cooking.

Grab a bite and take a walk. The whole town feels like an open-air museum and makes you feel like spending the night in a period bed-

and-breakfast, waking up to stroll the wonderful, walkable streets.

Access

There is off-street and on-street parking near the waterfront. Several large parking lots are available approximately one block from Front Street.

The city has two parks on Taylor Creek: Grayden Paul Park at the end of Pollack Street, two blocks east of the waterfront, and Jaycee Park at the east end of Front Street, which has parking for approximately 30 cars and two small boat ramps.

Beaufort is the departure point for several of the concession ferries carrying passengers to Cape Lookout National Seashore and the Rachel Carson preserve, directly across Taylor Creek from the waterfront. The park service can advise you on carriers and their schedules, and the Beaufort Docks harbormaster can give you additional docking information.

The following ferry services (Beaufort to Cape Lookout Lighthouse and Shackleford Banks) dock along Front Street: Island Ferry Adventures, Beaufort, NC, 252-342-7555; Mystery Tours, Beaufort, NC, 252-728-7827; and Outer Banks Ferry Service, Beaufort, NC, 252-728-4129.

Carteret County and local sport fishermen have established a boating access site to the Newport River and Beaufort Channel. To reach the site, cross US 70 going north on Turner Street, cross the railroad tracks, and turn left on West Beaufort Road. The ramp and parking area are at the end of the road.

Web addresses: <www.nc coastalmanagement.net/Access/sites.htm>; <www.protectthe beach.com/parking.html>

Handicapped Access

The waterfront is readily accessible for handicapped travelers, as are some of the shops and restaurants on Front Street.

Information

For information on accommodations, contact Crystal Coast Tourism Authority, 3409 Arendell Street, Morehead City, NC 28557, 800-SUNNYNC (800-786-6962), 252-726-8148; or the Carteret County Chamber of Commerce, 801 Arendell Street, Morehead City, NC 28557, 252-726-6350.

Web addresses: <www.historic beaufort.com>; <www.sunnync. com>; <www.nccoastchamber. com>

North Carolina Maritime Museum

If you want to plunge into the maritime history of the state, then this is the place to "wet" your curiosity. Indeed, become saturated. In the last couple of years, the museum has been topping off its extraordinary permanent exhibits with a celebrity booking—artifacts from the eighteenth-century sailing ship, *Queen Anne's Revenge*. For the nautically challenged, this was the flagship for Edward Teach, better known as Blackbeard, who lifted his flag and lost his head near Ocracoke in 1718.

The museum is the repository for the artifacts recovered from the wreck, which is in the ocean off of Beaufort Inlet. Items on display include the ship's bell, cannonballs, pewter plates, navigation instruments, and wine bottles. Thousands of artifacts have been recovered, and display will follow their conservation.

The museum focuses on North Carolina nautical traditions and how the various seafaring livelihoods developed indigenous forms and expression. There is particular attention to the boatbuilding tradition and the styles of boat developed to effectively work the shallow sound waters.

Inside, the museum unfolds as a well-organized and displayed nautical attic. Mounted game fish ornament the walls, and shells by the thousands are cataloged in cases in the auditorium. These popular and eye-catching exhibits are a backdrop to the museum's central features—the stories of boats and those who sailed them.

There are several authentic wooden boats made by area boatbuilders, exquisite replicas of faithful ships and designs, and detailed scale models of famous vessels. The story of waterfowl hunting, decoy carving, and the hunting tradition is depicted in one corner. Perhaps the most moving of all the exhibits is the story of the lighthouses and the crews of the U.S. Life-Saving Service. One poignant vignette in this exhibit is about the Gold Life-Saving Service Medal awarded to Rasmus S. Midgett for single-handedly saving ten members of the barkentine *Priscilla* on August 18, 1899, from the Gulf Shoal station on Hatteras Island.

The Maritime Museum also practices what it preaches in the Harvey Smith Watercraft Center across the street. In this large warehouse with a viewing balcony, artisans work on a variety of wooden boats, repairing and restoring some and creating others from the keel up. The boatbuilding and restoration exhibit is an outgrowth of one of the museum's important preservation efforts to find representative North Carolina sailing and working craft and to preserve the skills that built them as well.

One of best aspects of this museum is that the nearly 18,000-square-foot building fits right in with the scale and feeling of Beaufort's Front Street. The building tips its architectural hat at the styling of the U.S. Life-Saving Service Stations and the Beaufort vernacular as well. Inside, in the rich honeyed finishes of a wooden vessel, is a treasure ship for sea lovers.

Equally amazing is how busy and outgoing the museum's outreach program is. Throughout the year, the museum sponsors programs in-house and provides invaluable access to the cultural and ecolog-

ical history of the coast through its field-trip programs. The museum publishes calendars of its programs three times a year. The trips are by reservation, and the fee varies. In the past, the museum has offered different workshops in the Cape Lookout Studies Program, which uses the former U.S. Coast Guard Station on Cape Lookout as an education center and overnight facility. Fees for these programs include ferry travel to the cape. Programs have also been held at the Rachel Carson component of the North Carolina National Estuarine Research Reserve, directly across Taylor Creek from Beaufort. With Duke University Marine Laboratories, the museum co-sponsors trawl and dredge trips to collect research specimens for the laboratory. These are working trips, a behind-the-scenes look at marine biology, and should not be mistaken for pleasure cruises.

The bottom line: it's both a great place to gawk and to get involved as time permits.

The museum contains an excellent bookstore and gift shop and is one of the largest dealers in nautical charts on the East Coast. The museum also sponsors a research library.

Access

The museum is open 9 A.M. to 5 P.M. Monday–Friday, 10 A.M. to 5 P.M. Saturday, 2 P.M. to 5 P.M. Sunday. There is no admission fee.

Handicapped Access

The museum is accessible for handicapped travelers.

Information

For information, contact North Carolina Maritime Museum, 315 Front Street, Beaufort, NC 28516, 252-728-7317.

Web address: <www.ah.dcr. state.nc.us/sections/maritime>

Carrot Island and Bird Shoal

The narrow, protected channel serving Beaufort's waterfront is Taylor Creek, an ordinarily shallow passage that has been dredged to 13 feet by the U.S. Army Corps of Engineers. The spoil from the dredging has been deposited on Carrot Island and Bird Shoal, which, along with Town Marsh, Horse Island, and Middle Marsh, form the 2,675-acre Rachel Carson component of the North Carolina National Estuarine Research Reserve system.

The filled areas from the dredging notwithstanding, these islands and their flats are relatively unspoiled sanctuaries, right in the middle of an area of rapid growth. The reserve, with its many varied habitats, provides excellent refuge for a diversity of wildlife, especially birds. Knowledgeable counters have noted more than 200 species here, 23 of which are endangered, threatened, or decreasing in number. The site is an important feeding ground for Wilson's plover in summer and the piping plover in winter.

Historically, residents have used these islands for recreation and for horse pasturage. There are horses there now, but they are feral animals descended from horses released in the 1940s, when it was common practice to allow livestock to graze on these islands. The present herd of 48 animals is the optimal number for the reserve, and it will be kept constant and actively monitored for their health and damage to the ecology of the islands.

It should come as no surprise, but these isolated hammocks almost became condominiums. In 1977, however, the proposal was thwarted, and the North Carolina Nature Conservancy purchased 474 acres of Carrot Island, the principal high ground. Since that time, the remainder of the marsh, tidal flats, and barriers have been secured, protecting both the charm of the Beaufort waterfront and the integrity of the sites.

Carrot Island, Town Marsh, Bird Shoal, and Horse Island form the 3-mile-long, less than one-mile-wide part of the reserve directly opposite Beaufort. Middle Marsh, nearly 2 miles long and 650-acres, forms the eastern segment of the reserve, across the North River channel.

During the summer months, the North Carolina Maritime Museum occasionally conducts guided interpretive walks on Bird Shoal. Guided walks are typically conducted by reserve personnel Tuesdays and Thursdays during the summer months. There is no charge, and the tours depart from the Education Office of the North Carolina Research Reserve office at Duke University Marine Laboratories on Piver's Island.

Access

Check with the harbormaster at Beaufort Docks for ferry transportation to the reserve if you are not going with a tour group.

Information

For information, contact North Carolina Coastal Reserve, 135 Duke Marine Lab Road, Beaufort, NC 28516, 252-728-2170.

Web address: <www.ncnerr. org/pubsiteinfo/siteinfo/rachel carson/rachel_carson.html>

Duke University Marine Laboratories

If you walk to the west end of Front Street in Beaufort and look across the water, you will be looking at the close, village-like campus of a major oceanographic research institution. Duke University in Durham, North Carolina, staffs a marine science laboratory for undergraduate and graduate degree programs in marine sciences and related subjects. The campus is on Piver's Island, which it shares with a National Marine Fisheries Station. A boat dock is reserved for the use of the two institutions. Although the campus is open to the public for selected programs and talks, it is a research and teaching facility that is not designed to accommodate visitation.

It was from the campus of Duke University Marine Laboratories that Rachel Carson wrote part of her superb seashore ecological book, *The Sea Around Us*. Carson drew heavily on her visits to nearby Bird Shoal and Carrot Island, which are now set aside as the Rachel Carson component of the North Carolina National Estuarine Research Reserve.

Information

The property is not closed, but it is an academic facility that is generally not set up for public visitation. For information, call the Office of the Director, Duke University Marine Laboratories, 252-504-7503.

Web address: <www.nicholas. duke.edu/marinelab/about/index. html>

Radio Island

Radio Island is one of the best of the informal and undeveloped access sites in the area. The site is in the thick of the port action, within easy bait-casting distance of the channel and blessed with protected waters for swimming. It has traditionally been a local access area.

Recently, the North Carolina State Ports Authority acquired a significant portion of Radio Island and restricted access into the area. It subsequently leased a 12-acre site to Carteret County for use as public access. The county installed approximately 72 parking spaces and restricts access to daylight hours. The lease specifies that the State Ports Authority can terminate the lease for any infraction of the posted rules governing use and access, so obey the posted regulations.

There are no concessions, so carry what you need to be comfortable.

Access
Radio Island is reached by turning south off of US 70 at the first median break east of the high-rise bridge over the Newport River, which is opposite the turn to the Newport River regional access area. Turn on the island, travel for several hundred feet, and turn left on the paved road.

Handicapped Access
There are designated handicapped spaces in the parking lot. The water, however, is a good distance over sandy terrain from the parking lot.

Information
For information, contact Division of Coastal Management, P.O. Box 27687, Raleigh, NC 27611, 919-733-2293.

Web addresses: <www.nc coastalmanagement.net/Access/ sites.htm>; <www.protectthe beach.com/parking.html>

Newport River Regional Access Area

You can pull over to fish or sunbathe by the Newport River at the regional access site on the northeast side of the causeway, at the east end of the high-rise bridge over the river. This is a fully developed regional facility, with restrooms, a boardwalk, picnic tables, a dune crossover, and trails leading to riverfront fishing sites. The site provides excellent opportunity for fishing and crabbing along the Intracoastal Waterway, which follows the Newport River here.

The access area is built on a dredge-spoil site, which seems stable and is certainly serving good use now. The boardwalk overlooks the state port terminal at Morehead City. It is a surreal view, the many domed storage buildings interlocked with catwalks and conveyor-belt delivery tracks. A dune ridge trail leads among plantings of seaside goldenrod and other pioneering plants to views of the north side of the basin and the Newport Marsh.

Access
The access area closes at sunset.

Handicapped Access
The site is fully accessible for handicapped travelers.

Information
For information, contact Division of Coastal Management, P.O. Box 27687, Raleigh, NC 27611, 919-733-2293.

Web addresses: <www.nc coastalmanagement.net/Access/ sites.htm>; <www.protectthe beach.com/parking.html>

Morehead City

There is no false pretense about my appreciation for Morehead City—I head straight for the Sanitary Fish Market and Restaurant on Evans Street. I enjoy the waterfront view, the polished hardwood floors, the bottomless pitcher of iced tea, and the never-ending basket of hushpuppies. The idea is not original, but I feel like I'm doing my part to support the historic elements of Morehead City and every college kid who ever needed a summer job. And after I eat, I go for a stroll, well, maybe a roll along the waterfront.

Morehead City's boardwalk is amazingly squeaky-clean for a working charter center, the home port of one of the largest sportfishing, commercial fishing, and diving fleets on the East Coast. The waterfront hums: kiosks are covered with local information, diners wander about after their restaurant meals, charter crews tend to their boats. You can choose from Gulf Stream outings or head-boat trips for bottom-fishing excursions. Several annual fishing tournaments use the waterfront as their headquarters. It's an active waterfront that stays accessible and somewhat dressed up, too.

Because it is on Bogue Sound, Morehead City is more an auxiliary destination than a prime vacation spot. It is a town that has made the most of its safe anchorage and reliable channel to the sea. While vacationers prefer to spread their towels on the resort beaches of Bogue Banks, they still spill over the sound to eat, fish, and shop along the waterfront.

The high ground of cedar-covered Sugarloaf Island is the backdrop to the moorings. It is visible between the facades of buildings and from some of the restaurants. Across the street are shops and restaurants that can help fill an afternoon before eating dinner.

Parking is tight, so it makes some sense to consider parking on Arendell Street, the main commercial street, and walking the short distance to the waterfront. South of Waterfront Junction, at the corner of Sixth and Arendell Streets, is the entrance to the city park parking lot.

If you come to Morehead City from the west on US 70, the highway eventually parallels railroad tracks, eastbound lanes on one side, westbound lanes on the other. This continues through the center of the town, reminders of the formative role of the railroad in Morehead City's history. The tracks still carry the freight, a sign that the port of Morehead and the 150-year-old dream of its founder remain vital.

Governor John Motley Morehead, who served from 1841 to 1845, literally made tracks in North Carolina as a rail baron. By the 1850s, rail lines to Carteret County terminated at Beaufort, the major

shipping and shipbuilding community of the central coast.

Morehead foresaw the need to develop another deep-water port (Wilmington was the only one), so he purchased 600 acres in this area in 1853. Served by the railway, Morehead City quickly became a fashionable resort during the Victorian era, eventually becoming a major port much later. After substantial financial commitments by the state to improve docking facilities and the harbor channel, Morehead City became the dependable deep-water port its founder envisioned.

Morehead City began growing as a vacation location when the railway came to town. In 1883 the famed Atlantic Hotel opened and became known on the East Coast as a major resort destination, a place of gala ballroom dancing. The lights by Bogue Sound in Morehead belonged to social luminaries. In this golden age of railroads, Morehead City attracted the barons of incredible industrial wealth steadily through the 1920s.

On April 15, 1933, the lights went up in a blaze when the Atlantic Hotel caught fire. (Photographs of the hotel and the fire may be seen at the Carteret County Museum of History.) The fire and the Great Depression dramatically altered the role Morehead City would play in the social life of the East Coast. The Jefferson Hotel now stands on the site of the Atlantic Hotel. The Atlantic Hotel was served by the railroad, and the Morehead City Train Depot stood slightly west

at the block of Sixth and Arendell Streets. In 2004 the terminal went for a ride, moved for restoration to the park at Tenth and Arendell, across the street from the History Place and closer to the center of the present commercial district.

The hub of the social activity has always been the east end of the community, but most folks arrive from the west. The highway travels through attractive tree-lined streets and residential neighborhoods that back up to Bogue Sound. What was long considered the western town limit is where US 70 and Bridges Street close, an area known as Camp Glen. During World War I, this was an army encampment.

Slightly east of where the railroad slips into the median of Arendell Street, the Crystal Coast Tourism Authority has a visitor and information center. Look for an A-frame building on Arendell Street at the Morehead City municipal park. This should be your first stop for information on programs, facilities, and current events in the area.

The municipal park is a handsome setting; live oaks shade its picnic areas, and there is free boat ramp serving Bogue Sound. The memorial obelisk behind the visitors center honors Josiah Bogue, who deeded to his daughter the land known as Shepherd's Point, which became the site of Morehead City.

If you're in a hurry to go to the beach, zip east to Twenty-fourth Street and turn right over the bridge. If you are curious about old Morehead City, turn into the municipal park and drive east on Evans Street. You will be in a neighborhood of bungalow cottages and permanent homes, many of which are holdovers from the first wave of second-home construction and the continual resettling of Morehead City as a retirement community. These soundside homes are sheltered by the native live oaks and stand shoulder to shoulder, close enough to be cozy but not quite crowded. The homes on Sunset Drive, a bulge into the sound, are larger but have a weathered presence that evokes vacation places such as Martha's Vineyard. Evans Street is not a shortcut; it is a tour through a neighborhood, so be careful of your speed.

Morehead City's residential neighborhoods continue on the eastern side of the bridge/causeway leading to Bogue Banks. The mainland bulges two more blocks to the southeast of Twenty-third Street, where Shepard Street, which carries you to the commercial district, and Shackleford Street, the waterfront road, run parallel to Arendell Street.

The historical commercial center of town lines both sides of the train tracks. The History Place, at Eleventh Street, marks just about the center of the main business district. This part of town is compact with a small-town character reminiscent of coastal plain communities like Washington or Scotland Neck. The buildings sit close to the road with street side parking.

Shepard Street angles north from its soundside location to join Evans at Seventh Street, and the pace of the community picks up here, signaling the beginning of the waterfront. At the corner of Evans and Eighth Streets is the Mediterranean villa–styled fire/police station; next door is the Quonset-hut headquarters of the U.S. Marine Corps Shore Patrol. Across Shepard Street a duck crossing sign signals the beginning of Morehead City's thriving waterfront and tourist service business district, which runs along the sound to Fourth Street and slightly beyond.

There is something here for everybody, particularly if you are interested in eating seafood, buying seafood, or catching seafood. You can park, if you are lucky, in the municipal lot at the city park at Sixth Street and Evans, where there are also public restrooms. It's crowded in the summer: do not arrive here at 6:30 P.M. and expect to find a parking space easily or restaurant seating without a wait. This is where beach vacationers come to eat.

The community has the beat of a busy gateway. Any traffic that snags your patience today pales by comparison to that before the high-rise bridge to Bogue Banks opened in the early 1990s. Crossing Bogue Sound was a rite-of-passage traffic stall on eastbound US 70 because all lanes led to a swing bridge. In summer, water traffic ruled, and recreational sailors in Bogue Sound opened the bridge on their vacation and slammed the roadway shut on yours. Ahh, sum-

mertime in Morehead City, idling in traffic on blacktop hot enough to dent with a finger—it was a fine test of a car's cooling system and a parent's patience.

The new bridge speeds the access for everyone, swimmers and boaters alike, but at the faster speeds, you miss the opportunity to soak in the soundside bungalow view offered by the side streets of Arendell Street. Traffic still can be dicey at night when the trains do much of their maneuvering back and forth. Trains use the middle of town—the limits of the switching yard end at just about Sixth Street—to align cars onto the proper spur. They can block the intersection of US 70 and the bridge road for a bit.

The Morehead City Terminal, which is open to the public for tours during weekdays, serves ocean-crossing vessels from all seafaring nations. It is also a major shipping port of call for the U.S. Marine Corps from nearby Camp Lejeune.

Heading east on US 70, you cross the tracks and vault over the Newport River Bridge to Beaufort. Here you can sometimes see an immense pile of an indistinguishable material. The product is hardwood chips from the North Carolina coastal plain forest, destined for Asia to make fine papers. A tremendous covered building on the north side of US 70 is a shelter for phosphate, mined near Aurora.

Access

Morehead City has no beach access and only limited locations for public access to sound waters. Swimming is not recommended in these locations.

The North Carolina Wildlife Resources Commission maintains a boating access ramp to the waters of Bogue Sound at a city park located at Thirty-fifth Street. There is another boating access location approximately 1.5 miles east on US 70 after the junction with NC 24. The access area is near the western city limits on the right-hand side as you travel east. You will see a glimpse of water as you drive toward the city; slow down at that point and look for the diamond-shaped sign indicating the access location.

Handicapped Access

The Morehead City waterfront and docks are accessible for handicapped travelers, and many of the charter vessels dock at ramped locations. There are designated handicapped parking spaces within the municipal parking lot at Sixth Street.

Information

For information on accommodations, contact Crystal Coast Tourism Authority, 3409 Arendell Street, Morehead City, NC 28557, 800-SUNNYNC (800-786-6962), 252-726-8148; or the Carteret County Chamber of Commerce, 801 Arendell Street, Morehead City, NC 28557, 252-726-6350.

Web addresses: <www.townof morehead.com>; <www.sunnync. com>; <www.nccoastchamber. com>

The History Place— Carteret County Historical Society

While it is not possible to package everything that makes a county into a single building, a portrait of the richness of downeast life is certainly possible. This is exactly what the History Place in Morehead City, an outgrowth of the Carteret County Historical Society, accomplishes. It is a museum, research center, and archive of the people and events of this extraordinary coastal county.

Once housed west of town on the grounds of Carteret Community College in the original school building that served World War I–era Camp Glen, the museum has made an uptown move to a new, stylish headquarters at the corner of Eleventh Street and Arendell Street.

An enthusiastic combination of citizen donations and volunteer work has assembled a delightful cross-cultural portrait of Carteret County. In the past, the museum has been the recipient of one of the state's highest awards for historic preservation work at its prior location. It carried the same attitude to its new home, renovating an old grocery store building that once was home to a Colonial Store. The museum retains the original ceilings and displays promotional items used by Colonial Stores when the grocery chain was a staple in the South. Generous citizens donated the funds to provide the clock tower.

In fact, generous citizens donated time and materials to move the collections to the new quarters, including the museum's signature anchor. A construction company had volunteered to move the anchor, once thought to be from the U.S. navy ship *Aphrodite* lost at sea but now believed to be from a similar ship, and found the task a bit much. Two construction companies, two cranes, twenty men, and four days later, the anchor was weighed to its new location, a prime spot for souvenir photographs.

In 2004 Morehead City relocated the original Morehead City Train Depot to the park across Tenth Street from the History Place. The museum acknowledges the renovated depot with a working, circa nineteenth-century model train that circulates in the gallery of the museum's exhibit space.

The museum captures the flavor of earlier Morehead City with reconstructions of a Victorian parlor, a doctor's office, and an old general store. Details about Morehead City's history and the railroad are one feature exhibit; so is the history of local shrimp boats. The span of exhibits reaches back to include the Tuscarora Indians and showcases Native American artifacts.

Access

The museum is open Tuesday–Saturday, 10 A.M. to 4 P.M.

Handicapped Access

The museum is accessible for the handicapped.

Fishing on the inlet at Fort Macon. Courtesy of North Carolina Division of Parks and Recreation.

Information

For information, contact Carteret County Museum of History, 1008 Arendell Street, Morehead City, NC 28557, 252-247-7533.

Web address: <www.thehistory place.org>

Bogue Banks

Bogue Banks, approximately 25 miles long, is the longest island south of Cape Lookout, and since the mid-1970s, it has become one of the most popular beach destinations in the state. The reasons are simple: it is the only easily accessible developed beach between Ocracoke and the beaches of Topsail Island, approximately 35 miles to the south, and the beach itself is wide, the gradient flat, and the wave action typically gentle. On summer turnover days, when new weekly home rentals start, the traffic to the bridges at Morehead City and Cape Carteret crawls.

The proximity to population centers and the greatly improved beach access locations are two additional keys to Bogue Banks's popularity as a destination. If you go to Bogue Banks, it is evident that the island itself has some other natural appeals. The most noticeable feature is the trees; much of the island is covered with a stable maritime forest. The second noticeable feature is the height of some of the dune ridges.

Bogue Banks, like Shackleford Banks to the east, is a beach ridge barrier island. The short definition is that, for complicated geological reasons (ample sand supply from Cape Lookout, favorable geologic understructure, and favorable orientation), there is a spine of high ground along its length. At one time, nearly continuous high

	Fee	Parking	Restrooms	Lifeguard	Camping	Showers	Beach Access	Hiking	Trail	Handicapped	Boating	ORV Access	Fishing	Programs	Historic	Sand Beach	Dunes	Upland	Wetland
Fort Macon Museum and State Park		•	•				•	•	•	•			•	•	•	•	•	•	•
Regional Access: Fort Macon		•	•	•		•	•			•			•			•	•		
Regional Access: Les and Sally Moore	•	•	•			•	•			•	•	•				•	•		
Atlantic Beach ("The Circle")	•	•		•												•			
Regional Access: West Atlantic Blvd.	•	•	•	•		•	•			•	•	•				•	•		
Regional Access: Iron Steamer Pier	•	•	•				•						•		•	•			
Theodore Roosevelt State Natural Area		•						•	•					•	•			•	•
N.C. Aquarium, Pine Knoll Shores		•	•					•	•	•				•	•			•	•
Regional Access: Salter Path		•	•			•	•			•			•			•	•	•	
Indian Beach		•					•				•	•				•	•		
Indian Beach ORV Access		•				•	•				•	•				•			

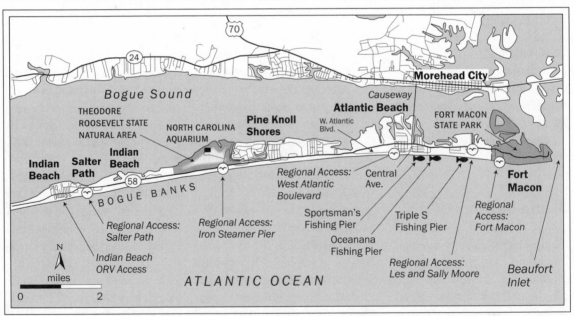

Map 19. Bogue Banks: Fort Macon to Indian Beach

dune fields fronted the ocean, but some of these have been leveled for building. The dune fields sheltered inland portions of the island from damaging salt winds; this and the high elevation allowed a maritime forest to develop. A contributing influence to its appearance is the prevailing north-south seasonal winds that strike Bogue and Shackleford Banks at right angles to the line of the beach. This pushes sand loosened by the waves into dunes. Contrast this to the low-profile islands of North and South Core Banks in Cape Lookout National Seashore, where the prevailing wind blows parallel to the beach, streaming sand across its front and making dune formation difficult.

The raw stuff of Bogue Banks —dense forest, high dune ridges, and a gentle beach gradient—are dreamed-about components for a barrier island, especially if the economy is tied to tourism. Spoiling the perfect picture is the fact that east to west; Bogue Banks is wrestling with the controversial tandem of beach erosion/beach nourishment. For a beach tourism town, losing the beach is tough; replacing the sand is even tougher, and the rancor does not make it any better.

The problem is perhaps more complicated here because dredging practices at the government-maintained shipping channel of Beaufort Inlet deprive the beach system of a natural supply of sand by dredging it then piling it in spoil islands in the sound or pumping the spoil offshore. (Atlantic Beach receives free sand from the dredging because it is within the official boundaries of the project area.) The upshot for visitors is that recent beach nourishment projects have been physically and aesthetically successful (after a rough start) and that by accepting federal assistance for the nourishment, communities have agreed to build new beach accessways with convenient parking.

While visiting the island is mostly about the beach, there are a variety of cultural and natural attractions to round out a trip. It is a 25-mile beach smorgasbord. There is a pre–Civil War fort, an aquarium and state natural area, luxury condominiums, an amusement park, shopping centers, a go-cart track, jungle golf, beachfront hotels, fishing piers, and trailer parks. There are marinas, sailing schools, and wild places that will stay that way except for observation trails. In some locations, dunes soar 15 to 20 feet above the tide line; in others, the dunes are as flat as beaten biscuits. There are a lot of different looks. There are four incorporated communities—Atlantic Beach, Pine Knoll Shores, Indian Beach, and Emerald Isle—and one stubbornly independent settlement—Salter Path. "Salter Pathers" adhere to traditional fishing and attitudes about fishing as a means of making a living.

Bogue Banks was first named for settler Josiah Bogue—the land that became Morehead City came from his family. The history begins with the quiet livelihood of small fishing communities on the soundside of the island and roars through a second-home explosion following the 1971 opening of the west-end bridge from Cape Carteret. Looking at the island today, it is difficult to believe that recreation and second-home construction did not become a force here until well after World War II. A bridge between Morehead City and Bogue Banks led to the creation of the playground of Atlantic Beach in the late 1920s. However, most of the remainder of the island, from Atlantic Beach west, belonged to two people, Alice Green Hoffman and Henry Fort, who, followed by their respective heirs, controlled the island up until the 1950s.

Alice Hoffman became the most colorful, notorious, and ironically beneficent owner of land here. Her domain, and she treated it as such, extended from Atlantic Beach to present-day Salter Path. She constructed a large estate with elaborate gardens on the soundside of the island, in what is now Pine Knoll Shores. (The estate was razed long ago, but for some time the foundation was visible along Oakleaf Drive, near the intersection of Hawthorne Drive.) Her disagreements with local fishermen (she sued for trespass and lost) led to the legal establishment of Salter Path.

At her death, she willed the land to her niece, Mrs. Theodore Roosevelt Jr. The Roosevelt heirs sold most of the land, which was subsequently developed, but they dedicated 290 acres to the state for the Theodore Roosevelt State Natural Area. Indirectly, Hoffman returned a portion of the property she had sued to protect to the people of North Carolina for their enjoyment.

Hoffman's next-door neighbor in an insular sort of way was Henry Fort, an entrepreneur from Pennsylvania who planned to build a tremendous resort on his property, which encompassed a great deal of the island west of Hoffman's estate. He needed a bridge to serve his development but was never able to get permission from the state for construction. His plans summarily died with the Great Depression.

The development of Atlantic Beach began in earnest with the economic boom following World War II. However, even though the island was accessible by bridge, very few people owned cars. The concept of extended vacations seems to have grown both as an idea and reality with the steady climb of the postwar industrial economy. The few folks who could drive to the island did not travel much farther than Atlantic Beach or the points east of there. The only road to the west, continuing to Salter Path, was not paved, and not many travelers wanted to go to Salter Path, anyway.

By the early 1950s, the demand for land was rising, but the island was essentially still not available. This changed in the mid-1950s when the heirs to the Henry Fort property sold the western half of the island and when Alice Hoffman died, leaving her property to

the Roosevelt family, who began selling their lands also. In effect, all of Bogue Banks west of Atlantic Beach was placed on the market at a time when the economy cycled high.

Within thirty years, it was a done deal, and access was becoming a problem because of the great numbers of people visiting each summer and because providing access to the beaches was an afterthought. As one Emerald Isle town official commented, "A few simple things a long time ago would have made a difference. If we had extended the right-of-way of the north-south streets to the water, we would have had plenty of access." But they didn't; Bogue Banks construction surged forward, and more and more of the beach became hard to reach.

You can develop a feeling today for which areas of the island date from earlier times. Careful siting of structures within the existing dunes and maritime forest yielded quickly to more expedient lot-clearing attitudes that were harsher on the land. Much of the wetlands adjacent to the causeway at Atlantic Beach were filled in to increase the number of home sites. The island showcases every barrier environment from low, narrow, treeless lengths, windswept and unsheltered, to salt-pruned and sculpted forests of live oak and yaupon. There are tall, grassed dunes and expanses of low plains of American beach grass. The older settlements such as Salter Path are on

comparatively high ground in the soundside forests; the newer developments are everywhere. The character of the development is as varied as the island environment. There are cushy second- and permanent-home estates and trailer parks, high-rise condominiums and mom and pop private campgrounds.

The two high-rise bridges—from Morehead City and Cape Carteret—loop NC 58 over the sound, along the spine of the island, and back to the mainland. It is a very leisurely loop—the speed limit on NC 58 is 45 miles per hour and closely enforced, particularly in Indian Beach, where it drops to 35 miles per hour. During summer, speed limits can be reduced further. Since you can rarely see the ocean from the highway, it is often difficult to tell that you are on an island. Some of the more intriguing stretches of the drive occur when the road tunnels through the salt-sculpted trees. The twisted trunks flash by at eye level, and the sheared tops undulate like closely cropped topiaries.

Access

Access has long been problematic at Bogue Banks given the popularity of its oceanfront. Generally, the problem has been that although there are clearly reserved public ramps to the beach, places to park are few and far between.

This has changed markedly, beginning at the first of this century, and the reason has been beach nourishment funding. The U.S. Army Corps of Engineers, who oversees beach nourishment programs, requires public access in exchange for public funds to nourish the beach, specifically, beach access plus available parking in reasonable walking distance every $\frac{1}{2}$ mile throughout the project area. The need for sand has trumped the need for privacy.

Carteret County's Shore Protection Office has assisted in the acquisition of funding for nourishment projects and has also had input into the access question. The end result for the beach and people wanting to use the beach is outstanding.

As a public service, the shore protection office maintains a website (<www.protectthebeach.com>) that has an excellent sequence of maps of Bogue Banks showing all the public access areas. The link is easy to follow, and the maps are easy to read.

Pine Knoll Shores previously had no public access but a Corps-funded nourishment project has brought three sites (plus parking) to the community. The new accessways, which are marvelous boardwalks through the maritime forest, are outstanding walks in their own right—no matter that they end in splendid (newly nourished) beach.

Fort Macon State Park, the largest and one of the most popular access locations on the island, serves Beaufort Inlet and the beaches at the east end of the island.

Atlantic Beach maintains two regional access sites, the Les and Sally Moore Regional Access at New Bern Street and the new West Atlantic Boulevard Regional Access just west of the "circle."

The most widely used facility is at Salter Path, featuring 65 parking spaces on 22 acres with a bathhouse and dune crossover.

The somewhat restricted access situation has come by an unexpected bonus in the form of misfortune and generosity of several pier owners.

The Iron Steamer Pier, so named for its landmark blockade-runner hulk visible at low tide, sold off one-half of its property to Pine Knoll Shores, which maintains a 60-space public parking beach access site there. The pier was demolished at the end of 2004, but the name persists at the access site.

Hurricanes destroyed the Indian Beach Fishing Pier in 1996, and the parking lot there at Indian Beach RV Park has become an access point.

Emerald Isle Regional Access, west of Twenty-fifth Street, is adjacent to the site of the Emerald Isle Fishing Pier. A plaque commemorates this island landmark's story with the simple inscription: "Former site of the Emerald Isle Fishing Pier. Established 1955. Destroyed by Hurricane Bertha July 1996 [and] Hurricane Fran September 1996."

Handicapped Access

The regional access sites at Fort Macon, Atlantic Beach, Salter Path, and Emerald Isle are accessible to handicapped travelers and have restrooms. Both the Fort Macon and the Salter Path access sites have terrific views from elevated, ramped dune crossovers.

The West Atlantic Boulevard access location in Atlantic Beach has handicapped spaces adjacent to a boardwalk and restrooms, and it provides access to the Atlantic Beach boardwalk as well as the oceanfront.

Information

For information, contact Crystal Coast Tourism Authority, 3409 Arendell Street, Morehead City, NC 28557, 1-800-SUNNYNC (800-786-6962), 252-726-8148.

Web addresses: <www.protect thebeach.com/parking.html>; <www.nccoastalmanagement.net/ Access/sites.htm>

Fort Macon Museum and State Park

We waited on a 97-degree day for the park ranger to begin his interpretive program on Civil War firearms. The walls of the citadel loomed above the parade ground, trapping the heat and casting a sliver of shade extending 3 feet from the base of the casement wall. About 80 people stood in the shade, waiting, our backs against the wall.

Out walked the park ranger carrying a vintage 50-caliber Civil War rifle.

State park ranger Paul Branch gives an interpretive program on Fort Macon's history. Courtesy of North Carolina Division of Parks and Recreation.

"My, y'all are cooperative," he boomed. "I walk out here with a rifle, and y'all are already standing against the wall. . . ."

Thus began a concise, informative, and entertaining chat on Civil War weapons and tactics, emphasizing the challenges of the ten-step loading and firing sequence when the heat is oppressive and people are shooting at you. The talk lasted about 30 minutes and then, timing himself (under 30 seconds), the ranger loaded a blank, took aim at a distant casement, and fired.

The sound that roared from the muzzle hit the opposite casement wall and bounced back—80 people cleared the ground.

"Imagine the noise of a battle," he said. It's still unimaginable, but far more vivid thanks to the talk.

Without doubt, the way to get the most out of a visit to Fort Macon, the state's most visited park, is to attend one of the interpretive talks. The competent park staff makes the old walls come alive again.

Fort Macon at one time commanded the approach to Beaufort Inlet and dominated the east end of Bogue Banks. It is kind of eerie. The main entry into the fort is a brick road, reinforced with stone wheel tracks, installed to bear the weight of caissons and cannon carriages, that descends from the heights of the earth ramparts. You enter through the walls of the outer ramparts, cross a moat on a wide wooden bridge, and then enter into the fortification. Inside the citadel, the bricked facades of vaulted casemates, the underground barracks, rim a geometrical parade ground. Three staircases ascend from the parade ground to the top of the citadel. On a 97-degree day, it is oppressive and medieval.

Should you visit on a day when

no children are playing tag along the ramparts—unlikely during the summer season—it is hauntingly quiet. From the parade ground, the only view is of the sky. It is necessary to ascend to the gun emplacements at the top of the citadel or on the covertway, the outer wall, to see the ocean.

The most surprising view atop the covertway is toward the entrance road. Engineers so skillfully sited and constructed the fort that you don't notice it when driving by to reach the parking lot. From the gun emplacements, you can see the field of fire that the location controlled.

The army built the fort between 1826 and 1834, using nearly 15 million bricks. While designed to secure the inlet militarily, the cannon were useless against the sea. Erosion and hurricanes had claimed earlier fortifications, so as the construction finished, the army determined that the fort needed fortifications, too. During the 1840s, a young West Point graduate by the name of Robert E. Lee designed and supervised the construction of the jetty that still works to protect the inlet and also provides great recreation for visitors.

During the Civil War, Confederate troops quickly seized Fort Macon. On April 25, 1862, the Union took it back after an eleven-hour siege. Following the war, the fort served as a penitentiary. The jail cells are under the outer ramparts.

In 1924 Congress permitted the state of North Carolina to take possession of Fort Macon to become its second state park—for the sum of one dollar. The facility languished until the Civilian Conservation Corps restored it during the mid-1930s, officially opening in 1936. While the fort is the centerpiece of the park, there are 389 acres in the entire preserve, encompassing the eastern end of Bogue Banks. The entrance drive passes through much of the park.

Exhibits inside the fort detail typical Civil War artillery, most of which was found on the grounds. Exhibits also include furnished officer's quarters, more stylishly comfortable than one would imagine, considering the starkness of the vacated casemates. A new exhibit is a reconstructed barracks from World War II, when the fort garrisoned a coastal artillery defense troop that had gun emplacements seaward of the fort walls. It takes a little more than an hour to wander the hallways and battlements. Watch your step as you walk through the casemates—the bricked floor is uneven.

The Elliot Coues Nature Trail, a self-guided walk through a maritime shrub thicket, leads up to higher ground that is the beginning of a maritime forest. Unusual, multibranched eastern red cedars, which hold their branches very low to the ground, grow along the trail, as does a beautiful specimen of prickly ash or Hercules club, a spiny tree pioneering in sandy soil. After leading you through this emerging forest with its varying ecological niches, the trail reaches the high dune ridge and beach overlooking the inlet and then returns to the parking lot at the fort. The stroll takes about 45 minutes.

One obvious park attraction is the beachfront on Beaufort Inlet. Nearby is a large regional access facility with a very lengthy stretch of beach. Fishing and bathing are permitted in the park. The inlet location provides both choice beach and angling. A very high dune system fortifies the seaward edge of the park; some individual dunes reach more than 40 feet high. Lee's jetty caps the east end, arresting erosion at the inlet and protecting the fort. The jetty also creates some shallower, calmer waters for swimming, but as with any inlet, caution should be observed when swimming here. The parking lot at the fort is close to the jetty. You have a direct access to the inlet and can watch the port traffic using Beaufort Inlet. Shackleford Banks of Cape Lookout National Seashore is across the inlet.

There is also a U.S. Coast Guard Station on the grounds of the park, which you will see before you reach the fort. The station is not closed to the public, but no public services are offered.

Access

The park is open 8 A.M. to 9 P.M. during June, July, and August. During April, May, and September, the park is open 8 A.M. to 8 P.M., and during October–March, 8 A.M. to 6 P.M. The fort is open 9 A.M. to 5:30 P.M.

The regional access site at the park is the major access point on Bogue Banks. The entrance to the site is a right turn soon after entering the park, which winds through the maritime shrub thickets into a dune field and a splendid 300-car parking lot. The access area includes showers, restrooms, concessions, telephones, and a boardwalk dune crossover. Programs by park rangers are occasionally offered at the site. The guarded swimming areas are open 10 A.M. to 5:50 P.M. during June, July, and August.

There is also a smaller parking area at the fort, near the inlet waters. The breaking-wave beach is south from the fort area. It is a hike to the beach from this lot.

Since Fort Macon is the most visited park in the state system, to be sure of a parking place, you need to be there before 10 A.M. on summer weekends.

Handicapped Access

Fort Macon is negotiable by handicapped travelers but not easily.

The regional access site is fully handicapped accessible.

Information

For information, contact Fort Macon State Park, P.O. Box 127, Atlantic Beach, NC 28512, 252-726-3775.

Web addresses: <www.ncs parks.net/foma.html>; <www. protectthebeach.com/parking/ html>; <www.nccoastalmanage ment.net/Access/sites.htm>

Atlantic Beach

Each turn of the coast has one place that pops and jumps with a higher-voltage vacation energy. Atlantic Beach fills that role for this length of North Carolina oceanfront. People convene here, collect here, figuratively wash up on shore here, and wish they could stay and play forever. Then Labor Day arrives, and it is time to go home.

The symbolic center of action is around the "circle"—the beachfront due south from the Morehead City bridge. It is not really a circle, but it has continually been the center of the action in Atlantic Beach since the first bridge was built from Morehead City in 1928. Captain John Newman Willis III, the first person to be born in the town of Atlantic Beach (his father was the first mayor), provides a detailed history of the community on the town website (<www.atlantic beach-nc.com>). Here is a sketch of his narrative.

Ironically, the bridge and the simultaneous opening of a complex of bathing and dance pavilions in the late 1920s spelled the economic end of two earlier beach bathing pavilions farther east that had been served by ferry lines from Morehead City. These earlier developments, reaching back to the late nineteenth century and the early years of the twentieth century, served the patrons of the Atlantic Hotel in Morehead City. One was at Money Island Beach (a city street name), where the Sportsman's Pier stands.

In 1922, during the times of segregation, Asbury Beach was developed around the construction of another bathing pavilion and ballroom just east of the Triple-S Pier by a gentleman named Asbury.

A fire and the Depression took out the original developments and bankrupted the owners, but in 1930, a new owner built two new bathhouses and dance hall called the Casino, and the beach was open again for business. (The road alignment in the circle dates from this era—it never was a circle.)

The final, formative chapter of Atlantic Beach came in this era when the land adjacent to the circle was subdivided for cottages. The street plan, from Durham Avenue in the west to Wilson Avenue in the east, is evident today.

As soon as the bridge opened, Atlantic Beach became the "center" of dancing and band music.

Today, the community center lacks the tight focus and concentrated purpose of the town's early resort decades. Instead, a mix of private clubs clusters around the outside of the "circle," emphasizing the sounds and suds preferred by a young crowd. What really dominates the skyline is a huge, lighthouse-sized water tower.

In the 1950s NC 58 opened along the length of Bogue Banks, allowing the community to spread out a bit. Old patterns persist, however, and the commercial and entertainment of much of Bogue Banks clusters at the junction of the bridge/causeway road and NC 58. The causeway is a healthy clue to the

Public beach access point at Atlantic Beach. Courtesy of North Carolina Division of Coastal Management.

mood and rhythm of the town; it screams a commercial welcome. You can rent a sailboard, charter a fishing trip, dine on fresh seafood, or buy a tee shirt. There is a type of touristy congestion at Atlantic Beach that has its own appeal, and you almost have to be in motion to appreciate it. From the central intersection of US 58, the town reaches east to Fort Macon State Park and west to its residential neighbor, Pine Knoll Shores. There are some unincorporated parcels between the two communities.

The streets in the older central section, between Durham and Wilson Avenues, form a grid. The causeway (named Morehead Avenue) becomes Central Avenue and runs to the water, ending in Atlantic Avenue, which is parallel to the ocean. East and West Drives fork off to either side of Central Avenue and curve to intersect Atlantic also. The three streets form a "Y" with Central Avenue in between them. An amusement park once occupied the open area between these roads, now replaced by a go-cart track. The rigid street matrix extends three blocks in either direction from the "circle." The "circle" and the boardwalk are still a beach-front focus. The boardwalk is concrete and not elevated, and it overlooks beach volleyball courts—at least between Raleigh Avenue and East Drive.

Previous expansion of the town limits was accomplished under protest. In an unsuccessful effort to thwart incorporation, the original developer of Money Island intentionally skewed Tryon, Dobbs, and Caswell Streets so they would not align with the corresponding streets in Atlantic Beach. As a result, not all the streets running parallel to the ocean align, which reduces through traffic in the

Cones, Coils, and Columns

I still have this unsatisfied childhood curiosity to look around the corner of a conch. When younger, I wanted to know how it held all that ocean I could so plainly hear. I kept trying to bend my eyesight even after learning that I didn't hold a conch but a whelk. Whelks, conchs, tulips—each of them is an example of one of nature's most exquisite blind alleys, known only to the nimble hermit crab and, of course, the creatures that made them.

My youthful curiosity evolved into an appreciation and fascination with the beauty of the coiling class of Mollusca known as gastropods or snails. The names don't do justice to the artistry. In a fantastic variation on a theme, nature took a simple form, the cone, and applied a simple formula, the coil, and then gave it a decorative twist. Snail quarters are some of the finest houses you will ever find. The Greeks knew it—they transcribed the spiral of a snail to become the volute or curved decorative capital appearing on the Ionic column.

The Greeks noticed that the coil of the whelk enlarged in an elegant manner. It seems proportional; indeed, it is proportional, as the French mathematical genius Descartes deftly discovered. He analyzed the graceful curve of snail shells, naming the mathematical function that describes it the equiangular spiral. Each successive coil of a snail's shell enlarges from the previous coil by a fixed proportion. A baby channel whelk is mathematically similar to a mature channel whelk; the proportions of the shells are the same—one is merely smaller than the other.

If you have ever opened the egg case of a whelk—the canvas-colored strings of rounded "pocketbooks" that look something like vertebrae—and found juvenile snails inside, then you have observed this mathematical precision. The spiral growth of the shell is logarithmic and numerically graphical (as if snails appeared cut from a digitized pattern).

To this self-regulating, enlarging shape, nature added curious ornaments, such as the knobs of the whelk, the flared lip of the queen conch, or the irregular mouth of the helmet shell—embellishments on the theme of cone and coil. Color and pattern adorn the snail further, but the greatest variation comes from the experimentation with the basic formula—the twisting, tapered tube.

If you can imagine that a cone is stretched out before you (or try one with modeling clay) and that you are the molluscan artist, first coil the cone in one plane, flat on the table, like the fiddlehead of a fern. This is the shell of the nautilus, native to gift shops on our coast. Next, coil the cone to the left. This is a sinistral shell (like that of the left-handed lightning whelk). Reverse the coil, and you have a dextral shell. Whichever hand's fingers cup behind the mouth of the shell when the thumb points in the same direction as the top of the shell determines its handedness. (This is important if you are cooking left-handed whelk chowder, for example.)

If the cone is fat and curls in a cushion, you have the coil familiar as the moon shell. Stretch the coil out for a great length in few revolutions, and you have the horse conch. Coil the cone tightly in a narrow taper, and you have created the auger.

Each snail species has its own rules for coiling and color pattern. Among individuals of a given species, color and patterning vary sufficiently to strike a note of individuality, but the coiled shape remains constant and telltale, as does the basic patterning of coloration.

neighborhood while confounding newcomers.

Atlantic Beach has the greatest number of hotel rooms on Bogue Banks, staying busy nearly year-round with convention and business gatherings. The hotels are interspersed with other property uses and are generally outside the boundaries of the original community plan. This softens the beach-front appearance, keeping a cottage feel to the center of the community. While national-chain hotels are present slightly west, the town has a lively condominium/apartment rental market and smaller family-owned motel business in the direction of Fort Macon.

Atlantic Beach is restive, rather than restful. It is busy in all directions—oceanfront and soundside. Toward the end of last century, while the beach was growing with taller, larger buildings, the sound-side bloomed with marinas and private communities.

Downtown Atlantic Beach is between times. The residential streets to either side, built long ago and honoring the natural dune line, perch above the "circle" in more ways than one. There is a steadiness about the houses that has been missing from the circle since the old-style pavilions disappeared.

In the summer the beach itself is the central focus, and this popular coast-to-sound city is wall-to-wall people. What still works about Atlantic Beach is the wide, gently sloping, frequently replenished sands of Bogue Banks. However,

even this has been tricky to hold on to.

Although a seawall had been constructed at Atlantic Beach following the invasion of Hurricane Hazel in 1954, there was no follow-up program to build up the beach. By the early 1980s, waves were slapping at some of the front-row cottages, particularly those east of the causeway.

Luckily, in 1986 the city received a windfall, or "dredgefall"—an entire island's worth of free sand. After the Environmental Protection Agency determined that a spoil island in Beaufort Inlet had too much sand and had to be moved, Atlantic Beach accepted the sand, which made nearly 200 yards of beach. The town carefully placed sand fences to retard sand movement, planted dune grasses, and posted the dunes. The result is a lot of beach. The seawall is no longer visible, now buried beneath new dunes. Although the replenishment has generally been a success, by the winter of 1991 erosion had again shortened the beach a good bit. One pier owner rejoiced at the erosion—the original filling had effectively "shortened" his pier by building beach under it.

Presently, the city is considered to be within the project area of the annual dredging required to maintain the channel serving the port of Morehead City. This means the town gets free sand whenever the channel needs dredging.

Second-home construction has prospered since the 1960s, and the

city and island have benefited from approaches that are more sensitive to building at the beach. Many housing units have been added, but there is still a great deal of open space because newer units are clustered. Some locations, such as the private property of the Dunes Club, visible from the Les and Sally Moore Regional Access Area, give you an idea of unaltered Bogue Banks.

A great deal of subdividing occurred before a program mandated public access. In the older parts of Atlantic Beach, there are walkways serving the neighborhoods, but as in the other island communities, they are inadequate to serve day-trippers since they provide no parking. The picture improves each year, but access is still at a premium, particularly if you drive your car over for the day.

Access

Atlantic Beach has ample dune crossovers and local paths serving hotels and cottages that are not on the oceanfront.

As of 2004, Atlantic Beach was one of three municipalities, along with Wrightsville Beach and Carolina Beach, that charge for parking or have leased parking management to a private parking authority to collect fees for public access parking. This practice is not strictly forbidden by the Coastal Area Management Act (in theory, any parking fees collected from an access location are supposed to be used to maintain and improve that location), and fortunately, it is not widespread. I feel that it clearly violates the spirit and intent of public access. Until this policy is changed, don't plan to park at the central lots in Atlantic Beach unless you have a bag full of quarters.

The going rate is $1.25 an hour, rigidly enforced with discouraging tickets (perhaps towing) for violations.

In addition, there is little parking on residential streets, so be careful where you leave your car.

The first area to check for a stopping place after crossing the bridge is around the "circle," which is directly ahead at the main intersection with NC 58 or Fort Macon/ Salter Path Road. This is the major public beach in the town, and there are lifeguards here during the peak season. There is angled parking along West and East Drives, with 300 spaces plainly marked and available on a first-come, first-served basis at the going parking rate. If you are creative, you might be able to invent a parking space out of some of the odd-shaped parcels of land remaining in the circle, but do so at your own risk.

One-half block west of West Drive is the West Atlantic Boulevard Regional Access, which puts you right in the heart of the old Atlantic Beach, and it is a beauty. There are about 75 parking spaces, restrooms, a bathhouse, and a deck that leads to the concrete boardwalk.

There is an off-road-vehicle ramp at the south end of Raleigh Avenue, the second road west of the causeway off Salter Path Road. The beach is closed to vehicular traffic between Good Friday and Labor Day. You must obtain a decal from the town and display it. Local restrictions on beach driving are explained when you purchase your sticker at town hall, and you are subject to all North Carolina driving and licensing laws.

Further west on Salter Path Road, shortly after passing the post office, the Sheraton provides parking for non-guests in a graveled oceanside lot either daily, weekly, or monthly at reasonable rates. The lot is attended and signed as a public access and includes more than 120 spaces. There may be a charge.

Sportsman's Pier at Money Island Road has a small private parking lot for pier users, with some overflow parking available for a fee. Fishermen receive a pass that allows them to park all day. The owners monitor the lot during the Good Friday–Labor Day season.

Oceanana Fishing Pier and Family Resort has a parking lot with more than 100 spaces. Fishermen get first preference, so it is advised that you check with the owners before parking.

Immediately west of the Dunes Club at New Bern Street is the Les and Sally Moore Regional Access Area. This is a heavily used access area with 51 parking spaces. There are restrooms and a boardwalk dune crossover leading to a children's play structure at the foot of the primary dunes.

The Triple S Pier at the end of Henderson Boulevard allows some overflow parking for folks who don't fish. Signs are posted to warn against parking in the neighboring motel lot, but the pier parking may be available by asking.

The causeway is a boating center. There are a number of marinas running fishing trips to the Gulf Stream and closer waters. There are also several locations for sailboat and sailboard rentals as well as sailing lessons. Private boats may launch as well.

Handicapped Access

Atlantic Beach will loan a beach wheelchair with advance notice. Call the fire department at 252-726-7361.

The following access locations in Atlantic Beach are fully handicapped accessible: Fort Macon Regional Access Area, the Les and Sally Moore Regional Access Area, and the downtown access area at West Atlantic Boulevard.

Information

For information, contact Crystal Coast Tourism Authority, 3409 Arendell Street, Morehead City, NC 28557, 800-SUNNYNC (800-786-6962), 252-726-8148.

Web addresses: <www.atlantic beach-nc.com>; <www.protectthe beach.com>; <www.nccoastal management.net/Access/sites. htm>

Pine Knoll Shores

Pine Knoll Shores begins at milepost 4 (Atlantic Beach Causeway is approximately milepost 2) on

How to Behave on a Pier

Maybe this should be how *not* to behave on a pier. The first thing you should know is that pier fishermen are territorial. They don't just fish from a pier, they stake a claim on a spot; first come, first served.

Several years ago, a grizzled, mackerel-slaying veteran of the fabled Kure Beach Fishing Pier groused about how pier fishing was going "all to hell." To paraphrase his colorful words, nobody knows how to fish well with others. He got no respect (perhaps another matter) and less room to land a fish, a real problem. If the fishing gods smiled and he hooked a real "rod bender," other anglers immediately rushed to his place on the pier to fish in the same vicinity. (Fish travel in schools, don't they?) He didn't need neighbors; he needed company, and he needed more pier real estate to land the fish. It was a Homer Simpson moment when the lines got tangled.

It is funny in retrospect, but only because such conduct tramples over all the tenets of pier behavior. (Think of a stranger spreading a blanket between you and the water when it's open beach as far as you can see. Grrrr.) Such actions are a sharp elbow to sociability in a sport well known for its solitary and contemplative waiting punctuated with bursts of activity. On a pier—a linear, two-sided world—a little courtesy goes a long way.

The fraternity of pier anglers has informal rules of etiquette, perhaps better described as pier protocol. It is a self-policing way of ordering the hoped-for bursts of adrenalin when fish begin biting.

Regulars know the truth about pier fishing: some days you catch them, some days you don't. It takes time either way, and it's nothing personal if you're skunked. The angler 30 feet away catching everything is probably not fishing any differently than you are. If you persist, your time will come as well. In fact, fishing embodies the rewards of patience and the arbitrariness of luck—great life lessons. Meanwhile, keep these things in mind:

— I always buy something from the pier owner—a soda, cheese crackers, bait. It lubricates conversation, and you might land a good tip.
— Some piers will rent all the gear you need if you just want to try pier fishing and do not own equipment.
— The first angler to arrive at a given length of pier has seniority. Ask this angler for permission before setting up shop immediately next to him or her.
— Unoccupied coolers, rods, and chairs stake claims for anglers who are temporarily absent. Honor the claim.
— As you set up your fishing station, allow plenty of elbow room between you and your neighbor.
— Don't intentionally cast across another angler's line.
— After you *accidentally* cast across another line, apologize and then *you* move around the victim to retrieve your lure.
— If you do this again, go home or move.
— If someone hooks a fish that really runs, reel in and provide the angler room to play the fish. Large fish will have to be walked to the beach.
— If you have questions, ask. If people don't want to talk, be quiet. A crowded pier is where some people go to be alone.
— Use headphones on portable radios and keep cell phone calls to a minimum.
— Mind your children. While you brought them there to teach them patience, patience and pier fishing are boring to small children. Small children can become boring to other fishermen.
— Watch where you and your children walk. Do not walk behind someone casting. Similarly, before casting, look behind you.
— Don't litter.
— If you are a spectator, don't stand behind anglers who are casting.
— After you backlash or throw your rig off, just turn red and get on with it. Everybody has done it, but they will laugh anyway.
— When you catch a big fish, be gracious. It is like winning the lottery; everybody will share your joy and stifle their envy. Crow about it and you'll make the pier real chilly.

some of the highest land and most mature maritime forests on Bogue Banks. Except for the town sign, there is no noticeable change immediately upon entering the community from the east. There are several hotels and motels along the oceanfront side of US 58, and there is little clue that these are about the only commercial buildings in the city limits (there's also at least one bank). This is a hint about Pine Knoll Shores, which is virtually a residential island on the island. It has always exerted strong controls over land use through zoning restrictions and, until the early years of this century, restricted beach access to members of local homeowners' associations and their guests. In this respect, it was similar to the private residential community of Southern Shores in Dare County. Both are incorporated, but the residential communities are essentially large subdivisions. The city limit signs are the only visual cues that you have left Atlantic Beach.

Pine Knoll Shores occupies some gorgeous maritime forest property, but it is difficult to get a measure of the richness because the evergreen vegetation, mostly yaupon trees, live oaks, and wax myrtle, forms such a thicket along the sides of US 58. The vegetation crowds the highway a bit, and the road seems to slash through the forest and reveals a wild, natural beauty in the salt-groomed tops of the vegetation and the smooth, mottled trunks of the yaupons. Occasionally, driveways wander into the interior of the forests offering a glimpse of

the changes of elevation and deep shade of the interior woods. Rarely can you see a home.

North of the highway, the tree mix of the forest becomes more diverse, adding pine trees, youthful hardwoods, and understory trees, a full canopy and subcanopy layers to the forest cover. The town hall, off of Pine Knoll Boulevard, sits in a beautiful wooded setting. Nearby, practically next door, sprawls the remarkable mature woodland of the Theodore Roosevelt State Natural Area. The stellar town attraction, the North Carolina Aquarium and its hiking trails, are sited in the forest as well.

Beginning in the late 1990s, Pine Knoll Shores suffered increased chronic beach erosion as well as catastrophic beach loss from severe storms. This has forced the town to join public efforts to pump sand and replenish their beaches (along with Indian Beach, Salter Path, and Emerald Isle) after an unsuccessful and costly effort to undertake beach nourishment privately. One condition of participating in publicly subsidized beach nourishment is that the recipient community must provide public beach access, the first such in Pine Knoll Shores.

Access
The new access areas in Pine Knoll Shores are tricky to spot. Parking for most of the new access walkways is located on the north side of US 58, necessitating crossing the highway to reach the beach access boardwalks.

There is a regional access with 60 parking places and restrooms west of the Iron Steam Pier and Hotel, approximately milepost 6.5.

The Oakleaf Drive access with 10 parking spaces is north of US 58, milepost 4.7 (the driver's landmark is the Christmas Store). The walkway passes between the Royal Pavilion Motel and the Atlantic Motor Lodge.

Memorial Drive access with 40 parking spaces is on the south side of US 58 near milepost 6; the entrance is marked by a sign. A house with two dolphin statues at the base of the driveway is due east.

Ramada Inn accessway has 25 spaces north of US 58 in a gated public complex at the Ramada Inn. The walkway passes west of the Ramada Inn.

Trinity Center access is at milepost 9.5 at the border with Indian Beach. The driver's landmark is the water tower that is the location of the parking.

The Sheraton permits parking and access for $5 per day.

Driving on the beach is not permitted in Pine Knoll Shores at any time.

Handicapped Access
None of the Pine Knoll Shores accessways are handicapped accessible to the beach.

Information
For information, contact Crystal Coast Tourism Authority, 3409 Arendell Street, Morehead City, NC 28557, 800-SUNNYNC (800-786-6962), 252-726-8148.

Web addresses: <www.townof pks.com>; <www.protectthebeach. com>; <www.nccoastalmanage ment.net/Access/sites.htm>

Iron Steamer Pier Access

In late 2004, the Iron Steamer Pier, a fixture at the western limits of Pine Knoll Shores since 1955, became a part of local history. The pier, formerly a part of a commercial complex including a hotel and restaurant, was razed to become housing, a victim of storms and a changing economy. The name honored the wreck of the *M. V. Prevensy*, a side-wheel steamer and blockade-runner that ran aground and wrecked here on June 9, 1864. Previously, a spur from the pier overlooked two eroded metal shapes, visible at low tide. The largest piece is the axle that turned the side wheel; the smaller is part of the boiler.

Access

There is a regional access location at the former site of the Iron Steamer Pier with 60 parking spaces and restrooms.

Web addresses: <www.townof pks.com>; <www.protectthebeach. com>; <www.nccoastalmanage ment.net/Access/sites.htm>

Theodore Roosevelt State Natural Area

The Theodore Roosevelt State Natural Area is the only location where

you can experience fully the natural richness of undeveloped Bogue Banks. The Roosevelt descendants inherited the 265-acre preserve from its litigious former owner, Alice Green Hoffman. Her lawsuit against the owners of cows that destroyed one of her gardens led to the legal establishment of Salter Path. When Hoffman died, she willed the land to her niece, Mrs. Teddy Roosevelt Jr. The family, in turn, dedicated it to the state as a natural area in memory of President Theodore Roosevelt.

The preserve is a coastal ecological laboratory under the administration of the staff of Fort Macon. As is the case with all state natural areas, part of the management scheme is to leave it alone; the public is given limited access. It has become a refuge on the island by default and a destination that makes for a stimulating side trip.

The North Carolina Aquarium is within its borders, sited at the edge of a small tidal creek and marsh, with the woods of the preserve walling it off from the rest of the island. The natural area preserves the many varied ecological niches that establish on an undeveloped barrier island, from fore dunes to maritime forest, freshwater bogs, salt marsh, and sound. Trails through the area provide visitors an opportunity to experience the full range of island vegetation and to possibly glimpse two of the preserve's rare inhabitants—resident ospreys and alligators.

A self-guided nature trail, also used for interpretive walks, starts

at the northeast corner of the parking lot, leading into the woods and eventually to the marsh. It is a good introductory hike to the thick-forested regions of the banks. The birds you will hear and see are usually land species.

Either bring plenty of insect repellent or wear long-sleeved shirts and long pants. Mosquitoes, no-see-ums, and deer flies abound. You should also be alert for snakes in warmer months.

Access

The gate to the area at the entrance of Roosevelt Drive off of Pine Knoll Boulevard usually opens by 8 A.M. and closes at 5 P.M. Parking for the natural area is at the North Carolina Aquarium.

Information

For information, contact Theodore Roosevelt State Natural Area, P.O. Box 127, Atlantic Beach, NC 28512, 252-726-3775, 252-247-2003.

North Carolina Aquarium, Pine Knoll Shores

This aquarium closed on January 1, 2004, for long-awaited renovations and expansions that will triple the square footage of exhibits. The expansion is to be completed and the building open by the spring of 2006.

The addition will bring new habitats and new animals to an aquarium that does an outstanding job of presenting the unique ocean life within Carteret County. Offshore, the Atlantic mingles both cold-water and warm-water creatures and plant life. The Gulf Stream cradles the warm-water species close to shore, while the cold-water fauna drift south past Cape Hatteras on the inland cold-water currents originating near Labrador. The currents and everything that rides them mix at Cape Lookout, creating a remarkable diversity of fishes, crustaceans, and other sea life.

Favorite exhibits like the touch-and-see tank, with urchins, horse-shoe crabs, channel whelks, knobbed whelks, and hermit crabs within arms reach of little fingers, will be included in the renovated quarters. The perennially popular exhibit on the endangered sea turtles will be back as well. The leatherback, loggerhead, green, and hawksbill turtles are known to nest on the islands that arc between Cape Lookout and the South Carolina border each year. The exhibit, which highlights the mystery of the turtles' migratory life, reinforces the staff's active efforts to boost public awareness of turtle nesting and to protect known nests from disturbance.

The aquarium will add habitat that represents the journey of water from the mountains to the sea. Newcomers to the aquarium will be mountain trout, river otters, and even a jellyfish gallery.

There will be two substantial additions. First, a 50,000-gallon ocean tank will feature the wreck of the *Queen Anne's Revenge*, Black-beard's famous flagship sunk off of Beaufort Inlet. Second, a sensational 306,000-gallon ocean tank will be completed with a partial replica of a 1942 German U-boat sunk offshore during World War II. The viewing gallery will be 60 feet long, and the stars of the show will be sharks, turtles, and schools of fish typical of the Carteret County coast.

Access

Signs along NC 58 at the western end of Pine Knoll Shores mark the turn for the aquarium. When the aquarium reopens in the spring of 2006, the hours will be 9 A.M. to 5 P.M. Monday–Saturday, 1 P.M. to 5 P.M. Sunday. There is ample parking.

Handicapped Access

The aquarium is fully accessible for handicapped travelers.

Information

For information, contact North Carolina Aquarium, Pine Knoll Shores, P.O. Box 580, Atlantic Beach, NC 28512, 252-247-4003.

Web address: <www.nc aquariums.com>

Indian Beach (East)

A portion of Indian Beach is adjacent to Pine Knoll Shores; the remainder is on the west side of Salter Path. Here, just west of Pine Knoll Shores, the island becomes narrower and the land is much more intensely developed. The several large condominium projects on the oceanfront are the most visible evidence of the change of communities. The unincorporated community of Salter Path splits the town. If you are driving west, the first section of Indian Beach is just under a mile in length, and then suddenly you are in Salter Path. There are no public access facilities in this portion of Indian Beach.

Information

For information, contact Crystal Coast Tourism Authority, 3409 Arendell Street, Morehead City, NC 28557, 800-SUNNYNC (800-786-6962), 252-726-8148.

Web addresses: <www.indian beach.org>; <www.protectthe beach.com>; <www.nccoastalman agement.net/Access/sites.htm>

Salter Path

Indian Beach sandwiches unincorporated Salter Path, practically in the middle of Bogue Banks. The sturdy homes—obviously not vacation homes—and a laissez-faire unfolding of land uses along a curving length of NC 58 signal Salter Path. You may also see the accumulations of maritime items you normally find in old fishing villages. Salter Path is the oldest settlement on the island, the only genuine "old ways" village.

Most of Bogue Banks witnessed a spit-and-polish beach buildup after 1971, when the high-rise bridge opened from Cape Carteret, but Salter Path did not. It is not quite as "shiny" as the rest of the island, but it isn't rusty either. Salter Path remains a fisherman's village, populated by folks who, in many respects, sail against a tide of change around them.

NC 58 curves through a vestigial live oak forest in a gradual arc from soundside to the oceanfront. Most of the village homes are on the soundside of the island. Several private campgrounds and private marinas provide access to Bogue Sound and, indirectly, to the beaches. What you may notice most about Salter Path is the advertisements for fresh fish. These folks still set their nets for a living, tying them off for a rise of the tide then pulling a seine net in beside the set net. The fish you buy in Salter Path is about as fresh as you will find on Bogue Banks.

The settling of Salter Path rivals the history of any coastal community for intrigue and curiosity. When Riley Salter settled on Bogue Banks in 1880, he certainly didn't intend to start anything; he just wanted to fish and be left alone. Salter and his neighbors, who sailed their goods, their dismantled homes, and their families to this yaupon and live oak–sheltered cove nearly in the middle of Bogue Banks, stayed busy fishing and living, even though they didn't have a deed or permission. The pace of life picked up considerably in the fall when great schools of mullet migrated close to the beach. The villagers mobilized, set nets, and hauled in fabulous catches. The women of the village cleaned and

gutted the fish, salting the catch in great barrels that they would leave on the beach until they could transport them to the soundside of the island. The path they wore through the island to the sound went by Riley Salter's house; hence, it was called Salter Path.

This was the beginning of a small, stubborn enclave that would continue to hold on to older ways even as it became surrounded by vacation destinations. When these move-weary families, driven by hurricanes and shifting sand dunes elsewhere, illegally established residence on the property of Bostonian John A. Royall at the turn of the century, they started a controversy that set them apart from other island residents. They were squatters. The land passed from Royall to Alice Green Hoffman, who built an estate in present-day Pine Knoll Shores. Hoffman sued the residents of Salter Path in 1923 because their cows had wandered onto her estate and destroyed a garden.

The court settlement, known locally as "The Judgment," decreed that the residents of Salter Path could remain, but their cows could not graze on the Hoffman estate. The village was restricted to the 81 acres the squatters occupied at the time, and direct ownership of the beachfront was not granted to any single person but to the village to use collectively, since they fished it that way. The ruling further maintained that only the current residents and their descendants could occupy the property. It did not give them title, however.

The villagers lived in a legal netherworld until 1979 when Carteret County conducted a tax assessment. The court again stepped in and sorted through the entangled ownership web, which included the residents of Salter Path and the heirs of President Theodore Roosevelt who had inherited the land from Alice Hoffman. The upshot was that Salter Pathers could now hold title to their property—and be taxed for it—which, believe it or not, was something new. Salter Path, which had been on the map for so long, was now on the books as well.

Access

Carteret County maintains a 22-acre access area in Salter Path beside NC 58, possibly the most beautiful access area along the coast. The area is clearly marked from the highway by the familiar access logo. The parking area is fronted by a picket fence, and the lot looks as though it belonged to a large residence. The access area includes 75 parking spaces, restrooms, a bathhouse, a deck, and a dune crossover walkway. The walkway is simply wonderful; you gradually, deliberately ascend above the trees of the property, emerging from the foliage to overlook a beautiful dune field. The undeveloped ocean frontage that you see from the boardwalk is the communal beach of Salter Path.

Not surprisingly, the area stays full from dawn to dusk during the summer season since it carries the burden of access demands for the central part of Bogue Banks, so arrive early.

Handicapped Access
The parking lot has designated handicapped parking spaces, and the access area is fully accessible by handicapped travelers.

Information
For information, contact Crystal Coast Tourism Authority, 3409 Arendell Street, Morehead City, NC 28557, 800-SUNNYNC (800-786-6962), 252-726-8148.

Web addresses: <www.protect thebeach.com>; <www.nccoastal management.net/Access/sites. htm>

Indian Beach (West)

The largest portion of Indian Beach is west of Salter Path. At Joseph Drive, you will see the town hall on the north side of the highway, a small building almost in the woods behind a tree-shaded parking lot at the edge of Paradise Bay. When the finger canals of Paradise Bay were excavated, the contractor uncovered a Native American burial ground, confirmation of very early occupancy of Bogue Banks, perhaps as a summer fishing village.

Indian Beach is laid-back and easy, a solid blue-collar beach with probably the highest density of trailers and campsites on the island. A small cluster of businesses seems tuned to serving year-round needs more than summer traffic.

The town is holding out against the second-home crush, although not completely. There is a wonderful visual juxtaposition here, one of the most vivid on any of the barrier islands. Near the western town limits of Indian Beach is a beautifully crafted, massive oceanfront retreat named Summer Winds, one of the few rental locations here. It communicates exclusivity and dwarfs the Ocean Front Trailer Court, its immediate neighbor. The transition is so abrupt that it looks like the island was grafted together with the seam between them.

The landscape changes as you drive west past Summer Winds. The natural tree line recedes inland as the island narrows, until you begin to move into the dune field of this very narrow part of Bogue Banks. The vegetation is mostly grass, and the landscape looks like rumpled plains. At the western edge of the town limits you have already visually moved into a different part of Bogue Banks. Before you know it, you are through the town; it is only a mile long.

Access
Indian Beach has the only off-road-vehicle access location in the middle of the island, with limited parking as well. The access ramp is at the end of SR 1192, the only paved road heading south. Look for the sign for Squatters Seafood. There are 25–30 parking spaces along the east side of the road at the ramp. The water is right at the foot of the accessway at high tide, and the sand is soft. You must have a

permit from the town before taking your vehicle on the beach, and you best have a four-wheel-drive vehicle.

Information
For information, contact Crystal Coast Tourism Authority, 3409 Arendell Street, Morehead City, NC 28557, 800-SUNNYNC (800-786-6962), 252-726-8148.

Web addresses: <www.indian beach.org>; <www.protectthe beach.com>; <www.nccoastal management.net/Access/sites. htm>

Emerald Isle

The western third of Bogue Banks is the town of Emerald Isle, more an assemblage of distinct neighborhoods than it is a homogeneous community. The seasonal population figures explain part of the story: while approximately 3,200 live here year-round, in summer the population swells to 50,000. Real estate/beach tourism is the largest player in the town economy: Emerald Isle is a place where vacationers rent homes by the week. This is what makes the town go round.

A full grasp of the seasonality comes with trying to get on the island before 3 P.M. on Saturday or Sunday during the summer season. Mainland traffic backs up at Cape Carteret, for at least 1/2 mile to a mile, waiting for a green light to cross the bridge vaulting US 58 over Bogue Sound.

Just waiting in traffic raises

	Fee	Parking	Restrooms	Lifeguard	Camping	Showers	Beach Access	Hiking	Trail	Handicapped	Boating	ORV Access	Fishing	Programs	Historic	Sand Beach	Dunes	Upland	Wetland
Emerald Isle		•	•				•			•		•	•			•	•	•	•
Regional Access: Emerald Isle		•	•				•			•			•			•	•		
Cedar Street Park		•								•									•
Regional Access: Emerald Isle West		•	•			•	•			•						•			

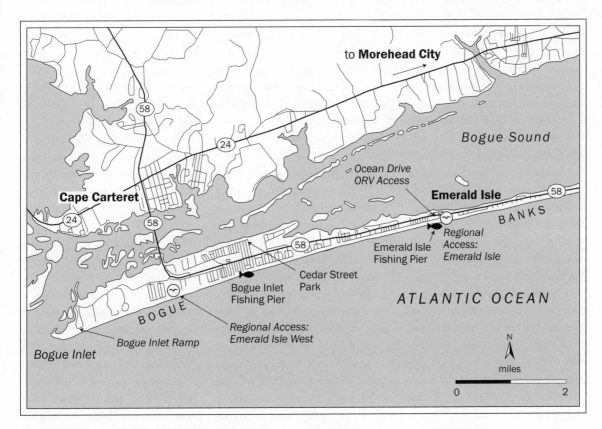

Map 20. Bogue Banks: Emerald Isle to Cape Carteret

expectations, and Emerald Isle meets them with a pleasant low-key, nonassertive manner. There is no big downtown, vibrant amusement park, or other city center of activity and recreation. The town is simply houses close to the beach throughout.

What do people do? After several years of family vacations there, I can say that Emerald Isle operates as an everyone-entertain-themselves beach. Mostly, people play in the ocean—all day. Our family, at least, cocoons by the sea; hanging out where the crowds are is just not a part of our scene, and it looks like we keep up with Joneses on this front. While we sometimes scoot away to dine out or make a field trip to Cape Lookout, our week evaporates before doing all the things we planned to do, a sign of a good vacation that is too short. Emerald Isle is filled with families doing the same thing. My morning runs to "the point" at Bogue Inlet give me the solid impression that it is a beach for children.

As a town, Emerald Isle is neutral; it doesn't grab you, grab at you, or push you away. There is some showiness in new home construction, but most ostentation is patently tied into the rental market.

Physically, Emerald Isle shows a good deal of natural variation within the 11-mile length of the town, and this makes it look like it is several different places. In fact, it is continuously small residential groupings along US 58, which threads nearly the entire length of the town.

The eastern end of town, beginning at Indian Beach, includes three miles that are among the narrowest of Bogue Banks. In the past, severe storms have cut the island twice along this length. The first paved road after the town sign is First Street, and the streets continue to be numbered, rhythmically spaced, through Nineteenth Street. Along these streets, you see houses in an old dune field. One block south, Ocean Drive runs parallel to NC 58 in the trough between houses on the parallel peaks of the dune field, a passage that ends as you approach the wooded section of the island. You can see the ocean at the end of nearly every numbered street.

The road moves out of the open-sky dune fields to a forested mid rib, several blocks inland from the beach. Occasionally, glimpses of ocean blink as a bright flash at the end of one of the wooded side streets. Except for a few commercial clusters, NC 58 stays in the woods.

US 58 passes a shopping center and makes a slow arc south to cross the bridge leading to Cape Carteret. There are nearly 2 miles worth of island west of that curve in the road, and it still looks like woods. Turning south on Coast Guard Road, at milepost 21, an easy drive—often with bicyclists and runners—passes through a towering forest marked by salt-wind damage. These are the newer subdivisions, and the houses are distinctly more upscale than most other homes in the community. This is also probably one of the most stable parts of the island. Once you are out of the tall woods and into the dunes, the remainder of the community is unabashedly summer second homes and rental property. This is mostly a tourist drive, but there are a few places to park legally and use crosswalks to reach the beach. There once was an off-road-vehicle access ramp serving the inlet, but hurricanes wiped out the island beyond the accessway and a shifted inlet, recently relocated west away from the island, caused the elimination of this access.

The town incorporated in 1957, and a small commercial interlude along NC 58 at the intersection of Bogue Inlet Drive still seems to be the figurative center of the community. It has seniority at least. If you turn east on Bogue Inlet Drive, you reach the Bogue Inlet Pier and several small motels. If you turn west, you reach the sound.

Given the summer influx of people and considering other resorts, you might anticipate more enterprises that are commercial. In fact, stores and services are few, modest, and practical, places such as groceries, hardware stores, and gas stations. Although newer shopping areas have been added one mile west of Bogue Inlet Drive, "beach boutique" doesn't thrive in Emerald Isle. Given the size and age of the community, this sets it apart from the rest of the Bogue Banks towns. It feels permanent here.

Perhaps because so much of the economy is tied to vacation rental, the resident community keeps to itself. Oddly, Emerald Isle is not memorable, but it is constant. Repeat visitors experience little change, but few surprises and predictability is a good trait for a vacation community. It is stable, beautiful-beach ordinary. You could rent for a week, know the neighbors by day two, and suddenly be packing to leave, wondering where the week went. It is a nice beach for decompression.

Ironically, while it is the first place you come to from the western bridge, it does not easily accommodate day travelers or overnight guests. Motel/hotel space is limited, and adequate parking for beach access is confined to two large regional access sites.

Access

If you are renting a non-oceanfront home in Emerald Isle, ask the real estate company or owner for the exact location of the nearest accessway. Personal plans should include walking to the access area from your rental.

Emerald Isle has a tremendous number of pedestrian access locations but a horrible parking shortfall. Nearly every street that is perpendicular to NC 58 terminates in an access location that is designed to serve the residents of the street and nearby neighborhoods, but there is no place to park your car. The city did not require that the right-of-way of perpendicular streets extend across Ocean Drive to the tide line. This would have left great land resources in the public domain.

The town continually evaluates its access program to see what it can improve and is moving to increase useable access steadily. It is trying to improve local access sites by providing a parking space or two and providing additional handicapped access parking at the end of some streets.

Here is a listing of access locations. It is likely that more access sites will be improved in the near future.

At the east end of the city, Third Street Park, which is closer to Fourth Street, has 10 parking spaces and is open 7:30 A.M. to 9 P.M.

Emerald Isle Eastern Regional Access site is at the former location of the Emerald Isle Pier. Turn south (toward the ocean) on US 58 at milepost 15 between the Pier Point and Ocean Reef Condominium developments. This large site has 245 parking spaces, a bathhouse, and restrooms and is handicapped accessible. A plaque adjacent the site marks the location of the Emerald Isle Pier, constructed in 1955 and destroyed by a sequence of hurricanes (Bertha and Fran) in 1996.

The Cedar Street Park is a soundside park with a pier with comfortable benches and a magnificent view of the sound. Turn north on Cedar Street, which is four blocks east of Bogue Inlet Drive. There are 4 parking places and a small garden lining the path leading to the pier. There is another treat as well. Directly across the sound is an auxiliary navy landing field. You may be sitting quietly at this park when a navy or marine jet rises si-

lently above the northern horizon, the sound following afterward. The jets sometimes turn east directly above the park, looping their flight pattern back to Morehead City to align for another touch-and-go.

On Black Skimmer Drive opposite the city hall is an off-road-vehicle ramp.

There is parking for a fee at Boardwalk by the Sea Arcade. To reach this amusement center, turn south off of NC 58 onto Islander Drive, turn east onto Reed Drive, and then turn south on Boardwalk Drive. In addition to parking, there are showers and concessions.

There is parking for a fee available at Bogue Inlet Pier. Check with the owner about where to park. There is some vacant land nearby, and you may leave your car there to use the beach.

Emerald Isle Western Regional Access site is accessible by taking the second right after crossing the bridge from Cape Carteret. This is near the Islander Hotel and is sometimes referred to as the Islander Access. The site has 250 parking spaces, a bathhouse, restrooms, and showers. There are 3 handicapped parking spaces, but no handicapped access to the beach. It is a busy spot, but the beach is lovely here. Amusements and refreshments are within walking distance.

Station Street Park at the intersection of Station Street and Coast Guard Road has 15 parking spaces. It provides access to the western end of Bogue Banks by using the Channel Drive dune crossover, approximately 300 yards from the parking area.

You must obtain a permit from the town to drive on the beach, and driving on the beach is not permitted between Memorial Day and Labor Day. The town recently defeated a proposal that would have banned all oceanfront driving.

Handicapped Access

Emerald Isle will loan a beach wheelchair with advance notice. Call the fire department at 252-726-7361.

The town plans to improve three or four existing dune crossovers to make them accessible to handicapped travelers and designate handicapped parking spaces at the same locations.

The new regional access area at the Emerald Isle Fishing Pier has a ramp that makes it accessible for handicapped travelers. When this access site is completed, it will have handicapped accessible restrooms.

Cedar Street Park is negotiable by handicapped travelers. There is a gentle gradient from the parking area to the dock.

Information

For information, contact Crystal Coast Tourism Authority, 3409 Arendell Street, Morehead City, NC 28557, 800-SUNNYNC, (800-786-6962), 252-726-8148.

Web addresses: <www.emerald isle-nc.org>; <www.protectthe beach.com>; <www.nccoastal management.net/Access/sites. htm>

Cape Carteret to Cedar Point

NC 58 intersects with NC 24 at Cape Carteret, a commercial center for many Bogue Banks visitors and residents. NC 24 east heads back to Morehead City, a trip that looks fairly long, but in the summer vacation season it can be much less tedious and quicker than driving the length of Bogue Banks on US 58. This road is named Freedom Way, in honor of the marines in Camp Lejeune who served in Operation Desert Storm.

Driving west (and south) on NC 24 takes you to Swansboro through the hamlet known as Cedar Point. A sign claims that Cedar Point was established in the early 1700s, but there is not much visible from the roadway that evokes that era.

During the summer, produce stands along this highway do a bustling business.

Lost with the recent road widening were handsome plantings of old red cedar trees. These windswept, sculptured evergreens stamped the name Cedar Point into memory.

Access

There is a boat-launching ramp along the causeway on NC 24 crossing the White Oak River farther south.

Hook, Line, and Rulebook

Coastal fishing as one of the last free forms of recreation passes into history on January 1, 2006. This is the effective date of North Carolina's saltwater fishing licensing requirement, which applies to all anglers 18 years of age and older. As of this writing, the final details of the regulations are not complete, but here are a few things that seem certain:

— The fee is $15 per year; however, a $1, one time per year, seven-day license may be purchased as well.
— The license may not be transferred or assigned.
— Children under 18 and in school do not need a license.
— Lifetime licenses are available. The fees are:
    Age 0 through age 5—$100
    Age 6 through age 10—$150
    Age 11 through age 17—$250
    Age 18 and above—$500.
— The license is required for *any* type of recreational fishing activity, including fishing, crabbing, clamming, or collecting oysters.
— The license covers personal use only; the catch may not be sold.
— Fishermen using this license will be held to the state's Recreational Size and Possession Limits that govern the legal numbers and sizes of any catch. Note: These limits change frequently.
— The license covers fishing in Coastal Fishing Waters, which include the sounds, coastal rivers, and their tributaries out to three miles. Recreational fishermen who catch fish in the Exclusive Economic Zone (3 miles–200 miles offshore) will be required to possess this license to land fish in state waters.
— This saltwater fishing license is required in addition to the Wildlife Resources Commission Lifetime Fishing License that an individual might already have.

The license is a new management tool. Prior to this requirement, the state could only estimate the numbers of recreational fishermen, and their impact on fish stocks was anecdotal. The license will provide actual numbers that can help fisheries personnel better manage fish and shellfish populations.

The license revenues will go into the North Carolina Saltwater Fishing Fund, which will be administered by an eleven-member board of trustees. The board will issue grants for a broad range of programs and proposals that benefit saltwater fishing directly and indirectly.

Three different agencies govern fishing on North Carolina's coast: the North Carolina Wildlife Resources Commission governs inland creeks, bays, and rivers; the Division of Marine Fisheries governs coastal creeks, bays, rivers, sounds, and the ocean out to 3 miles; both of these agencies govern joint creeks, bays, and rivers; and finally the National Marine Fisheries Service governs ocean fishing beyond the 3-mile limit.

In many ways, the license simplifies fishing—everybody will have to have one. If you are over 18 and going fishing in a boat, buy the license. In areas jointly administered by the North Carolina Wildlife Resources Commission, called Joint Waters, both licenses will be required.

Although the entrance to restricted waters will be posted, it is prudent to know where you are going and what you are going after before you start out. Check with local marinas or tackle shops for any restrictions you are likely to encounter.

Size, limit, and closed water restrictions will change frequently. It is the fisherman's responsibility to abide by these regulations. Break the rules and get caught, and the price can be steep in dollars as well as in forfeited equipment.

While fines have not yet been determined, it can be costly. When I purchased a saltwater fishing license in South Carolina several years ago, I was admonished to mind the state restriction on summer flounder because recently a fisherman with six undersized flounder was fined $200 per fish.

Crabs

The new license is required for crabbing or "chicken-necking" for crabs off of a dock or pier. Crabs must meet a 5-inch minimum (tip-to-tip across the shell). You may catch

50 a day, not to exceed 100 crabs per vessel per day.

Oysters

The new license is required. The oyster season is usually in the fall. Because of pollution-decimated populations, some waters may be closed. It is advised that you check with the North Carolina Division of Marine Fisheries to determine the areas in which oystering is permitted.

Oysters must be a minimum of 3 inches in length, and you may catch one bushel a day, not to exceed two bushels per vessel per day.

Clams

The new license is required. Clam season is open year-round. You may collect 100 per day per person or 200 per day per vessel without a commercial license. The clams must have a minimum thickness of one inch.

Shrimp

You may only use a cast net to shrimp, and the license is required. You may fish in closed or open shrimping waters. In closed shrimping waters, the limit is 100 shrimp per person per day for any purpose. There is no limit in open shrimping waters.

Fish

Fishing limits are based on the species. Three popular game fish, striped bass, red drum, and southern flounder, could hook you if you don't know the regulations. They are closely regulated because of declining numbers.

Striped bass is zealously regulated with different seasons in different waters and different limits in each. Check with the Division of Marine Fisheries before you go.

There are spring and fall seasons. As of this writing, if you are fishing in the sounds or rivers, any fish 18 inches long from nose to tail is safe. In the Roanoke River, fish must meet this minimum, and no fish between 22 and 27 inches may be kept.

In the Atlantic Ocean, there is a 28-inch minimum.

How many you may catch depends on where you are fishing. Check with the Division of Marine Fisheries for exact information.

Red drum migrate through the surf zone in fall and spring. The minimum size is 18 inches; the maximum size is 27 inches. You may keep no more than one per day. In addition, you may not gig, spear, or gaff red drum.

Both red drum and striped bass are illegal to possess beyond the 3-mile limit (in the Exclusive Economic Zone, 3–200 miles), regardless of where they are caught. Do not transport either of these fish into these waters. If you catch one in federal waters, you must release it.

North Carolina is the southernmost range for summer flounder and the northernmost range for southern flounder, and so it has to manage both. Summer flounder, a popular fish for recreational fishing that is typically caught in the ocean, has been overfished in recent years, and recovery is dependent on adhering to the limits. The best way to be safe is to return all flounder caught in the ocean that are less than 14 inches in length. You may keep 8 fish per day that are larger than 14 inches. There are some locations in inland waters where 13-inch flounder may be kept. However, if you don't know your fish or where the demarcation line happens to be, it is just easier to throw anything less than 14 inches back. Then you can sound noble when you lie about the big fish you released.

Bluefish must be a minimum of 10 inches, and you may keep no more than 5 that are longer than 24 inches per day, something that could happen quickly in a bluefish "blitz."

It's a good idea to know what you're catching. If you have any doubts about the legality or the identity of the fish you've caught, then either ask someone or release it.

Piers, tackle shops, and marinas can advise you of these restrictions, but the only sure way to comply is to have a copy of the regulations.

For information, contact the North Carolina Division of Marine Fisheries, 3441 Arendell Street, Morehead City, NC 28557, 252-726-7021. A 24-hour toll-free line is available for specific questions; call 800-682-2632 (North Carolina only).

Web address: <www.ncfisheries.net>

Onslow County

The publicly accessible barrier islands of Onslow County are at opposite ends of the county coastline and equally opposite in character.

The northernmost island in the county, Bear Island, is the site of Hammocks Beach State Park, which may be the gem of the entire state park system. Parked between Bogue Inlet and Bear Inlet, it is accessible only by ferry, and it is the one island in the state, in the view of some marine biologists and coastal ecologists, that most closely approximates an island remaining in an unaltered, natural condition. Unlike many islands along the southern third of the coast, it is blessed with ample sand supply and a favorable orientation to wind. Though subject to the typical "nibblings" of inlet migration and occasional smack-downs by hurricanes, the beach is healthy and tends to increase in width.

(Shacklefoot Island and Onslow Beach in the center of Onslow's coast are a part of Camp Lejeune. Use of the beach varies from base recreation to landing sites and target ranges.)

On the other hand, Topsail Island, the more easily accessible barrier island in the south of the county, is rapidly becoming the new hot beach for home and condominium construction. Topsail Island is 22 miles long, the second-largest barrier island in the south-central coast after Bogue Banks. Onslow County can lay claim to more than half of that length, which falls in the community of North Topsail Beach. The southern remainder of the island is in Pender County in two communities: Surf City and Topsail Beach. North Topsail Beach and Surf City are neighbors.

Construction has been on fire on Topsail Island in general and North Topsail Beach in particular since the close of last century. This is particularly true of the island north of the NC 210 bridge to the mainland. Several large condominium developments have been built on New River Inlet Road, north of the bridge. South of the bridge, vacation rental construction and single-family homes are erupting along NC 210. Drive along NC 210 and even New River Inlet Road, and it would seem that all the prerequisites for an easy, gentle-beach lifestyle are here and waiting, perhaps even more available

Fisherman unloading the day's catch of oysters. Courtesy of the author.

because the island is still out of the mainstream. It is easy to sense that the island is on the cusp of a boom, and there seems to be a "get it while you can" energy driving the building.

The frenzy of construction—some longtime residents are ambivalent about the changes that have come with it—is not tempered at all by any memories of 1996. That is when Topsail Island took a one-two hurricane punch in an eight-week period.

Bertha, an 85-mile-per-hour Category I storm that crossed Cape Fear to the south on July 12, 1996, eroding a stressed dune line, threatening NC 50 and NC 210, and overwashing New River Inlet Road, turned out to be a setup for something worse—Hurricane Fran. On September 6, 1996, this Category III behemoth, with whirling winds in excess of 135 miles per hour, made landfall in Brunswick County to the south. Its powerful northeast quadrant piled a tremendous storm surge and splintering winds onto Topsail Island. It crushed the island, temporarily severing it in two locations, planing the dune line flat, and destroying 80 percent of the buildings.

Emergency aid poured in and everyone scrambled to successfully reestablish the easygoing ocean-side living of Topsail Island. Today, my reaction at driving the island is, "Wow, what a difference a decade makes."

By appearances, North Topsail Beach (and the rest of Topsail Island) have recaptured some of that somnolent charm that bewitched so many folks before, although this reincarnation has substantially more shine. There is no denying how inviting the southeast-facing beach can be—wide, flattened profile, and gentle waves. Not only is the resource outstanding, the island is not at all crowded, making it a ripe beach plum to be picked in this southern arc of the state's coastline. Now that improved roads make it easier to reach, North Topsail Beach is dizzy with building.

There are a few things missing from the idyllic picture—at least three fishing piers for one, and most of the 10-foot-high dune line that ran the length of the island. The dunes have come back in most locations, though not as substantial as before, yet the island once again casts a far-away, bucolic spell on those who come here; more are deciding to stay.

The 1996 hurricane hammering awakened the island from a longtime lull. It has been surprisingly stable since 1954 when Hurricane Hazel erased 210 out of the 230 homes on the island. That it was so few homes is a good indication of how off the beaten path the island happened to be. Topsail took a backseat to other islands in the development footrace, probably because this part of the coast has been lightly traveled in the past.

Coastal geography isolated Onslow County and its beaches from the flow of state commerce in the nineteenth century. A not so obvious reason why is that the low, densely vegetated interiors of Onslow and neighboring Pender Counties defied road building. There are not many even today.

When the deep-water ports of Wilmington and Morehead City became the destinations of railroads from the Piedmont, this directed any smidgen of attention away from these two sparsely populated and forested counties between the burgeoning ports.

Even the dredging of the Intracoastal Waterway in the 1930s failed to stimulate growth on the islands. If anything, the new "moat" made access to the islands more difficult, discouraging growth. While widely scattered building began on Topsail Island in the mid- to late 1930s, Onslow County's oceanfront acreage remained sleepily rural until the 1940s. Then World War II brought a tremendous military presence, effectively ending its isolation and altering the traditional use of some of its beachfront.

Camp Lejeune Marine Corps Base, built on the banks of the New River as the headquarters for the Second Marine Division, became a primary amphibious training base. It absorbed the barrier island Onslow Beach for its purposes. Holly Ridge, southwest of Jacksonville, became the focal community for Camp Davis, an artillery and antiaircraft training base that had nearly 200,000 personnel. While some of the old buildings are visible, the base, now reacquired for Camp Lejeune, is being reclaimed by coastal vegetation.

The establishment of Camp Lejeune led to the military's widening US 17 to Wilmington to facilitate troop movement. Meanwhile, during World War II, the military purchased Topsail Island to eventually set up a secret rocket-testing program, code-named Operation Bumblebee. When that program ended, the military left their bunkhouses, a launching pad, concrete observation towers, and a rocket assembly building on a comparatively untouched Topsail Island. At that time, the island was linked to the mainland by a pontoon bridge over the Intracoastal Waterway. Although a swing bridge carrying NC 210 and NC 50 into Surf City replaced the pontoon bridge, several of the original military structures remain, recycled into different uses today.

The military remains the biggest player in the county; Camp Lejeune encompasses more than 153,000 acres and nearly one-half of the county's oceanfront. In an ambitious expansion in 1991, Camp Lejeune added 42,000 acres of a pocosin area known as Great Sandy Run between Verona and Holly Ridge, an area that is between US 17 and US 50. Plans for the area are still unknown at this time, but it would seem that in an era of base consolidation, Camp Lejeune will not be one of the bases deactivated. The base functions as its very own city of 30,000 and is open to public most of the time. The marines occasionally close roads in the base as a safety measure when they have live training with the tools of their trade.

The beachfront communities and Camp Lejeune are not the only locations in the county to experience changes. Sneads Ferry, once a small mainland community south of Camp Lejeune, is growing resorts and second homes while maintaining its fishing and agricultural base. An attraction to the area is available land and boating access to the Atlantic Ocean through New River Inlet. Fulcher Landing and Swan Point have bloomed with houses as newcomers take advantage of these factors.

Being able to easily boat to the Atlantic Ocean has been a drive of construction in North Topsail Beach. It has only been recently that natural and building pressures have begun to tax the physical resources of the island. The major issue is chronic oceanfront erosion, which is compounded by an extraordinarily flat island profile on the north end of North Topsail Beach and the fact that nearly 6 miles of that part of the island fall in a federal Coastal Barrier Resources Act (CoBRA) zone. The parts of the island within the CoBRA zone are ineligible for federal flood insurance and beach nourishment. At this time, North Topsail Beach is implementing different strategies to raise funds for an expensive per capita strategic beach nourishment.

Even in this rapidly changing atmosphere, the beaches of Onslow County are both easily accessible and hold a delight of basic beach pleasures, gentle surf, sun, and good fishing.

Access

Onslow County has superb access facilities. Nearly all of them had to be rebuilt following the 1996 hurricanes, but they are in full service now.

Onslow County Parks and Recreation maintains four regional access areas in the newly incorporated community of North Topsail Beach. These are numbered in the order of construction.

Onslow Beach Access Site number 1 is slightly south of the Topsail Dunes development, on the north side of New River Inlet Road. After crossing over to Topsail Island on the high-rise bridge on NC 210, turn left on SR 1568 (New River Inlet Road) and continue north about 4 miles. There are 30 parking spaces and pay telephones. A dune crossover across the road leads past Topsail Dunes to a very flat beach.

Access site number 2 is a major regional access location 4 miles south of the NC 210 bridge. It has an elevated wood pavilion on the oceanfront with a ramp to the beach for handicapped users. There are concession areas, showers, restrooms, and parking for 250 cars. There is also a soundside parking area across the highway.

Access site number 3 is farther north at the end of the private road that winds past the St. Regis Hotel at the mouth of the New River.

This area offers 30 parking spaces and fishing access to the inlet on approximately 700 feet of New River Inlet frontage.

Onslow Beach Access Site number 4 is approximately one mile north of NC 210 on SR 1568 (New River Inlet Road), where the roadway "S" curves inland, away from the old roadbed. This access area has an elevated wooden deck on the ocean, restrooms, showers, concession area, and parking for 100 vehicles.

The North Carolina Wildlife Resources Commission maintains several fishing and boating access sites in the county. Access to the Intracoastal Waterway is on the north side of the NC 210 high-rise bridge that crosses the waterway to reach Topsail Island. To reach the Turkey Creek access area, which also serves the Intracoastal Waterway, from the junction of US 17 and NC 50 in Holly Ridge, go north on US 17 for 4 miles to Folkstone, turn east on SR 1518, travel 1.5 miles, turn south on SR 1529, go nearly 2 miles, and turn south on SR 1530. The area is almost a mile from the turn.

Handicapped Access

Access sites 1, 2, and 4 have designated handicapped parking places, restrooms with facilities for handicapped travelers, and ramped access over the dunes.

Information

For information, contact Onslow County Tourism, P.O. Box 1226, Jacksonville, NC 28541-0765, 910-455-1113, 800-932-2144; or Greater Topsail Area Chamber of Commerce and Tourism, 13775 Highway 50, Suite 101, or P.O. Box 2486, Surf City, NC 28445-2486, 910-329-4446, 800-626-2780.

Web addresses: <www.onslowcountytourism.com>; <www.topsailcoc.com>; <www.nccoastalmanagement.net/Access/sites.htm>

Swansboro

Swansboro has the bundled-up coziness of a New England seafaring settlement. It began as a fishing community, and surprisingly, it still retains much of that flavor. You can easily amble through its narrow streets in a morning stroll.

Small clapboard houses march down the hill to the banks of the White Oak River, which opens to the sea through Bogue Inlet. The open water begins at the end of a wandering passage through channels threading salt marsh islands. The inlet has been open and navigable since the first settlers arrived in the mid-eighteenth century. The community grew around a local plantation known as the Wharf and thrived in its early years as a port for the trading of naval stores, cotton, and timber. By the Revolutionary War, it was the only town on the coast between Beaufort and Wilmington.

The General Assembly passed articles of incorporation for the community in 1783 and formally named the town Swannsborough (shortened in 1877), honoring Samuel Swann, a former Speaker of the House from Onslow County. Shipping and shipbuilding dominated the economy following incorporation. In Bicentennial Park, on the north side of NC 24, a statue honors Captain Otway Burns, a daring privateer during the War of 1812 who was born nearby. In 1818 Burns built the *Prometheus*, one of the first steam-powered vessels constructed in the state, in Swansboro. Burns is better known in Beaufort, where he is buried in the historic cemetery, the Old Burying Ground, and is also honored in the naming of Burnsville in Yancey County.

Many of the older buildings in Swansboro are marching into their third century, renovated for reuse. Several mercantile buildings on Front Street now house craft and antique retailers. The town itself unfolds with richer and richer discoveries as you stroll outward from the center. At the town library in the city hall building, you may make a copy of a local history booklet that will direct you on a walking tour of the individual homes. There is a small copy fee. The library opens at 9 A.M. Monday–Saturday and closes at 8 P.M. on Monday, Tuesday, and Thursday, 6 P.M. on Wednesday and Friday, and 1 P.M. on Saturday.

Access

Swansboro has no beach access, but charter fishing and head-boat fishing trips depart from the village docks to both sound and open water. There are several marinas

	Fee	Parking	Restrooms	Lifeguard	Camping	Showers	Beach Access	Hiking	Trail	Handicapped	Boating	ORV Access	Fishing	Programs	Historic	Sand Beach	Dunes	Upland	Wetland
Swansboro		•	•								•		•		•			•	•
Hammocks Beach State Park	•	•	•	•	•	•	•	•	•		•		•	•		•	•	•	•

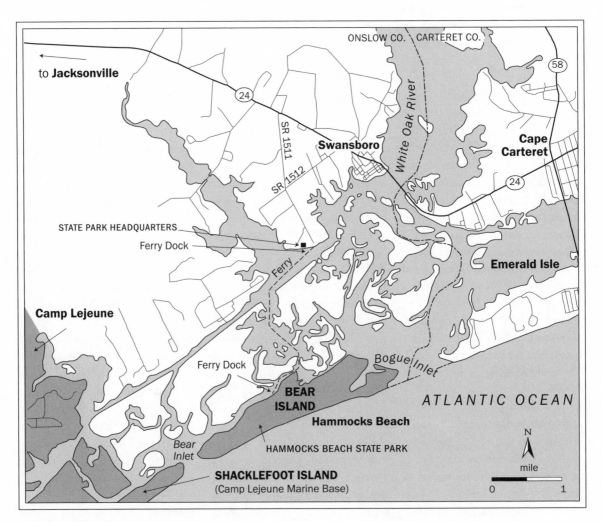

Map 21. Swansboro and Bear Island

Primitive (hike/canoe-in) campsite on Bear Island, Hammocks Beach State Park. Courtesy of North Carolina Division of Parks and Recreation.

and boat ramps that provide access to the White Oak River.

There is a town dock extending into the White Oak River at the end of West Main Street. A floating dinghy dock serves the boaters traveling the Intracoastal Waterway.

At Cedar Point on the Intracoastal Waterway, one mile north of Swansboro on NC 24, the North Carolina Wildlife Resources Commission maintains a boating access area with a launching ramp.

Handicapped Access
Bicentennial Park is accessible for handicapped travelers.

Information
For information, contact Onslow County Tourism, P.O. Box 1226, Jacksonville, NC 28541-0765, 910-455-1113, 800-932-2144.

Web address: <www.onslow countytourism.com>

Hammocks Beach State Park

The most natural of all the barrier islands in the state may be Bear Island, now set aside as the central feature of Hammocks Beach State Park. Lying 2 miles off the mainland

across a bewildering salt marsh maze, it is accessible only by private boat or toll ferry from the park headquarters on the mainland. The crossing is pleasant but slightly disorienting if you are not accustomed to navigating in a salt marsh.

The beach here is as wild and wonderful as any in North Carolina, and because access is restricted, it is about as empty as a beach can be, too. Even though it took a hit during the 1990s hurricanes, it has recovered nicely and still rates as one of the last, best places on the North Carolina coast.

Bear Island is 3 1/2 miles long

and a mile wide, with approximately 900 acres of varied habitat, including salt-tolerant trees and shrubs along the marsh side. The most imposing feature is the sand dunes, which vary between 25 and 50 feet in height. The island has possibly the largest intact natural dune field in the state. There are no restrictions on walking among the dunes, and they offer more than enough quiet places for sunning. The dune area is extremely hot, however. Park rangers have observed that not too many visitors linger amid the dunes during the busy season. All good and well because there is more to explore elsewhere.

The island is moving inland and has migrated over ancient sound and lagoon sites, which are now seaward of the island. Many of the shells found here are between 7,000 and 9,000 years old, having been uncovered by wave action.

During the first half of the twentieth century, William Sharpe, a New York neurosurgeon, owned Bear Island, its marshes, and considerable acreage on the mainland as a recreational hunting and fishing area. John Hurst, a black hunting guide who lived in Onslow County, originally directed Sharpe to the property and became his preferred guide. Sharpe wanted to will the property to Hurst and his wife, Gertrude, in 1949, but at her request, he left Bear Island and marsh holdings to the North Carolina Black Schoolteachers' Association. In 1961 the association gave the land to the state for a park.

In 1999 200-acre Huggins Is-land in the mouth of the White Oak River became a part of the park following its purchase from citizens who wanted it to be preserved. The island has an amazing range of habitats, including a rare freshwater seep and stately, sizeable live oak trees. Abandoned furrows from farming long ago are still visible. The island will be maintained as a preserve, and ecological and archaeological inventories are scheduled in the near future. Rangers provide an interpretive overview at the park headquarters, and there is a kayak loop trail that circumnavigates the island.

Your exploration of the park begins at the handsome headquarters and interpretive center at the ferry dock overlooking the extensive marsh and labyrinth of channels. Exhibits in the headquarters provide a glimpse of the type of environments that can be experienced in the park.

Park visitation stays at capacity during the summer season, but this is not to say that the island stays full. The capacity of the park is determined by the number of people that the ferry can return to the mainland before the park closes, and the ferry capacity fills long before the island does. You can virtually disappear into the surf and sand on the island, but be back at the ferry dock before the last departure, unless you have a camping permit.

There are 14 designated family campsites on the island, all of which are also available for individual campers, and 3 group camp-sites. Four of the family sites are located at the north and south points of the island, primarily to serve campers arriving in private boats. The other 10 are scattered along the length of the island just behind the primary dunes. The campsites are available on a first-come, first-served basis by securing a permit at the park headquarters before going to the island. The permitting process prevents quarrels over campsites. Because of the popularity of camping here, almost every weekend campsite is taken by the end of the day on Friday. Weekday camping is not nearly as competitive. Since the park is a favored nesting site for the loggerhead sea turtle, the park restricts camping during the three-day full moon period of the nesting season in the months of June, July, and August.

There are a central bathhouse and restrooms approximately $1/2$ mile from the ferry landing. Bring plenty of insect repellent and suntan lotion. When planning your visit, remember that camping is primitive, and you must carry in what you will use.

Access

To reach the park headquarters, west of Swansboro turn south off of NC 24 onto SR 1511, which goes directly to the headquarters. You may also turn east at Hardee's outside Swansboro, follow this road even after the pavement ends, turn left at the stop sign (onto SR 1511), and the park headquarters are directly ahead. The park office opens at 8 A.M. for permitting. The ferry service runs weekends only during May and September; Memorial Day through Labor Day the ferry operates every hour Monday–Tuesday and every half hour Wednesday–Sunday. The fee is $2 for adults, $1 for children. Usually, by 1:30 P.M. the ferry stops taking visitors to the island because it cannot get them off before closing. Only by arriving early in the morning are you assured of a campsite or a full day on the island.

The group campsites may be reserved and are limited to 12 people per site. There is a fee. Campers must use only the assigned campsite. No open fires are permitted; all cooking must be done on a camp stove. Water is available from the central bathhouse. If you secure a campsite far from the bathhouse, you may wish to have an expandable water container to cut down on refill trips.

Handicapped Access

The park visitors center is fully handicapped accessible.

There are steep steps down to the ferry, but once these are negotiated, mobility-impaired passengers may ride the ferry to the island.

The island itself should be considered inaccessible for mobility-impaired travelers.

Information

For information, contact the park office at 1572 Hammocks Beach Road, Swansboro, NC 28584, 910-326-4881.

Web address: <www.ncsparks. net/habe.html>

Camp Lejeune

A city of more than 30,000 covering more than 153,000 acres (including 26,000 acres of water), Camp Lejeune is the training base for the U.S. Marine Corps Second Marine Expeditionary Force and the Second Marine Division. It is an amphibious training ground that surrounds the New River nearly from the historic river crossing town and port of Jacksonville to the New River Inlet, which opens to the Atlantic. It is also growing. In 1991 the secretary of the navy authorized funds for the purchase of nearly 42,000 acres of land southeast of the current boundary, US 17, from Jacksonville to Holly Ridge.

Camp Lejeune includes the islands and beachfront that comprise the middle third of Onslow County's oceanfront, Brown's Island and Onslow Beach. These beaches are not accessible to the general public, but a visitor would find a remarkable transition area for the coast. Bear Inlet separates Hammocks Beach State Park from Brown's Island, also referenced as Bear Island or, an older designation, Shacklefoot Island. Very similar in topography and landscape to the park, Brown's Island is also backed by extensive salt marsh along the Intracoastal Waterway. Brown's Inlet separates this island from the landform known as Onslow Beach, which is an island in that the Intracoastal Waterway separates it from the mainland. If you look at a map of the entire coast, Onslow Beach is a bulge in the otherwise smooth

arc from Cape Lookout to Cape Fear. This is the location where it appears most likely that the barrier islands have completely migrated back to the mainland.

The Beirut Memorial stands along the Jacksonville-Lejeune Boulevard (NC 24), paying tribute to the 268 marines and sailors from Camp Lejeune who died in the 1983 barracks bombing in Beirut, Lebanon. The granite memorial wall, set in a grove of oak trees and dogwoods, lists the names of the casualties of the bombing along with three service members who died in Grenada. The memorial is never closed.

NC 172 travels through the southern portion of the base. You do not see much as you approach the entry checkpoint except exquisite coastal plain woods and a few houses outside the base perimeter. After the guard waves you through, pay attention to the highway and warning signs. In a few locations, Camp Lejeune posts one of the state's most memorable cautionary signs. It is a yellow diamond, just like a deer-crossing sign, only this shows the silhouette of a tank. "Tank Crossing" is painted on the road across a massive crossing area as if to caution you not to hurt one. Obey the restrictions imposed by the sentries and any temporary signs that are posted. It is not the sort of place to wander aimlessly or to get out of the car and go for a hike in the woods. Camp Lejeune conducts live-fire drills, sometimes across highways, and you could wander into an impact area, that is, the area where live ammunition hits the ground and explodes. Although the marines are extremely conscientious and thorough about posting warnings and restricting access to dangerous parts of the base, if you disregard the warnings, you could end up somewhere you don't want to be.

Access

Visitors may take a self-directed driving tour through the base that takes several hours to complete. Check in at the Lejeune Visitors Center (Building 812) near the main gate off of NC 24 in Jacksonville. It is advised to call ahead to be certain the tour is permitted, 910-451-2197.

Web address: <www.lejeune. usmc.mil/mcb>

Sneads Ferry

Sneads Ferry, one of the oldest settlements in the county, is fundamentally a simple place that is complicated to define. The name applies to an aggregation of small crossroad neighborhoods (and now, new second-home developments, even a golf course) that are between NC 210 and NC 172 and the New River. The older part of Sneads Ferry is a modest-sized village off of NC 172 with a cluster of small stores, a skating rink, community center, fairgrounds, and a few churches, well away from the water of New River.

The nearest marinas are southeast of Sneads Ferry. Nearby Fulcher Landing and Hatch Point

on the New River are the principal commercial fishing docks in the area with several seafood companies and a restaurant. Swan Point is a commercial and recreational boating center downriver from Fulcher Landing, taking advantage of the Intracoastal Waterway leading to the New River Inlet.

The first licensed ferry operator here, Edmund Ennett, started the passenger business in 1725. Robert W. Snead arrived in 1760, took over the ferry, and opened a tavern. His name stuck to the vicinity, even after the bridge over the New River was built in 1939, upriver from the ferry landing.

The town sprawls freely amid fields and coastal forests, but you don't feel a sense of place, a condition once compounded by the absence of road signs. Despite the uncentralized evolution of the community, there is a key organizing element, a central post office. Sneads Ferry has significant shrimp fishery business, but second-home development and construction are becoming more important. Several expansive and expensive developments with amenities such as golf-course living and waterside homes have grown handsomely in the last decade. Although the new locations have a Sneads Ferry address and are visible from NC 210 and the Intracoastal Waterway, the original community is off the more traveled roads and much lower-key.

Access

There is no direct access to the oceanfront, but there are several

private marinas that offer charter head-boat fishing. There are also boat ramp locations on the Intracoastal Waterway at Swan Point and a private boat ramp at Fulcher Landing.

Information

For information, contact Onslow County Tourism, P.O. Box 1226, Jacksonville, NC 28541-0765, 910-455-1113, 800-932-2144.

Web address: <www.sneads ferry.com>

Topsail Island

Topsail Island is the beach for Onslow and Pender Counties. If you are arriving from Jacksonville or points northeast, NC 210 arcs over a high-rise crossing of the Intracoastal Waterway and lands in North Topsail Beach, still a good ways south of the island's north end. (The marsh of the Intracoastal Waterway is curiously channeled in a geometric pattern creating a series of fingers of water.) From the south and west, most visitors arrive by way of NC 50. This highway crosses to Topsail Island into the heart of Surf City. The passage over the Intracoastal Waterway here is on one of the few remaining swing bridges in North Carolina.

It is a long island, 22 miles in fact; only Bogue Banks on this part of the state's coast is longer. It features a south-facing oceanfront, and the island actually aligns more northeast-southwest.

Topsail Island is the midpoint of

	Fee	Parking	Restrooms	Lifeguard	Camping	Showers	Beach Access	Hiking	Trail	Handicapped	Boating	ORV Access	Fishing	Programs	Historic	Sand Beach	Dunes	Upland	Wetland
North Topsail Beach	•	•				•	•			•	•		•			•	•		•
Public Boating Access: North Topsail Beach		•									•		•						•
Regional Access: Onslow No. 1	•	•					•			•			•			•	•		
Regional Access: Onslow No. 2	•	•				•	•			•			•			•	•		•
Regional Access: Onslow No. 3	•							•					•			•			
Regional Access: Onslow No. 4	•	•				•	•			•			•			•	•		
Permuda Island Coastal Reserve								•			•		•					•	•

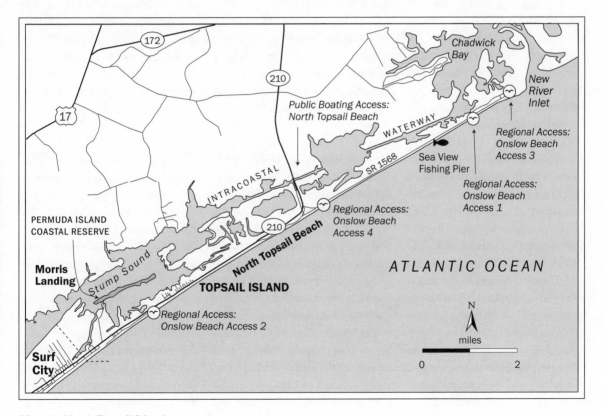

Map 22. North Topsail Island

the westward crescentic arch that begins at Cape Lookout and ends with Cape Fear. This body of water is called Onslow Bay, and the deepest part of the arc is in the vicinity of Topsail Beach. So much water makes for plentiful crabs, shrimp, water-skiers, and marinas. Most marinas, as you would expect with such a lengthy island, are at the ends where the natural inlets are, thereby reducing the cruising time necessary to reach open ocean, where the mackerel, bonito, and other popular game fish swim.

It seems like a simple picture, but there is room for confusion. Topsail Island stretches through two counties, Onslow and Pender, and three incorporated communities: North Topsail Beach in Onslow County, Surf City in Onslow and Pender Counties, and Topsail Beach in Pender County. The multijurisdiction confusion most frequently comes up during calls for emergency services by vacationers. Folks literally don't know where they are other than on Topsail Island.

For the record, North Topsail Beach is at the northeast end of the island; Surf City is in the middle; and Topsail Beach is at the southeast end. The island population is approximately 3,500 people; Surf City is largest community with about 1,700 citizens. Even with the increased building of recent years, the island still feels roomy, especially in the shoulder seasons.

Geologically, Topsail Island is nearly welded to the mainland; the sound waters to the north are narrow and filled with marsh. In fact, north of the New River, only the channel of the Intracoastal Waterway maintains Onslow Beach as an island. The marsh indicates that the sound is beginning to silt in, and peat deposits on the beach reveal that the island has indeed migrated inland over ancient sounds.

The island once had a single dune line, not a dune field, that extended along its length. Severely damaged by the 1996 hurricanes, it is now an abrupt escarpment rising sharply from back of the beach, where it exists at all. Topsail is generally blessed with a wide, flat beach that has gentle wave action. This makes it possible to find fragile shells such as sand dollars intact. The island is also a shelling hot spot for the much more durable ancient shark's teeth, by patiently sifting handfuls of shell "hash."

Loggerhead turtles frequently lumber ashore on Topsail. The popular work of the Karen Beasley Sea Turtle Rehabilitation and Rescue Center in Topsail Beach has done much to educate residents and visitors about how to enjoy the beach and share it with these nocturnal nesters. In the past, as many as 100 nests have been confirmed on the island, but in immediate past years the total has dropped inexplicably.

The low-density oceanfront housing and wide, gentle beaches offer favorable conditions for these seagoing reptiles to dig nests at the high tide lines between April and May. The comparatively undeveloped beach provides a darkened skyline for the turtles, a key they use to judge the safety of a potential nesting site. It is customary when renting on the oceanfront on Topsail Island to turn off all oceanside house lights at night as a simple act of assistance to the turtles. The nesting is monitored by local volunteers and is one of the celebrated natural summer rituals of the island. Hatchlings usually emerge in August.

The island has a great curiosity: abandoned reinforced concrete towers along the length of the island, beginning with the first tower in Topsail Beach. The U.S. Navy built these monumental structures in the 1940s as observation platforms for the nascent rocket-testing program, Operation Bumblebee, headquartered at Topsail Beach. Six towers still stand and probably will forever. The first tower at Topsail Beach is a private residence; another was once incorporated into the structure of the Ocean City Fishing Pier. The pier is now destroyed. Because they were used to document the flight of early rockets, the towers were precisely located in relation to each other, and the longitude and latitude of their location was exactly recorded. In fact, the U.S. Coast and Geodetic Survey used the first tower as a sea-level monitoring station.

Visiting Topsail Island is still a trip into the past, a visit to a beach thirty years ago. The island has predominantly modest single-family cottages, and the focus of activity is the beach. Some resort-style construction is finding its way to Topsail Island, particularly at North Topsail Beach, but for the most part, east to west, sound to sea, Topsail is folksy and casual. Its discovery was inevitable, but then, it really hasn't been hiding.

Access

Onslow County maintains several regional beach access locations on the island in North Topsail Beach.

There is a boating ramp and access location serving the Intracoastal Waterway on the north side of NC 210 after you cross onto the island.

Handicapped Access

Onslow Beach Access Site numbers 1, 2, and 4 in North Topsail Beach are fully accessible to handicapped travelers.

Information

For information, contact Onslow County Tourism, P.O. Box 1226, Jacksonville, NC 28541-0765, 910-455-1113, 800-932-2144; or Greater Topsail Area Chamber of Commerce and Tourism, 13775 Highway 50, Suite 101, or P.O. Box 2486, Surf City, NC 28445-2486, 910-329-4446, 800-626-2780.

Web addresses: <www.onslow countytourism.com>; <www.top sailcoc.com>; <www.nccoastalman agement.net/Access/sites.htm>

North Topsail Beach

North Topsail Beach began on January 1, 1990, and officially became the lengthiest community on Topsail Island, extending from the New River Inlet to the city limits of Surf City, a distance of slightly more than 12 miles. The incorporation came about in response to recent building trends at what was then North Topsail Shores, the portion of the island north of the NC 210 bridge. This is one of the most threatened locations on the North Carolina coast.

On September 6, 1996, Hurricane Fran confirmed the worst fears of the coastal geologists and wiped the sands of North Topsail Beach clean. It is difficult to describe the destruction, except to say it was practically total.

More remarkable is the recovery of the community since Fran's visit. People rebuilt destroyed homes, and many more newcomers have joined the community that has a population of just fewer than 1,000. The recovery has occurred in spite of the disadvantage that 6 miles of the community are in a CoBRA zone, making them ineligible for federal flood insurance or beach nourishment funds.

North Topsail Beach has extensive development north of the NC 210 bridge (most of the taller buildings were approved prior to incorporation) along New River Inlet Road, and at the southern three miles of the town, a location known as the Ocean City fishing area. There are scattered homes and small developments in between these two concentrations of vacation homes. There is no commercial center; most folks drive north to the intersection of NC 172 and NC 210 (nicknamed "four cor-

ners") for their needs. It is also close enough to Jacksonville to be commuter country.

The beach here is low and flat, and the wave energy is low. North Topsail Beach can state that it has some of the cleanest, least commercial beaches on the coast, and this is certainly evident by driving the island. The recent building push has brought a new, ornate beach architecture to the shores, homes engineered to withstand hurricane-force pounding. Some of these houses reign as isolated getaway castles in the middle of American beach grass, plush but lonely.

North Topsail Beach faces substantial long-term erosion north of NC 210. New River Inlet Road, SR 1568, has been relocated inland from its oceanfront location because storms undermined it during the winter of 1991.

Access

All the streets perpendicular to NC 210 provide pedestrian access to the beach. A few of these areas have parking spaces available. There are dune crossovers at the ends of Fifth Avenue, Ninth Avenue, Fifteenth Street, Twenty-first Street, Twenty-third Street, Chestnut Street, Reeves Street, Sixth Street, and Seventh Street.

Onslow Beach Access Site number 1 is slightly south of the Topsail Dunes development, on the north side of New River Inlet Road. After crossing over to Topsail Island on the high-rise bridge on NC 210, turn left on SR 1568 (New River

Inlet Road) and continue north about 4 miles. There are 30 parking spaces and pay telephones. A dune crossover across the road leads past Topsail Dunes to a very flat beach.

Access site number 2 is a major regional access location 4 miles south of the NC 210 bridge. It has an elevated wood pavilion on the oceanfront with a ramp to the beach for handicapped users. There are concession areas, showers, restrooms, and parking for 250 cars. There is also a soundside parking area across the highway.

Access site number 3 is farther north at the end of the private road that winds past the St. Regis Hotel at the mouth of the New River. This area offers unimproved parking and fishing access to the inlet on approximately 700 feet of New River Inlet frontage.

Onslow Beach Access Site number 4 is approximately one mile north of NC 210 on SR 1568 (New River Inlet Road), where the roadway "S" curves inland, away from the old roadbed. This access area has an elevated wooden deck on the ocean, restrooms, showers, concession area, and parking for 150 vehicles.

Handicapped Access
North Topsail Beach will provide a beach wheelchair with advance request. Call the police department at 910-328-0042.

Onslow Beach Access Site numbers 1, 2, and 4 are accessible to handicapped travelers.

Information
For information, contact Onslow County Tourism, P.O. Box 1226, Jacksonville, NC 28541-0765, 910-455-1113, 800-932-2144; or Greater Topsail Area Chamber of Commerce and Tourism, 13775 Highway 50, Suite 101, or P.O. Box 2486, Surf City, NC 28445-2486, 910-329-4446, 800-626-2780.

Web addresses: <www.onslowcountytourism.com>; <www.topsailcoc.com>; <www.north-topsail-beach.org>; <www.nccoastalmanagement.net/Access/sites.htm>

Permuda Island Coastal Reserve

Permuda Island is a marshy island that rises slightly above sea level in Stump Sound west of North Topsail Beach. The island is about 1.5 miles long, with its center nearly due west of the Onslow Beach Access Site number 2. The state owns the 50 acres of upland on Permuda Island, and it is included in the North Carolina Coastal Reserve program.

The island is a mix of habitats, including stunted trees such as red cedar, live oak, and yaupon, and abandoned agricultural fields that are reverting to woodland. The island marsh and mudflats provide habitat for willets, American oystercatchers, egrets, herons, black skimmers, and sandpipers. It is also known that early Native Americans used the island as a seasonal fishing and shellfish-gathering enclave.

The island narrowly escaped modernization in 1983, when a proposal to develop it met tremendous, prolonged opposition. Development, opponents argued, would irreparably damage the shellfish harvest in Stump Sound. In January 1985 the North Carolina Coastal Resources Commission officially designated Permuda Island as an Area of Environmental Concern because of the significant archaeological features on the island, including a centuries-old Native American living site.

The Nature Conservancy eventually purchased the island for $1.7 million. In January 1987 the state purchased half of the island from the Nature Conservancy, completing the purchase and taking control the following September. There are no plans to change the traditional use of Permuda Island for fishing or hiking.

Access
The closest marina is at Morris Landing in Bethea, at the end of SR 1538. You could also probably slip a canoe into Stump Sound from Onslow Beach Access Site number 2, but there is no boat-launching ramp.

Information
For information, contact North Carolina Coastal Reserve, 5600 Marvin K. Moss Lane, Wilmington, NC 28409, 910-395-3905.

Web address: <www.ncnerr.org/pubsiteinfo/index.html>

Plane Speaking

By the time you hear them, they are gone. Military jets outrun their sound, and when you hear the roar, the planes are in another part of the sky. Fortunately for us big kids, military pilots train in the skies above our coast. This makes for a different kind of "bird-watching." Here are some field guide keys.

Most training occurs around the bases of Cherry Point Marine Air Station near Havelock or Seymour Johnson Air Force Base in Goldsboro. Oceana Naval Air Station in Virginia Beach has wide-ranging fliers that sometimes cruise the northern banks. Your chances to plane-watch increase if you are near these bases or near Stumpy Point in Dare County, a practice range used by several services.

There is a proposal to create a multipurpose training base near Creswell in Pamlico County, extremely close to Pungo Lakes National Wildlife Refuge. This controversial proposal is bitterly opposed because of the potential cost and conflict with migratory waterfowl. If the base is built, jet traffic will be widespread over the Albemarle Sound region.

The two most important keys to identifying these birds are tail configuration and wing shape.

Twin-Tail Planes

There are four twin-tailed fliers: the F-15 Eagle (air force), the F-14 Tomcat (navy), and the F-18 (navy and marines), and the YF-17 Stealth fighter (air force). The F-15 and F-14 are both large planes and can be easily confused if you've not seen them before. They may be distinguished by the following characteristics.

F-15: The twin tails (vertical stabilizers) are extremely tall in proportion to the body; one has a light or sensor in the tip. The profile is sleek and flat with a high-domed canopy. It may have one or two fliers. The wings are rigid, and small ailerons at the rear extend past the tail to form a noticeable "notch." Even though this is a large plane, it is very agile with a streamlined wedge shape that is unmistakable because of the high tail. These planes are usually spotted over the coastal plain near Goldsboro.

F-14: The twin tails are not as tall and are more in proportion to the body; they also have a slight cant outward. In profile, the plane seems to have thick, heavyset "shoulders," yet it is streamlined. It has a similar domed canopy with two fliers. Wings are variable and may be swept back. The outer half of the wings appears to emerge from sleeves and seems stiff when fully extended. The wings fold back to form a delta (triangular) configuration with the rear ailerons. There are two exhausts, and the tail profile is even. This is a brooding, powerful flier that seems compact and very explosive, more brutal in appearance than the F-15. Most are based in Norfolk, Virginia, and so are most commonly sighted over the northern banks; however, one may be occasionally spotted over Emerald Isle practicing landings at Bogue Field.

F-18: The twin tails that are set forward of the rear wings and ailerons are an immediate giveaway. This is a much smaller craft than the other two as well. The tails are canted at an angle much like holding up two fingers. The twin engines' exhaust extends far past the vertical tails. The wings are fixed, and the plane has a long nose extending in front of the single-seat cockpit. The F-18 is more waspish and lithe than the F-15 and F-14. The F-18 is rarely seen over the northern banks, but it is more likely near Havelock/Jacksonville.

YF-17: The Stealth fighter will not be mistaken for any other plane. It looks like a flying angular horseshoe crab with two canted tails. It doesn't fly fast. It is spooky-looking, and the first thought that comes to mind is how does it fly? This plane is rarely spotted, though it is possible near Goldsboro.

Single-Tail Planes

The most likely seen single-tail planes are the F-5 (navy), A-6 (navy), and AV-8 (marines). Several others, the A-4, F-4, and A-7, have been retired.

F-5: This plane has one seat and is recognized by its stiletto profile and short wings that extend straight from the middle of the plane. It looks like a dart. There are twin intakes and twin exhausts. This is a small, lithe, swift flier. The navy uses it as a trainer (with two seats) and to simulate enemy tactics. The F-5 is usually seen over the northern banks.

A-6: This twin-engine plane, with two seats side by side, has a bulging front end that tapers rapidly to a thin fuselage. The engine intakes are under the wings, which are long for the body. The A-6 is a navy attack jet, and it is a deliberate, steady flier. It may be seen near Stumpy Point, though it is close to retirement.

AV-8: This is the Harrier, a vertical-takeoff jet with single tail and seat. It is heavy through the middle with variable-angle thrust deflectors under the wings. The wings have distinctive ribbing. Although "chunky," it is still streamlined, with some speed in the lines of the plane. Camouflage coloring is a good tip-off. These jets practice takeoffs at the auxiliary field at Bogue. The AV-8 is an efficient, deliberate flier, though not really remarkable, and can be seen near Havelock and Stumpy Point.

Pender County

Driving south on the racetrack of I-40 provides a fleeting glimpse of what awaits on the slower secondary roads that lead from the interstate to Topsail Island, the beach in Pender County. The interstate, paralleling the Seaboard Coastline Railroad tracks to Wilmington, divides Pender County; to the west are well-tended fields, to the east, tangled, impenetrable woods. A highway map confirms this pattern, showing immense roadless areas, which is where the wild things are. Pender County is for growing things, tamed or otherwise.

Rivers have scored this county as well. East of I-40, the Northeast Cape Fear River bisects the county north and south, a winding braided passage feathering to wetlands on either side of its channel. The interstate and its companion rail line ride atop gently sloping ridges that drain to the river floodplain. Across the county, on its western border, winds the Black River. As the twentieth century waned, scientists discovered a key to the past climate on its banks: bald cypress trees more than 1,700 years old. Core samples from the trees document drought, flood, and fire. Between these two waterways and their broad wetlands stretch the prime farmlands of Pender County, some of the finest in the state.

There's no "bad" land in Pender County, even that which shows as big empty spots on the highway map. It's land that is special because of its forbidding nature, and it becomes a drive-by story of traveling to Topsail Island.

Much of Pender County's roadless areas are included in the vast evergreen shrub bogs managed as game lands by the North Carolina Wildlife Resources Commission. These are fascinating ecosystems, recognized as unique by pioneering botanists two centuries ago, but even now not fully appreciated or understood. Characterized by boggy conditions, but not necessarily peat-forming, these great expanses have been called variously evergreen shrub bogs, pocosin, or bays for both the bay-shaped leaves of the characteristic evergreen shrubs and the elliptical ponds within them. The predominance of broad-leaved, single-veined evergreen plants is one of the noteworthy characteristics of these regions. To the inexperienced eye, all the plants look alike; so do most of the places within the game lands.

These two tracts—Angola Bay and Holly Shelter—present different management challenges to wildlife officials. Angola Bay, in the northeast part of the county, is the wilder of the two, covering 22,600 acres of forbidding wetland with no roads and few fire lanes. In contrast, Holly Shelter, in the east-central part of the county, has 64,740 acres actively managed for big game and waterfowl hunting. It, too, is a wild, generally poorly drained area, but there is better access to the interior than in Angola Bay. Both are rich in fragrant flowering shrubbery and rare herbaceous plants, and the North Carolina chapter of the Nature Conservancy has moved to preserve some of the unique botanical niches associated with these two state holdings.

These nearly impenetrable wild tracts shaped the settlement of the county by thwarting commerce and easy transportation. Fortunately, there has been a high and drier ridge that parallels the coast southeast of the Holly Shelter game land. This serviceable route became the King's Highway, an old post road between Wilmington and New Bern. Eventually, it became the route of US 17. Southeast of US 17, the land drains into the sounds behind the barrier beaches of Topsail and Lea-Hutaff Islands.

The coast of Pender County, like that of neighboring Onslow, has been below beach development radar until recently. The county's only resort beach is on Topsail Island. It amounts to slightly less than half of the island and includes two communities: Surf City, the central, most populous community, and Topsail Beach, the sleepy community at the southeast end of the island. NC 50 and NC 210 cross the Atlantic Intracoastal Waterway at Surf City on one of the last remaining swing bridges in the state. At the Surf City stoplight—until recently the island's sole stoplight—the roads part ways. NC 210 turns northeast and NC 50 heads southwest.

The isolation of Topsail Island—though people have summered here since before the 1930s—has made the island beaches economically more "accessible" than many other locations for summer "second homes." There are several mobile home and camper parks on the island. The last decade, though, has seen a slow but steady increase in construction, both in numbers of homes built and in size and scale of dwellings. Surf City and Topsail Beach are steadily growing. In recent years more folks have moved here permanently, choosing to work off island in Jacksonville or Wilmington, both manageable commutes for oceanfront living.

The island is widest in Surf City, and this is the portion of the island with best frontal dunes as well, but the island profile is still low. Hurricane Fran flattened the island's meager dune line, before taking chunks out of the road and generally cleaning out all or parts of all the structures on the island. It left several oceanfront buildings in Topsail Beach, tottering over the swash line. (Hurricane Hazel in 1954 destroyed 210 of 230 island homes.)

Until the summer of 1996 (Hurricanes Bertha and Fran), Topsail Island summered for 42 years beside a benevolent ocean. The pair of storms took a shovel-cut out of the dunes, leaving a steep, sharp incline to the still gentle beach. The six miles between Surf City and Topsail Beach were spared the worst of those storms. Topsail Beach, then with far fewer houses than Surf City, seemed to be the less for wear and tear, except for the oceanfront, where nearly all homes were highly damaged and where many had the island itself washed out from underneath.

Today, 1996 is a year long forgotten. The same gentle beach that spurred storm victims to rebuild has steadily lured newcomers to the island. The island profile has not changed; it is still low, but it now has a steeper face to the dune line, if one exists at all. The beaches again are ample, flat, and washed with soft, easy wave action.

The six miles between communities have more houses and more people. The towns have essentially the same appeal, offering a different expression of the characteristically low-key and understated beach experience that is the hallmark of Topsail Island. There are a couple of noticeable differences: Topsail Beach is always less crowded and is closer to the inlet.

There are nominally two islands remaining in southern Pender County, Lea and Hutaff Islands, southwest from Topsail Island. Both of these barrier spits are very low, highly erodible, and generally not very stable. They are accessible only by boat. The historic inlets between the three islands—New Topsail Inlet between Topsail and Lea Islands and Old Topsail Inlet once separating Lea and Hutaff Islands—provide rich fishing, even though the depths of the channels shift around enough to make boating a challenge. Each of the inlets is migrating south, though at different rates, which means that each of the islands is gaining ground by accretion on its southern end. However, such added landmass has been shown to be unstable over time for any use other than as a delightful beach.

All three islands have wide marshes to the west. Finger canals poke into the marsh on Topsail Island in several locations. Once the marsh and sound waters supported a rich fishery because the small, rural, mostly wooded watershed filtered rainwater runoff, maintaining a clean, healthy estuary. However, the sound waters are now showing deterioration from construction pollutants, the destruction of the woods, and the increasing numbers of people and boats using the sound. Certain portions of the sound may soon be closed to shellfishing.

Back on the mainland, the land between Holly Ridge and Hampstead east of US 17 has gone to golf. The resort real estate market in Pender County is becoming an increasingly important player in the local economy, which will no doubt result in changes along the coastline.

Access

Pender County maintains two regional access locations in Surf City. The first is at Broadway Street north of the city center. The access area has parking for 50 cars and a bathhouse with restrooms and showers.

The other regional access is at New Bern Avenue, which runs from Topsail Drive to the oceanfront, three blocks northeast of the center of Surf City (where NC 210/50 becomes Roland Avenue) and intersects Topsail Drive. There are 22 parking places, a gazebo, restrooms, showers, and a dune crossover at the site.

Neighborhood parking is also at Wilmington Street and at 508 North Shore Drive.

Handicapped Access

The regional access site at New Bern Avenue is accessible to handicapped travelers and includes a ramped dune crossover.

Information

For general information on Pender County, contact County of Pender Tourism Department, P.O. Box 5, Burgaw, NC 28425, 888-576-4756.

For information about Angola Bay and Holly Shelter game lands, contact North Carolina Wildlife

Resources Commission, 1703 Mail Service Center, Raleigh, NC 27699-1703, 919-733-3391.

Greater Topsail Area Chamber of Commerce and Tourism, 13775 Highway 50, Suite 101, or P.O. Box 2486, Surf City, NC 28445-2486, 910-329-4446, 800-626-2780.

Web addresses: <www.visitpender.com>; <www.topsailcoc.com>; <www.ncwildlife.org>; <www.nccoastalmanagement.net/Access/sites.htm>

Surf City

This six-mile-long oceanfront community, founded in 1949, was way out in front of the 1960s chart-topping single of the same name by Jan and Dean, but if there is an easy-come, easy-go community that captures the song's mood and attitude about a super summer at the beach, it might very well be this beach.

The waves aren't nearly as big, but the small-town, summer of '63 feeling still lingers at Surf City. City fathers are striking a careful blend of today and yesterday, too. The town motto is "Big enough to be competitive, but small enough to be happy!" I'll vote for that, and if I have to set my watch back a decade or two, I'll gladly do that as well. Surf City has its priorities straight, and chilling out is obviously high on the list.

This community of some 1,700 people (20,000 in summer) could have been the movie set for the boy-meets-girl-at-the-beach summer movie of forty years ago. There are just enough amusements and hangouts and not quite enough parking to keep things moving on summer nights, stirring up the evening the way the under-21 beach crowd wants it to be—or at least the way us older folks remember wanting it stirred.

Surf City is the most populated of Topsail Island's three communities. It is compressed around the junction of NC 210 and NC 50; the latter continues southwest through the wide and most heavily developed portion of Topsail Island to Topsail Beach. The northern city limits of Surf City actually extend over the Pender County line at Broadway Avenue into Onslow County for about two miles and include portions of Old Settlers Beach. To the southwest, Surf City borders Topsail Beach.

The swing bridge over the sound provides one of the highest vantage points at this end of the island, offering a quick glimpse of the modest center strip of this beachfront community. The swing bridge, one of the last on North Carolina's coast, fits the town's character. This is the kind of community where having to wait for a boat to motor along the Intracoastal Waterway fits right in with its anachronistic charm.

There is a handsome soundside park to the south of the main road with a band shell, picnic shelters, and walkway along the water. Marinas cluster the shores, and in the heart of downtown, businesses dot the grid of streets outward from the main intersection, which happens to have the island's only stoplight. There are amusements, beachwear shops, restaurants, and an Internet café that offers web access 24/7. The development pattern creates commercial nodes of services and shops along the strand. Low-rise commercial services provide the island welcome. The town hall is two blocks north on NC 210.

While Surf City is not really small, it projects a small-town atmosphere, and much of this has to do the intimate grid of streets. The community is not wide from surf to sound, the roads are two-lane, and buildings are close to them. The few generic beach commercial buildings seem too large for the place. North of city center is a condominium complex that looks blocky, chunky, and overwhelming. Surf City's charm revolves around the idiosyncratic individualism of restaurants, stores, houses, and motor inns that embody the era in which they were built. This style better reflects the individualism that brought and kept people here initially. Pressure is not a part of the experience here, and if you are seeking urban intensity, Surf City may frustrate you slightly. Don't go unarmed—take a good book, boat, fishing rod, or cast net.

On September 5, 1996, the strongest winds and highest storm surge of Hurricane Fran piled into Surf City, destroying most oceanfront buildings, including the fishing piers. The Surf City Fishing Pier rebuilt, but the others, Barnacle Bill's, Scotch Bonnet, and Ocean City, which incorporated

	Fee	Parking	Restrooms	Lifeguard	Camping	Showers	Beach Access	Hiking	Trail	Handicapped	Boating	ORV Access	Fishing	Programs	Historic	Sand Beach	Dunes	Upland	Wetland
Regional Access: Surf City		•	•			•	•			•			•		•	•	•		
Soundside Park Surf City		•	•						•	•	•		•						•
Topsail Beach		•	•				•				•		•		•	•	•		•

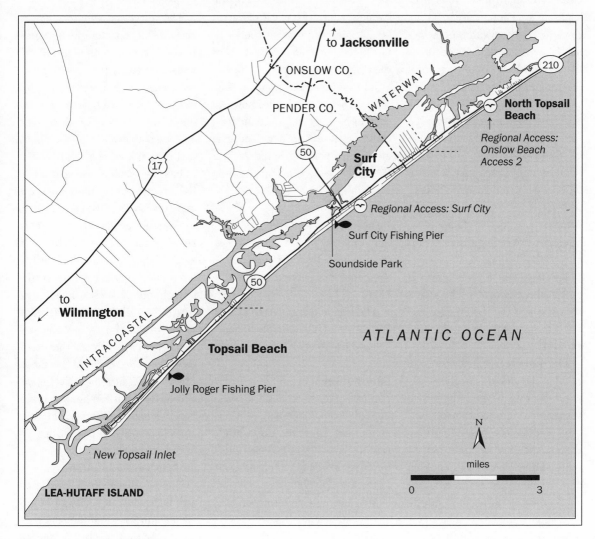

Map 23. South Topsail Island

one of the early rocket-testing towers), did not. This was more than a loss to fishermen since these piers were important recreational centers in the earlier, sleepier years of this beach community.

So far, Surf City redux is not wandering too far from its halcyon origins. Some individual homes have that "I've arrived" heft, but less is still more here. Topsail Island's general popularity is hitting close to this easygoing home for many. At a gasoline-tackle shop, the owners were muttering about the first "throw-away homes," where someone bought a house and lot and gave the house away to build something completely new on the lot. Some folks want to be there that bad, and others are not sure if they are ready for them to arrive.

Access

There are two regional access sites in Surf City.

The first is at Broadway Street north of the city center. The access area has parking for 50 cars and a bathhouse with restrooms and showers.

The other regional access is located at the end of New Bern Avenue, northeast of where the bridge brings you into downtown Surf City. The facility has 22 parking spaces, showers, restrooms, a gazebo, and a dune crossover. Next door is one of the seven concrete observation platforms used during Operation Bumblebee. The tower is boarded up and is plainly posted no trespassing.

There are also signed neighborhood access points with a number of parking places available at many of the streets that dead-end into Shore Drive, the road directly behind the dune line. Several parking lots on Shore Drive south of the central fishing pier, within easy view, have more spaces. You may have a better chance finding parking at Wilmington and Kingston Avenues southwest of the pier than at the smaller areas in the more populated portions of town toward the Onslow County line.

Informal access is also available. Surf City Pier has been known to open its parking lot for beachgoers; check with the owner. There is also some parking spillover into the grocery store lot on the next block inland.

Handicapped Access

Surf City will loan a beach wheelchair with advance request. Call the police department at 910-328-7711.

The regional access site at New Bern Avenue is accessible to handicapped travelers.

Information

For information, contact Greater Topsail Area Chamber of Commerce and Tourism, 13775 Highway 50, Suite 101, or P.O. Box 2486, Surf City, NC 28445-2486, 910-329-4446, 800-626-2780.

Web addresses: <http://surf city.govoffice.com>; <www.visit pender.com>

Topsail Beach

I love the drive to Topsail Beach because there are so few beach drives like this remaining. It is a long ride through an oceanfront subdivision; there are no stores, no hotels, and no amusements, just a pleasant passage through three miles of Surf City homes before entering the city limits of Topsail Beach.

The drive is windows down, arm outside, lazy tour along Shore Drive (NC 50) with intermittent houses on either the oceanfront or the soundside of the road. The island narrows after passing from the wider portion of Surf City, and the soundside lots reach back to the marshy edge of the island.

In a few locations, these residential streets seem to tunnel into the maritime forest, boring a path to the sound. The illusion from Shore Drive is that you are traveling at a much higher elevation than the water. Sometimes that is true. At the town limits of Topsail Beach, the road crests along the back ridge of the frontal dunes, and the seaward houses perch on the precipice above the beach. At this point, Shore Drive becomes North Anderson Boulevard. When you reach downtown Topsail Beach, the road is no longer at the oceanfront but instead parallels Ocean Boulevard, directly behind the dunes.

Topsail Beach is a tight and tidy little town, a series of homesteads and vacation outposts built for the love of the beach, tucked behind a remarkably high and intact dune line that stretches almost the length of the city limits. A water tower marks the center, more or less. Ocean Boulevard and its beachfront houses continue to the southwest until they meet the natural chiseling away of real estate closer to the inlet. It is so very laid back everywhere.

North Anderson changes to South Anderson at the intersection of Banks Channel Court. There is a bike path along the soundside of Anderson leading into the central business portion of Topsail Beach. The Jolly Roger Motel and Pier mark the approximate central business district and certainly the historic part of the island. The patio of the motel is on the site of the launching pad of rocket tests conducted here by the navy in the 1940s, named Operation Bumblebee. The original building of the motel dates from that era.

The rocket assembly was in the soundside building now known as the Arsenal Centre. The rockets moved from this assembly station to the launching pad underground. The reinforced concrete observation towers were used to track the flight of the missiles. Other buildings still standing here served in support of the effort, identifiable by the vintage architecture and the lean square chimneys in the middle of the buildings. When the military abandoned Topsail, it returned the island and sold the buildings to the former owners, and the resort era began. It has grown to a whopping 800 residents year-round.

Sleepy though it may be, Topsail Beach is becoming better known because of the hard work of the volunteers at the Karen Beasley Sea Turtle Rescue and Rehabilitation Center. This is one of two facilities on the East Coast dedicated to the care and rehabilitation of injured sea turtles. Effective and dedicated from the get-go, the center has rapidly gained stature and, unfortunately, patients from many locations. Scheduled releases of recovered turtles are big events in Topsail Beach when the healed turtles, adopted and named by the volunteers who nursed them to health, are allowed to crawl back into the ocean and swim away. A release in early June 2004 was attended by more than 1,000 people. Five turtles departed for the wilds again in September of the same year with a send-off of hundreds. Located behind Topsail Beach Town Hall, the center allows visitation as schedule and staffing permit. Visitors are welcome to stop by and support the effort by donating or purchasing tee shirts and other turtle-themed mementos. It is best to call for visiting hours at 910-328-3377 or visit online at <www.seaturtle hospital.org>.

Another unique stop is the Topsail Island museum "Missiles and More," located in the assembly building used between 1946 and 1948 when Topsail Beach genuinely was a center for rocket scientists. Falling squarely in the "believe it or not" category is the fact that the principle of the ram jet

engine, the mainstay of supersonic flight today, was developed and proved on Topsail. Among other exhibits are parts of the original test rockets that washed ashore, as well as a color video of actual missile launchings at the time.

The "more" of Missiles and More is details on the natural and cultural history of Topsail Island, a name, by the way supposedly bequeathed when pirates were based in its sound waters.

The southwest end of the island has had a tough time with erosion, but the beach is still lovely and much less crowded (by Topsail standards) than closer to the center of town. As at New Topsail Inlet, the beach is building, which is extending the island. Serenity Point, a new development on land that in 1938 was the location of the inlet, faces nearly 100 yards of new, wide, flat beach. It is the best beach in the town now and the place to head, particularly for fishing and shelling. Sit down in an expanse of "sea hash," as the multicolored debris of shell fragments is known, and carefully sift through it with an eye for sharp, triangular shapes—tiny ancient shark's teeth. Topsail is a hot spot for them, and a practiced eye can turn some time on the beaches here into a pocketful of treasures.

Access

There are no regional access locations in Topsail Beach. Each street that is perpendicular to the oceanfront terminates in a dune crossover, and there are a few parking spaces available near each. There is a parking area at Serenity Point that leads by boardwalk and stairs up over the dune line, providing access to the inlet and the newly accreted beach at the southwest end of the island. You must get there early to squeeze into one of the parking spaces.

According to law enforcement officers in Topsail Beach, parking is permitted pretty much anywhere as long as you observe the following commonsense rules:

— Don't park where signs indicate no parking.
— Pull your car completely off the pavement.
— Park at least 15 feet from a water hydrant.
— Don't block anyone's driveway, sidewalk, or service area.
— Don't park on anyone's property without permission.

Several marinas offer boating access to Topsail Sound. There are four fishing piers that offer angling, including one soundside pier.

An unimproved off-road-vehicle access is at the ocean terminus of Drum Avenue.

Handicapped Access
Topsail Beach will loan a beach wheelchair with advance request. Call the police department at 910-328-4851.

Information
For information, contact Greater Topsail Area Chamber of Commerce and Tourism, 13775 Highway 50, Suite 101, or P.O. Box 2486, Surf City, NC 28445-2486, 910-329-4446, 800-626-2780.

Web addresses: <www.topsail coc.com>; <www.visitpender. com>

New Topsail Inlet and Lea-Hutaff Island

New Topsail Inlet is beyond the beach west of the Serenity Point development in Topsail Beach. From the inlet, you can see a residence on neighboring Lea-Hutaff Island, once separate islands, now joined, named after the previous owners.

Lea-Hutaff Island, the next island in the sequence along the Pender County coast, is generally small and low, but it does have some upland. Nearly forty lots were platted on the island as recently as the 1980s.

Old Topsail Inlet was in this vicinity, more or less splitting the mass into separate islands, but it has shoaled past usefulness, and the islands are practically one. To the south of the hyphenated land is Rich Inlet, separating Lea-Hutaff Island from Figure Eight Island.

The complex supports nesting loggerhead sea turtles and hundreds of nesting terns, skimmers, and shorebirds. In season, thousands of migrant shorebirds stop off to feed and rest during their long flights. The island has never had any severe disturbance by man and is considered one of the last and best undeveloped barrier islands on the North Carolina coast.

The two islands combined have a total of 5.6 acres of high ground backed by extensive marsh that is an important estuary. A coalition of conservation groups, led by Audubon North Carolina and including the North Carolina Coastal Land Trust, the state of North Carolina, and the U.S. Fish and Wildlife Service, has purchased most of the islands and marsh. Audubon North Carolina is managing this coastal complex for the benefit of the wildlife that uses its unspoiled beaches and marshes for nesting and habitat.

Access
The islands are reachable by boat. Access to certain parts of the islands may be restricted during certain nesting seasons.

Information
Contact Audubon North Carolina, 123 Kingston Drive, Suite 206A, Chapel Hill, NC 27514, 919-929-3899.

Web address: <www.nc audubon.org>

Hampstead

Oh, how I miss old Hampstead, where a two-lane US 17 passed through a whisper of a community. Moss-draped trees, some with an arching reach across the road, crowded and enclosed this passage where the highway speed limit dropped to 45 miles per hour as though a mark of respect.

Five lanes where two once were can alter the visual quality of a community beyond reclamation. So it went as US 17 grew to five lanes in during the mid-1990s.

There is a small shopping center and the beginnings of a commercial hub where NC 210 turns to the west. Several roads lead east to marinas.

It is said that George Washington stopped at Hampstead during his southern tour in 1791, and south of town, beside the right-of-way, the Daughters of the American Revolution have designated a live oak tree as the site of his encampment. NC 210 turns to the west at Hampstead, leaving behind seafood packers and wholesalers and a small Mormon graveyard.

Access
There is no direct access from Hampstead to the waters of Stump Sound, but there are private marinas at the ends of the secondary roads that lead east from US 17.

Information
For information, contact County of Pender Tourism Department, P.O. Box 5, Burgaw, NC 28425, 888-576-4756; or the Hampstead Chamber of Commerce, P.O. Box 211, Hampstead, NC 28443, 800-833-2483.

Web address: <www.visit pender.com>

Poplar Grove Plantation

James Foy established Poplar Grove Plantation in 1795, which is now in the small town of Scott's Hill. Following a fire that destroyed the original home, his son Joseph M. Foy built the present plantation manor in 1850. A pioneer in peanut cultivation, Foy rebuilt the family fortunes of the 685-acre landholding through the economic sways of the Reconstruction era. The manor house, long central in the affairs of the plantation, exemplifies antebellum plantation architecture and lifestyle in the area. The building, which is on the National Register of Historic Places, has been open to the public for tours for eleven years. The handsome structure is on the southeast side of US 17 and cannot be overlooked.

The grounds are open to the public without charge, but there is a fee for the guided tour of the manor. The elevated first-floor living quarters of the manor house are an example of architectural adaptation to the humid climate of the coastal plain; the high floor level caught the prevailing winds and channeled them through the house for cooling.

For many years, the manor house was also a restaurant, but a new restaurant has been constructed on the grounds, freeing the interior of the house for exhibits. In addition to the house, there are several outbuildings open to the public, including a tenant house, kitchen, blacksmith shop, salt works, and turpentine display.

Access
Poplar Grove is alongside US 17 in Scott's Hill. The plantation is open February–December, 9 A.M. to 5 P.M. Monday–Saturday, 12 P.M. to 5 P.M. Sunday.

Handicapped Access
Because of its age and architectural styling, the manor house is not very accessible. The barn and craft center have accessible restrooms for handicapped travelers.

Information
For information, contact Poplar Grove Plantation, 10200 US 17 North, Wilmington, NC 28411, 910-686-9518.

Web address: <www.poplar grove.com>

What's behind the Breakers?

Telling a child that a great machine sends waves crumpling over his or her feet is closer to the truth than you might think. Most of the waves you see are products of the wind.

However, the wave-building wind may not be the same zephyr tousling your hair. Imagine a becalmed sea, hundreds, perhaps thousands of miles away from you. A breeze gusts the ocean's surface, pushing the water into ripples and creating an effect similar to when you blow on the surface of a bowl of soup. The breeze continues, and the ripples, gathering energy from the wind, pile together to build into waves that travel across the sea to froth at your feet. The friction of air moving over water is sufficient to begin an ocean wave, but the effectiveness of the wind to forge waves depends on the average velocity of the wind, the duration of the wind, and the fetch—the reach of open water—that the wind traverses. The stronger the wind, the longer it blows, and the greater the distance of open ocean across which it pushes the water, the greater the waves that reach the shore.

Wind is neither predictable nor simple, nor are waves, although all waves have some characteristics in common.

Each ripple spawned by wind has a steep windward side that acts as a sail. Should the wind gust too sharply, the top of the youthful wave shatters, spilling over its leading surface or exploding in spray. A stormy coastal day reveals a frothing sea, because the wind shears the crests of waves and spits them about.

If you know what to look for, you can stand on the beach and make an educated guess about where waves originated. Sharp, peaked waves, spilling whitecaps as they march landward before breaking with a "groan," are probably young waves created by a nearby offshore storm. A wave that rolls into a crest that uniformly pipe-curls over and breaks with a roar before pummeling the surf zone is ending a journey from far away.

Have you ever seen a diamond-like pattern in the arriving waves? It is a wild sight, slightly abstract and sometimes overlooked. This occurs when intersecting groups of waves that originated from distant compass points do not march straight into shore. The groups are called wave trains. Each has its own rhythm, wavelength, period of repetition, and height. When separate wave trains intersect and continue their individual tracks, the eye sees a diamond pattern of crests.

When a wave train overtakes another, the separate crests may combine to form a large single wave, or the crest of one may combine with the trough of the other, minimizing the effect. Have you ever noticed that every fourth or fifth wave (or some other count) is larger than average (surfers sure do!)? The larger wave is probably the combined overlap of two different wave trains.

In a boat offshore, waves are felt as swells, which travel at an average rate of 3.5 times their period, the distance between successive crests in seconds. Thus, a wave with a 20-second period travels at about 70 miles per hour. (The lon-

gest period of a swell ever reported was 22.5 seconds, corresponding to a wavelength of 2,600 feet and a speed of 78 miles per hour— a serious wave.)

The wind can blow in any direction, and waves can begin from any direction. Why, then, do they usually arrive at the beach, breaking mostly parallel to shore? Waves refract or begin to "bend" as soon as the depth of the water is about one-half their wavelength. In addition, the wave responds to shallows by shortening its length, increasing its height, and reducing its speed, just like a man running uphill, who chops his steps, lifts his knees higher, and slows down.

The most dramatic evidence of this phenomenon is at Cape Point, the spit of land extending southeast into the ocean at Cape Hat-

teras. The fishermen who line the two sides of the spit witness the spectacular clash of waves, which originate far out at sea. As the leading edge of these waves reaches the first shallows of Cape Point, the faster-traveling edges, which are in deeper water to either side of the spit, refract around the shallows, bending until you witness a spectacular head-to-head explosion of water.

The movement of water at the edge of land will always be one of the most enthralling and restful images on earth. The mystery of waves, their possible origin, the transoceanic crossings, and the shapes and patterns that never repeat will always be the attraction of the beach—a product of the great wave machine that gently tousles your hair.

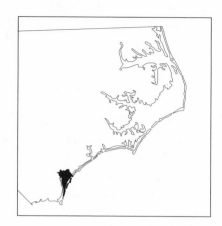

New Hanover County

Wilmington makes New Hanover the most urban of the North Carolina coastal counties. The city has a romantic allure, but those not familiar with the state sometimes wrongly assume that it is a coastal city on the ocean. In fact, North Carolina's most dependable and only natural deep-water port perches on the banks of the Cape Fear River, its historic center some 10 miles west of the nearest beach. (It is even further from open ocean by way of the river.)

Wilmington is a coastal destination of a different sort; it is a city rich in mercantile history and blessed with an abundance of architectural character. It has also had an astonishing renaissance that began building in the 1980s. Do *Dawson's Creek* or *One Tree Hill* sound, let alone look, familiar? If they seemed all so real, it is because much of those television programs were filmed in the "Wilmington area," where the creative forces of North Carolina's film industry, the third-largest in the country, have made home base. The movie and television credits for Wilmington scenery continue to roll on and show no signs of stopping. It has the local economy on a roll as well.

The resurgence of the community has generated growth, and riverside Wilmington, once 10 miles from the nearest beach, has burgeoned nearly to the ocean. The town is filling the middle of the county between the Cape Fear River and the Intracoastal Waterway and is now spreading north into the dense, dark, and often soggy forests of northern New Hanover County.

There is a cultural division in New Hanover County between Wilmington residents and beach residents. Many who work in Wilmington live, vacation, or own homes on the barrier islands or along the Intracoastal Waterway in the county. They have very definite opinions about land use and beach accessibility there. Different feelings are strongly held by those who live on the barrier islands all year and make a living from tourism or real estate. What serves tourism and real estate sometimes comes in conflict with or is not sympathetic to the visual character of a community. This comes out in tussles over land planning issues such as zoning.

There are also conflicting currents regarding the needs of a resident populace, the demands of a tourism-based economy, and the ongoing civic dialogue in many communities about "who we are or want to be." While there is not a clear-cut Mercedes/dune buggy divide, there is enough of a schism that it spills over into the beach access debate in the form of parking fees. In New Hanover County, the public beach is not always free.

A wave of retirement development and business growth in the county has brought together folks with common, but insular, interests. Golf-course communities selling housing with access to the Intracoastal Waterway are booming. There is a resurgence in time-share condominiums, which are more numerous in the beachfront communities. These communities tend to attract socially homogenous folks, making it possible to pick the atmosphere of your waterfront development. Much of this is occurring on the outskirts of Wilmington proper, while drawing on the recent cache of the name, the splendid climate, and accessible water to fuel their success.

Even though New Hanover County is the smallest coastal county, there are approximately 27 miles of oceanfront, most of which is on barrier islands. There are three islands north to south: Figure Eight, Shell Island/Wrightsville Beach, and Masonboro Island. They are completely different from one another. Figure Eight is a low-density, exclusive, private island for homeowners and guests; Wrightsville Beach/Shell Island is a historic playground that is a populated resort beach; and Masonboro Island is completely untouched by building. The Intracoastal Waterway and extensive salt marsh separate all three islands from the mainland.

Heading south from Wilmington, US 421 crosses Snows Cut, the channel of the Intracoastal Waterway gouged by the U.S. Army Corps of Engineers in the 1930s to connect Myrtle Grove Sound with the Cape Fear River. The channel lopped off the southern tip of the county from the mainland, creating a fourth island, sometimes referred to as Pleasure Island. It includes the communities of Carolina Beach, Kure Beach, and Fort Fisher, along with Carolina Beach State Park and Fort Fisher State Recreation Area.

Before Snows Cut, this was a peninsula of the mainland, and though now technically an island, it is still the ever-narrowing neck of land that separates the Cape Fear River from the Atlantic Ocean. It is here that North Carolina's characteristic barrier island coastline temporarily ends in the town of Carolina Beach. While the northern portion of Carolina Beach is a barrier spit, the southern portion is solid mainland peninsula and remains so south through Kure Beach to Fort Fisher. There is a difference in the oceanfront; the dunes are smaller because the oceanfront land is actually a modest bluff. This is particularly noticeable in Kure Beach.

New Hanover County also includes two components of the North Carolina National Estuarine Research Reserve, Masonboro Island and Zeke's Island. Masonboro Island is a 6-mile-long, low barrier south of Wrightsville Beach, accessible by boat. Zeke's Island is at the end of US 421, beyond the Fort Fisher/Southport ferry dock, and contains a 4-mile-long barrier spit that extends south from the Federal Point access area. Because of these "free" beaches, admittedly not readily accessible, New Hanover County has quite a balance in the types of beach experience available to visitors.

Since the late nineteenth century, New Hanover County islands and beaches have been popular

Catching a wave at Kure Beach. Photograph by Erin Whittle; courtesy of Cape Fear Coast Convention and Visitors Bureau.

resort and vacation getaways. Close enough to be "bedroom communities" for Wilmington, there is more of a permanent character in appearance and attitude in some of these locations. Wilmington has the jobs, and the resort beaches have the atmosphere. It is hard to resist being able to be in the ocean or sailing at 5:45 P.M. every day.

The towns of Wrightsville Beach, Carolina Beach, and Kure Beach are well-established, self-sufficient communities with a varying degree of dependency on tourism that increases with the distance from Wilmington. Wrightsville Beach, the closest, has practically a suburban feeling, with a relationship to Wilmington that is similar to the relationship of Virginia Beach to Norfolk. Farther south, Carolina Beach is definitely "beachy." There are fewer year-round residents, and streets are quiet between Labor Day and Memorial Day. Kure Beach, more distant still, is a grand place to find surf and solitude and is extraordinarily quiet after the summer season.

It is possible to pick your mix of mood and atmospherics at the beaches in New Hanover County. Couple these with the improving access provided with the completion of I-40 from Raleigh to Wilmington, and you have a run on the beach. An ocean once so far away is now 2 1/4 hours from Raleigh.

Access

The individual municipalities maintain access sites in New Hanover County. There are four regional access locations at Wrightsville Beach, one at Carolina Beach, and a very large regional access area at Federal Point, south of Fort Fisher.

The New Hanover County Parks and Recreation Department has provided numerous access locations in Wilmington Beach.

The county also maintains a 24-acre park, Snows Cut Park, off of River Road on the northwest side of US 421 (before you cross the Intracoastal Waterway to Pleasure Island). There are four boat-launching ramps, restrooms, picnic shelters, tables, grills, and a gazebo.

New Hanover County jointly maintains the regional beach access area at Fort Fisher with the state.

Masonboro Island is accessible only by boat and is frequently and traditionally used by residents for recreation.

The approach to Zeke's Island is accessible by car. Park at either the Federal Point regional access area or at the North Carolina Wildlife Resources Commission boat ramp south of the Fort Fisher/Southport ferry dock.

Handicapped Access

All of the regional access sites are accessible to handicapped travelers. The Federal Point access area has the shortest distance to the water from the end of the dune crossover ramp.

Information

For information, contact Cape Fear Coast Convention and Visitors Bureau, 24 North Third Street, Wilmington, NC 28401, 910-341-4030, 800-222-4757.

Web addresses: <www.cape-fear.nc.us>; <www.nccoastalmanagement.net/Access/sites.htm>

Wilmington

One key to understanding Wilmington's importance in the state is detailed in the Wilmington Railroad Museum in a renovated Atlantic Coastline warehouse on the river. In 1840 Wilmington was one terminus of the "World's Longest Railroad," the Wilmington and Weldon Railroad, which linked the Cape Fear River to the Albemarle region at Weldon on the Roanoke River. It was this rail line that was "the lifeline of the Confederacy" during the siege of Petersburg.

Wilmington is capitalizing on its past mercantile prominence, digging into the stored wares and gutted trade houses of dusty decades to develop a refreshing, entertaining presence. It feels vital, beating with the pulse of a city building a commercial future around and within its heritage.

Its environment certainly does not hamper it. Shaded by moss-draped trees, surrounded by floral gardens, and saturated with historic buildings and sites, Wilmington draws visitors both as a city and as a center of history. The fact that some of the finest beaches, swimming, and fishing are barely a half hour to the southeast does not hurt its attractiveness in the least.

Approaching from the north, US 17 (accessible from I-40) deposits you directly into the heart of Wilmington, where it becomes Market Street. This uncommonly serene entry to a downtown area follows a planted median and carries you past one of your first stops, the Cape Fear Museum at 814 Market Street. This introduction (admission charged) to area history sets the stage for walking the town later and firmly fixes Wilmington's prominence.

Wilmington's place in North Carolina's history is ample and secure. There are more historic markers here than in any other city in the state (including one noting the birthplace of Whistler's mother). Commerce has grown on these riverbanks since the early 1730s, and for several years in the eighteenth century, the town served as the state capital. Until 1910, it was the state's largest city.

Historically, the economy of the city was based on mercantile trade such as the production and shipping of naval stores from nearby pine forests. The secure harbor made Wilmington the only reliable natural deep-water port in the state. During the Civil War, the Confederacy tried to keep the port open and constructed Fort Fisher to defend the entrance. Blockade-runners—privateers who knew the local waters and could press into the port at night—kept Wilmington a productive, though limited, port of call nearly throughout the war in spite of Union efforts to thwart shipments.

Let serendipity guide your discovery of Wilmington. First discover a parking place—perhaps near the visitors center in the restored 1892 courthouse at Princess and Third Streets across from Thalian Hall, the city hall building. Inside the courthouse is the headquarters of the Cape Fear Coast Convention and Visitors Bureau. Collect the several self-directing flyers, spend fifteen minutes in the courthouse to absorb an introductory video on the Wilmington area, then head to the water via Market or Princess Street.

Wilmington's commercial heart lies along the river, of course, and the street to walk is Front Street. The Cotton Exchange, between Grace and Walnut Streets, is a boutique crafted out of old cotton warehouses. It provides a multileveled descent to public parking along cobbled Water Street and the promenade along the Cape Fear River. The backdrop to the setting is the magnificent USS *North Carolina* at berth across the river.

At Water and Market Streets are public restrooms and a visitors center. You may also take a 1 1/2-hour sightseeing cruise of the waterfront on the *Henrietta III* (adults $6, children $4). There is also a small launch that will cross the river to the battleship *North Carolina*.

Wilmington's historic district extends south from the downtown until it gradually becomes almost completely residential. At Water and Ann Streets is Chandler's Wharf, a shopping exchange in historic structures. The cobblestones end, and a boardwalk sidles along the river. Head uphill and you ascend into the midst of the historic residential area beside the Governor Edward B. Dudley mansion. Dudley won the first statewide gubernatorial election in 1836 and was the president of the Wilmington and Weldon Railroad, which, at 161 miles long, was the longest continuous track in world in 1840. The Dudley mansion is one of several fine houses along Front Street. Because of the number of historic markers in this area, it is better explored on foot than by car. On Third Street, you can also stroll through the magnificent Greenfield Gardens, an extraordinary landscape of trails and plantings crafted around a lake. You may even rent a paddleboat there.

Access

There is ample parking in downtown, but you have to attend to the parking meters.

Handicapped Access

Wilmington is a surprisingly "hilly" city and handicapped accessibility varies. There are handicapped restrooms at the visitor information center at Water and Market Streets in Riverfront Park. The following are some of the more noted attractions in Wilmington that are accessible to handicapped travelers.

At Chandler's Wharf, 2 Ann Street, the streets are cobblestone, but some restaurants in the complex have ramped entrances. There are handicapped accessible restrooms in the Wharf building.

The Cotton Exchange, 321 North Front Street, is moderately accessible, but assistance would be best. Shops on the upper level are accessible from Front Street. Parking is on Water Street.

Greenfield Gardens, South Third Street, 910-341-7855, are very accessible, and wheelchairs are available with advance notice.

The Cape Fear riverboats *Henrietta III* and *Capt. J. N. Maffit*, docked at the foot of Market Street at Riverfront Park, 910-343-1611, are accessible with staff assistance.

Web address: <www.cfrboats.com>

The Cape Fear Museum, 814 Market Street, 910-341-4350, is fully accessible.

Web address: <www.capefearmuseum.com>

The Thalian Hall Center for the Performing Arts, Third and Princess Streets, 910-763-3398, is accessible.

Web address: <www.thalianhall.com>

At the USS *North Carolina* Battleship Memorial on the Cape Fear River, 910-762-1829, the main deck, museum, and memorial area are accessible.

Web address: <www.battleshipnc.com>

Information

For information, contact Cape Fear Coast Convention and Visitors Bureau, 24 North Third Street, Wilmington, NC 28401, 910-341-4030, 800-222-4757.

Web addresses: <www.ci.wilmington.nc.us/welcome.htm>; <www.cape-fear.nc.us>

Figure Eight Island

Figure Eight Island is a naturally low-profile barrier island with some upland that had modest natural stands of trees. The entire island is backed by the extensive marshes of Middle Sound. This is a private island—a gated community—exclusively developed with some extraordinary, large, fine homes. Only homeowners and their guests have access by crossing a private drawbridge across the Intracoastal Waterway and a causeway through the marsh with clearance from a security service on the mainland. The security and isolation make the island attractive for celebrity vacationers.

If you catch a glimpse of the island from the mainland or from neighboring Shell Island (the north end of Wrightsville Beach), there is the illusion that the houses rise out of the salt marsh and sand flats that buttress the island's edge. From Shell Island, the view is stark because there is very little natural tree and shrub growth that would tie the houses back to the island, better blending them into its profile.

There is no doubting the quality of the island's location and the care taken with the land planning. The roads thread atop a sparsely vegetated spine with spurring side streets that serve marsh front or oceanfront houses. Particular care was taken to preserve much of the natural vegetation at the island's north end, adjacent to Rich Inlet, which has been set aside as a preserve for island residents.

The island, as do many others, tussles with erosion, particularly at its inlets. Rich Inlet on the north end of the island has a channel that shifts around a lot naturally, exacerbating wear and tear on that end, depending on its location. The south end of the island, which looks past Mason Inlet to Shell Island, began accreting sand in a low, wide fan at an astonishing rate in the late 1990s as the inlet practically sprinted south. Though beneficial to Figure Eight, the migration had catastrophic effects on Shell Island property owners.

In 2002 the inlet was moved 3,000 feet north providing substantial relief to Shell Island residents.

Access
Only homeowners and their guests can drive on the island. Boaters or swimmers may use the wet sand beach.

Wrightsville Beach and Shell Island

There is a settled-in quality about Wrightsville Beach, and it has a self-assurance that comes with age and perseverance. It comes by this attitude honestly. Since 1889, when a rail line began steadily chugging across Banks Channel bringing bathers to its shores, Wrightsville Beach has been the place of choice for Wilmingtonians to live and play. It incorporated ten years later and promptly had to rebuild after a hurricane welcomed the new city to life by the sea.

Rebuild it did. A local power company, Tide Water Power, turned the railroad into an electric trolley. Its president, Hugh MacRae, built an entertainment pavilion at the last trolley stop, named it Lumina, and rimmed it with lights, and so Wrightsville Beach bathed in the joys of living and playing by the sea.

Then Hurricane Hazel came in 1954, and the oceanfront houses were rebuilt again.

Every time it has had to right itself from the toss of a storm, Wrightsville Beach has carried forward bits and pieces of its pre-storm days in the form of architectural detailing and its original city form. The houses look sturdy, permanent, and lived in. There are not many designed in the resort beach idiom that hangs a "Rent Me" sign on the front. Instead, most say "welcome" or "home." Wrightsville Beach looks like a neighborhood by the sea instead of a vacation resort. It is this continuity that gives evidence to the perseverance of its citizenry and creates its confident persona.

The streetcar access early made it a beach for anyone. Tide Water Power subdivided the beachfront and began building sturdy cottages for "everyman" in 1907. In 1911 John

Sand Dollars

Beach nourishment promises to be the most divisive coastal issue of the next decade. The topic is every bit as polarizing as 2004 presidential politics; the subject is contentious, and the debate is sharp.

Beach nourishment is the process of replacing the sand on a beach. The process is straightforward. Typically, sand dredged from a borrow site (sometimes offshore, sometimes from inlet channels) is pumped as a wet slurry and deposited on the ocean berm. While each beach nourishment project is unique, the basic process extends and elevates the beach. Doing so provides a place for people to walk and spread their towels, and it provides an additional buffer and measure of safety for oceanfront property.

The last point is the most controversial. North Carolina law plainly forbids the building of any beach-hardening structures such as groins, jetties, rock revetments,

or other reinforcing measures that are designed to hold an edge against the ocean. (The lone exception to date is Fort Fisher State Historic Site.) Beach nourishment is thus one of the few options available to oceanfront property owners to ameliorate the effects of chronic erosion caused by rising sea level or to repair the damage caused by storms. The other options are relocation or loss of property.

It is expensive, costing between $2 million and $5 million per mile of beach to be nourished. Current trends seem to indicate that any given nourishment project may only be an interim solution to the intractable problem of rising sea level.

Nourishment projects are carefully defined and are designed to weather in and mimic a natural sand beach as much as possible. A 2002–3 project from the eastern end of Emerald Isle provides some examples. Installed during the win-

ter before the 2003 vacation season, the project widened the beach by approximately 180 feet. Based on the average annual tidal rise, the project started at a point on the beach that was 7 feet above mean sea level, tapering gradually seaward from there (starting higher creates a drop-off where the new sand meets the water).

The final cost was $3.78 per linear foot or slightly under $2 million per mile. By the summer of 2004, the project had weathered in nicely in spite of some initial misgivings over the quality of the source material, which included large clam shells and was gray in color (typical coastal sand is tan to brown because of the shell matter).

The problem of source sand can sour users on a project quickly. It can also cause it to fail. If the sand grain size of the source material differs too much from naturally occurring material, it will not remain in place for the designed life of

---

Quince Myers purchased one such house that stayed in his family until 1954. If you want to see what oceanfront living was like one hundred years ago, then stop in the Wrightsville Beach Museum of History at 303 West Salisbury Street; the museum is in John Quince Myers's

oceanfront cottage. This splendid, ambitious, small museum captures the story of the early years of the resort and features an exquisite scale model of the 1907 Oceanic Hotel, the 1897 Seashore Hotel, and the 1905 Lumina—Wrightsville Beach at the turn of the last century.

Visit Wrightsville Beach once and it's easy to see the reasons for the popularity of the place. The beach here is wide and flat and has long been favored by families with small children because of the gentle wave action. The community capitalizes on the commutable dis-

the project, which is typically eight years.

Beach nourishment has been going on along the coast for some time. Wrightsville Beach and Carolina Beach have received several nourishments, conducted by the U.S. Army Corps of Engineers, the agency responsible for the supervision of this type of shoreline maintenance project. Atlantic Beach is regularly nourished as a part of harbor maintenance for the port of Morehead City.

Historically, the federal government subsidizes most of the expense. There is every indication, however, that this is changing. Federal budgets proposed for 2005 had very little money for beach nourishment, and as of this writing, several resort communities in North Carolina had joined suits against the government on this matter. What is evident is that while sea level is rising, the federal budget is sinking in debt.

The acrimonious debate around this topic is polarizing. Opposing it are those who see it as a taxpayer-funded subsidy that benefits only a few property owners who gain small personal fortunes when their threatened property is provided with a nice, wide beach. Opponents also contend that beach nourishment rewards unwise behavior, is environmentally harmful, and costs more over time than relocating or buying and removing the threatened structures.

Proponents reply that the real beneficiary is the public; that only publicly accessible beaches receive nourishment, that there is a more than favorable cost-benefit ratio because of the tourism economy, that it is the most manageable and least expensive option because of existing land values, that environmental damage, if any, is brief and minimal, and that nourished beaches restore nesting habitat that had vanished.

What seems certain is that beach nourishment will continue to be needed at increasing costs. In the future, the federal government may no longer be willing (or able) to provide the subsidy it has in the past. In anticipation of reduced federal money, resort communities faced with eroding beaches are increasing property taxes and imposing occupancy taxes in an effort to stockpile sufficient funds to undertake projects on their own. The cost will be staggering. North Topsail Beach, ineligible for federal monies because it is in a Coastal Barrier Resources Act (CoBRA) redline zone, is looking at $25–30 million in 2004 dollars for its six-mile project. Homeowners would have to pick up the tab.

At some point, whether it is in time or in dollars, the issue of rising sea level/coastal erosion/beach nourishment will prompt a reform in coastal development policy. It is a matter of dollars and sense.

tance by encouraging year-round visitation, astutely providing easy access to the oceanfront. It does send a mixed message, however; the community views public parking spaces, even those provided by the Coastal Area Management Act access grant funding, as a civic re-source and enforces parking fees aggressively through a parking management agency.

US 74 and US 76 share a drawbridge crossing the Intracoastal Waterway to carry you across Harbor Island to the town following the early streetcar route. The roads fork shortly after the drawbridge at a roundabout; US 74 continues north closer to the Shell Island portion of Wrightsville Beach. This is Salisbury Street (the museum will be on the right), and the road crosses Banks Channel where Salisbury Street dead-ends

	Fee	Parking	Restrooms	Lifeguard	Camping	Showers	Beach Access	Hiking	Trail	Handicapped	Boating	ORV Access	Fishing	Programs	Historic	Sand Beach	Dunes	Upland	Wetland
Wilmington		•	•							•	•			•	•			•	
Wrightsville Beach and Shell Island	•	•				•	•			•			•			•	•		
Public Boating Access: Wrightsville Beach		•									•		•						•
Regional Access: North Lumina	•	•	•			•	•			•						•			
Regional Access: Moore's Inlet	•	•	•			•	•			•			•			•	•		
Regional Access: Salisbury St.	•	•	•			•	•			•			•			•	•		
Regional Access: Lumina Ave.	•	•	•			•	•			•			•			•	•		
Masonboro Island Research Reserve							•	•			•		•			•	•	•	•

directly at the Johnnie Mercer Fishing Pier. There is public parking here. If you turn north, you continue to the Shell Island section of the community.

Fifty years ago, present-day Wrightsville Beach was a neighbor to Shell Island. In 1965 the intervening Moore's Inlet was filled in, and the combined geography became one community. "Shell Island" is still used in local conversation.

A Holiday Inn (locals called it "Holiday Inlet") once stood in the approximate location of the old Moore's Inlet channel (commemorated by Moore's Inlet Street). Hurricane Fran so damaged the motel that it was razed, and a new one was constructed in its place.

The island narrows near the site of the old inlet, which restricts de-velopment to the east side of Lumina Drive. Extensive salt marsh is visible to the west. The only beach-front high-rise construction within the corporate limits of the island is on what was once Shell Island. These taller buildings obscure the view of the ocean, and revised zoning laws adopted in 1974 confine high-rise and mid-rise construction to those buildings you see today.

Lumina Avenue passes the Shell Island Resort and loops out at the north end of the island in a modest-sized turnaround. The area north of the turnout is one of the most dynamic headlands in North Carolina.

In 1991 I walked approximately $^1/_4$ mile north from a parking area in this location and did not reach Mason Inlet. Beyond it spread the fan of tidal flats accreting to Figure Eight Island. Within a few years, the fast migrating inlet had caused the erosion of all useable beach from the parking area and threatened the Shell Island Resort. These dire circumstances led to a dredging and relocation of Mason Inlet approximately $^3/_5$ of a mile north, providing a large tidal-flat buffer for the Shell Island headland that has been designated the Mason Inlet Bird Sanctuary. Audubon North Carolina is under contract to New Hanover County to manage the sanctuary that includes the tidal shoals and eastern half of the sandy spit extending north from Shell Island Resort. For now, it seems, the relocation of the inlet is providing the safety buffer Shell Island needs.

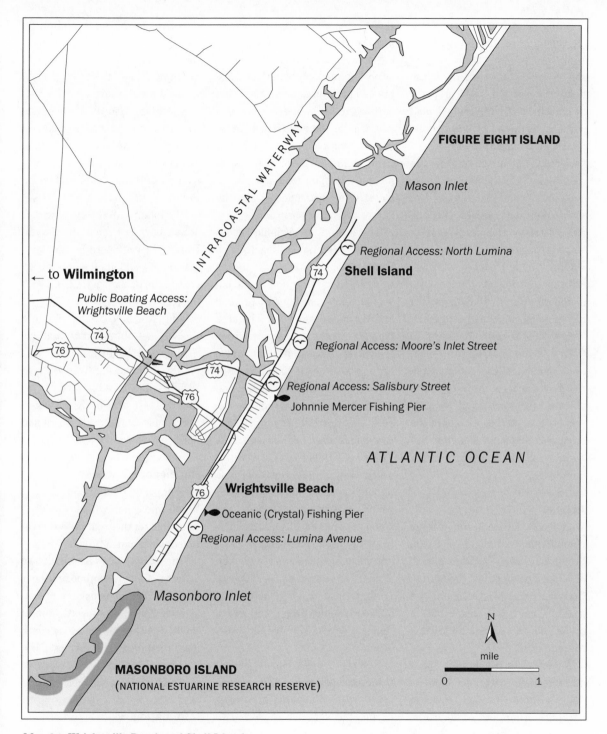

FIGURE EIGHT ISLAND

Mason Inlet

Regional Access: North Lumina

Shell Island

INTRACOASTAL WATERWAY

to **Wilmington**

Public Boating Access:
Wrightsville Beach

Regional Access: Moore's Inlet Street

Regional Access: Salisbury Street
Johnnie Mercer Fishing Pier

ATLANTIC OCEAN

Wrightsville Beach

Oceanic (Crystal) Fishing Pier

Regional Access: Lumina Avenue

Masonboro Inlet

N

mile

0   1

MASONBORO ISLAND
(NATIONAL ESTUARINE RESEARCH RESERVE)

Map 24. Wrightsville Beach and Shell Island

At the same time, it has resulted in shoaling of the Intracoastal Waterway at the mouth of Mason's Creek. Homeowner associations representing 1,044 property owners from Figure Eight Island and the north end of Wrightsville Beach have agreed to pay the associated maintenance costs for the thirty-year life of the project. There is no intention of maintaining Mason's Creek as a navigable channel, and recreational boaters quickly learned that it shoals rapidly.

Once you are parked, you will enjoy one of the gentler beaches in the state in surroundings that have a comfortable patina to them. Wrightsville Beach is "cottagey" in feeling, regardless of the height of the buildings. Even at the high-rise zoned lands of the Shell Island portion, the prevailing perception is "low," perhaps because the dune system is wide enough to balance visually the mass of the larger buildings.

Access

Wrightsville Beach is one of three communities that charges for public parking, even in access areas developed using public funds from Coastal Area Management Act grants. This is not illegal, but, in my opinion, it violates the spirit of the legislation.

Nevertheless, Wrightsville Beach accommodates large numbers of daily visitors through metered parking. Bring lots of quarters; the rates are steep and discouraging. Locals who go there don't park there. Parking is expensive

(2004 rates were $50 per week, $8 per day, and $1.25 per hour). Parking policies are rigorously, expensively enforced. If you park in a designated parking area or attend to a parking meter, you are okay anywhere in Wrightsville Beach. Stray out of unmarked spaces, leave your car blocking a drive or on the pavement of the main roads, or allow a meter to expire, and you run the risk of a ticket or towing.

There are four regional access sites on Wrightsville Beach/Shell Island. The first is south of the Lumina Club Townhouses, sandwiched between Lumina Avenue and Waynick Boulevard. The area has 86 parking spaces, restrooms, showers, a gazebo, and a dune crossover. At East Salisbury Street, almost directly at the end of US 74, there is a regional access site with 192 parking spaces, restrooms, showers, and a gazebo. There are 30 metered spaces with a 4-hour limit at 2698 North Lumina on Shell Island. This regional site, which has restrooms, showers, and a dune crossover, fills quickly during the season. There are 29 parking places, restrooms, showers, and a dune crossover at 2498 North Lumina, next to the Holiday Inn at Moore's Inlet Street, the fourth regional access site of this resort beach.

Several neighborhood access points offer parking and dune crossovers with lifeguarded beaches during the summer season. Two are located at the eastern end of the following streets: Jack Parker Boulevard (20 spaces), with a dune

crossover to the south end of the island and Masonboro Inlet, near the U.S. Coast Guard Station; and South Sea Oats Street (39 spaces), with a dune crossover.

There are also unimproved access areas with lifeguarded beaches located at Heron Street and Stone Street and many signed pedestrian paths throughout Wrightsville Beach.

The Johnnie Mercer Fishing Pier at Salisbury Street and the Crystal Fishing Pier at South Lumina provide fishing and limited parking access to the oceanfront. Check with the pier owner before parking.

The North Carolina Wildlife Resources Commission maintains fishing and boating access area on the Intracoastal Waterway at Wrightsville Beach, adjacent to the US 74/76 drawbridge. Parking is available, and there is no launch fee.

Handicapped Access

Wrightsville Beach will loan a beach wheelchair with advance notice. Contact the parks and recreation department at 910-256-7925.

The access sites south of the Lumina Club Townhouses near Oceanic Pier, at Salisbury Street, at Jack Parker Boulevard, and at South Sea Oats Street are accessible for handicapped travelers. The first two have accessible showers and restrooms.

Information

For information, contact Cape Fear Coast Convention and Visitors Bureau, 24 North Third Street, Wil-

Beachgoers prepare for a day at Masonboro Island. Photograph by Michael Wolfe; courtesy of Cape Fear Coast Convention and Visitors Bureau.

mington, NC 28401, 910-341-4030, 800-222-4757.

Web addresses: <www.townof wrightsvillebeach.com>; <www. cape-fear.nc.us>; <www.nccoastal management.net/Access/sites. htm>

Masonboro Island National Estuarine Research Reserve

In 1952 present-day Masonboro Island was isolated from Caro-lina Beach by the artificial open-ing of Carolina Beach Inlet for eas-ier open-water access. This proved to be a blessing for Masonboro Is-land because it cut off direct access from the mainland, precluding con-struction. The island remains pris-tine, frequented only by fishermen and beach lovers who enjoy the comparative solitude along the sev-eral miles of beachfront.

Masonboro Island is one of the four components of the National Estuarine Research Reserve sys-tem in North Carolina. Acquisi-tion of the 5,097 acres of island and mainland began in 1985 and is still underway. (In December 2003 the Society for Masonboro Island, a nonprofit organization instrumen-tal in protecting the island, volun-tarily merged with the North Caro-lina Coastal Land Trust, citing the fact that their goals had largely been accomplished.) The few par-cels that have not yet been pur-chased do not restrict use or enjoy-ment of the island.

Approximately 453 acres of the preserve is natural dune and woodlands, and 166 acres are spoil islands next to the Intracoastal Waterway. The remainder of the island is marsh and tidal flats.

The island remains an astonishing sight in the rapidly developing coast. Except for a jetty created by the U.S. Army Corps of Engineers to stabilize Masonboro Inlet at the north end, there are no artificial structures. The largest undisturbed barrier along the southern portion of the North Carolina coast, Masonboro is markedly different physically from both Shackleford Banks in Carteret County and Bear Island (Hammocks Beach State Park) in Onslow County, its unaltered companions.

Masonboro is an "overwash" island, with a low, essentially dune-free profile. The wide beaches and the solitude they provide are a haven for loggerhead turtles and piping plovers, two endangered species that can nest in comparative safety along the undeveloped shores. Gray foxes, river otters, raccoons, and opossums live in the upland portion of the island, which is safe enough from storm overwash to sustain a maritime forest habitat.

Although Masonboro Island has never supported a settlement, it may be that this was the first land in the New World sighted by a European explorer. Some historians believe that the island noted by explorer Giovanni da Verrazano several miles north of the mouth of the Cape Fear River in a 1524 report to his sponsor, Francis I, included present-day Masonboro Island.

Access

Access to Masonboro Island is by boat only. You will have to bring everything you need with you; there are no concessions of any kind and very little shade. No vehicles are allowed on the island.

Information

For information, contact North Carolina National Estuarine Research Reserve, 5600 Marvin K. Moss Lane, Wilmington, NC 28409, 910-395-3905; or Division of Coastal Management, P.O. Box 27687, Raleigh, NC 27611, 919-733-2293.

Web address: <www.ncnerr.org/pubsiteinfo/siteinfo/masonboro/masonboro.html>

Snows Cut Park

Snows Cut Park is a 24-acre park maintained by New Hanover County on the water on the north side of Snows Cut, which links the Cape Fear River and Myrtle Grove Sound. To reach the park, turn right on River Road immediately before the Intracoastal Waterway bridge. The park has four boat-launching ramps, restrooms, picnic shelters, tables, grills, and a gazebo.

Information

For information, contact New Hanover County Parks and Recreation Department, 414 Chestnut Street, Room 101, County Administration Annex, Wilmington, NC 28401.

Web address: <www.nhcgov.com/PRK/PRKmain.asp>

Pleasure Island

Snows Cut is a passage for the Intracoastal Waterway created in the 1930s by the U.S. Army Corps of Engineers to link the Cape Fear River and Myrtle Grove Sound. Technically, the peninsula south of Snows Cut is an island. For a number of years the area, which includes the communities of Carolina Beach, Kure Beach, and the unincorporated beaches of New Hanover County, Fort Fisher, and Fort Fisher State Recreation Area, has been jointly marketed as Pleasure Island.

US 421 is the major access road and is locally renamed as Lake Park Boulevard shortly after the crossing of the Intracoastal Waterway. When you drive into Carolina Beach, the Chamber of Commerce is plainly signed, a small building on the right side of the road. If you want to avoid the heavier summer traffic, turn right on Dow Road at the first intersection shortly after crossing Snows Cut. Dow is a two-lane soundside road bordering Carolina Beach State Park and will probably be less congested than US 421. Turn left on Harper Avenue to reach downtown Carolina Beach or continue to Ocean Boulevard for Wilmington Beach or Avenue K for Kure Beach.

Access

The individual municipalities manage access locations on Pleasure Island, and New Hanover County maintains several locations between Carolina Beach and Kure

A lone fisherman on a dock near the marina at Carolina Beach State Park. Courtesy of North Carolina Division of Parks and Recreation.

Beach. Specific access locations are noted following the municipal listings below. For a rule of thumb, sleep north and swim south; the farther south on US 421, the more convenient the access.

The North Carolina Wildlife Resources Commission maintains a fishing and boating access area on the Intracoastal Waterway at Carolina Beach, one mile east of US 421 at the south end of the bridge over the waterway. Parking is available, and there is no launch fee.

Information

For information, contact the Pleasure Island Chamber of Commerce, 1121 North Lake Park Boulevard, Carolina Beach, NC 28428, 910-458-8434.

Web address: <www.nccoastal management.net/Access/sites. htm>

Carolina Beach State Park

The 761 acres of Carolina Beach State Park are on the north end of Pleasure Island, approximately one mile northeast of Carolina Beach and 10 miles south of Wilmington. Heading south, shortly after US 421 crosses the Intracoastal Waterway at Snows Cut, turn right onto Dow Road. At the water tower, turn right onto SR 1628, which leads to the park.

Carolina Beach State Park is bounded by the Cape Fear River to the west, Snows Cut to the north, and Dow Road, which bisects the peninsula. The park provides boating access and camping and, most important, functions as a preserve and interpretive facility, exploring the natural history of the coastal plain.

This is one of the most biologi-

	Fee	Parking	Restrooms	Lifeguard	Camping	Showers	Beach Access	Hiking	Trail	Handicapped	Boating	ORV Access	Fishing	Programs	Historic	Sand Beach	Dunes	Upland	Wetland
Snows Cut Park		•	•							•	•		•					•	•
Pleasure Island		•	•	•	•	•	•	•	•	•	•	•	•	•		•	•	•	•
Carolina Beach State Park		•	•		•	•		•	•	•	•		•	•			•	•	•
Public Boating Access: Carolina Beach		•									•		•						•
Carolina Beach, North End		•					•					•	•			•	•		•
Regional Access: Sandpiper Lane	•	•	•	•		•	•						•			•	•		
Kure Beach		•	•				•						•			•			
Regional Access: Hamlet Avenue	•	•	•	•		•	•						•			•	•		

cally diverse parks in the entire state system and showcases thirteen different plant communities on its network of extensive interpretive trails. If I had to pick only two trails from the group, they would be the Sugarloaf Trail and the Fly Trap Loop.

Sugarloaf Trail skirts south from the park marina along the east bank of the Cape Fear River. One of the joys of the trail is the bird life, but only quiet hikers will be able to see egrets, herons, and kingfishers along the salt marshes and sandy riverbank before they startle. After a mile-long easy walk along a packed-sand trail, hikers arrive at the Sugarloaf, a large relic sand dune of Pleistocene age that is stabilized by live oak trees nearly 55 feet above sea level. Sugarloaf has long been a navigational landmark for Cape Fear sailors, appearing on maps drafted in the mid-eighteenth century. Farther along the trail, there are several limestone sink ponds, formed when the underlying coquina rock collapsed after being dissolved by groundwater percolation and the new surface depression filled with water. The trail then loops back to the marina, and spur trails return to the camping area.

Fly Trap Loop leads through boggy ground populated by the carnivorous Venus flytrap, sundew, and pitcher plants, which prefer the high moisture and spongy organic soil in limited areas of the coastal plain. The Venus flytrap is found only within a 75-mile radius of Wilmington and nowhere else in the world. If you call the park in May, the rangers will be glad to tell you when the flytraps will flower, a point in their life cycle that makes these diminutive predators more visible.

The remainder of the park is generally a combination of evergreen shrub savanna and sandy ridge vegetation. The juxtaposition of these strikingly varied environments is readily seen in the short Fly Trap Loop. In mid- to early spring, the flowers of the sweetbay magnolia, which prefer the dark soil of the wetter areas of the park, perfume the trails. In mid- to late summer, the fragrant flowers of loblolly bay, an upright broadleaf evergreen tree, are in full bloom. In the drier sandy ridge habitats, wire grass and long-needle pine join blackjack oak to form the familiar sandhills associations.

Carolina Beach State Park pro-

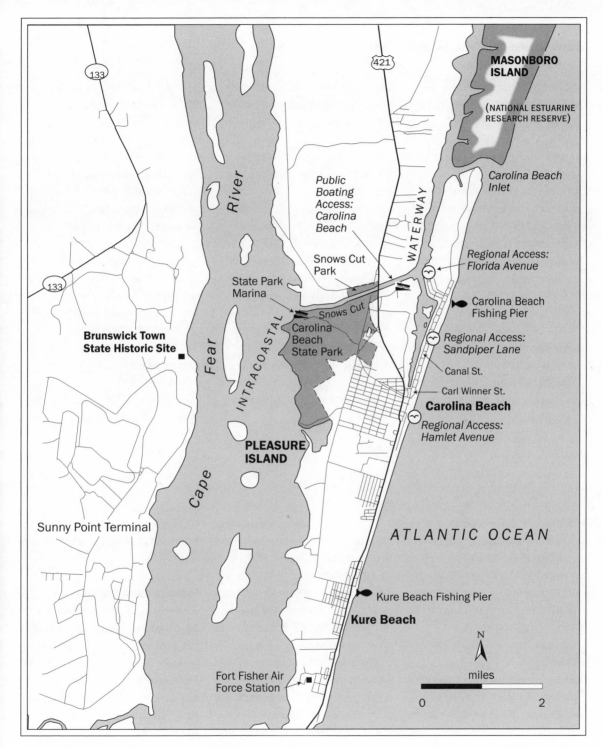

Map 25. Pleasure Island

Blue Skies for the Brown Pelican

I remember seeing brown pelicans in the early 1960s, and then I saw none for nearly two decades. Now they are back, steadily increasing in numbers and pushing their home range north. These magnificent birds have permanent roosts (the brown pelican does not migrate) on dredge spoil islands as far north as Oregon Inlet, a historic first. It is all the more remarkable because the species hovered on the brink of extinction in the 1970s. The brown pelican is a companion story to the resurgence of many raptors following the banning of the pesticide DDT in the early 1970s.

And *how* they are back—gracefully, elegantly, wondrously lazing and dipping, gliding by the beach. To see a squadron pass, wing to wing or in an echelon grouping, feather-to-froth above the waves, is to witness the deliberate passage of great, dignified kites. So effortless is their habit of flight that pelicans appear to be magically suspended, pulled past the beach by invisible strings. They rule the skies above our coastal waters.

If you aren't sure you have ever seen a pelican, here is the first clue: the birds are huge. They are the largest birds you are likely to see at the coast. A pelican flies with great dignity, pulling its head back on its shoulders, tucking its nearly one-foot-long beak into its chest. It is, in a word, unconcerned, and certainly above it all.

That the pelican has grace in the air seems impossible given its awkward, practically prehistoric appearance. The overlarge bill that is its meal ticket cuts into its appeal. You cannot use cute or cuddly to describe one. Surprisingly though, pelicans can be adroit, nimble, and beak-bashingly brave when hungry.

The second-best thing to a pelican flyby is dinnertime at the wave trough. Pelicans are picky eaters, feeding almost exclusively on mullet, menhaden, and silversides (a small baitfish). They feed opportunistically with the subtlety and elegance of a dropped brick.

Pelicans fold their wings, tip their tail feathers up, and drop, no, crash into the water from heights of 30

vides one of the few public places to see these particular ecosystems and glimpse North Carolina plant communities that have been reduced to vestigial locations even though they were once abundant in the coastal plain.

Access

The park is open daily November–February, 8 A.M. to 5 P.M.; in March and October it closes at 7 P.M.; in April, May, and September, the park closes at 8 P.M.; and June–August it closes at 9 P.M.

The park provides camping and boating access to the Cape Fear River and Intracoastal Waterway. The 83 tent/trailer campsites are first-come, first-served; groups may reserve sites. There is a central bathhouse and restrooms but no utility hookups.

The marina has 44 slips available for daily, weekly, or monthly rental. A full-service store and snack bar at the marina stocks such items as insect repellent, sunscreen, sunglasses, flares, and fishing tackle. The marina also has restrooms.

There is also a boat launching ramp and parking for vehicles with trailers.

Handicapped Access

The marina is fully accessible to handicapped travelers, including ramped access to the restrooms and the store. The campground restrooms are not readily accessible, and the trails are compacted sand, not easily negotiable in a wheelchair.

feet or more. It is a teeth-jarring spectacle to witness and would crumble the pelicans' hollow bones except that they are protected by all-natural bubble wrap: air sacs under their skin that also help them, with beaks full, to bob to the surface like a cork. Dinner comes up in the scoop sack beneath the beak, the water is squeezed out, and the fish is swallowed whole. The pelican rises and, if still hungry, crashes the lunch counter again.

It's quite a show because brown pelicans have a wingspan of nearly 7 feet. Ordinarily, their flying habit is so lazy to be hypnotic, but when the dinner bell rings, it becomes reckless abandon. There's a sudden climb, a precipitous plunge,

and a satisfied push back from the table.

The brown pelican's recovery was rapid once it got underway. The key was the banning of DDT, a chemical compound that persisted up the food chain. When pelicans retained high levels by eating contaminated fish, the residual systemic DDT reduced the calcium in their eggshells, which resulted in crushed eggs and nesting failure. Today, with this threat removed, the bird flourishes in North Carolina because of suitable nesting habitat.

In the early 1980s brown pelicans began nesting on older dredge spoil islands with grassy cover in Pamlico Sound. Adults construct nests about one foot high made

of grass. Usually, they lay two or three eggs in spring that hatch in a month. The parents feed the chicks regurgitated fish. Volunteers who help biologists band the new chicks report that the rookery islands are aromatic to a fault, a scent that can linger in the laundry for two wash cycles.

Happily, the recent pelican colonies seem permanent. A census in 1990 counted 2,912 nests in seven separate colonies. There are an estimated 4,000 nesting pairs today, and the population is considered stable. In spite of its nonchalant flight, the brown pelican is doing much better than just sliding by.

Information

For information, contact Carolina Beach State Park, P.O. Box 475, Carolina Beach, NC 28428, 910-428-8206.

Web address: <www.ncsparks. net/cabe.html>

Carolina Beach

If I had a few beach weekends in my teens and twenties left over, I would put Carolina Beach high on my list of destinations. It has the look of a

place for beach questing, for long "see-nic" (as in "see and be seen") strolls and places to hang out. The place seems to buzz, jump, and pop with an energy that is distinctly collegiate. The town persona is neon and beach music. This is not a mauve and taupe town; it is turquoise and tangerine.

What I really like about Carolina Beach is that it is the only oceanfront community that has a clear oceanfront center of action, the several blocks either side and between Cape Fear Boulevard and

Harper Avenue. There is a lively urban density to the central area where awnings hover over narrow passageways and the streets are so narrow that cars have to crawl. There is just a lot to do here—live-music nightspots, miscellaneous vendors, whatever, which I say because it doesn't matter what the shops are because the attraction is the compression of the space. It has a carnival midway feeling, requiring the fuel of coconut oil, night breezes, and jostling crowds to be alive. The boardwalk does just that

Soundside Trail, Carolina Beach State Park. Courtesy of North Carolina Division of Parks and Recreation.

at night, especially in the annual Beach Music Festival, when shaggers shuffle into town in a dance-loving mass. In the off-season, Carolina Beach takes a breather; it is an empty stage without the people.

Something is working right for the town—a Courtyard Marriott that sports a slightly retro look dominates the southern edge of the oceanfront center steals the show, really, yet seems to fit right in. The blocks of Carolina Beach Avenue south of the Marriott (awkward to reach from the north because of one-way streets) are engaging to drive along and stare; they are a

mix of new and old places that fade in mood from vivace to adagio as you drive south from town center.

Carolina Beach has been a resort /entertainment destination since the late nineteenth century. The town incorporated in 1925, and there are fading reminders of those early years. The median of Harper Avenue carried trolley lines not so long ago. You could ride the rails directly to the center of downtown.

One block north of Harper Avenue is Carl Winner Street, which serves as an informal dividing line between the peninsula and barrier island sections of Carolina Beach.

North of Carl Winner Street, the oceanfront of Carolina Beach is actually a barrier island separated from the peninsula by Myrtle Grove Sound. South of Carl Winner street, Carolina Beach is on the peninsula referred to as Pleasure Island.

Most of the barrier island between Myrtle Grove Sound and the Atlantic is residential, and the sound serves as the boating and fishing center of activity for Carolina Beach. Since the mid-1980s, the barrier beach portion of has changed most radically: smaller cottages with approximately 50 feet of road frontage were razed to build mid-rise condominium units. The increase in building height combined with narrow streets offering little on-street parking creates an urban feeling. The type of buildings also makes it hard to see the water until traveling almost to the end of Carolina Beach Avenue. (There are a few long-established motels and hotels north of Carl Winner Street well before reaching the condominium boom.)

When the beach is in full vacation roar, the drive to the north end of Carolina Beach Avenue and the return by Canal Street can be tedious. Parking fills up quickly, and access remains the province of those who have rented.

The outfall for all this built-up energy is the North End, where Canal Street and Carolina Beach Avenue North run out of pavement. The sandy spit that continues north is where all the action begins and exists, 24/7. The undeveloped barrier is between Carolina Beach Inlet and the Atlantic Ocean. It is passable only by foot and four-wheel-drive vehicle and is a terrific resource created by the opening of the inlet. It is out of the city limits of Carolina Beach.

Until late summer of 2004, the North End was mercifully (for the beach-driving party set) under the jurisdiction of New Hanover County, which was strapped to enforce regulations that kept behavior and off-road vehicles in bounds. In early September 2004 Carolina Beach took over the responsibility

for managing the area that earlier in the summer was named, "Freeman Park." There had been an increasing need to rein in some off-road behavior.

A new management plan enforced by the town will require vehicle owners to purchase a permit to drive at the North End. There will be restrictions on where vehicles may go, and Carolina Beach police will be present and enforcing additional regulations as needed. It is a win all the way around.

The North End and easy ocean access were the big gain from opening Carolina Beach Inlet, but its opening interrupted the replenishing natural flow of sand from points north of the inlet. This has exacerbated erosion at the north end of the community where, in the past, a rock revetment was built to anchor the north end. (Hurricane Fran took out the sand, exposing much of the revetment.) Nevertheless, the post-Fran beach has a very wide, low dune line and a fairly gentle beach. At its intersection with Starfish Street, Carolina Beach Avenue angles east, and because of erosion, the beach decreases in width the closer you get to the Carolina Beach Fishing Pier. This angling of the road and the erosion led to the beach armoring mentioned above.

Carolina Beach has an entirely different appearance and character south of Harper Avenue. This part of the town, with its grid of place-name street names, is the higher-ground haven for traditional

cottage homes, rooming houses, apartments, and small motels. This part of the city feels more relaxed and inviting; it is not nearly as close or confining. The open feeling is reinforced by Carolina Beach Lake Park, a freshwater lake set aside and developed as a city recreation area and a reminder that this part of the town was once mainland.

In 2001 Carolina Beach annexed part of the unincorporated area of New Hanover County previously known as Wilmington Beach. This extended the southern town limits from Tennessee Street, five blocks south to the centerline of Alabama Street.

Access

On the north end of town, there is a regional access with 50 parking spaces at Carolina Beach Avenue North and Pelican Lane and another with 25 parking spaces at Carolina Beach Avenue North and Sandpiper Lane. Another regional access with restrooms and 50 parking spaces is at Carolina Beach Avenue South and Hamlet Avenue; one with 100 parking spaces is at Carolina Beach Avenue South and Atlanta Avenue; and another with 54 spaces, restrooms, and showers is at Carolina Beach Avenue South and Alabama Street, the southern town limits.

Eight large parking lots with over 500 spaces are within walking distance of city hall and permit all-day parking for $1. Of the total, nearly 400 spaces are within two blocks of the oceanfront. A handout available at city hall shows the locations, nearly all of which are off of Canal Street.

Only a few access locations on the northern extension have parking spaces, and they fill quickly. These neighborhood access points are at the east ends of the following streets that run perpendicular to the beachfront: Sea Oats Lane (2 spaces), Sand Fiddler Lane (4), Periwinkle Lane (4), Pelican Lane (2), and Driftwood Avenue (3).

South of Harper Avenue, parking is more plentiful at the oceanfront ends of most east-west streets in the old Wilmington Beach area between Tennessee and Alabama Streets.

Handicapped Access

Carolina Beach will loan a beach wheelchair with advance notice. Call the parks and recreation department at 910-458-8216.

The regional access site at the center of town is handicapped accessible, as are five dune crossovers off of the boardwalk.

The east end of the following streets have handicapped access locations: Sand Dollar Lane (7 designated handicapped parking spaces), Sand Piper Lane (5), Sea Gull Lane (3), Scallop Lane (4), and Spartanburg Avenue (2).

Information

For information, contact Cape Fear Coast Convention and Visitors Bureau, 24 North Third Street, Wilmington, NC 28401, 910-341-4030, 800-222-4757.

Web addresses: <www.carolina beach.org>; <www.cape-fear.nc. us>; <www.nccoastalmanagement. net/Access/sites.htm>; <www. carolinabeach.org/pages/parking. html>

Wilmington Beach/ Hanby Beach

In 2001 Wilmington Beach and Hanby Beach, two contiguous unincorporated areas of New Hanover County, were annexed by Carolina Beach to the north and Kure Beach to the south, respectively.

The annexations made official the seamless fade from Carolina Beach into the unincorporated part of New Hanover County and then into Kure Beach. Today as you drive south on US 421, the corporate limits of Carolina Beach end at the centerline of Alabama Street, which runs perpendicular to the beachfront (and has a regional access). Once you past the centerline of Alabama Street continuing south, you enter the portion of the beachfront community of Kure Beach that was once known as Hanby Beach.

A few high-rise buildings sprout here, but they are far enough apart to allow a glimpse of the ocean. The streets perpendicular to the ocean are named for states, except for Ocean Boulevard near the middle of the community. The streets parallel to the oceanfront are named for game fish that local anglers here frequently catch—or dream of catching.

The steep dune profile often impedes your view of the water from US 421. You almost have to park and use one of the dune crossovers to see the beach. Wilmington Beach has a steeper berm profile than Carolina Beach. The fact that it is mainland coast accounts for some of the difference. The water here seems more active, with more energy and bolder wave action.

Kure Beach

Kure Beach is expanded. The new northern city limit is now the centerline of Alabama Street, the result of an annexation of the old unincorporated New Hanover County community of Hanby Beach. It is a logical fit; a change that, except for the city limit signs, is essentially "invisible" to travelers passing through. The Hanby Beach section of Kure Beach returns a "cottage" feeling to the drive south to Fort Fisher.

The town of Kure (pronounced "cur-ree") Beach was established in 1947, spreading south from where Avenue K intersects with US 421. There is a stoplight here, as well as an oceanside extension of Avenue K that leads to the Kure Beach Fishing Pier, the oldest pier in the state. In this vicinity is a small café and a quick mart, and this, in brief, is downtown Kure Beach.

The community has a wonderful old-timey feeling about it that is as substantive as it is different from the historic beach cottages in Nags Head. By comparison, Kure Beach is simpler. The cottages are neither as old nor as architec-

A family enjoys a walk near the southern town limits of Kure Beach. Courtesy of Cape Fear Coast Convention and Visitors Bureau.

Name That Wave

Anyone who has been walloped unexpectedly by a wave knows that not all waves are alike. There are four identifiable types (there is no "sneaky" wave, however), and each one looks and acts differently when it gets to the beach.

Bubbles and turbulent water bubbling down the face of the wave identify spilling waves. These waves seem to effervesce away over a long distance, the result of a shallow, sloping bottom.

Collapsing waves are usually low and very close to the beach; the lower half of the wave plunges abruptly, and the wave plays out up the beach. It makes a "plop" or "ploosh" sound when it collapses. These usually occur where the beach profile is short and steep.

A surging wave peaks noticeably. but then the bottom moves rapidly forward to push the water up the beach, sort of flipping it onto the sand. The wave seems to pulse forward.

A plunging wave is a surfer's wave, where the crest curls over creating an air pocket and then plunges into a trough. Plunging waves are the most spectacular and, in our mind's eye, the true beach wave. They occur when a swell approaching shore reaches a water depth 1.3 times the height of the wave. At this point, the wave has shortened and its height has increased, but there is insufficient water (because of the shallow depth) for the swell to continue. The water particles at the top curl over and crash from lack of support.

There is personal sense of waves being "big," but what does that mean in real measurements? It's possible to "guesstimate" the height of breaking waves in the following manner: Walk toward the ocean and stop when you reach a spot on the beach where the top of the breaking waves is level with the horizon. This makes you part of the yardstick.

To "guesstimate" the wave height, compute the height measured between your eye level and the lowest point on the beach where the water recedes after a wave breaks. This dimension is equal to the height of the breaking wave as measured between its peak and trough (whew). It's a mouthful, but not so challenging. Just remember that your eye level is approximately $5^1/_2$ inches less than your height, and add this to your best estimate of the measurement between the low point of the wave and where you are standing.

What surprises me most about this little exercise is that our personal frame of reference for a "big" wave is usually a wave size much less than our height. Waves feel a lot bigger than they really are.

---

turally distinctive, but they are no less genuine and character-defining for Kure Beach. The community seems to be sitting back and watching everybody else rush past—going someplace else, when everything anyone needs is right here. It makes me think of someone sitting in a front porch rocker as the world rushes madly on. It seems as if you could go to bed early and sleep late here without much interference. The selling point here is the ocean, and if that is all you need to enjoy a beach getaway, then Kure Beach is the place for you.

Atlantic Avenue, which runs parallel to the ocean for several blocks east of US 421 (easily reached east of the Docksider Inn one block north of the Kure Beach pier), provides a character study of the town. It is a side trip that is like looking through a window to another time.

Kure Beach sits on a mainland bluff that has protected its cottages from storm damage. In spite of this natural elevation, though, Kure Beach has taken its thrashings. Prior to Hurricane Hazel in 1954,

Atlantic Avenue, now a beachfront street, was two blocks away from the waves.

The community's stormy history contrasts with its day-to-day ambience as a relaxed place with a low vacation pulse. There are a number of motels and rental accommodations available.

In 1923 L. C. Kure constructed the pier, then promptly rebuilt it the following year after it collapsed. The pier has been rebuilt several times since then because of hurricane damage (repaired again, for example, after Hurricane Fran), but it continues to serve the many anglers who want to fish amid a sense of history and perseverance. A wonderful grizzled group hangs out on the pier for hours in the worst of weather waiting for the summer and fall king mackerel runs. By listening in, you can learn a lot about fishing and a lot about what's wrong with the town, state, world, etc.

The western city limits of Kure Beach extend to the Cape Fear River through the maritime woodland west of Ninth Avenue and Dow Road, the edge of the developed resort. Most of this area will stay undeveloped because it is a required buffer zone between the town and Sunny Point Army Terminal, a military fuel/ammunition depot across the Cape Fear River. South of Kure Beach, west of the highway, the U.S. Air Force maintains an electronic surveillance station. Part of the base is turned over to become beach access housing for air force personnel.

There is a quirky spot that has been taken in by the expansion of the city limits north—the former LaQue Test Center. This is surely one of the more surreal pieces of industrial art to ever exist beside any oceanfront highway on any coast; hands down, it is one of the most surreal in North Carolina.

The testing center is on the oceanside of US 421; a driveway is draped with cable to signal no entrance, but then who would want to go there—it looks like a *Far Side* junkyard. This is the place with air conditioner fan covers bolted to metal supports; the same with pieces of appliances. The facility was once operated by a subsidiary of Inco of Toronto and was founded in 1935 by scientist Francis LaQue. The whole idea was to test metal in the sea spray of the marine environment to see how resistant it was to the corrosion of water, salt, and rays of the sun. Such tests take a very long time, hence the longevity of the testing site. At one time, there was active (such as it is) testing of the metal braces of varying composition that have been used in the refurbishing of the Statue of Liberty. It is smaller than it used to be, but still camp as it can be.

In July 2004 the Federal Emergency Management Agency tapped its funds for pre-disaster mitigation for $2.7 million of the $3.6 million required to purchase and demolish the Riggings, a troubled condominium project at the south end of Kure Beach. Owners of the Riggings's 48 condominiums will pick up the remaining $900,000. The property owners intend to rebuild on land they own across the street.

The Riggings had been caught between a rock and an eroding place. A rare natural outcrop of coquina rock seaward of their property, a state natural heritage site, prohibited nourishment of the beach. After the condominiums are demolished, the land, where permanent structures will be banned, will be turned over to Kure Beach as a public access area.

Access

Beach access sites are not clearly designated but are plentiful. Parking is available at the oceanfront ends of Avenues E through N.

Handicapped Access

The town of Kure Beach will loan a beach wheelchair with advance request. Call the town hall at 910-458-8216.

Information

For information, contact Cape Fear Coast Convention and Visitors Bureau, 24 North Third Street, Wilmington, NC 28401, 910-341-4030, 800-222-4757.

Web addresses: <www.cape-fear.nc.us>; <www.kurebeach.cc>; <www.nccoastalmanagement.net/Access/sites.htm>

Fort Fisher State Historic Site

Three miles south of downtown Kure Beach, Fort Fisher greets you with a surprising sight—a live oak forest. The wandering limbs support foliage that is salt sculpted, sheared, and molded by sea winds into topiaries that seem to hover in a canopy over US 421. The visitors center parking lot is to the west, as are the remaining earthworks and reconstructions of the fort, but your eye is drawn east to the sea, visible through the coiling, rough bark of the live oaks.

Fort Fisher was the southern counterpart of Fort Macon in Carteret County. Unlike its brick companion, Fort Fisher was an earthwork fortification that protected the important navigation waters of the Cape Fear River. Confederate forces succumbed to a merciless assault here on January 15, 1865, in one of the largest land-sea battles ever fought on U.S. soil.

Should you walk to the oceanfront, you will see that the devastation suffered by the Confederate troops pales when compared to the assault on the site by the ocean. Ninety percent of the original earthwork fort has fallen into the sea. In fact, the original embankments extended south seaward from the present parking lot at the Fort Fisher State Recreation Area. The rubble-armored coast protecting the United Daughters of the Confederacy monument, which is located at the approximate headquarters of the Confederate forces, gives evidence of the desperate struggle against the natural forces.

In an effort to stop the final destruction of the fort, the North Carolina General Assembly amended its administrative rules on erosion-control structures to permit the construction of a revetment that will protect the scant remnants of the fort. This is the only exception to a state law that forbids armoring the coast to prevent erosion damage.

Ironically, it may be a Natural Heritage Site nearby that is exacerbating the erosion of the landmark earthwork fort. About 1/4 mile north of the monument on the beach is a rocky outcrop, the only natural outcrop of its kind on the North Carolina coast. The outcrop is made of coquina rock, a hard limestone composed of the fossilized shells of a small bivalve, which originated during the Pleistocene era, somewhere between 10,000 and 2 million years ago. The exposed rock disrupts the normal north-south flow of sand, thereby creating mild erosion to the north and very pronounced erosion to the south, toward the fort.

There is no admission fee to visit the fort and view its significant artifacts, including battle and commemorative swords associated with the fort's history. Outside, there is an interpretive walk with twelve wayside exhibits and a restored gun emplacement, Shepherd's Battery, with a fully functional heavy seacoast cannon that fired a 32-pound projectile. The site has several functioning period weapons that were in place at the fort. During public special events, these weapons are fired. The state also maintains an underwater archaeological research laboratory on the grounds that studies preservation and restoration techniques for artifacts recovered from underwater sites across the state.

Access

The fort is open April 1–October 31, 9 A.M. to 5 P.M. Monday–Saturday, 1 P.M. to 5 P.M. Sunday; November 1–March 31, 10 A.M. to 4 P.M. Tuesday–Saturday, 1 P.M. to 4 P.M. Sunday.

There are 75 parking spaces at the visitors center. From the visitors center, you may walk along the beach to reach the coquina outcrop. Much of the outcrop is in front of a private development that has some parking spaces on the west side of US 421.

Handicapped Access

The visitors center is accessible to handicapped travelers, but the restrooms are not modified.

Information

For information, contact Fort Fisher State Historic Site, 1610 Fort Fisher Boulevard South, Kure Beach, NC 28449, 910-458-5538.

Web address: <www.ah.dcr. state.nc.us/sections/hs/fisher/ fisher.htm>; <www.nccoastal management.net/Access/sites. htm>

Fort Fisher State Recreation Area

The Fort Fisher State Recreation Area includes the Fort Fisher State Historic Site. The remainder of this

	Fee	Parking	Restrooms	Lifeguard	Camping	Showers	Beach Access	Hiking	Trail	Handicapped	Boating	ORV Access	Fishing	Programs	Historic	Sand Beach	Dunes	Upland	Wetland
Fort Fisher State Historic Site		•	•				•	•	•	•			•	•	•	•	•	•	
Fort Fisher State Recreation Area		•	•	•		•	•	•	•	•		•	•			•	•	•	•
North Carolina Aquarium, Fort Fisher		•	•				•	•	•	•				•	•	•	•	•	•
Federal Point		•						•	•		•	•			•	•	•		•
Zeke's Island Research Reserve							•	•					•	•	•	•	•		•
Fort Fisher Ferry	•	•	•																•

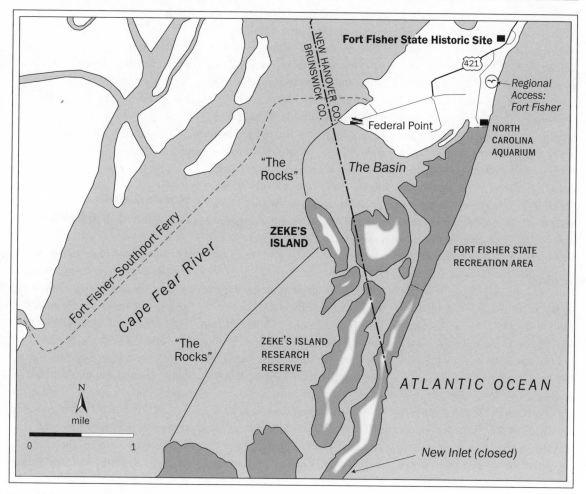

Map 26. Fort Fisher to Zeke's Island

287-acre preserve provides access to more than 4 miles of beautiful and comparatively unused beach immediately south of the fort. Approximately $^1/_{10}$ mile from the fort on SR 1713, there is a major regional access facility with nearly 200 parking spaces, restrooms, showers, refreshments, and a dune crossover that leads first to a sun shelter/gazebo and then to a splendid beach. During the summer months, the beach has lifeguards from 10 A.M. to 6 P.M. daily. There is excellent surf fishing here, and there is a vehicular dune crossover ramp, frequently used by surf fishermen to travel south to the sandy barrier spit of the Zeke's Island preserve, which is the northern headland of New Inlet.

South of the access area, the beachfront becomes a barrier island (technically, a barrier spit) backed by the waters of the Zeke's Island preserve. The spit once ended at New Inlet, which opened to the Cape Fear River, but that has shoaled, so it is possible to walk the six miles to Bald Head Island from Fort Fisher State Recreation Area.

In what turned out to be a contentious resource management change in 2004, the North Carolina Parks Department declared restrictions in access to the barrier strip for all-terrain vehicles because drivers threatened the nesting of certain endangered species. This was the first time in memory that the spit had ever been closed; an uproar that went all the way to the North Carolina General Assembly followed. The current policy restricts driving on the barrier strip from dawn to dusk between March 16 and September 14; the remainder of the year, the spit is open 24 hours.

The mainland peninsula, known as Federal Point, arcs west. US 421 follows the general bowing of the mainland to the terminus of the highway at the Fort Fisher/Southport ferry dock and the North Carolina Wildlife Resources Commission boat ramp at "the Basin" of Zeke's Island preserve.

The dune crossover at the access area elevates you above the vegetation in the trough behind the primary dunes and provides an educational stroll, more than 150 feet long, ending at the gazebo shelter overlooking the waves. Salt-sheared wax myrtle and sea oats/beach grass are the predominant plants, along with blanket flower, dollar weed, and other dune-loving plants. The monument at Fort Fisher is visible to the north; looking south, the barrier spit stretches to the horizon.

Access

There is a major regional access location and vehicular dune crossover. The entrance is just north of the aquarium. The general hours are dawn to dusk, year-round. In summer there are lifeguards at the beach near the access area.

All-terrain-vehicle access to the spit south of the regional access site is restricted to permitted vehicles only. Permits are $10 per day or $40 per year. Between September 15 and March 15, access is 24 hours a day, 7 days a week. Between March 16 and September 14, crucial dates for nesting birds and sea turtles, the spit is open in daylight only. Access will be through a card-operated gate, and additional personnel have been added to enforce the new restrictions.

Handicapped Access

The recreation area will loan a beach wheelchair with advance request. Call 910-458-5798.

This access area is designed to be accessible for handicapped travelers.

Information

For information, contact Fort Fisher State Recreation Area, P.O. Box 243, Kure Beach, NC 28449, 910-458-5798.

Web address: <www.ncsparks. net/fofi.html>

North Carolina Aquarium, Fort Fisher

The huge Cape Fear Conservatory, with its living vignettes of the Cape Fear River watershed, beginning well upstream in the Piedmont, is the superb and unexpected journey offered in the expanded Fort Fisher aquarium. Step into the exhibit area and you find yourself on a path leading through a giant terrarium. Beside the walk grow the trees, shrubs, and vines of rare ecosystems such as the Carolina Bays. Peer closely and you can see box turtles wresting through the natural leaf litter and carnivorous plants perched on the edge of the bog. Turtles and snakes rest in enclosed cases next to their habitat, and the plight of rare fishes such as the shortnosed sturgeon are highlighted in tanks adjoining the walkway.

Rivers, of course, flow down to the sea, and the aquarium completes its symbolic Piedmont to ocean floor journey in the adjacent building. Exhibits here present the flora and fishy-fauna of the varied ocean habitats in the Cape Fear estuary and the waters of the Atlantic beyond.

Could you stand eye to eye with a shark and not blink? Could you pick a safe shark from a dangerous one? The North Carolina Aquarium allows you the opportunity to pick the wrong shark in a safe place. The 20,000-gallon shark tank that exhibits these sleek, machine-eyed predators and additional tanks with other large game fishes are among the educational highlights at the aquarium.

If the sharks don't capture your imagination, step into the dark of a moray eel's cave or become transfixed watching "Shadows on the Sand," a shallow tank featuring locally native skates and rays.

The aquarium is carefully tucked into the upland region of the Fort Fisher State Recreational Area. As do its counterparts in Manteo and Pine Knoll Shores, the aquarium explores the mysteries and wonders of the ocean. Exhibits concentrate on the marine and terrestrial life of the southern coast of North Carolina. Multiple programs are offered throughout the year, and the 200-seat auditorium stays busy with daily lectures and films.

The Hermit Trail leads to an abandoned bunker where a well-known hermit lived for a number of years. Excursions vary widely and include bird-watching in the salt marsh and a look at the other side of the aquariums. Some of the more popular programs require advance reservations.

Access

The aquarium is open 9 A.M. to 5 P.M. daily. It is closed Thanksgiving Day, Christmas Day, and New Year's Day. Admission is $7 for adults, $6 for seniors and active military, $5 for children 6–17; children 5 and under are free.

Handicapped Access

The aquarium is fully accessible to handicapped travelers, including the restrooms. A wheelchair is available at the aquarium. Some of the exterior pathways are accessible to persons using wheelchairs.

Information

For information, contact North Carolina Aquarium at Fort Fisher, 900 Loggerhead Road, Kure Beach, NC 28449, 910-458-8257.

Web address: <www.nc aquariums.com>

Federal Point

There is no "point" at Federal Point anymore. The name has lost its precision since erosion, construction, and the many different agencies owning land here have not only altered the terrain but renamed and resurveyed portions of it as well.

It is generally conceded that Federal Point is the terminus for US 421, but it is not specified whether the point is at the Fort Fisher/Southport ferry dock, at the turnaround at the nearby boat ramp, at the old Civil War gun emplacement adjacent the dock, or perhaps within some of the wild acreage south of the road and bordered by the waters of "the Basin" in Zeke's Island preserve. It does seem fairly clear that the barrier spit of Fort Fisher State Recreation Area is not included as a part of Federal Point. It seems that Federal Point historically was the most southeastern part of the mainland, which, because of Snows Cut, is now an island.

Access

It is accessible if you can find it. Park at the boat ramp past the Fort Fisher ferry dock or at the ferry dock. At this point, Federal Point is all around you.

Zeke's Island National Estuarine Research Reserve

The northern border of Zeke's Island National Estuarine Research Reserve begins at the traffic turnaround or the boat ramp at the end of US 421. Looking southwest from the ramp at low tide, you will see a breakwater known as "the Rocks" at the westernmost boundary of the preserve. The large bay of water inside the rocks is called "the Basin." If you follow the breakwater, you will reach a small, sandy spit, high enough to support some shrubby growth, which is Zeke's Island. Be sure to set out for the island only at ebbing tide; "the Rocks" are not passable at high tide. Also, wear old clothes, carry water and bug spray, and walk very carefully—the wet, algae-covered rocks are treacherously slippery.

Zeke's Island is probably the most accessible component of the reserve system. It is approximately 1,165 acres of islands, marsh, tidal flats, shallow estuarine waters, and a barrier spit. It is an unusual spot because of the Basin, which is continuing to fill with sediment. When I hop-skipped to the rocks one time, there were several clammers raking the waters within the Basin.

The three islands and their attending flats are the important components of the reserve. Zeke's Island is 42 acres, low, with some high ground with live oaks and red cedar trees; North Island, once a barrier island south of New Inlet that is now parallel to the barrier spit, has about 138 acres; and No Name Island, southeast from Zeke's Island, has about 3 acres. The beach barrier spit, has about 64 acres of dunes and uplands. Extensive marshes and tidal flats spread out from each of the islands.

The varied environment features extensive tidal flats that are extremely important to both the log-gerhead turtle and many shorebird species. Because of the relative isolation, bird life is abundant in the tidal flats, and many species of herons, along with brown pelicans, are regulars. It is an extensive and important preserve, not only because of its wealth of habitat features, but also because it is so close to other proven habitats such as Ferry Slip Island and Battery Island, which are important rookeries.

Zeke's Island supported a gun emplacement during the Civil War. "The Rocks," extending from the mainland near the Fort Fisher/Southport ferry dock to Zeke's Island and then south to just north of Smith Island, comprise a breakwater or jetty constructed by the Army Corps of Engineers between 1875 and 1881. Designed to reduce shoaling in the Cape Fear River from the old New Inlet, which was just south of the present North Carolina Aquarium, connecting the Cape Fear River and the Atlantic, and Corncake Inlet, the jetty also effectively closed New Inlet and resulted in the slow silting of the Basin. Zeke's Island grew following the construction of the jetty and became a fishing center and the site of a turpentine factory. The great hurricane of 1899 destroyed the wharf and fishing operations.

The Basin has become increasingly shallow during this century. The migration of New Inlet since the construction of the jetty left a growing spit of sand south of Federal Point. In fact, the jetty has finally worked—New Inlet has shoaled, and it only took a hundred years.

Ironically, the jetty has proven to be an ecological bonus, creating a rocky shore that would not otherwise be found in these waters. Indeed, if you don't mind hopping on rocks, you can enjoy a lengthy excursion alongside the Cape Fear River.

Access

US 421 provides access to the major departure points for Zeke's Island. The highway ends at the North Carolina Department of Transportation parking for the Fort Fisher/Southport ferry. The North Carolina Wildlife Resources Commission maintains a boat ramp at the northern shore of the Basin near the ferry dock. Zeke's Island may be reached by walking "the Rocks" or by boat.

From the regional access at Fort Fisher State Recreation Area, you may walk or drive to the barrier-spit portion of the preserve and, if intrepid, venture south to New Inlet in its present location, nearly 3.5 miles south of the aquarium.

Information

For information, contact North Carolina National Estuarine Research Reserve, 5600 Marvin K. Moss Lane, Wilmington, NC 28409, 910-395-3905; or Division of Coastal Management, 1638 Mail Service Center, Raleigh, NC 27699-1638, 919-733-2293.

Web address: <www.ncnerr.org>

Fort Fisher Toll Ferry

The Fort Fisher / Southport toll ferry at the end of US 421 provides one of those marvelous interludes in the routine of a trip that only ferry rides seem capable of providing. But don't expect this one to be a quick hop in either direction for a night out on the other side of the river. The last departures are 6 P.M. from Southport and 6:50 P.M. from Fort Fisher. This is a daytime connector that runs every 50 minutes between April 1 and October 31 and every 1 hour and 40 minutes the remainder of the year. You may walk around while the ferry is crossing. The passage will be more enjoyable and informative with a bird guidebook, a bag of soda crackers for the gulls, and binoculars.

The ferry replaces about 40 miles of driving. It is definitely the rapid transit of north/south travel if you choose to hug the beachfront. The route crosses the Cape Fear River, North Carolina's major river channel, and the ferry sometimes shares the channel with impressive freighters and other open-ocean vessels entering or leaving the port of Wilmington. The passage takes about 30 minutes and offers excellent views of Zeke's Island, Bald Head Island, and Oak Island. Like a mariner, you can mark the transit with two familiar landmarks, Old Baldy, the lighthouse on Bald Head Island, and the newer Oak Island light that replaced it. Between and beyond them are the open ocean and the hazardous navigation of Frying Pan Shoals.

One particularly intriguing site on the west bank of the Cape Fear is the abandoned brick cone of Price's Creek Lighthouse, visible slightly downriver from the large commercial docks of Pfizer Chemical. Shortly after passing the Price's Creek Lighthouse, which was once used to help navigate the channel to Wilmington, the ferry docks in a sheltered slip just a few miles north of Southport. You've ridden a ferry, crossed a river, and landed in Brunswick County, the southeastern-most county in the state.

Information

To contact the ferry docks, call 910-457-6942 (Southport) or 910-458-3329 (Fort Fisher).

Web address: <www.ncferry. org>

Intracoastal Interstate

Wherever you go to the beach in North Carolina, you will cross the Atlantic Intracoastal Waterway. There is no way to avoid it and even less reason to notice it much beyond the fact of crossing a body of water by means of one of the high-rise bridges that link the barrier islands to the mainland.

Yet this remarkable ditch represents one of the more ambitious and successful civil-engineering projects ever completed by the U.S. government. It provides a safe, protected waterway route for light boats and barges that are not suited for the open ocean. If you are a boater and like lengthy, varied cruises, the Intracoastal Waterway in North Carolina has to be a magical trip. If you are going to the beach, however, it is a hurdle.

The waterway is an old idea. George Washington surveyed a canal route through the Dismal Swamp in the mid-1750s, and a completed canal in 1803 led to boomtown years for Elizabeth City. Other early barge/canal projects connected the Neuse and Newport Rivers north of

Beaufort in the early nineteenth century to shorten the commercial route between that city and New Bern.

The German U-boat attacks during World War I made a sheltered sea-lane a necessity, and the project was pressed to completion by 1936. It had immediate impact along its route. At Oak Island, for example, the waterway actually impeded access to the coast because it made an island. The project lopped the tip off the mainland south of Wilmington at Snows Cut, which linked Myrtle Grove Sound and the Cape Fear River. This made an island, Pleasure Island, of the mainland resorts of Carolina Beach, Kure Beach, and Fort Fisher.

The waterway reaches 3,000 miles from Massachusetts to Brownsville, Texas, using both natural waterways and artificial canals to provide a continuous navigable passage. Approximately 330 miles are in North Carolina. From Virginia to Morehead City, the waterway is considerably inland from the barrier beaches. From Morehead City south, however, the Intracoastal

Waterway routes directly landward of the barrier beaches. This part of the coast is where you are most likely to be aware of the inevitable crossing.

Since the 1970s, there has been an improvement in the crossings. Modern two- and four-lane bridges have taken the place of the old swing bridges. The faster, higher-capacity crossings fulfill the need for better hurricane evacuation. This minimization of the waterway has provided an unexpected bonus: a cure for "seasonal vexation disorder," the agonizing waits at swing bridge crossings while pleasure boats cruise through the open bridge, indifferent to the annoyance of idling motorists.

The waterway is less than 90 feet wide at most crossings, but that was enough to become a very effective moat. Some crossings, such as Coinjock in Currituck County, became legendary, if not notorious. The entire eastern seaboard seemed to back up on the north side of the waterway, waiting for the bridge to drop back in place and the crossing warning arms to lift on holiday weekends. When the bridge opened, it was like waving the green flag at a NASCAR race, and it sent fuming tourists roaring to the beach. In the early 1980s, a barge rammed into this bridge, jamming it and causing traffic of all kinds to grind to a halt until repairs were made.

The most intractable bottleneck was between Morehead City and Atlantic Beach, particularly before the new bridge at Cape Carteret opened. In the summer Bogue Sound waterway traffic was nearly as endless as the automobile traffic on the causeway. The bridge would flip open and shut like it was part of a pinball machine. Traffic would snarl westward on US 70 to the Morehead City limits on weekends. Waiting to cross Bogue Sound had the same inevitability as April 15 and was considered with the same affection.

You have a few more years yet to snag a drawbridge on busy routes. The waterway travels the length of the Alligator River in Dare and Tyrrell Counties, and the long bridge over the river on US 64 still must lift for boating traffic, which, thankfully, is comparatively light there. Perhaps the most famous bridge remaining is the narrow pontoon bridge serving Sunset Beach. Although proclaimed a hazard in the event of hurricane evacuation and soon to pass into history, the bridge is a cause célèbre with residents and visitors. It literally and figuratively cuts the tie with the mainland and makes Sunset Beach slightly isolated, inconvenient, and old-timey.

That's the landlubber's point of view. If you look at the waterway through the eyes of a boater, it's a different experience indeed. In North Carolina the Intracoastal Waterway provides many of the public boating access sites that serve the sounds and open ocean. Many of the North Carolina Wildlife Resources Commission boat ramps are located along its length, usually within easy access to coastal highways. Communities on the waterway close to inlets frequently have private marinas that use it to advantage. Calabash, for example, is a fishing community on Calabash Creek with access to Little River Inlet by means of the waterway. Throughout its length, the waterway offers excellent crabbing from piers or banks. Fishing can be good as well, depending on where you are along the waterway's course.

Towns along the waterway, such as Belhaven, Beaufort, and Southport, have their own tourist traffic that comes to call by boat. These places pick up a decided cosmopolitan air during the fall and spring migrations of yachts traveling between northern and southern coastal ports.

It is hard to think of the Intracoastal Waterway as a "working road," but that is its primary purpose. Currently, it is troubled. The Army Corps of Engineers is having difficulty securing funds for dredging maintenance, and at some inlet crossings, such as Lockwoods Folly Inlet, the waterway has shoaled to one-third of its proposed navigation depth. With funding doubtful, the utility of the waterway is increasingly diminished.

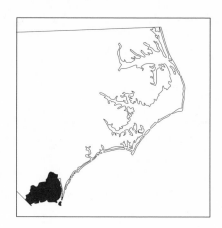

Brunswick County

There is either a low-profile conspiracy to keep Brunswick County a secret, or it is wonderfully adept at attracting new residents without changing the appealing character that attracted them initially. The most southern of the coastal counties, it is at once the most convenient and out of the way—highways lead you there, but finding its coastal pleasures requires more determined navigation. This awkward access explains part of its constancy over the past several decades of growth; the most compelling reason, however, may be that most residents like it the way it is.

US 17, the major highway serving the area, whisks travelers north to Wilmington or south to Myrtle Beach, South Carolina, inland from the coast. There is no enticing clue along its route about the how pleasant and easygoing this down-to-earth county with five sunny islands happens to be. In fact, the best of Brunswick County is found from its unhurried two-lane roads. Plan for some lazy travel with the opportunity to explore some curiosities.

Sleepy charm is the rule, especially in the older communities blessed with inlet or beach access. Southport, the oldest established community, has a briny patina along its waterfront that yields to homey picket-fence-perfect residential streets. It sets a tone that reads "small town near open water" instead of resort. The other waterfront communities in the county make every effort to mimic this tone.

Brunswick County seems content resisting the commercial intensity pushing north from their megawatt resort neighbor, Myrtle Beach. Myrtle Beach roars and glows into the night; Brunswick County dials down to a whisper and a twinkle after dusk. Why, on Ocean Isle Beach, volunteers hand out pamphlets requesting that guests dim oceanfront house and porch lights during the April to June nesting season for loggerhead turtles. Low lights and low-key beachfront development improve the odds that these intrepid reptiles will annually lumber ashore to lay eggs as they historically have. This gentle nudge to do a small part to help turtles reflects the attitude of the island beachfront communities. While not strictly "all natural, all the time," the communities prefer life by the sea to be

Southport's old boat harbor is as authentic as they come. It's still a working dock for commercial fishing vessels as well as the Cape Fear River pilots. Courtesy of the author.

sleepy, unplugged, and family-oriented. The Brunswick County Tourism Development Board is more direct: their promotional flyers brag, "Things don't change much around here." Folks have come to count on it.

There are more than 50 total miles of gently sloping oceanfront on five different islands in the county, and a quirk in coastal geography blesses most of those miles with a southern exposure. East of the Cape Fear River, at a portion of the Smith Island Complex known as the private resort of Bald Head Island, North Carolina's coast elbows sharply northwest from its nearly due south alignment. West of the Cape Fear River, the four remaining Brunswick islands—Oak Island, Holden Beach, Ocean Isle Beach, and Sunset Beach—align in a gentle arc that bends from southeast to southwest. This makes aligning a beach chair for the maximum summer tan uncomplicated (facing the ocean is facing south), and it leads to the wry observation that on Brunswick beaches, as on Bogue Banks, the sun also rises from the left and sets to the right.

Complimenting the tan-favorable compass alignment of the five islands is a barely sloping ocean bottom, which in turn means generally benign surf. These wide, flat, and generally children-friendly beaches are the foundation of the county's popularity as a family destination. While Myrtle Beach is certainly a family destination, the Brunswick island communities build their vacation appeal around simple pleasures instead of staged entertainment, outlet shopping, and amusements. There is no way to emphasize too much how these islands are a world of difference from Myrtle Beach.

There are a couple of geographic curiosities about Brunswick County: First, the southernmost location in the state is on Bald Head Island. Relative to the rest of North Carolina's coast, the Brunswick Islands are considerably west. In fact, the former Bird Island, the latest jewel of the North Carolina Coastal Reserve, is due south of Raleigh, which seems wholly improbable, but then this is the county where the sun sets on the right. . . .

In the last decade, Brunswick County has been among the top five counties in the state in the percentage of population increase. In part, this trend results from people finding a hospitable place where the balmy winters of the coastal South become reliable—daytime winter temperatures average in the mid- to high fifties—as well as the county making its mark as a golfing mecca. In a region once known for agriculture, Brunswick County has grown some of the finest golf courses in North Carolina, proudly proclaiming that it is the "Golf Coast" of the state. Residential golf-course community development started gradually as the idea migrated north from Myrtle Beach. Today, Brunswick County can tick off approximately forty championship golf courses, crafted by some of the nation's finest golf architects. Even though most of these golf courses are part of residential communities, many are open for public play. One of these communities, St. James, between Southport and Supply, incorporated in 2003.

It seems like a lot of golf and growth, but while the past rate of growth has been rapid, the permanent population is still modest. Less than 80,000 people call the 907 square miles of Brunswick County home. That is about one person for every seven acres. Outside of the incorporated communities, it still has a rural atmosphere.

The several islands and tidal rivers that complicate the coast here have naturally divided the county into sections that easily associate because of geography. Mainland Southport, recently incorporated St. James, and Oak Island, with its two communities of Caswell Beach and Oak Island (Long Beach and Yaupon Beach merged in 1999), are close and work easily together, supporting many activities including a mutual chamber of commerce. Oak Island, the most populous community in the county, is still very village-like in feeling in spite of its 11-mile length.

The private resort of Bald Head Island, which forms the north headland of the Cape Fear River channel, also shares some resources with these two communities: Indigo Plantation in Southport provides the landing for the private passenger ferry that serves Bald Head Island.

The Lockwoods Folly River, its wetlands, headwaters, and pine pocosin woodlands are a physical barrier between the communities in the western part of the county and the nexus of Southport/Oak Island. Holden Beach, Ocean Isle Beach, Shallotte, Sunset Beach, and Calabash have sufficiently common interests and proximity to naturally form a separate identity.

While three island communities, Holden Beach, Ocean Isle Beach, and Sunset Beach, have incorporated parts of the mainland, life on the islands exists apart from the mainland. Even today, they seem suspended in a different era—of some thirty years ago. The developed beach has a tempo and mood that is more in step with earlier, less frenetic times.

Once known as the South Brunswick Islands, these three island communities support their own chamber of commerce headquartered in Shallotte. It is a bit confusing, but trying to drive from Shallotte to Oak Island or Southport or vice versa reveals the practicality of the division. All roads leading directly to the beaches are North Carolina secondary roads. When you arrive, in most instances, you will find houses, but you will not find crowds.

NC 133, which links Wilmington and Southport, is a lazy, winding passage. It is the aged and venerable shore route and passes by Orton Plantation and Gardens and Brunswick Town State Historic Site. Orton Plantation is an eighteenth-century rice plantation well known for its extensive gardens. The gardens are at the peak of seasonal show in mid-spring, when an almost unsurpassed azalea planting erupts in bloom. Lesser-known Brunswick Town State Historic Site is the historical heart of Brunswick County. In 1725 the town was laid out as one of the new colony's premier cities. By 1760, more than 250 citizens and 60 structures formed the nucleus of the town, a wealthy community by the standards of the time. The British army razed it in 1776 as punishment for the residents' resistance to British rule. Brunswick Town was never resettled, and slowly the woodlands have reclaimed it. Now visitors can walk the sand beds of streets long gone, view the foundations of the houses overlooking the Cape Fear River, and learn the story of the community in a visitors center that houses archaeological relics of the site.

On the wild side, Brunswick County is something of a botanical wonderland, possibly hosting more species of restricted distribution than any other county in the state. The diversity of habitats covers the range from the Smith Island Complex, with extensive maritime forests, to the sinkhole ponds of the Sunny Point Terminal fuel and ammunition depot. The largest breeding colony of egrets, herons, and ibises in the state is on Battery Island, off of Southport, and the marshes of Brunswick County host the state's limited alligator population. Green Swamp, a 15,700-acre Nature Conservancy property, features one of the best, and last, longleaf pine savannas in the state. Within its borders, northeast of Shallotte and east of NC 133, are fourteen species of insectivorous plants. One of the newest natural features open to the public is Boiling Spring Lakes Nature Preserve, in the community of Boiling Spring Lakes. This 5,000-acre preserve showcases several of the most important ecosystems found in Brunswick County. It is one of the best places to stop for a stroll and a better understanding of this magnificently wild coastal county.

In the last several years, the loss of the natural dune line and the steady annual erosion exacerbated by powerful storms have imperiled oceanfront structures on several of the islands. (Erosion has also reduced the amount of oceanfront that could serve as suitable sea turtle nesting sites.) Beachfront restoration, mostly in the form of beach nourishment projects, has been successful at arresting the continuation of the erosion and has, in fact, restored useful, useable beach before cottages that, in some places, had the high tide rushing underneath. To further protect their investment, the municipalities have enacted strict dune protection ordinances with fines sufficient to gain one's attention if not deter dune destruction.

Access

The municipalities on the islands provide beach access. The sites are listed after each specific section below.

Orton Plantation is off of NC 133 south of Wilmington. It is open daily 8 A.M. to 6 P.M. This is a private residence, but the gardens and grounds are open to the public. There is an admission fee. For information, call 910-371-6851.

Web address: <www.orton gardens.com>.

Brunswick Town State Historic Site is off of NC 133, south of Orton Plantation. It is open April 1–October 31, 9 A.M. to 5 P.M. Monday–Saturday, 1 P.M. to 5 P.M. Sunday; November 1–March 31, 10 A.M. to 4 P.M. Tuesday–Saturday, 1 P.M. to 4 P.M. Sunday. For information, call 910-371-6613, 910-392-3189.

Web address: <www.ah.dcr. state.nc.us/sections/hs/ brunswic/brunswic.htm>

Boiling Spring Lakes Nature Preserve is off of NC 87 in Boiling Spring Lakes. The trail begins at the community center, which is on the south side of the lake in the community of Boiling Spring Lakes. For additional information, contact the Nature Conservancy, Wilmington, NC, 910-762-6277.

Web address: <www.tnc.org/ northcarolina>

Handicapped Access

The resort communities of Brunswick County will loan a beach wheelchair with advance request. Contact information is listed with the individual communities.

Orton Plantation is handicapped accessible, but some of the paths are gravel or packed sand and are not easily negotiable by handicapped travelers.

The auditorium in the museum at Brunswick Town State Historic Site is handicapped accessible; the grounds have paved paths near the ruins of St. Philip's Anglican Church.

The Boiling Spring Lakes Nature Preserve is not handicapped accessible.

Information

For information about the Southport/Oak Island attractions, contact Southport Visitors Center, 113 West Moore Street, Southport, NC 28461, 910-457-7927; or Southport/Oak Island Chamber of Commerce, 4841 Long Beach Road Southeast, Southport, NC 28461, 800-457-6964.

For information about the islands of Holden Beach, Ocean Isle Beach, and Sunset Beach, contact North Carolina Brunswick Islands Chamber of Commerce, P.O. Box 1186, Shallotte, NC 28459, 800-795-7263, 910-754-6644.

Web addresses: <www.south port-oakisland.com>; <www.nc brunswick.com>

Southport

The waterfront seating in Southport's Ship Chandler restaurant offers a canoeist's-eye view of the comings and goings in the shipping channel of the Cape Fear River. I was dining as the tide ebbed, and a freighter glided downriver toward the ocean beyond Fort Caswell and Smith Island. It came closer and closer, so close it seemed the crew could have counted the hush puppies on my plate. The freighter swung to port around Battery Island then back to starboard to clear Fort Caswell. Gulls swirled above its wake as it powered seaward.

It was a fitting floor show for a Southport seafood dinner. This sturdy village is the home base for the harbor pilots who guide seagoing vessels up and down the Cape Fear River. Ocean traffic is a part of Southport's riverside panorama. Look inland and you will find a settled riverfront town in the quiet, resilient way of Atlantic and Beaufort.

Without being saccharine, the "quaint little fishing village" clichés are apt for Southport. Two-story, classically proportioned wooden

	Fee	Parking	Restrooms	Lifeguard	Camping	Showers	Beach Access	Hiking	Trail	Handicapped	Boating	ORV Access	Fishing	Programs	Historic	Sand Beach	Dunes	Upland	Wetland
Brunswick County		•	•				•			•	•		•		•	•	•	•	•
Southport		•									•		•		•			•	
Bald Head Island (private)	•	•	•				•								•	•	•	•	•
Bald Head Island State Natural Area							•	•			•		•			•	•	•	•

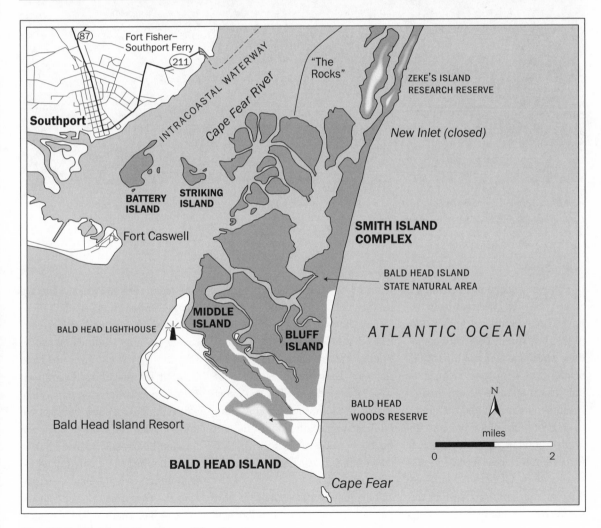

Map 27. Smith Island Complex and Southport

Few towns offer the pure, simple charm of Southport's friendly Victorian neighborhoods a few short blocks from the Cape Fear River. Courtesy of the author.

houses line shaded streets. Moore Street, the road into town from the Fort Fisher/Southport ferry dock, passes by a serene *Our Town* cemetery, where moss-draped live oaks shade the headstones. Residential streets march in a grid inland from the riverfront, and the close-in neighborhoods have homes with shaded porches and trees musical with crickets and cicadas. If the streets were not paved, you could imagine a driving rain pelting the sandy soil, puddling and melting away.

Up from the river comes the smell of marsh and fish, air as genuine as the happenstance way the waterfront has been cobbled into use. If there is something about Southport that seems ideal, romantic, and Tom Sawyeresque, read *The Old Man and the Boy* by Robert Ruark. This thoroughly charming book draws heavily on the author's boyhood experiences with his grandfather, J. B. Ruark, a Southport resident.

The movie and television studios of Wilmington and Hollywood have employed Southport's scenic appeal in at least six movies, and vignettes of the town have made the small screen as well.

Since 1748, when soldiers established Fort Johnston, folks have lived by the Cape Fear River in what is present-day Southport. From its sheltered basin, they sailed the Cape Fear River channel and followed the river to open water. Southport makes a good home: it perches high on the mainland, 26 feet above sea level. Bay Street follows the riverfront, along the natural bench or shoulder that is below the higher elevations of town center, where Moore Street (NC 211) and Howe Street intersect. Bay Street is the heart of the sea-based economy of Southport, where marinas, seafood markets, and restaurants line the riverfront. The pert little pilot boats that ferry the pilots to the oceangoing vessels requiring their assistance are docked at East Bay Street.

Looking north from Bay Street, you will notice a large white Georgian building dominating an expanse of lawn. This is the officers' quarters, and the only remaining building, of Fort Johnston, established in 1748 as a protection against privateering from French and Spanish vessels. The original fortification also provided protection for the swelling numbers of settlers at Smithville, as it was called until 1899, honoring General Benjamin Smith. Whigs burned the original fort in 1775, chasing out royal governor Josiah Martin who fled by British vessel. The federal government rebuilt the fort in 1794–1809, and the town incorporated in 1805. As you might suspect, Confederate forces seized the fort in 1861. The strategic importance of the fortification and the town lay in their proximity to the river channel. Fort Caswell on Oak Island, Fort Fisher across the river, Fort Johnston, and other smaller gun emplacements kept the port of Wilmington open by creating a formidable gauntlet for Union forces entering the Cape Fear River.

The Whig forces that gave Josiah Martin a fiery send-off began a revolutionary tradition here. The officers' quarters building is a centerpiece for the official North Carolina Fourth of July celebration, which attracts more than 40,000 visitors to Southport each year.

Visit Southport at another time of year and you may very well wonder where such numbers of guests could congregate. The antique and curio stores of the town center invite exploration in less pressing throngs.

Stop in at the visitors center at 113 West Moore Street and pick up a copy of the Southport Trail, a self-guided walking tour that weaves past the notable buildings in the town.

The North Carolina Maritime Museum at Southport at 116 North Howe Street, a block north from Moore Street, details the river history that swirled around Southport, including that of the gentleman pirate, Stede Bonnett, who was captured here on September 26, 1718, and tanker *John D. Gill*, which was torpedoed off Southport on March 12, 1942.

As mentioned above, the Ship Chandler restaurant is a Southport seafood standby with definitely the best view in town. Another seafood house with a longtime following is Mr. P's, which has left its waterfront location to move to Howe Street across from the water tower.

One natural note: Battery Island, southeast from Southport in the Cape Fear River, is an Audubon North Carolina–managed preserve. The locally known sandbar, closed to human access, has enough feathers in early spring to give it lift. The 100-acre island serves as the nesting ground for nearly 15,000 white ibis and 500 pairs of other shore-wading birds. Seasonally, Audubon North Carolina will sponsor guided bird-watching boat tours, but the island is otherwise closed to visitation.

Access

There is a wonderful public pier extending from Bay Street into the Cape Fear River. There are two gazebos on the pier and, weather permitting, a lot of youthful fishermen. The pier is easily manageable by wheelchair, as is the town and many of the stores, although there are no public restrooms for handicapped travelers.

Information

For information, contact Southport Visitor Information Center, 113 West Moore Street, Southport, NC 28461, 910-457-7927; or Southport/Oak Island Chamber of Commerce, 4841 Long Beach Road Southeast, Southport, NC 28461, 910-457-6964.

Web addresses: <www.cityof southport.com>; <www.southport-oakisland.com>; <www.nc audubon.org/nccas_sanc3.html>

Smith Island Complex

The southeastern promontory of what is today known as Bald Head Island put the fear in sailors, which led to the naming of the Cape Fear River. Giovanni da Verrazano discovered it in 1524, and it appeared on a 1590 map as "Promontorium tremendum," which has a more substantive sound to it than the official name Smith Island Complex, of which Bald Head Island is part.

Bald Head is as far south in the state as you can go and close enough to the coast-hugging flow of the Gulf Stream to be nearly a world unto itself. On a coast that is extraordinary for its astonishing number and variety of islands, Bald Head is itself extraordinary. It is accessible only by the ferry that runs round-trip from Indigo Plantation in Southport or by private boat.

Bald Head Island is certainly one of a kind within the state for its inventory of natural riches, and it may rival some of the islands of South Carolina and Georgia for the private development that simultaneously protects and makes available the island experience. It has been as prominent in the maritime history of the state as it is now in the evolution of a constructive blend of conservation and development.

While the name Bald Head Island refers to the largest of three parallel sand ridges in the Smith Island Complex, it is also the name of the resort that has been built into this extraordinary maritime mosaic. Access is only by ferry, and no cars are allowed on the island. There is a golf course (designed by George Cobb) that threads the middle portion of the island. The homes here are substantial and expensive; vacation rentals are priced accordingly. The development is low rise and low density; in the wooded sections of the island, houses are discreetly sited. In addition to the open space provided by the golf course and its surrounds, a 174-acre parcel of magnificent upland forests has been set aside as part of the North Carolina Coastal Reserve.

Bald Head Island has its own local government and a very active conservation society, the Bald Head Conservancy. For all its marvelous attributes, part of the island beachfront is in a struggle with erosion. As of the summer of 2004, portions of South Bald Head Wynd, the main oceanfront street along the island's south beach, were closed off and threatened with destruction by erosion. Although this beach has always been flat, lacking significant dunes and exposed to overwash, Bald Head Island residents assert that erosion has accelerated dramatically since 2002, following a deepening of the Cape Fear River channel. In fact, there was not much beach on the south beach during the summer of 2004. The U.S. Army Corps of Engineers disputed a cause/effect relationship, but nonetheless a sand disposal project during the winter of 2004–5 "disposed" of sufficient sand to establish 100 feet of beach at high tide. The sand, of course, covered the field of sand-bag groins.

The oldest state maps note the name of the island as Smith Island for Landgrave Thomas Smith, who acquired it in 1690. By the time the state wished to construct a lighthouse here to serve the Cape Fear River, Benjamin Smith (the name-sake of Smithville, later Southport, and perhaps an heir of Thomas) grazed sheep and cattle here. The civic-minded Smith offered 10 acres to the state as a site for the lighthouse in 1789, provided that there were suitable protections for his cattle. By 1794, the grazing privileges had been protected by the General Assembly, and the light was completed and already deemed as inadequate. By 1817, another lighthouse, the present-day "Old Baldy," had been constructed and continued to illuminate the Cape Fear River entrance until it was decommissioned in 1903 for a taller lighthouse at the eastern end of the island. Old Baldy is the oldest standing lighthouse in the state, predating the Ocracoke light by six years. The name Bald Head originated from mariners' observations of the white sandy prominences at the southwest corner, adjacent to the oldest channel of the Cape Fear River and hence visible from the sea.

Although the lighthouse is the most storied feature, the remainder of the island is the featured story. There are more than 12,000 acres in the complex of marsh, tidal creeks, relic dune ridge lines, maritime forests, and beachfront within the accepted boundaries of Smith Island, which extend north from Cape Fear to Corncake Inlet, separating Smith Island from the barrier spit of Zeke's Island North Carolina National Estuarine Research Reserve in New Hanover County. Smith Island is the most northern habitat for the semi-

Lighthouses

For more than two centuries, lighthouses have guided mariners' navigation of North Carolina's coast. The towers are true landmarks, structures visible and identifiable by day by their color or pattern and by night by their characteristic signal. In this era of electronic navigation, the lighthouses are working reminders of the state's maritime history.

Six lighthouses serve the coast, marking, north to south, Currituck Banks, Oregon Inlet, Cape Hatteras, Ocracoke Inlet, Cape Lookout, and the Cape Fear River.

North to south, the first light is the red-brick tower at Corolla, known as the Currituck Beach Lighthouse. It was first lighted on December 1, 1875. The 162-foot-tall tower is one of two on the coast that you may climb to the 150-foot-high focal-plane catwalk. Outer Banks Conservationists, Inc., received the deed for the lighthouse in 2003, based on the organization's long history of restoration and site management. The group charges a small fee to ascend the tower and uses the proceeds for the restoration of the lightkeeper's quarters and the grounds. The Currituck Beach Lighthouse is one of the best restoration stories on the Outer Banks.

South of the Currituck light is the horizontally striped frustum of Bodie Island Lighthouse, which has served Oregon Inlet since 1872. Its beacon is visible 19 miles at sea, and its repeated signal—2.5 seconds on, 2.5 seconds off, 2.5 seconds on, 22.5 seconds off—pulses from a focal plane height of 156 feet above the sandy base. The restored lightkeeper's quarters now serve as a visitors center for Cape Hatteras National Seashore. By 2007, the National Park Service plans to open the tower to would-be climbers—all 214 steps. Until then, take time to gaze up the elegant spiral of the stairs. It is quite a view.

The Cape Hatteras Lighthouse, at 208 feet tall, is one of the tallest brick lighthouses in the world and a cause célèbre among lighthouse aficionados. The two beacons inside—once whale oil lamps—make one full rotation every 15 seconds, which is visible as one flash every 7.5 seconds. Built in 1873, the black-and-white barber-pole-striped light replaced an 1802 tower. Although it was 1,500 feet from the ocean when it was built, the ocean was 50 yards away by 1999.

In February of that year, contractors separated it from its foundation, placed it on rollers, jacked it up, put it on tracks, and moved it 2,899.57 feet to its new home. After the move, the light was illuminated again the following November. The Coast Guard maintains the light, but the tower belongs to the National Park Service, which carefully controls the ascent. Tickets to climb can be purchased at the headquarters building on the lighthouse grounds. The original lightkeeper's quarters serves as an interpretive visitors center.

The Ocracoke Lighthouse, dating from 1823, is the oldest continually operating lighthouse in the state. The squat, stuccoed tower is 75 feet tall, and the focal plane of the light is at 65 feet, visible 14 miles out to sea. At one time, it served the busiest inlet, Ocracoke, and port, Portsmouth, in the state.

The Cape Lookout Lighthouse, south of Ocracoke on South Core Banks in Cape Lookout National Seashore, guards the entrance to Morehead City, warning mariners of the treacherous waters to the southeast known as Cape Lookout Shoals. Placed into service in 1859, this lighthouse became the model for the other majestic beacons along the coast. Its diamond-patterned black-and-white markings are incorrectly thought to be a mistake. Although its pattern seems to be more suited to Cape Hatteras because of its offshore Diamond Shoals, in 1873 the lighthouse board did specify that the Cape Lookout Lighthouse be "checkered."

The oldest lighthouse standing in the state is the Bald Head light on Smith Island, constructed in 1795. Although it is no longer illuminated, the tower once signaled the entrance to the Cape Fear River, North Carolina's only natural deep-water channel, ominously guarded by the shifting sands of an offshore sandbar known as Frying Pan Shoals.

Shortly after construction, the Bald Head light became obsolete because of a shift in the Cape Fear channel much farther north to a new inlet south of present-day Smith Island. A new lighthouse was authorized by Congress and placed in service in 1816, and the Bald Head light was retired. Eventually, the inlet shoaled, and the channel shifted again to the southwest of Smith Island. By 1848, a new pair of lights (no longer evident) on Oak Island became the primary navigation aid to the mouth of the Cape Fear.

On May 15, 1958, the current Oak Island Lighthouse was placed into service. This is one of the most powerful beacons in the world, visible 24 miles out to sea. The flash activates 4 times at one-second intervals, followed by 6 seconds of darkness.

The distinctive day marks, black on top, white in the middle and gray at the bottom, are actually finished into the tower's concrete surface instead of being painted.

tropical vegetation that characterizes the Sea Islands of South Carolina and Georgia. The tidal waters and salt marsh north of the semitropical maritime forests are immense, and a diverse population of resident and migratory wildlife populates the many habitats, including alligators. Nearly all of the acreage, except for the 2,000 acres developed as part of the Bald Head Island Resort, is protected by the state or under the auspices of the Nature Conservancy.

In the early 1970s there was much controversy over the proposal to develop Bald Head Island. It nevertheless has become a self-sustaining resort, with the natural features of the island—the marsh and mix of forests—as a focal element of the resort experience. The island offers single-family homes, condominiums, a community center, a golf course, swimming pools, and a small store. The limited numbers of rental rooms available, the care taken to preserve the island's natural features, and the restriction to boat-only access make the island exclusive but not excluding. You are as welcome as a day guest as you would be if you rented a villa or private home for an overnight or weekend stay. There is a museum, a lighthouse, and a vast natural area of barrier island upland to explore.

The 14 miles of beach attract visitors from both the land and the sea. The island has long been a prime nesting location for pelagic turtles, primarily the loggerhead turtle. Federal and state naturalists carefully monitor the three-month summer nesting season, from June through August. Helping these different groups live together has been a primary function of the Bald Head Conservancy, a private, nonprofit organization, which, in conjunction with the University of North Carolina at Wilmington, provides a full-time naturalist on the island who is responsible for assisting with the annual turtle watch. The conservancy is one of the few private organizations authorized to participate in the federal tagging program for pelagic turtles. The naturalists note the location and type of nest, count the number of eggs, and place protective screening over the nest to thwart predators such as raccoons. If possible, they tag the mother turtle. The hatchlings emerge in approximately sixty days from nesting, enter the open ocean, and begin their lives at sea. In 1990 187 nests were recorded on the island, 20 of which were lost to predation. Two nests were green turtle nests, a much more rare species than the well-known loggerhead.

The Bald Head Conservancy is also a management partner with North Carolina's Division of Coastal Management in overseeing the 174-acre Bald Head Woods Reserve, part of the North Carolina Coastal Reserve system. The conservancy is also active in securing additional land on the island to protect through private donations and purchase.

Access

Although Bald Head is promoted as a private resort, anyone can rent a villa or cottage on the island, and you may visit the island for a day trip. You may reach the island and the lighthouse by ferry from Southport at the Indigo Plantation. The fee for the ferry crossing is around $15 round-trip. Ferry departures are on the hour year-round, 8 A.M. to 6 P.M.

Handicapped Access

Bald Head Island will loan a beach wheelchair with advance request. Contact the fire department at 910-457-4310.

The island does accommodate mobility-impaired travelers. Contact the resort to see about access assistance and available rentals on Bald Head that may be suitable for handicapped visitors.

Information

For information, contact Bald Head Island Information Center, 5079 Southport-Supply Road, Southport, NC 28461, 800-234-1666, 910-457-5000.

Web addresses: <www.baldhead island.com>; <www.villagebhi. org>; <www.ncnerr.org>

Bald Head Island State Natural Area

The North Carolina Division of Parks and Recreation manages the more than 10,000-acre state natural area composed of labyrinthine tidal creeks, marsh, bays, and uplands between Bald Head Island and Fort Fisher. The land, which includes 9,000 acres of marsh and 1,000 acres of uplands and dunes, was deeded to the Nature Conservancy in the 1970s by several owners. The conservancy in turn gave it to the state of North Carolina. The tract includes Bluff Island, one of three upland ridges (the other two are Middle Island and Bald Head Island) that, along with marshes, comprise the Smith Island Complex.

In the 1990s additional upland acreage was added to the natural area through a combination of donation and purchase by the state. The Bald Head Island Conservancy also participates in the management of the natural area.

Access

Access is by boat only. The North Carolina Wildlife Resources Commission boat ramp at Federal Point provides the most direct access, although the island is readily accessible by crossing the Cape Fear River from Southport.

Information

For information, contact Fort Fisher State Recreation Area, P.O. Box 243, Kure Beach, NC 28449, 910-458-5798. Additional information

may be available from the Bald Head Island Conservancy, P.O. Box 3109, Bald Head Island, NC 28461, 910-457-0089.

Web address: <www.bhic.org>

Oak Island

Oak Island, the first of the Brunswick County barrier islands that you reach by driving south from Wilmington or Southport, incorporates the communities of Caswell Beach and Oak Island on its 13-mile beachfront. The town of Oak Island dates from the 1999 merger of Yaupon Beach and Long Beach.

The island, which touches the Cape Fear River at one end and Lockwoods Folly Inlet at the other, aligns east-west. It has an extensive ridge of high ground, and a tidal creek, Big Jim Davis Canal, drains from the center of the island to Lockwoods Folly Inlet. This splits the western half of the town of Oak Island and gives a split-tail shape to the land itself. It also cleanly divides Oak Island into a beachfront barrier and upland forest. At the east end of the island, on the west bank of the Cape Fear River, is the North Carolina Baptist Assembly Grounds, which include the weathered ramparts and old buildings of Fort Caswell. Also at this end are a U.S. Coast Guard Station and the Oak Island Lighthouse, the most recently constructed light to aid navigation in the Cape Fear River and the brightest light in the United States. The Oak Island light is plainly visible from Southport,

	Fee	Parking	Restrooms	Lifeguard	Camping	Showers	Beach Access	Hiking	Trail	Handicapped	Boating	ORV Access	Fishing	Programs	Historic	Sand Beach	Dunes	Upland	Wetland
Caswell Beach		•	•				•			•			•			•	•		
Oak Island Lighthouse		•													•				
Fort Caswell	•	•													•	•	•		•
Public Boating Access: Oak Island		•									•		•						•
19th Place East Walkway		•						•	•	•									•
Tidal Way Trails Park		•	•						•		•		•						•
Regional Access: 46th St.		•	•			•	•			•			•				•		
Robin Schuster Park		•	•								•		•						•

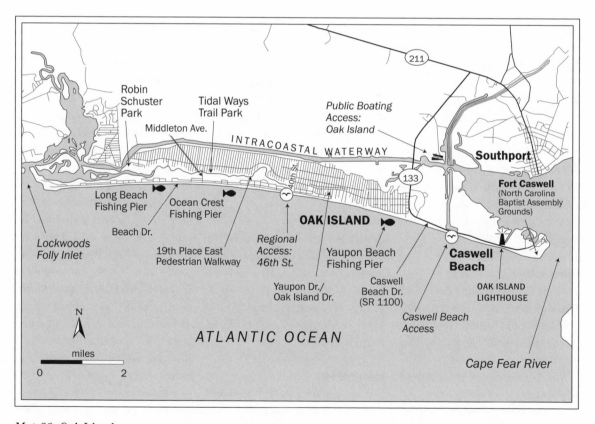

Map 28. Oak Island

as are some of the buildings at the Baptist assembly grounds, but the Southport vantage embraces only the eastern part of Oak Island and views it across a great swatch of salt marsh at that.

NC 133, also known as Long Beach Road, is the only route onto the island, heading south from its intersection with NC 211 approximately 2.5 miles west of Southport. On the west side of NC 133, just south of the junction, is the Southport/Oak Island Chamber of Commerce welcome center. It is a good first stop for information about the attractions and accommodations of the island communities and the surrounding area as well.

The highway crosses the Intracoastal Waterway over a high-rise bridge. Below the bridge on the mainland are the rusting ruins of a menhaden-processing plant, whose pungent odor used to signal the arrival to Oak Island. The bridge provides an elevated glimpse of the island. It is a tree-covered landscape, and there is only a hint of housing peeking through the treetops in the distance. The bridge ends in a tree-covered section of Oak Island, and the route proceeds to a traffic light.

Be ready for the name change from Long Beach Road to Caswell Beach Drive; and if you do not turn at the light, the route makes a sweeping curve east into the residential community of Caswell Beach. The U.S. Coast Guard Station, the Oak Island Lighthouse, and the North Carolina Baptist As-

sembly Grounds are at the end of the road.

A turn right, or west, at the traffic signal will put you on what once was (or may still be) Yaupon Drive, which eventually becomes Oak Island Drive. The name Yaupon Drive predates the merger, and the street name was used up to Seventy-ninth Street, the old city limits of Long Beach. At that point, Yaupon Drive became East Oak Island Drive. The takeaway here is that if you turn west at the stoplight, you enter Oak Island, regardless of the street name.

Access

The individual communities maintain the access locations on the island. Specific sites are noted following the descriptions of the communities below. Generally speaking, access is better the further west you drive; Caswell Beach is small, and access is very limited, serving primarily homeowners, rental visitors, and guests.

The North Carolina Baptist Assembly restricts visitation to its grounds, but travelers may drive through to view the remnants of the fort.

The North Carolina Wildlife Resources Commission maintains a fishing and boating access area on the Intracoastal Waterway at Oak Island. From Southport, follow NC 211 west to NC 133. Turn south on NC 133, turn left on SR 1101, and the area is down the road on the left. Parking is available, and there is no launch fee.

Information

For information, contact Southport/Oak Island Chamber of Commerce, 4841 Long Beach Road Southeast, Southport, NC 28461, 800-457-6964.

Web address: <www.southport-oakisland.com>

Caswell Beach

After crossing the Intracoastal Waterway onto Oak Island, NC 133 becomes SR 1100, locally known as Caswell Beach Drive, and begins a gradual curve east into the community of Caswell Beach. The town hall stands just inside the city limits. The salt sculpting of the vegetation visible from the road provides the earliest clue that the road will soon travel parallel to the oceanfront, behind the south-facing berm of Caswell Beach.

Caswell Beach is quiet, restful, and absolutely neutral about tourism, neither inviting nor uninviting. It makes few overtures to visitors. Probably more salt marsh than either upland or beachfront, Caswell Beach has no commercial district. The only concessions available are those at the country club on the north side of Caswell Beach Drive. Caswell Dunes, a private golf course on the north side of Caswell Beach Drive, and Oak Island Villas, on the beachfront shortly after the town hall, are the most visible developments within the corporate limits. With a year-round population of around 200, the community almost seems to be a confederation of cottages rather than an incorporated entity with municipal boundaries.

Caswell Beach Drive, running very close to the narrow 2.5 miles of beach, is the primary access for both the oceanfront and second-row homes in this municipality. The road passes a large channel cut through the salt marsh to the north, which is a cooling channel used by Carolina Power and Light's Brunswick plant, north of Southport. A pipe carrying cooling water from the plant passes under the road and continues 2 or 3 miles out to sea, where it discharges. Shortly past the channel, in the 700 block of Caswell Beach Drive, is a neighborhood access site on the oceanfront with parking.

The no-parking signs in Caswell Beach should be obeyed as some are in place to protect the town's underground drinking water lines. Ticketing is quick; besides, errantly parked cars have mired in the soft sands.

There are sharply peaked dunes and a widened nourished beach beyond. Caution should be taken when swimming at Caswell Beach. Oceanfront currents here can be dangerous because of the discharge effects of the Cape Fear River, especially if you choose to swim closer to the inlet.

Caswell Beach Drive passes the Oak Island Lighthouse and the U.S. Coast Guard Station at the east end of the island beyond the corporate limits of Caswell Beach. The road loops to an end before the gate and

attendant at the North Carolina Baptist Assembly Grounds.

Access

There is a neighborhood beach access site in the 700 block of Caswell Beach Drive with parking for around 80 cars, marked by the Coastal Area Management Act logo. Caswell Beach also has several neighborhood access locations in the west end of town.

Information

For information, contact the Southport/Oak Island Chamber of Commerce, 4841 Long Beach Road Southeast, Southport, NC 28461, 800-457-6964.

Web addresses: <www.caswellbeach.org>; <www.southport-oakisland.com>; <www.nccoastalmanagement.net/Access/sites.htm>

Oak Island Lighthouse and U.S. Coast Guard Station

Constructed in 1958, the Oak Island Lighthouse is the primary light for the Cape Fear River, replacing the old Cape Fear light on the eastern beach of Bald Head Island which, when first lighted in 1903, replaced "Old Baldy."

The Oak Island light is a statement of efficiency—tall enough to hold up the light, wide enough to accommodate enclosed stairs. The paint scheme is a curious banding, dark at the top to show against the daytime sky, white at the mid-

dle, and reddish-brown at the base. The light is 169 feet above ground, which is reached by ascending 132 steps within the tower. The light flashes four times every 10 seconds and has a range of 24 miles at sea. It is the brightest light in the United States.

What the light does not do, at least as romantically as its older counterparts elsewhere on the coast, is serve as a landmark. The very ornate Gothic gingerbread building across SR 1100 from the lighthouse is the old lightkeeper's quarters from an earlier era, which was auctioned, moved, and restored as a private residence.

There is a small parking area just downhill from the earthen berm supporting the lighthouse. A sign states that all visitors are to report to the officer of the day at the nearby U.S. Coast Guard Station, which has a twofold mission of search and rescue and navigation-aid maintenance from here to the South Carolina border. Although this base is not generally open to the public, group tours of the facility may be arranged in advance.

Behind the Coast Guard building is the dock serving the station's vessels, including a boat that tends the navigation equipment, a small boat for emergency calls, and a 44-foot motor lifeboat for rescue in severe seas.

Information

For information about scheduling a group tour of the U.S. Coast Guard Station, contact U.S Coast Guard, Oak Island Station, P.O. Box 1030,

Long Beach, NC 28465, 910-278-5592.

North Carolina Baptist Assembly Grounds/ Fort Caswell

Caswell Beach Drive ends at the gates to the grounds of the North Carolina Baptist Assembly, a coastal retreat that serves primarily as a summer camp for Baptist youths. The assembly includes the remnant earthworks of Fort Caswell, constructed in 1826 to guard the entrance to the Cape Fear River. The fort was seized in 1861 by Confederate forces and remained in their hands until taken in 1865 by conquering Union troops.

During the Spanish-American War and both World Wars, this point of land was again garrisoned and fortified against coastal invasion. The fortifications visible on the island are a mishmash of additions and improvements added to the brick portions of the works, which date from the Civil War. The concrete bunkers that dot the seaward side of the headland are vestiges of the twentieth-century fortifications.

Many of the structures in current use at the assembly grounds are refurbished U.S. Army barracks and outbuildings. The architecture is unmistakable, and the orderly layout of the buildings and grounds leeward of the revetments confirms the longtime importance of this piece of ground to military planners. From a deep-water channel overlook on the assembly grounds, you can see the maritime trade of the Cape Fear River that passes along the easternmost tip of the island to and from port in Wilmington.

Access

During the summer, the assembly grounds are reserved strictly for the youths attending camp and are closed to visitors. However, from Labor Day to Memorial Day, you may drive through the assembly grounds to visit the fort for a $2 fee, which covers the cost of insurance that the assembly must carry because of the extensive and possibly dangerous fortifications on the grounds. All visitors must report to the office, a clearly signed refurbished barracks. The assembly reserves the right to restrict visitation and requests that visitors be considerate and respectful of the property.

Information

For information, contact North Carolina Baptist Assembly, Oak Island, NC 28465, 910-278-9501.

Town of Oak Island

After crossing the bridge over the Intracoastal Waterway on NC 133, Long Beach Road becomes Caswell Beach Drive and comes to an intersection. Turn right, or west, at the light to enter Oak Island on Oak Island Drive, formerly Yaupon Drive. From the light, it is nearly 10 miles from to the loop at the western extreme of Oak Island, by way of West Beach Drive.

Approximately 3,500 people call Oak Island their primary community. Second and retirement homes are abundant. Between Memorial Day and Labor Day, the rental business is predominant; thereafter, the retirement-home market sets the tone of the community. The wooded half of the island, north of the Big Jim Davis Canal, is the preferred location for retirement homes.

Much of the community's commercial services are along East Oak Island Drive in the several blocks before and after the intersection with Fifty-eighth Street. Gas up if you are headed west. It's a very long way to the western edge of the island, and it is no location to run out of fuel.

The first mile of the community is the former town of Yaupon Beach, a small, nearly 100 percent residential town of modest cottages. Most of old Yaupon Beach is in the woods. The first impression is of an inland, wooded subdivision with sandy soil. The tree cover of the upland portion of the island extends quite nearly to the oceanfront. The original town limits were at Seventy-ninth Street, and the beach has always been sequestered. It is necessary to sidestep through the residential areas to get a view of the water, a glimpse really, from Ocean Drive. It is immediately obvious that this is not the place to come looking for a Myrtle Beach–type of vacation. It isn't going to happen. The neigh-

Sea Oats (*Uniola paniculata*)

Sand dunes are a movable story, a single frame in the cinema of wind, water, and sand. Sand dunes are ephemeral in geologic time, yet they seem formidable to us, well, at least insurmountable to the short legs of a three-year-old. Sand dunes are a barrier island's first line of defense against storms, standing as a malleable response line that reduces a storm's impact by making it expend energy before it pushes inland.

Nature builds sand dunes with wind, time, and available sand. People use sand fences or heavy equipment to create dunes faster. Both nature and people, however, rely on sea oats (*Uniola paniculata*), the rugged pioneering plant adapted to the worst combinations of salt, wind, and drought, to hold on to their castles of sand.

Sea oats are coarse, pale green grasses that form tough clumps that die back to the surface of the dune each year. The plants thrive on tough circumstances, growing at the back reach of the tides—a sun-seared, grainy, and restless piece of real estate. They stake a claim on the harshest, most demanding environment on a barrier island and then tenaciously hold on. It is a lonely, inhospitable outpost so severe that sea oats practically go it alone.

In mid- to late summer, sea oats send up stems more than 3 feet tall that bear clusters of oatlike seed spikelets. The resemblance to grain is obvious, hence the descriptive common name. These plumes ripen to a golden color in September—usually a glorious contrast to the polarized light of the cobalt skies of early autumn. The plants wave their flags against the sea, even as the traditional tropical storm season advances.

The true value of sea oats is not what you see above ground but what "grows on" beneath the surface. Spreading by underground stems, sea oats can colonize over the top of a dune. Meanwhile, below the surface sand, the plants drop anchor. Sea oats spread vigorously through the core of the dune by means of an insinuating root system. It literally threads through the mass of sand. If sand covers up a plant, it sprouts lateral roots and volunteers new foliage above the taller dune surface. The root network is plainly visible where waves have sliced off part of oat-covered dune to expose the interior. By this arrangement, sea oats and the dune can survive all but the most damaging storm surge.

Ironically, the storms that could destroy sea oats provide the means for their survival. Studies reveal that sea oats seeds germinate best after a period of soaking in salt water. In other words, waves harvest the seeds, wash them in the salt water, and spit them back up on the dunes again, a curiously macabre recycling of the plant and, in some instances, the very island itself.

Sea oats are so important to the beach that the law prohibits harvesting the strands—you may not pick sea oats at any time. As sea oats go, so go the dunes. As dunes go, so go the islands. As you go, leave the sea oats behind.

borhoods of former Yaupon Beach are as reticent as oceanfront neighborhoods can be and charming in a simple, unsophisticated way.

The houses settle amid live oak trees mixed with loblolly pines and the town's namesake tree, the yaupon holly. In the areas close to the beach, the island woods yield to lower salt-sheared shrubs that in turn roll down into shrubby, grassy plains in a natural line that, if unaltered, would almost melt into the wet sand beach. The sandy berm of Yaupon Beach has a very low profile, giving the impression that the ocean could just slide smoothly up and into the center of the forest with little resistance. The gradient of the beachfront is appealing for its gentleness.

Do let curiosity draw you into some of these first neighborhoods. Barbee Boulevard is a delightful residential street with a live oak–filled planting dividing the northbound and southbound traffic lanes. Any other left turn off of Oak Island Drive leads to the water as well and with the same low-key neighborhood scenery.

Parking is available at the beachfront at the end of each named north-south street as well as at selected signed locations. If you turn left on Womble Street, you will reach the parking area serving the Yaupon Beach Pier and the pavilion area, the center of the low-energy beach.

This first section of Oak Island serves as a prologue for the remaining nine miles. Oak Island Drive burrows deeper into the island's length and carries the burden of being the commercial center for the island. It is easy to become so intent on getting to the beach, which is several blocks south of Oak Island Drive, that overlooking the larger portion of the island to the north is commonplace. The north side is all neighborhoods of numbered, straight-shot streets that go directly to the Intracoastal Waterway. One block from the waterway, Yacht Drive runs nearly the full length of the island.

One delightful side trip is to the Oak Island Memorial Waterway Park at Fifty-second Street and Yacht Drive, a civic garden in a wooded setting with a contemplative spirit. There is the Dot Kelly Memorial Butterfly Garden and an enlightening nature walk that introduces the trees of Oak Island. The park has restrooms and a boardwalk to a sitting area in the Intracoastal Waterway.

Here's a "heads up." Although every north-south street in the western half of the town leads to the ocean, don't try to use this direct approach between Seventy-ninth and Fifty-eighth Streets. Although these streets dead-end close to the water and there is parking, there is no connector to the adjacent block. You have to return to Oak Island Drive to reach the next street.

Fortune changes at Fifty-eighth Street Southeast, however. It goes directly to the water and intersects with the eastern end of Beach Drive, which continues to the southwestern end of the town at a wonderful parking turnout at South Lynn.

When you reach the water at Fifty-eighth Street, you will find the heart of this single-family residential beach community. There are few hotels and motels in Oak Island, and few commercial diversions from the experience of salt water and sand. Even the surf seems lazy. The oceanfront is a long beach strand of private cottages, with few "collecting spots," interrupted only by two fishing piers, the Ocean Crest Pier and the Long Beach Pier.

Generally speaking, ample beach access parking is provided for visitors, and most visitors secure access by weekly rental within walking distance of the wet sand beach. Oak Island has had a tough time with erosion and has had to turn to beach nourishment several times to stem the erosion rate and to actually provide sufficient beach width for nesting sea turtles.

Every third street from Fifty-eighth to Fortieth Street connects Oak Island Drive and Beach Drive. The intervening streets stop at East Pelican Drive, parallel to the beach inland. The town hall is on East Oak Island Drive, at the Forty-sixth Street intersection. There is a large recreational-vehicle parking area nearby and a major regional beach access parking area at the oceanfront terminus of Forty-sixth Street Southeast.

Fortieth Street is at the east end of the headwaters of the Big Jim Davis Canal, which divides the remainder of the island into a sandy barrier beach to the south and a wooded landmass to the north, separated from the mainland by the Intracoastal Waterway. You cannot cross the canal by automobile for another 40 blocks, until Middleton Avenue, where East Oak Island Drive changes to West Oak Island Drive before continuing for another 30 blocks.

Oak Island does provide a delightful walkway over the canal, accessible from Nineteenth Place East on the south shore of the canal and Twentieth Street Northeast on the north shore. There are several parking places along the residential streets, and a gazebo provides shade. The scenic walkway over the salt marsh and tidal creek displays a range of vegetation, beginning with a live oak and pine forest with a wax myrtle understory and grading through vegetation with increasing salt and water tolerance to the spartina marsh. Redwing blackbirds flit through the marsh grasses and shrubs, while ghost crabs scurry across the mud flats of the marsh. At low tide, oyster reefs are exposed, and mullet fingerlings swirl beneath the shadows cast by the walkway.

Further west, at Third Street Southeast, next to the Oak Island Recreation Center, which faces East Oak Island Drive, is the Tidal Way Trails Park. The park has a small boardwalk and a canoe-launching site on the canal with a gazebo and picnic tables. This is one of the few designated canoe-launching sites on the entire coast and allows easy launching for canoes and kayaks only.

The last convenient route to the beach is Middleton Avenue, which crosses to Beach Drive. Both east and west of Middleton Avenue, the streets perpendicular to the oceanfront are numbered erratically in increasing value, beginning with Second Place West to Sixtieth Place West toward Lockwoods Folly Inlet and Third Place East toward the town line. You can continue along Oak Island Drive until reaching Robin Schuster Park, a recreational facility at the western end of the island on the Intracoastal Waterway.

At the west end of the island, West Beach Drive forks in an ex-tensive development. Follow the left fork until the parking turn-out. This glorious accessway leads to the exquisite beaches of the island's west end. There is a magnificent dune field and a $1/2$-mile walk to the waters of the inlet. This little getaway has an extensive guided walk with interpretive plaques telling of the dune ecosystem. The paths have wooden lattice spread over them and are moderately accessible for wheelchairs.

Access

The largest parking area is at the pavilion at Womble Street and Ocean Drive.

The following north-south streets have access points: McGlamery Street, Sellers Street, Mercer Street, Norton Street, Trott Street, Keziah Street, Barbee Boulevard, Sherril Street, and Crowell Street.

Some parking for beach visitors may be available at the Yaupon Beach Pier on Womble Street. Check with the owner before you park there.

Oak Island has a major regional access area at the end of Forty-sixth Street, with 43 parking spaces, restrooms, a gazebo, and two dune crossovers.

There are many neighborhood access points as well. The following streets have dune cross-overs and parking: Seventy-ninth, Seventy-eighth, Seventy-sixth, Seventy-fourth, Seventy-second, Seventy-first, Seventieth, Sixty-ninth, Sixty-fourth, Fifty-eighth, Fifty-fifth, Fifty-second, Forty-ninth, Forty-third, Twenty-fifth Place East, Fifty-ninth Place East, Sixteenth Place East, Fourteenth Place East, Third Place East, South Middleton Avenue, Fifth Place West, Seventh Place West, Tenth Place West, Thirteenth Place West, Twentieth Place West, Twenty-third Place West, Twenty-seventh Place West, Thirtieth Place West, and Thirty-third Place West.

Paved bikeways along Oak Island Drive and Beach Drive have eased car/pedestrian/bicycle conflicts.

Handicapped Access

Oak Island will loan a beach wheelchair with advance notice. Call the recreation center at 910-278-5518.

The Southwinds Motel also has a beach wheelchair for its guests. Call 910-278-5442.

The regional access site at Forty-sixth Street is fully accessible for the handicapped, with accessible restrooms as well.

Information

For information, contact Southport/Oak Island Chamber of Commerce, 4841 Long Beach Road Southeast, Southport, NC 28461, 800-457-6964.

Web addresses: <www.oakisland nc.com>; <www.southport-oak island.com>; <www.nccoastalman agement.net/Access/sites.htm>

Green Swamp/Boiling Spring Lakes Preserve

To the untrained eye, the forests adjacent to NC 211 and NC 87 may appear like so much scruffy pine forest or swamp wasteland, when in fact these "throwaway" woods are some of the most botanically diverse wild lands in the state. The North Carolina chapter of the Nature Conservancy has two extraordinary preserves in Brunswick County that safeguard portions of these unique ecosystems.

North from Supply off of NC 211, Green Swamp is a 15,552-acre expanse of pine savanna and upland evergreen shrub bog, designated a National Natural Landmark by the U.S. Department of the Interior.

Once more than 200,000 acres, Green Swamp has been timbered, drained, and put to the plow, but in the 1970s, a major landowner, the Federal Paperboard Company of New York, donated nearly 14,000 acres to the Nature Conservancy, which has expanded its holdings to the current number of acres. What looks barren and unpromising to the eye is actually one of the richest plant habitats in the state, and it harbors the greatest number of carnivorous plants found in the country. The density and diversity of plant species within the swamp rank it as one of the finest unaltered habitats in the state. Ecologists have mapped at least two distinct types of pocosin here, differentiated by their various understory and tree species mix and by the amount of sphagnum moss.

This is a virtually roadless tract of land and just plain difficult to move around in. A topographic map shows the natural crown in the land, nearly like a ridge, that is north of Supply. The natural drainage moves away from the crowning earth. The permeated nature of the surface made road building and farming difficult.

In the town of Boiling Springs Lakes are the 5,000-plus acres of the Boiling Springs Lakes Preserve, co-managed by the North Carolina chapter of the Nature Conservancy and the Plant Conservation Program of the North Carolina Department of Agriculture.

An interpretive trail leads through a sample of this cross section of Brunswick County ecosystems that includes the xeric sandhill community (which may be familiar from the Pinehurst/Southern Pines area), Pond Pine Woodland community, and the Pocosin community. Each is characterized by different soils, moisture levels in the soils, and the unique plant and animal associations that adapt to those conditions.

A self-guided flyer keyed to the plant communities explains their importance as one moves along the trail. Because the trail exhibits so many plant associations typically found in Brunswick County, it offers one of the best opportunities to easily see and learn about them at your own pace and schedule.

Access

There is a parking area for Green Swamp 5 miles north of Supply on US 211. The North Carolina Nature Conservancy will be restricting access periodically to protect the habitat. Contact the southeastern office in advance to see about visitation or field trips. Boiling Spring Lakes Nature Preserve is off of NC 87 in Boiling Spring Lakes. The trail begins at the community center, which is on the south side of the lake in the community of Boiling Spring Lakes.

Information

For information, contact the Nature Conservancy Southeast Coastal Plain Office, Building 4, Unit E, 2725 Old Wrightsboro Road, Wilmington, NC 28405, 910-762-6277; or North Carolina Nature Conservancy, One University Place, Suite 290, 4705 University Drive, Durham, NC 27707, 919-403-8558.

Web address: <www.tnc.org/northcarolina>

Lockwoods Folly Inlet

Lockwoods Folly Inlet, the outlet of the Lockwoods Folly River, separates Holden Beach and Oak Island. The dark tannic river is considered by boating enthusiasts to be one of the most scenic tidewater rivers in the state. The slowly flowing waters thread through a maze of cypress and live oak trees draped by Spanish moss.

The river originates west of Boiling Spring Lakes in Brunswick County and flows northwest before looping underneath NC 211 a few miles east of Supply. The river you cross at this point does not draw much attention.

In the summer of 2004, shoaling in the inlet threatened navigation along the Intracoastal Waterway, which passes behind Oak Island, routes through the northern edge of the inlet, and then resumes its protected passage north of Holden Beach. Sandbars had reduced the depth to three feet. Without reliable funding for the U.S. Army Corps of Engineers, who is responsible for maintaining the navigable depth of the waterway, its usefulness as a commercial outlet is in jeopardy.

Access

Access to the river and the inlet is at Sunset Harbor, on the east bank of the river on the mainland.

Shallotte

Shallotte has grown to become the commercial hub of southern Brunswick County and now the gateway town for the burgeoning beach resort and golf course retirement communities nearby. Shallotte once served as the central shopping area for the three island communities of Holden Beach, Ocean Isle Beach, and Sunset Beach. The recent growth in those communities has led to new, more convenient locations on the mainland for stores and services, thus ending vacationers' dependency on Shallotte retailers. Several national chain hotels have accommodations here.

The bypass of US 17 around Shallotte does speed traffic if you are heading north or south on that roadway. The most direct way to Holden Beach and Ocean Isle

Beach still goes through Shallotte, however. Once past the community's commercially crowded main road, the routes to the beaches, NC 130 to Holden Beach and NC 179 to Ocean Isle, lead past the once-rural farmland that in the pre–golf course community era, was responsible for the fine fresh produce grown in the county. The roadside markets, should you see one, are good sources for seasonal vegetables and, in summer, fresh shrimp.

Information

For information, contact the North Carolina Brunswick Islands Chamber of Commerce, P.O. Box 1186, Shallotte, NC 28549, 800-795-7263, 910-754-6644.

Web address: <www.ncbrunswick.com>

Holden Beach

Holden Beach is across Lockwoods Folly Inlet from Oak Island, the next island west and the most easterly of the south Brunswick island group of Holden Beach, Ocean Isle Beach, and Sunset Beach. The quickest way to reach Holden Beach from Oak Island is to wade across Lockwoods Folly Inlet; the more conventional way means a looping roundabout drive through Supply and picking up NC 130 off of US 17 at Shallotte. Miss the turns (or the secreted signs) and you'll learn the secret of these westernmost islands in Brunswick County—they're more than slightly out of the way and out of the main-

stream. I estimate they are about twenty-five years' "relaxed," and that is a strong part of the appeal of Holden Beach.

In summer, Oak Island will swell with close to 25,000, visitors; Holden Beach on the other hand brims full but never seems so tightly packed. About 900 folks call the nearly 9-mile-long island home year-round, making it the most populated island in the trio. In summer, the population will grow to 10,000. Visitors have picked well: in 2004 *National Geographic Traveler* picked Holden Beach as one of its top family beaches in the country.

There is a grand view of the island from the high-rise bridge crossing the Intracoastal Waterway that replaced the old drawbridge, which had replaced a ferry. The overwhelming perception is of a spacious island resort with plenty of beach to go around and plenty of island to enjoy. Driving the island reinforces the view—it is a quiet cottage beach. Sure, there is a touch of grand and gaudy at the island's eastern and western extremes, but it is mostly a low-key, quiet beach. In the past, promotional literature proudly proclaimed, "You won't find much to do except swim, fish, and sunbathe." There's nothing wrong with that, and there's nothing much on the island to change that impression.

It's not void of alternate ways to vacation: There's a Surfside Pavilion, a video game amusement center with a county fair midway flavor, and there's also a pier. You

	Fee	Parking	Restrooms	Lifeguard	Camping	Showers	Beach Access	Hiking	Trail	Handicapped	Boating	ORV Access	Fishing	Programs	Historic	Sand Beach	Dunes	Upland	Wetland
Regional Access: Holden Beach	•	•				•	•			•			•			•			
Ocean Isle Beach		•					•						•			•	•		
Sunset Beach		•					•				•		•			•	•		

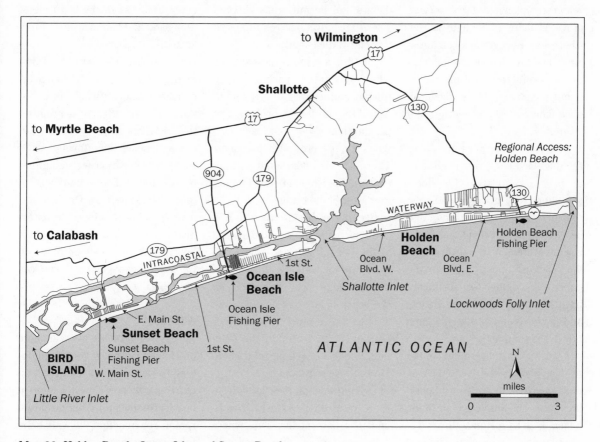

Map 29. Holden Beach, Ocean Isle, and Sunset Beach

walk the pier, you fish, you sunbathe—Holden Beach is uncomplicated this way.

The high-rise bridge assured both easy access and evacuation and stimulated second-home construction somewhat. It certainly has yet to bring any significantly tall or mid-rise buildings, hotels, or motels to the island. Holden Beach remains almost exclusively single-family cottages for rent or sale.

Holden Beach happens to have an unmatched history as a family beach. In 1756 Benjamin Holden purchased 100 acres between Lockwoods Folly Inlet and another closed inlet. Most of the island, parts of which were a commercial fishing center in the early twentieth century, has been in the family ever since. The digging of the Intracoastal Waterway severed Holden Beach completely from the mainland, and it also slowed development plans. A ferry service provided more immediate access (there is still a Ferry Road on the island), and this in turn was followed by a drawbridge. Since the 1950s, family members have slowly developed their real estate holdings into a summer resort.

Most of the services are along the mainland causeway leading to the bridge. There are tackle shops, gift shops, dry goods merchants, restaurants, sundry stores, and service stations. Along the Intracoastal Waterway are several seafood-packing houses open to the public. A number of shrimpers have homeport in Holden Beach, and shrimp is almost always a good buy in the summer season.

From the island terminus of the bridge, it is a short drive to the east end, where there are several parking places and ample access to the beach. Beach erosion at this end of the island threatens several homes, and efforts were made in the past to armor the headland of the island against the migration of Lockwoods Folly Inlet by constructing a bulkhead. If you are fortunate enough to secure one of the parking spots in the 300 block of North McCray Street, you can take advan-

tage of the solitude of the point. It is popular for bathers and surf fishermen who work the tidal changes for flounder and other fish. The inlet current is modest; strong swimmers need not fear the water here. Plentiful shoaling of the inlet and the gentle beach gradient create tidal pools that are excellent for younger children. At low tide, sand dollars and hermit crabs abound. There are no public restrooms at this end of the island.

There is a regional access area with substantial parking, restrooms, and cold showers underneath the high-rise bridge. The parking is a short walk from designated dune crossover locations. There are also additional parking places at the Holden Beach Fishing Pier, west of the bridge.

Because of beach erosion, Holden Beach has constructed a berm at the oceanfront, and there is a $500 fine for walking on the sand dunes. Dogs are prohibited on the beach from 9 A.M. to 5 P.M. and at other times must be leashed or restrained. In summer, the community has a beach patrol that enforces these regulations.

Driving west on the island, from the central business area, the island has several locations where it is very narrow and backed with marsh. There are also places where the island widens, and homes are subdivided in a grid of lots accordingly. Access is limited in these higher-density areas. If you do not intend to rent on the oceanfront, be sure to inquire about the exact distance to walk to the nearest pub-

lic path to the beach. There will be some cottages where access is annoyingly far away and requires walking along the island's main road to reach a crossover.

The west end of Holden Beach is closed to the public, and there is only limited access along West Ocean Boulevard until the guardhouse is reached. The guardhouse cuts off access to the last mile of the island and land access to Shallotte Inlet.

In 2004 Dr. Stephen P. Leatherman, also known as "Dr. Beach," certified Holden Beach as a National Healthy Beach, a program that requires monthly water testing and beach monitoring, along with an application fee submitted by the town. The voluntary program, sponsored by Dr. Leatherman, is being developed to recognize communities that keep their beaches in tip-top shape by using the best management practices available.

Access

Access for vehicles is inadequate on Holden Beach. If you do not intend to rent on the oceanfront, inquire exactly how close the nearest beach crossover is to your proposed rental. You may find the walk to be too inconvenient.

There is no parking on Ocean Boulevard, the main street parallel to the ocean. You may park on side streets, but your vehicle must be completely off of the pavement. Permission of the adjacent property owner is advised.

There is a regional access area

Water in Orbit

Why, if waves keep marching toward you at the beach, does the water not slosh up into the dunes? This simple question has a charmingly simple answer. While waves move through water horizontally, the actual water molecules move very little. Passing waves move floating objects back and forth, up and down, but never really transport them very far. If you could see seaweed swaying with passing wave action, you could readily observe this.

Waves are motion—energy—passing through a medium—the ocean. The actual particles of water in a wave move in a circular orbit, as shown in the diagram. This circular pattern of water particle movement was first observed by 1802 by German Franz Gerstner.

As a wave approaches a droplet, it carries the droplet in the direction of transport along with the crest of the wave. Then the trough of the wave follows, and the droplet moves against the direction of the wave for almost the same horizontal distance. During the swell, of course, the droplet is elevated and subsequently "dropped" as the swell passes and the trough approaches. In fact, the water particle returns almost to its original position.

The diameter of the circle is, of course, equal to the height of the wave. When a wave approaches shore, there is insufficient room for particles to make their circular path. The orbit flattens, and the droplets tarry at the top of the swell, pushed higher and ever forward with no support beneath them. The circle is broken, and the wave breaks on the sand.

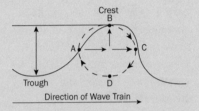

---

under the high-rise bridge, with 90 parking spaces, restrooms, cold showers, and dune crossovers a short walk away.

There is also a large parking area at the east end of the island in the 300 block of McCray Street, which has parking for 50 cars.

There are smaller parking locations and dune crossover sites at the south end of Heritage Harbor, Dream Harbor, and Colonial Beach Streets. Other designated access locations are at Avenue D, Avenue C, Avenue B, Avenue A, Holden Street, and Ferry Road.

Handicapped Access

Holden Beach will loan a beach wheelchair with advance notice. Call the town hall at 910-842-6488.

The regional access facility under the bridge, including the restrooms, is accessible to handicapped travelers.

Information

For information, contact North Carolina Brunswick Islands Chamber of Commerce, P.O. Box 1186, Shallotte, NC 28549, 800-795-7263, 910-754-6644.

Web addresses: <www.hbtownhall.com>; <www.ncbrunswick. com>; <www.nccoastalmanagement.net/Access/sites.htm>

Ocean Isle Beach

Ocean Isle Beach fits between Holden Beach and Sunset Beach in location and in length. It is also different in mood and atmosphere.

The first glimpse of the island, from the high-rise Odell Williamson Bridge that crosses the Intracoastal Waterway, is stark, even jarring. There is very little to soften the view of rooftops from the crest of the bridge, and there are a lot of houses on Ocean Isle Beach. The island is packed tight from a retirement and second-home building boom, especially in its middle third where finger canals protrude into the island's interior. The canals provide boating access to the Intracoastal Waterway for canal-fronting properties.

Once you reach beach level at First Street, the main road behind the first row of cottages, the first impression fades. Ocean Isle Beach has a neat, tidy central district featuring a waterslide, a splendid nature museum, and some small conveniences. Move away from the center of town, and the island becomes more welcoming, and the houses are not so tightly packed as they seemed from the bridge-top vantage point.

The community has some nice touches: there are sidewalks parallel to the beachfront along East First Street, an unusual urban element in a small vacation island. It always seems busy with joggers, walkers, and families strolling with children. Odell Williamson, who developed the island following his purchase after World War II, achieved a goal of making it a family destination. The fishing pier is squarely at the end of Causeway Drive. One block east is the Museum of Coastal Carolina, an excellent facility that concentrates on the natural history of North and South Carolina.

The island has the same east-west orientation as its neighbors and a gentle tan-all-day, south-facing beach. Ocean Isle Beach has a gentle gradient for most of its length that rises abruptly to a steep dune line that has been chiseled by the sea. It is an appealing, wide beach that, like many others in this part of Brunswick County, must contend with the problems of chronic erosion, particularly in mid-island. There have been collateral costs to the loss of stable dry sand beach. Ocean Isle Beach has an active sea turtle monitoring program, but these seasonal nesters have been hard-pressed to find suitable nesting sites above the high tide mark. In the early years of this century, beach nourishment projects restored sand in the eroded areas and provided the island an opportunity to establish anew a dune line landward of the high tide mark and to stabilize it with plantings.

The east end is the major playground for Ocean Isle Beach. There are numerous places to park, many that are not officially marked but that are obvious locations to pull completely off the road. Shallotte Inlet is intent on migrating west, and the island is fighting a wearying, never-ending battle with erosion as the inlet works its way down the island.

First Street stops dramatically at High Point and state maintenance ends, which indicates the difficulty of this end of the island. To continue east, it is necessary to move one block inland to Second Street, head east again; but it in turn ends abruptly at Shallotte Road, and it is necessary to move another block inland to Third Street, which is being undermined. This end of the island is being resolutely carved. During the September storms of 2004, the sea pulled the sand from beneath some of the homes, which were then condemned.

There are several distinct rows of pilings in the inlet area that are the remnants of failed headwalls or groins. Beyond these, there are overwash flats. The beach gradient is very flat, and it makes it a reasonably safe place for swimming. In summer, this end is covered with seashellers, fishermen, and children. Not surprisingly, the parking spaces at this end of the island are taken quickly.

The west end of the island has taller buildings—several mid-rise condominium towers, for example. The extreme west end is owned privately by Ocean Isle West, which prohibits land access to the inlet. There are both single-family detached cottages and condominiums for rent in this development.

Ocean Isle Beach approaches parking with an up-front, practical approach. There are marked places to park about every six blocks at the ends of streets running toward the ocean. And, like elsewhere, the ones closest to the center of town fill up first. Police officials at the town hall point out that even on the most crowded days a few spaces are usually open at the lots at the east end of the island.

In addition to serving residents, the artificial canals dredged into the soundside of the island provide harbor for a number of charter and head-boat fishing operations. The easy access to open water through Tubbs Inlet to the west or Shallotte Inlet to the east makes the charter and head-boat fishing fleets of Ocean Isle Beach a major vacation attraction.

Access

Your first opportunity to park is just as you arrive on NC 904 across the causeway at a central parking location directly ahead. There may be a charge.

The following streets have neighborhood access sites: Monroe Street, Concord Street, Newport Street, Raeford Street, Leland Street, Goldsboro Street, Chadbourn Street, Winnabow Street, Greensboro Street, and Beaufort Street.

Use common sense about parking in unmarked locations: do not block drives, sidewalks, flower beds, or side streets, and pull completely off the pavement. Dune crossovers are located at the south ends of High Point Street, Shelby Street, and Driftwood Drive.

Handicapped Access

Ocean Isle Beach will loan a beach wheelchair with advance notice. Call the police department at 910-579-4221.

Information

For information, contact North Carolina Brunswick Islands Chamber of Commerce, P.O. Box 1186, Shallotte, NC 28549, 800-795-7263, 910-754-6644.

Web addresses: <www.oibgov. com>; <www.ncbrunswick.com>; <www.nccoastalmanagement.net/ Access/sites.htm>

Sunset Beach

The sun has set on the drawbridge days at this delightful, low-key resort island. It is no longer a question of if, but when a new bridge, tall enough to permit boats to pass beneath, will replace the anachronistic traffic-clogging crossing over the Intracoastal Waterway. For years, the drawbridge, and the simpler times it represents, has been a symbol of what is different about Sunset Beach, which is that it is a simpler place, and it is growing—more beach.

The drawbridge juxtaposed two different worlds and was an apt transition between them. West of the drawbridge on the mainland, just a few miles along NC 179, is the entrance to Sea Trail Golf Resort and Conference Center, one of several golf-resort retirement developments in the neighborhood and in the town limits. The big contrast is that of the grasses—manicured, hybrid-grass fairways on one side of bridge, an expanse of needle rush and black rush on the other.

The drawbridge causeway provides one of the more intimate and truly delightful crossings along the coast. It ranks with the ferry rides on the Outer Banks in the way that it firmly underlines the change from mainland to island. Crossing to Sunset is a change in worlds, and the causeway serves as a reminder. The replacement bridge, when it comes, will be more efficient, but its elevated construction will eliminate the gradual entry onto the island provided by the causeway. Binoculars can be handy when crossing the causeway; there are wide spots where it possible to pull off and watch bird life in the marsh.

How about this for disorienting geographic trivia: Sunset Beach, the westernmost barrier island in North Carolina, is nearly due south of Raleigh. It floats in its own little world, and while the mainland of Brunswick County has gone to golf in a big, big way, Sunset Beach basks nonchalantly in the sun as its exquisite beach grows wider and wider. Nature is steadily *adding* sand to the 3-mile-long island. Today some "beachfront" houses are 600 feet away from the water behind an undulating field of dunes.

While this is generally true of the entire island, it is especially true of the portion west of the fishing pier. This end of the island is blessed with one of the widest dune zones in all of North Carolina. Elevated boardwalks, leading from public parking to the beach, traverse the impressive field providing an excellent vantage point for studying an example of an important ecological niche of barrier islands.

At one time, when you looked west from this access point, you could see the trickle of a tidal creek that was Mad Inlet. Beyond it was about 167 acres of high ground named Bird Island. Before Hurricane Bonnie in 1999 closed Mad In-

Sunset Beach has a gazebo-by-the-sea at its public accessway serving the oceanfront. Courtesy of the author.

let and Bird Island became a state natural area, it was a special sort of place for Sunset residents and guests.

At the west end, the town has constructed a boardwalk, which makes a steep ascent over the primary dune line. The beach has a gentle gradient, and the quality of the beach experience is paralleled in the state only by the most remote lengths of Outer Banks beachfront and the jewel of Hammocks Beach State Park in Onslow County. There is not quite as much isolation on Sunset, but there is plenty of peace and quiet. The oceanfront streets are so distant from the beach that there are no traffic sounds—no sounds at all really except those of the edge of the sea.

The homeowners of Sunset Beach displayed an extraordinary sensitivity to the dunes when building. In addition, for more than thirty years, the beach has been advancing out to sea. The fact that the island is growing, along with the fact that there are only 300 residents who live here full-time, makes Sunset Beach one of the least crowded of the Brunswick islands.

Access

There is all-day parking at the Walt and Doris, Inc., Sunset Pier for $5. The pier is just west of the south end of Sunset Boulevard.

The Fortieth Street access location has a dune crossover.

There are 25 unimproved access points at First through Eleventh Street and Twenty-seventh through Fortieth Street. Parking is permitted at all access locations even though no parking spaces are specifically provided.

The North Carolina Wildlife Resources Commission maintains a fishing and boating access area on the Intracoastal Waterway near Sunset Beach, at the end of Park Road, $1/2$ mile west from the junction of NC 904 and NC 179, in the Sea Trail development. Parking is available, and there is no launch fee.

Handicapped Access

Sunset Beach will loan a beach wheelchair with advance notice. Call the town hall at 910-579-3808.

Information

For information, contact North Carolina Brunswick Islands Chamber of Commerce, P.O. Box 1186, Shallotte, NC 28549, 800-795-7263, 910-754-6644.

Web addresses: <www.ncbrunswick.com>; <www.nccoastalmanagement.net/Access/sites.htm>

Bird Island

I don't know whether you've ever strolled to Bird Island to drop a note in the Kindred Spirit mailbox, but it's a trip worth making. Bird Island has just short of a mile of beachfront extending south from Sunset Beach. Beach walkers will head south, and after crossing the low flats of filled-in Mad Inlet, begin to look toward the dunes. There, nestled amid beach grass and sea oats is a simple mailbox and a board that serves as a bench. Inside the mailbox are paper and pen and opportunity to read some of the most touching and thoughtful messages of kindred spirits who have visited before you.

The Kindred Spirit is all the better now that Bird Island belongs to all.

Bird Island, with its thickly knitted forest and extensive sand flats and dunes, was the last privately owned barrier beach in North Carolina. Little River Inlet borders it to the southwest—in fact, part of the property is in South Carolina —and its northern neighbor is Sunset Beach. In 2002 the state of North Carolina completed purchase of Bird Island from the Price family in Greensboro. After a long struggle for preservation, the last barrier island on North Carolina's coast, nearly 1,200 acres of upland, dunes, flats, and marsh, has become a part of the North Carolina Coastal Reserve.

It is a short walk on lovely beach, terminating just before the jetty that protects the Little River Inlet.

Although the island was the starting point for the 1735 survey line dividing North and South Carolina, the island's most recent history adds color to this passive preserve.

"The idea of owning my own island appealed to me," Greensboro resident Ralph Clay Price explained long ago about his purchase of Bird Island. Price, son of Julian Price, the driving force behind the Jefferson-Pilot Corporation, had the money and the dream, and so, in the late 1950s, sight unseen, he purchased a 1,150-acre island, the most southern of all North Carolina barriers. He then built a bridge to the island from Sunset Beach, crossing the shallow creek known as Mad Inlet. The island has been without access since the 1960s when arsonists burned the bridge that Price built. The arsonists also spread tacks in the road to slow fire trucks rushing to the conflagration. The Price family never reconstructed the bridge. When Ralph Price died in 1987, he left the island to his wife.

In early 1992 Mrs. Price initiated new development plans for the island and applied for a permit to the Division of Coastal Management to rebuild the bridge to the island. This began a struggle between preservationists and the family over the fate of the island. In 2002 North Carolina completed the purchase of the property.

Access

Public access is primarily via the ocean beach on the Sunset Beach side, while boats may land on the beach associated with Little River Inlet on the South Carolina side.

Web address: <www.ncnerr. org>

Calabash

I have this personal routine about dining in Calabash: regardless of where I eat, I buy hush puppies from Beck's Seafood. The natty restaurant at the top of the street leading to the river offers delicious food, but the hush puppies, to my taste, cross to a new dimension. I'm good for a dozen a carry-out no matter when or where I eat.

Everybody probably knows by now that Calabash is synonymous with seafood dining, indulgence, or maybe overindulgence. The traditional Calabash seafood is lightly breaded, quickly deep-fried, bountifully served, and nominally priced. Dinners come with hush puppies, sweet iced tea, coleslaw, and a potato; the style of cooking has caught on because, frankly, it is tasty. Calabash is a town and an event. In the 1940s it was little more than a small fishing community where two local families, the Becks and the Colemans, held outdoor oyster roasts for folks. The logical extension of the outdoor feast was an indoor restaurant, and the two families eventually opened rival restaurants, but there was only congenial competition because the restaurateurs were (and still are) related.

The Calabash reputation spread by word of mouth, and one nationally known entertainer took a fancy to one of the restaurants and to the young woman in charge. Though flattered by the attention, she would not give her name. The good-natured entertainer said he would make her famous anyway. Thus, Jimmy Durante's enigmatic close, "Good night Mrs. Calabash, wherever you are."

Today, it really does not matter which family started the restaurant challenge; more than twenty restaurants here capitalize on the national reputation that Calabash developed in late 1960s and 1970s.

There is one turn in town, and it goes down to the banks of Calabash Creek. There, the shinier restaurant facades of NC 179 give way to the more reserved dockside settings in the older part of the community. The closer you get to the water, the closer you get to a taste of old Calabash. You might be confused about the multiple uses of old and original, but it is simple. Straight ahead on River Road is the Coleman's Original Calabash Restaurant, now run by the third generation of the original family. Beck's Seafood, at the top of River Road, is a contemporary of (and related by marriage to) the Old Origi-

nal. Down by the water, the Dockside Seafood Restaurant is another of the earlier restaurants.

You can walk out on the docks or wander into a seafood market and load up a cooler for the ride home. It feels like a tidewater fishing community, where everybody is a captain. You hardly even notice that you can see golf carts across the creek.

I have enjoyed delicious meals in the Dockside, Coleman's Original, Beck's, and the Seafood Hut. Truthfully, if you like Calabash-style cooking, you could fall off the back of a boat here and land a good seafood dinner. And you will be joining nearly one million diners a year. So come early, or you'll leave late.

Handicapped Access

Handicapped access varies with the individual enterprise, but nearly half of the restaurants have the entire dining area on one floor with fully accessible entrances. Restroom accessibility is limited.

Information

For information, contact North Carolina Brunswick Islands Chamber of Commerce, P.O. Box 1186, Shallotte, NC 28549, 800-795-7263, 910-754-6644.

Web addresses: <www.ncbruns wick.com>; <www.townofcalabash nc.com>

With Mollusk Aforethought

That glimmer of color in the sand, the rounded form emerging from the foam of a wave, is an abandoned home. For every shell that whispers sea sounds in our ears, there is another inspiring words of wonder in our minds. Some of the most creative architects I know are mollusks.

A mollusk is a soft-bodied creature that comes in six basic body styles, or classes. Three of those body styles produce the shells that we might reasonably expect to find on North Carolina beaches. Two mollusk classes, the Gastropoda, or snails, and the Pelecypoda, or bivalves, have the most species by far and generate nearly all of the shells. (The tusk shells, members of another class, are infrequently found.) The snails have one-piece shells with one opening; the bivalves are hinged shells such as oysters, clams, coquinas, and scallops.

A shell is first and foremost armor, developed to protect a mollusk's soft body parts. (Other shell-less mollusks such as squids and slugs have other survival strategies.) Why such differences in design and pattern? Probably in response to the environment in which the creature lives and perhaps whimsy—why should there not be variety for its own sake?

Most important, each different shell is a different creature—the shell is both the visual cue and de-fining taxonomy for creatures infrequently seen and morphologically very similar when caught outside their homes. In other words, you must judge a snail by its cover.

A shell's shape, color, and pattern of ornamentation provide clues about where the creature lives. Mollusks with ornately structured shells (murex, for example) live in calmer, lower-energy waters where waves won't damage the shell's protuberances. The streamlined channel whelk (which reminds me of the Guggenheim Museum) is aptly named for its high-energy home turf, where its smooth shell contours offer minimal resistance to wave action. Offshore from the churning barrier islands, below the effective level of daily wave action at the seafloor, more ornamentally inclined shell builders find water-motion levels compatible with their shell construction and are likely to flourish undamaged.

The ocean is tough on shells that are exposed to its tumbling action and to the lapidary effect of sand, which in North Carolina is composed of continental shelf sand and shell debris. A shell cannot resist the grinding effect, and, especially with no creature inside to replenish the worn surfaces and keep the shell anchored or moving upright, it weathers rapidly. Even the durable, thick-walled helmet shell and whelks can be tumbled to pieces in as few as three weeks. Bright shells, vibrant with color and comparatively unscathed, are probably very recently abandoned. A lingering fetid odor provides the ripest clue of recent abandonment.

Like any other creature, every mollusk adapts to a particular ocean environment. The type of seafloor, the water temperature, wave action, and other creatures that share the neighborhood play a part in which species will live successfully. Here's a generality to this point: sandy or muddy ocean bottoms give bivalves a break because they can burrow; harder seafloors typically support larger numbers of snails, which are mobile.

The evolutionary change that turned a two-piece fortress into a one-piece armored personnel carrier set some mollusks in motion. Snails inch across the ocean floor on their "foot," grazing or hunting less agile bivalves. Bivalves, on the other hand, must hide through burrowing or coloration. Bivalves are more general feeders; snails are specialty diners, and some, such as the Atlantic oyster drill, are efficient enough at feeding on their prey that they threaten oyster populations.

The Molluscan lifestyle produces extraordinary architecture, from humble bungalow to exuberant gingerbread Gothic, each of which, although resembling the neighbors, has a "personal" touch. Every shell creature takes a basic "floor plan" that includes the shape of the shell, the general color scheme, and the pattern of coloration and then does a personal home makeover. The individualization is akin to painting the trim on a house.

The workhorse for each shell-producing mollusk is an organ known as a mantle, a fleshy, cape-like covering that lines the inside of the shell and wraps around the remainder of the mollusk. The mantle makes the shell. The mollusk extracts calcium and magnesium carbonate from its food and, to a limited extent, from the water and gives the minerals in solution to the mantle. The mantle serves as the paintbrush, spreading the liquid carbonates (and other minerals) on the inside of the shell. In place, these compounds rapidly crystallize into complex, rigid lattices that make the shell. The spots, bands, and checkers of color are deposits of waste material into the shell lattice.

Mollusks experience periods of growth followed by rest. This shows in the shell in the form of ridges of enlarging dimension emanating from the hinge of the bivalve or the axis of the coil in snails. While the ridges of a shell reflect periods of growth, they are not annual measurements such as the concentric rings of a tree. The periods of shell growth may correspond to seasonal change but do not correlate on a calendar basis. While you can't determine a mollusk's age from its shell, you can pick up a good idea of periods of feast or famine.

Fortunately, when I am shelling, I forget about all this stuff. I don't pick up shells to illustrate or illuminate any of these points; I pick them up because they are pretty, amazing, interesting, and one of the most wonderful calling cards around. Plus, they make me smile.

Appendixes

Appendix A: Information

National Parks

Cape Hatteras National Seashore
1401 National Park Drive
Manteo, NC 27954-9451
252-473-2111
<www.nps.gov/caha/index.htm>

Cape Lookout National Seashore
131 Charles Street
Harkers Island, NC 28531-9690
252-728-2250
<www.nps.gov/calo/home.htm>

Fort Raleigh National Historic Site
c/o Superintendent, Cape Hatteras
    Group
1401 National Park Drive
Manteo, NC 27954
252-473-2111
<www.nps.gov/fora/raleigh.htm>

Wright Brothers National
    Memorial
1401 National Park Drive
Manteo, NC 27954
252-441-7430
<www.nps.gov/wrbr>

National Wildlife Refuges

Alligator River National Wildlife
    Refuge
P.O. Box 1969
Manteo, NC 27954
252-473-1131
<www.outer-banks.com/
    alligator-river>

Cedar Island National Wildlife
    Refuge
c/o Mattamuskeet National
    Wildlife Refuge
38 Mattamuskeet Road
Swan Quarter, NC 27885
252-926-4021
<http://mattamuskeet.fws.gov/
    cedarisland/>

Currituck National Wildlife
    Refuge
c/o Mackay Island National
    Wildlife Refuge
P.O. Box 39
Knotts Island, NC 27950
252-429-3100
<http://mackayisland.fws.gov/
    currituck/>

Mackay Island National Wildlife
    Refuge
P.O. Box 39
Knotts Island, NC 27950
252-429-3100
<http://mackayisland.fws.gov>

Mattamuskeet National Wildlife
    Refuge
38 Mattamuskeet Road
Swan Quarter, NC 27855
252-926-4021
<http://mattamuskeet.fws.gov>

Pea Island National Wildlife
    Refuge
P.O. Box 1969
Manteo, NC 27954
252-987-2394 (visitors center),
    252-473-1131 (office)
<http://peaisland.fws.gov>

State Parks and Recreation Areas

Carolina Beach State Park
P.O. Box 475
Carolina Beach, NC 28428
910-428-8206
<www.ncsparks.net/cabe.html>

Fort Fisher State Recreation Area
P.O. Box 243
Kure Beach, NC 28449
910-458-5798
<www.ncsparks.net/fofi.html>

Fort Macon State Park
P.O. Box 127
Atlantic Beach, NC 28512
252-726-3775
<www.ncsparks.net/foma.html>

Hammocks Beach State Park
1572 Hammocks Beach Road
Swansboro, NC 28584
910-326-4881
<www.ncsparks.net/habe.html>

Jockey's Ridge State Park
P.O. Box 592
Nags Head, NC 27959
252-441-7132
<www.ncsparks.net/jori.html>

North Carolina Division of Parks
and Recreation
512 North Salisbury Street
Raleigh, NC 27611
919-733-4181
<www.ncsparks.net>

State Natural Areas

Bald Head Island Conservancy
P.O. Box 3109
Bald Head Island, NC 28461
910-457-0089
<www.bhic.org>

Bald Head Island State Natural
Area
c/o Fort Fisher State Recreation
Area
P.O. Box 243
Kure Beach, NC 28449
910-458-8206
<www.bhic.org>

Theodore Roosevelt State Natural
Area
P.O. Box 127
Atlantic Beach, NC 28512
252-726-3775, 252-247-2003

North Carolina
Coastal Reserve

North Carolina Coastal Reserve
Coordinator
North Carolina National Estuarine
Research Reserve
5600 Marvin K. Moss Lane
Wilmington, NC 28409
910-395-3905
<www.ncnerr.org>

North Carolina Division of Coastal
Management
North Carolina Department of
Environment and Natural
Resources
1638 Mail Service Center
Raleigh, NC 27699-1638
919-733-2293, 888-4RCOAST
<http://dcm2.enr.state.nc.us>;
<www.nccoastalmanagement.
net>

State Historic Sites

Brunswick Town State Historic
Site
8884 St. Philip's Road Southeast
Winnabow, NC 28479
910-371-6613
<www.ah.dcr.state.nc.us/
sections/hs/brunswic/
brunswic.htm>

Currituck Beach Lighthouse and
Lightkeeper's Quarters
Outer Banks Conservationists,
Inc.
P.O. Box 361
Corolla, NC 27927
252-453-8152
<www.currituckbeachlight.com>

Fort Fisher State Historic Site
P.O. Box 68
1610 Fort Fisher Boulevard South
Kure Beach, NC 28449
910-458-5538
<www.ah.dcr.state.nc.us/
sections/hs/fisher/
fisher.htm>

North Carolina Division of
Archives and History
4620 Mail Service Center
Raleigh, NC 27699-4620
919-733-7862
<www.ah.dcr.state.nc.us/
sections/hs/default.htm>

North Carolina Maritime Museum
315 Front Street
Beaufort, NC 28516
252-728-7317
<www.ah.dcr.state.nc.us/
sections/maritime>

Roanoke Island Festival Park
1 Festival Park
Manteo, NC 27954
252-475-1506, 252-475-1500
<www.roanokeisland.com>

Aquariums

North Carolina Aquariums,
Administrative Office
417 North Blount Street
Raleigh, NC 27601
919-733-2290
<www.ncaquariums.com>

North Carolina Aquarium at Fort
Fisher
900 Loggerhead Road
Kure Beach, NC 28449
910-458-8257
<www.ncaquariums.com>

North Carolina Aquarium at Pine
Knoll Shores
P.O. Box 580
Atlantic Beach, NC 28512
252-247-4003

North Carolina Aquarium on
   Roanoke Island
P.O. Box 967
Manteo, NC 27954-0967
252-473-3494
<www.ncaquariums.com>

Ferries

For general information on
   all ferries, locations and
   departures call 1-800-BY-
   FERRY (800-293-3779)

Cedar Island, 252-225-3551
Hatteras, 252-928-3841
Knotts Island, 252-232-2683
Ocracoke, 252-928-3841
Pamlico River, 252-964-4521
Swan Quarter, 252-926-1111

<www.ncferry.org>

Boating and Fishing Access

North Carolina Wildlife Resources
   Commission
1703 Mail Service Center
Raleigh, NC 27699-1703
919-733-3391, 800-662-7350
<www.ncwildlife.org>

Saltwater Sportfishing Restrictions

North Carolina Division of
   Marine Fisheries
3441 Arendell Street
Morehead City, NC 28557
252-726-7021, 800-682-2632
<www.ncfisheries.net>

General Tourism

North Carolina Association of RV
   Parks and Campgrounds
605 Poole Drive
Garner, NC 27529
919-779-5709
<www.kiz.com/campnet/html/
   cluborgs/nccoa/nccoa.htm>

North Carolina Bed and
   Breakfasts and Inns
P.O. Box 1029
Carolina Beach, NC 28428
800-849-5382
<www.ncbbi.org>

North Carolina Division of
   Tourism, Film, and Sports
   Development
301 North Wilmington Street
Raleigh, NC 27601
919-733-8372, 800-847-4862
<www.visitnc.com>

National Seashore Campground Reservations

Biospherics, Inc., 800-365-CAMP
<http://reservations.nps.gov>

Mainland Attractions

Belhaven Memorial Museum
210 East Main Street
Belhaven, NC 27810
252-943-6817
<www.beaufort-county.com/
   Belhaven/museum>

Historic Albemarle Tour, Inc.
P.O. Box 1604
Washington, NC 27889
252-926-2950, 800-734-1117
<www.albemarle-nc.com/hat>

Bath State Historic Site
207 Carteret Street
Bath, NC 27808
252-923-3971
<www.ah.dcr.state.nc.us/
   sections/hs/bath/bath.htm>

Historic Halifax State Historic Site
St. David and Dobbs Street
Halifax, NC 27839
800-522-4282
<www.ah.dcr.state.nc.us/
   sections/hs/halifax/halifax.
   htm>; <www.visithalifax.com>

Port O'Plymouth Museum
Historical Society of Washington
   County
302 East Water Street
Plymouth, NC 27962
252-793-1377
<www.livinghistoryweekend.com/
   port_o.htm>

Somerset Place State Historic Site
2572 Lake Shore Road
Creswell, NC 27928
252-797-4560
<www.ah.dcr.state.nc.us/
   sections/hs/somerset/
   somerset.htm>

Tryon Palace Historic Sites
   and Gardens
610 Pollock Street
New Bern, NC 28560
252-514-4900, 800-767-1560

Northern Coast

Greater Hyde County Chamber
of Commerce
P.O. Box 178
Swan Quarter, NC 27885-0178
252-926-9171, 888-493-3826
<www.hydecounty.org>

Ocracoke Island Visitor
Information
P.O. Box 456
Ocracoke Island, NC 27960
252-928-6711
<www.ocracokevillage.com>

Outer Banks Visitors Bureau
One Visitors Center Circle
Manteo, NC 27954
252-473-2138, 877-OBX-4FUN
(877-629-4386)
<www.outerbanks.org>

Outer Banks Chamber of
Commerce
P.O. Box 1757
Kill Devil Hills, NC 27948
252-441-8144
<www.outerbankschamber.com>

Central Coast

Beaufort Historical Association
P.O. Box 1709
Beaufort, NC 28516
252-728-5255
<www.historicbeaufort.com>

Carteret County Chamber
of Commerce
801 Arendell Street
Morehead City, NC 28557
252-726-6350
<www.nccoastchamber.com>

Crystal Coast Tourism Authority
3409 Arendell Street
Morehead City, NC 28557
252-726-8148, 800-SUNNYNC
(800-786-6962)
<www.sunnync.com>

New Bern/Craven County
Convention and Visitors Center
P.O. Box 1713
New Bern, NC 28563-1413
252-637-9400, 800-437-5767
<www.visitnewbern.com>

Onslow County Tourism
P.O. Box 1226
Jacksonville, NC 28541-0765
910-455-1113, 800-932-2144
<www.onslowcountytourism.com>

Topsail Area Chamber of
Commerce and Tourism
13775 Highway 50, Suite 101, or
P.O. Box 2486
Surf City, NC 28445-2486
910-329-4446, 800-626-2780
<www.topsailcoc.com>

South Coast

Cape Fear Coast Convention and
Visitors Bureau
24 North Third Street
Wilmington, NC 28401
910-341-4030, 800-222-4757
<www.cape-fear.nc.us>

North Carolina Brunswick Islands
Chamber of Commerce
P.O. Box 1186
Shallotte, NC 28459
910-754-6644, 800-795-7263
<www.ncbrunswick.com>

Southport/Oak Island Chamber
of Commerce
4841 Long Beach Road Southeast
Southport, NC 28461
800-457-6964
<www.southport-oakisland.com>

Appendix B:
Festivals and Events

The following is a selected list of festivals and events in coastal communities. Events are listed in calendar order within the month. Most of the numerous local Fourth of July celebrations are not listed. Check with the local chamber of commerce or visitors bureau for exact dates or for other events. The North Carolina Division of Tourism also provides a listing by calling 1-800-VISITNC or consulting the calendar at <www.visitnc.com>.

April

Biennial Pilgrimage-Tour
of Homes
Edenton
800-775-0111

Friends of *Elizabeth II* Antique
Faire
Roanoke Island Festival Park
Manteo
252-475-1506
<www.roanokeisland.com>

North Carolina Azalea Festival
Water Street
Downtown Wilmington
910-794-4650
<www.ncazaleafestival.org>

Beaufort Music Festival
Downtown Beaufort Waterfront
Beaufort
252-728-6894
<www.beaufortmusicfestival.com>

Plymouth Living History Weekend
Historic Civil War Battle
Reenactment
Plymouth
252-793-1377
<www.livinghistoryweekend.com>

May

Hang Gliding Spectacular and
Air Games
Jockey's Ridge State Park
Nags Head
877-359-8447
<www.kittyhawkkites.com>

Outer Banks Jaycees Beach
Music Festival
Roanoke Island Festival Park
Manteo
252-473-4600
<www.roanokeisland.com>

Southport Heritage Day
Southport
910-457-7927

June

River Walk Festival
Downtown Court Street-Linear
Park
Jacksonville
910-937-7222

Ocrafolk Music and Storytelling
Festival
Ocracoke
252-926-9171, 252-928-3411
<www.ocrafolkfestival.org>

Junior Sailing Program
North Carolina Maritime Museum
Beaufort
252-728-7317
<www.ah.dcr.state.nc.us/
sections/maritime/
default.htm>

Wilmington Nautical Festival
Downtown Wilmington's
Riverfront
910-341-3237
<www.nauticalfestival.com>

July

Cape Fear Blues Festival
Wilmington
910-350-8822
<www.capefearblues.com>

Civil War Reenactment
Fort Macon State Park
Atlantic Beach
252-726-3775
<www.ncsparks.net/foma.html>

Fourth of July Celebration
Swansboro
910-326-1145

North Carolina Fourth of July
Festival
Southport
Southport/Oak Island Chamber
of Commerce
910-457-5578, 800-457-6964

Surf, Sun, and Sand Celebration
Wrightsville Beach
Wrightsville Beach Parks and
Recreation
910-256-4744

August

National Aviation Day
Kill Devil Hills
252-441-7430

Sneads Ferry Shrimp Festival
Sneads Ferry Fairgrounds
910-327-0432

September

Topsail Island's Autumn
with Topsail
Topsail Beach
Topsail Island Chamber
of Commerce
800-626-2780
<www.topsailcoc.com>

Spot Festival
Hampstead
910-270-4568

October

Albemarle Craftsman's Fair
Elizabeth City
252-335-7276

Colonial Day at Brunswick Town
Brunswick Town State Historic
Site
Winnabow
910-371-6613
<www.ah.dcr.state.nc.us/
sections/hs/brunswic/
brunswic.htm>

Mumfest
Tryon Palace Historic Sites and
Gardens
New Bern
252-514-4900, 800-767-1560
<www.tryonpalace.org>

Harvest Time at the Beaufort
Historic Site
Beaufort
252-728-5225
<www.historicbeaufort.com>

Annual Swansboro Mullet Festival
Swansboro
910-353-0241

North Carolina Oyster Festival
Ocean Isle Beach
910-754-6644, 800-426-6644
<www.brunswickcountychamber.
org>

North Carolina Seafood Festival
Morehead City
252-726-6273
<www.ncseafoodfestival.org>

Outer Banks Stunt Kite
Competition
Jockey's Ridge State Park
Nags Head
877-359-8477
<www.kittyhawkkites.com>

Pleasure Island Seafood, Blues,
and Jazz Festival
Fort Fisher State Recreation Area
Kure Beach
910-458-8434

Sometime in October Film
Festival and Screenplay
Competition
Wilmington
910-200-2439
<www.cfifn.org>

Surf Fishing Weekend Workshop
North Carolina Aquarium
Pine Knoll Shores
252-247-4003
<www.ncaquariums.com>

November

Fort Branch Civil War Battle
Reenactment
Hamilton
252-792-4902, 800-776-8566
<www.fortbranchcivilwarsite.
com>

Holiday Flotilla
Banks Channel
Wrightsville Beach
910-455-3555
<www.ncholidayflotilla.org>

Wings Over Water
Kill Devil Hills
252-441-8144
<www.wingsoverwater.org>

December

Christmas by the Sea Festival
Southport/Oak Island Chamber
of Commerce
910-457-6964

Historic Edenton Candlelight
Tours
Edenton
800-775-0111

Christmas Celebration/
  Candlelight Tours
Tryon Palace Historic Sites and
  Gardens
New Bern
252-638-1560
<www.tryonpalace.org>

Core Sound Waterfowl Weekend
Harkers Island
252-728-1500
<www.coresound.com>

Old Wilmington by Candlelight
Wilmington
Lower Cape Fear Historical
  Society
910-762-0492

Appendix C: Saltwater Fishing Tournaments

Saltwater fishing tournaments are held along the entire North Carolina coast. They are an important part of local tourism, and new events emerge each year. Entry fees can be stiff, but the larger the entry fee, the greater the prize money, and the prizes can be lucrative. The competition is intense but good-natured. This list is simply a starting point. Consult the local chamber of commerce or visitors bureau that serves your intended destination or check the calendar at <www.visitnc.com> or call 800-VISITNC.

May

Memorial Weekend Tournament
Pirate's Cove Marina
Manteo
252-473-3610, 800-422-3610
<www.fishpiratescove.com>

Cape Fear Open Marlin
    Tournament
Wrightsville Beach
910-256-6550

Hatteras Village Offshore Open
Hatteras
800-676-4939
<www.hatterasoffshoreopen.com>

June

Big Rock Blue Marlin Tournament
Morehead City
252-247-3575
<www.thebigrock.com>

Big Rock Lady Angler Tournament
Morehead City
252-247-3575
<www.thebigrock.com>

Fisherman's Inn Marina Cobia
    Tournament
Harkers Island
252-728-2265

Hatteras Harbor Blue Water Open
    Billfish Tournament
Hatteras
252-986-2166

Hatteras Invitational Marlin
    Tournament
Hatteras
252-986-2454

Cobia Tournament
Pirate's Cove Marina
Manteo
252-473-3610, 800-422-3610
<www.fishpiratescove.com>

U.S. Open Pier Fishing
    Tournament
Southport/Oak Island Chamber
    of Commerce
Southport
910-457-6964, 800-457-6964
<www.usopenpiertournament.
    com>

July

Morehead City Rotary Club King
    Mackerel Tournament
Morehead City
252-726-8033

August

Pirate's Cove Billfish Tournament
Manteo
252-473-3610, 800-422-3610
<www.fishpiratescove.com>

Offshore Fishing Club King
    Mackerel Tournament
Topsail Beach
910-329-4446
<www.topsailcoc.com>

North Carolina Ducks Unlimited
    Billfish Tag and Release
    Tournament
Anchorage Marina
Atlantic Beach
336-668-2736

September

Allison "White" Marlin Release
    Tournament
Manteo
252-473-3610, 800-422-3610
<www.fishpiratescove.com>

Atlantic Beach King Mackerel
    Tournament
Atlantic Beach
800-545-3940
<www.abkmt.com>

Hatteras Village Surf-Fishing
    Tournament
Hatteras
252-986-2579
<www.hatterasonmymind.com>

Oregon Inlet Billfish Release
    Tournament
Nags Head
252-441-6301

Pirate's Cove White Marlin
    Release Tournament
Manteo
252-473-3906, 800-367-4728

U.S. Open King Mackerel
    Tournament
Southport
910-457-5787, 800-457-6964
<www.usopenkmt.com>

October

Atlantic Beach Surf-Fishing
    Tournament
Atlantic Beach
800-622-6278

Big Rock Sailfish Challenge
Morehead City
252-247-3575
<www.thebigrock.com>

Cape Lookout Albacore Festival
Radio Island Marina
Morehead City
252-726-3773
<www.claf.org>

Nags Head Surf-Fishing Club
    Invitation Tournament
Nags Head
252-441-5464

Outer Banks King Mackerel
    Festival
Manteo
252-473-3906, 800-367-4728

U.S. Open King Mackerel
    Tournament
Southport
910-457-5787, 800-457-6964
<www.usopenkmt.com>

November

Bob Bernard Open Individual
    Tournament
Cape Hatteras Anglers Club
Hatteras
252-995-4253

Taft's Poem

For Taft Lee Morris

February 2, 1979–February 4, 1989

Once,
The silver sea slip foamed around your ankles
And high above your sun-towed head the man-birds roared,
And rolling split the sky.
We built castles and the sea pulled them in
And laughingly, we built them again
In brash defiance.
We hallowed pools for your splashing and small fish
Caught to stock your private puddle-sea.
To this mooring, you brought ropes,
Tangled, tentacled frondlings, and with sticks and boat bones
Secured your palace of sand.
You came to this at three
And I, at thirty-three,
Had not grown enough to know you.
A thousand questions flowed
And I of answers stood silent for one.

Your gentle mother told you
Your spirit will live forever.

You knew and smiled.
I know now and cry still.

For once,
The silver sea slip foamed around your ankles
Slid past your toes and ebbed,
Leaving forever your palace of sand
Grain by grain
Behind.

> Glenn Morris
> February 7, 1989

Index